ANALYSIS OF THE SEXUAL IMPULSE

LOVE AND PAIN

THE SEXUAL IMPULSE IN WOMEN

BY

HAVELOCK ELLIS

PREFACE TO SECOND EDITION.

This volume has been thoroughly revised for the present edition and considerably enlarged throughout, in order to render it more accurate and more illustrative, while bringing it fairly up to date with reference to scientific investigation. Numerous histories have also been added to the Appendix.

It has not been found necessary to modify the main doctrines set forth ten years ago. At the same time, however, it may be mentioned, as regards the first study in the volume, that our knowledge of the physiological mechanism of the sexual instinct has been revolutionized during recent years. This is due to the investigations that have been made, and the deductions that have been built up, concerning the part played by hormones, or internal secretions of the ductless glands, in the physical production of the sexual instinct and the secondary sexual characters. The conception of the psychology of the sexual impulse here set forth, while correlated to terms of a physical process of tumescence and detumescence, may be said to be independent of the ultimate physiological origins of that process. But we cannot fail to realize the bearing of physiological chemistry in this field; and the doctrine of internal secretions, since it may throw light on many complex problems presented by the sexual instinct, is full of interest for us.

HAVELOCK ELLIS.

June, 1913.

PREFACE TO FIRST EDITION.

The present volume of *Studies* deals with some of the most essential problems of sexual psychology. The *Analysis of the Sexual Impulse* is fundamental. Unless we comprehend the exact process which is being worked out beneath the shifting and multifold phenomena presented to us we can never hope to grasp in their true relations any of the normal or abnormal manifestations of this instinct. I do not claim that the conception of the process here stated is novel or original. Indeed, even since I began to work it out some years ago, various investigators in these fields, especially in Germany, have deprived it of any novelty it might otherwise have possessed, while at the same time aiding me in reaching a more precise statement. This is to me a cause of satisfaction. On so fundamental a matter I should have been sorry to find myself tending to a peculiar and individual standpoint. It is a source of gratification to me that the positions I have reached are those toward which current intelligent and scientific opinions are tending. Any originality in my study of this problem can only lie in the bringing together of elements from somewhat diverse fields. I shall be content if it is found that I have attained a fairly balanced, general, and judicial statement of these main factors in the sexual instinct.

In the study of *Love and Pain* I have discussed the sources of those aberrations which are commonly called, not altogether happily, "sadism" and "masochism." Here we are brought before the most extreme and perhaps the most widely known group of sexual perversions. I have considered them from the medico-legal standpoint, because that has already been done by other writers whose works are accessible. I have preferred to show how these aberrations may be explained; how they may be linked on to normal and fundamental aspects of the sexual impulse; and, indeed, in their elementary forms, may themselves be regarded as normal. In some degree they are present, in every case, at some point of sexual development; their threads are subtly woven in and out of the whole psychological process of sex. I have made no attempt to reduce their complexity to a simplicity that would be fallacious. I hope that my attempt to unravel these long and tangled threads will be found to make them fairly clear.

In the third study, on *The Sexual Impulse in Women*, we approach a practical question of applied sexual psychology, and a question of the first importance. No doubt the sex impulse in men is of great moment from the social point of view. It is, however, fairly obvious and well understood. The impulse in women is not only of at least equal moment, but it is far more obscure. The natural difficulties of the subject have been increased by the assumption of most writers who have touched it—casually and hurriedly, for the most part—that the only differences to be sought in the sexual impulse in man and in woman are quantitative differences. I have pointed out that we may more profitably seek for qualitative differences, and have endeavored to indicate such of these differences as seem to be of significance.

In an Appendix will be found a selection of histories of more or less normal sexual development. Histories of gross sexual perversion have often been presented in books devoted to the sexual instinct; it has not hitherto been usual to inquire into the facts of normal sexual development. Yet it is concerning normal sexual development that our ignorance is greatest, and the innovation can scarcely need justification. I have inserted these histories not only because many of them are highly instructive in themselves, but also because they exhibit the nature of the material on which my work is mainly founded.

I am indebted to many correspondents, medical and other, in various parts of the world, for much valuable assistance. When they have permitted me to do so I have usually mentioned their names in the text. This has not been possible in the case of many women friends and correspondents, to whom, however, my debt is very great. Nature has put upon women the greater part of the burden of sexual reproduction; they have consequently become the supreme authorities on all matters in which the sexual emotions come into question. Many circumstances, however, that are fairly obvious, conspire to make it difficult for women to assert publicly the wisdom and knowledge which, in matters of love, the experiences of life have brought to them. The ladies who, in all earnestness and sincerity, write books on these questions are often the last people to whom we should go as the representatives of their sex; those who know most have written least. I can therefore but express again, as in previous volumes I have expressed before, my deep gratitude to these anonymous collaborators who have aided me in throwing light on a field of human life which is of such primary social importance and is yet so dimly visible.

HAVELOCK ELLIS.
Carbis Water,
Lelant, Cornwall, England.

ANALYSIS OF THE SEXUAL IMPULSE.

Definition of Instinct—The Sexual Impulse a Factor of the Sexual Instinct—Theory of the Sexual Impulse as an Impulse of Evacuation—The Evidence in Support of this Theory Inadequate—The Sexual Impulse to Some Extent Independent of the Sexual Glands—The Sexual Impulse in Castrated Animals and Men—The Sexual Impulse in Castrated Women, after the Menopause, and in the Congenital Absence of the Sexual Glands—The Internal Secretions—Analogy between the Sexual Relationship and that of the Suckling Mother and her Child—The Theory of the Sexual Impulse as a Reproductive Impulse—This Theory Untenable—Moll's Definition—The Impulse of Detumescence— The Impulse of Contrectation—Modification of this Theory Proposed—Its Relation to Darwin's Sexual Selection—The Essential Element in Darwin's Conception—Summary of the History of the Doctrine of Sexual Selection—Its Psychological Aspect—Sexual Selection a Part of Natural Selection—The Fundamental Importance of Tumescence—Illustrated by the Phenomena of Courtship in Animals and in Man—The Object of Courtship is to Produce Sexual Tumescence—The Primitive Significance of Dancing in Animals and Man— Dancing is a Potent Agent for Producing Tumescence—The Element of Truth in the Comparison of the Sexual Impulse with an Evacuation, Especially of the Bladder—Both Essentially Involve Nervous Explosions—Their Intimate and Sometimes Vicarious Relationships—Analogy between Coitus and Epilepsy—Analogy of the Sexual Impulse to Hunger—Final Object of the Impulses of Tumescence and Detumescence.

The term "sexual instinct" may be said to cover the whole of the neuropsychic phenomena of reproduction which man shares with the lower animals. It is true that much discussion has taken place concerning the proper use of the term "instinct," and some definitions of instinctive action would appear to exclude the essential mechanism of the process whereby sexual reproduction is assured. Such definitions scarcely seem legitimate, and are certainly unfortunate. Herbert Spencer's definition of instinct as "compound reflex action" is sufficiently clear and definite for ordinary use.

A fairly satisfactory definition of instinct is that supplied by Dr. and Mrs. Peckham in the course of their study *On the Instincts and Habits of Solitary Wasps.* "Under the term 'instinct,'" they say, "we place all complex acts which are performed previous to experience and in a similar manner by all members of the same sex and race, leaving out as non-essential, at this time, the question of whether they are or are not accompanied by consciousness." This definition is quoted with approval by Lloyd Morgan, who modifies and further elaborates it (*Animal Behavior*, 1900, p. 21). "The distinction between instinctive and reflex behavior," he remarks, "turns in large degree on their relative complexity," and instinctive behavior, he concludes, may be said to comprise "those complex groups of co-ordinated acts which are, on their first occurrence, independent of experience; which tend to the well-being of the individual and the preservation of the race; which are due to the co-operation of external and internal stimuli; which are similarly performed by all the members of the same more or less restricted group of animals; but which are subject to variation, and to subsequent modification under the guidance of experience." Such a definition clearly justifies us in speaking of a "sexual instinct." It may be added that the various questions involved in the definition of the sexual instinct have been fully discussed by Moll in the early sections of his *Untersuchungen über die Libido Sexualis.*

Of recent years there has been a tendency to avoid the use of the term "instinct," or, at all events, to refrain from attaching any serious scientific sense to it. Loeb's influence has especially given force to this tendency. Thus, while Piéron, in an interesting discussion of the question ("Les Problèmes Actuels de l'Instinct,"*Revue Philosophique*, Oct., 1908), thinks it would still be convenient to retain the term, giving it a philosophical meaning, Georges Bohn, who devotes a chapter to the notion of instinct (*La Naissance de l'Intelligence*, 1909), is strongly in favor of eliminating the word, as being merely a legacy of medieval theologians and metaphysicians, serving to conceal our ignorance or our lack of exact analysis.

It may be said that the whole of the task undertaken in these *Studies* is really an attempt to analyze what is commonly called the sexual instinct. In order to grasp it we have to break it up into its component parts. Lloyd Morgan has pointed out that the components of an instinct may be regarded as four: first, the internal messages giving rise to the impulse; secondly, the external stimuli which co-operate with the impulse to affect the nervous centers; thirdly, the active response due to the co-ordinate outgoing discharges; and, fourthly, the message from the organs concerned in the behavior by which the central nervous system is further affected.[1]

In dealing with the sexual instinct the first two factors are those which we have most fully to discuss. With the external stimuli we shall be concerned in a future volume (IV). We may here confine ourselves mainly to the first factor: the nature of the internal messages which prompt the sexual act. We may, in other words, attempt to analyze the *sexual impulse.*

The first definition of the sexual impulse we meet with is that which regards it as an impulse of evacuation. The psychological element is thus reduced to a minimum. It is true that, especially in early life, the emotions caused by forced repression of the excretions are frequently massive or acute in the highest degree, and the joy of relief correspondingly great. But in adult life, on most occasions, these desires can be largely pushed into the background of consciousness, partly by training, partly by the fact that involuntary muscular activity is less imperative in adult life; so that the ideal element in connection with the ordinary excretions is almost a negligible quantity. The evacuation theory of the sexual instinct is, however, that which most popular vogue, and the cynic delights to express it in crude language. It is the view that appeals to the criminal mind, and in the slang of French criminals the brothel is *le cloaque.* It was also the view implicitly accepted by medieval ascetic writers, who regarded woman as "a temple built over a sewer," and from a very different standpoint it was concisely set forth by Montaigne, who has doubtless contributed greatly to support this view of the matter: "I find," he said, "that Venus, after all, is nothing more than the pleasure of discharging our vessels, just as nature renders pleasurable the discharges from other parts."[2] Luther, again, always compared the sexual to the excretory impulse, and said that marriage was just as necessary as the emission of urine. Sir Thomas More, also, in the second book of *Utopia*, referring to the pleasure of evacuation, speaks of that felt "when we do our natural easement, or when we be doing the act of generation." This view would, however, scarcely deserve serious consideration if various distinguished investigators, among whom Féré may be specially mentioned, had not accepted it as the best and most accurate definition of the sexual impulse. "The genesic need may be considered," writes Féré, "as a need of evacuation; the choice is determined by the excitations which render the evacuation more agreeable."[3] Certain facts observed in the lower animals tend to support this view; it is, therefore, necessary, in the first place, to set forth the main results of observation on this matter. Spallanzani had shown how the male frog during coitus will undergo the most horrible mutilations, even decapitation, and yet resolutely continue the act of intercourse, which lasts from four to ten days, sitting on the back of the female and firmly clasping her with his forelegs. Goltz confirmed Spallanzani's observations and threw new light on the mechanism of the sexual instinct and the sexual act in the frog. By removing various parts of the female frog Goltz found that every part of the female was attractive to the male at pairing time, and that he was not imposed on when parts of a male were substituted. By removing various of the sense-organs of the male Goltz[4] further found that it was not by any special organ, but by the whole of his sensitive system, that this activity was set in action. If, however, the skin of the arms and of the breast between was removed, no embrace took place; so that the sexual sensations seemed to be exerted through this apparatus. When the testicles were removed the embrace still took place. It could scarcely be said that these observations demonstrated, or in any way indicated, that the sexual impulse is dependent on the need of evacuation. Professor Tarchanoff, of St. Petersburg, however, made an experiment which seemed to be crucial. He took several hundred frogs (*Rana temporaria*), nearly all in the act of coitus, and in the first place repeated Goltz's experiments. He removed the heart; but this led to no direct or indirect stoppage of coitus, nor did removal of the lungs, parts of the liver, the spleen, the intestines, the stomach, or the kidneys. In the same way even careful removal of both testicles had no result. But on removing the seminal receptacles coitus was immediately or very shortly stopped, and not renewed. Thus, Tarchanoff concluded that in frogs, and possibly therefore in mammals, the seminal receptacles are the starting-point of the centripetal impulse which by reflex action sets in motion the complicated apparatus of sexual activity.[5] A few years later the question was again taken up by Steinach, of Prague. Granting that Tarchanoff's experiments are reliable as regards the frog, Steinach points out that we may still ask whether in mammals the integrity of the seminal receptacles is bound up with the preservation of sexual excitability. This cannot be taken for granted, nor can we assume that the seminal receptacles of the frog are homologous with the seminal vesicles of mammals. In order to test the question, Steinach chose the white rat, as possessing large seminal vesicles and a very developed sexual impulse. He found that removal of the seminal sacs led to no decrease in the intensity of the sexual impulse; the sexual act was still repeated with the same frequency and the same vigor. But these receptacles, Steinach proceeded to argue, do not really contain semen, but a special secretion of their own; they are anatomically quite unlike the seminal receptacles of the frog; so that no doubt is thus thrown on Tarchanoff's observations. Steinach remarked, however, that one's faith is rather shaken by the fact that in the *Esculenta*, which in sexual life closely resembles *Rana temporaria*, there are no seminal receptacles. He therefore repeated Tarchanoff's experiments, and found that the seminal receptacles were empty before coitus, only becoming gradually filled during coitus; it could not, therefore, be argued that the sexual impulse started from the receptacles. He then extirpated the seminal receptacles, avoiding hemorrhage as far as possible, and found that, in the majority of cases so operated on, coitus still continued for from five to seven days, and in the minority for a longer time. He therefore concluded, with Goltz, that it is from the swollen testicles, not from the seminal receptacles, that the impulse first starts. Goltz himself pointed out that the fact that the removal of the testicles did not stop coitus by no means proves that it did not begin it, for, when the central nervous mechanism is once set in action, it can continue even when the exciting stimulus is removed. By extirpating the testicles some months before the sexual season he found that no coitus occurred. At the same time, even in these frogs, a certain degree of sexual inclination and a certain excitability of the embracing center still persisted, disappearing when the sexual epoch was over.

According to most recent writers, the seminal vesicles of mammals are receptacles for their own albuminous secretion, the function of which is unknown. Steinach could find no spermatozoa in these "seminal" sacs, and therefore he proposed to use Owen's name of *glandulæ vesiculares*. After extirpation of these vesicular glands in the white rat typical coitus occurred. But the capacity for *procreation* was diminished, and extirpation of both *glandulæ vesiculares* and *glandulæ prostaticæ* led to disappearance of the capacity for procreation. Steinach came to the conclusion that this is because the secretions of these glands impart increased vitality to the spermatozoa, and he points out that great fertility and high development of the accessory sexual glands go together.

Steinach found that, when sexually mature white rats were castrated, though at first they remained as potent as ever, their potency gradually declined; sexual excitement, however, and sexual inclination always persisted. He then proceeded to castrate rats before puberty and discovered the highly significant fact that in these also a quite considerable degree of sexual inclination appeared. They followed, sniffed, and licked the females like ordinary males; and that this was not a mere indication of curiosity was shown by the fact that they made attempts at coitus which only differed from those of normal males by the failure of erection and ejaculation, though, occasionally, there was imperfect erection. This lasted for a year, and then their sexual inclinations began to decline, and they showed signs of premature age. These manifestations of sexual sense Steinach compares to those noted in the human species during childhood.[6]

The genesic tendencies are thus, to a certain degree, independent of the generative glands, although the development of these glands serves to increase the genesic ability and to furnish the impulsion necessary to assure procreation, as well as to insure the development of the secondary sexual characters, probably by the influence of secretions elaborated and thrown into the system from the primary sexual glands.[7]

Halban ("Die Entstehung der Geschlechtscharaktere," *Archiv für Gynäkologie*, 1903, pp. 205-308) argues that the primary sex glands do not necessarily produce the secondary sex characters, nor inhibit the development of those characteristic of the opposite sex. It is indeed the rule, but it is not the inevitable result. Sexual differences exist from the first. Nussbaum made experiments on frogs (*Rana fusca*), which go through a yearly cycle of secondary sexual changes at the period of heat. These changes cease on castration, but, if the testes of other frogs are introduced beneath the skin of the castrated frogs, Nussbaum found that they acted as if the frog had not been castrated. It is the secretion of the testes which produces the secondary sexual changes. But Nussbaum found that the testicular secretion does not work if the nerves of the secondary sexual region are cut, and that the secretion has no direct action on the organism. Pflüger, discussing these experiments (*Archiv für die Gesammte Physiologie*, 1907, vol. cxvi, parts 5 and 6), disputes this conclusion, and argues that the secretion is not dependent on the action of the nervous system, and that therefore the secondary sexual characters are independent of the nervous system.

Steinach has also in later experiments ("Geschlechtstrieb und echt Sekundäre Geschlechtsmerkmale als Folge der innerskretorischen Funktion der Keimdrusen," *Zentralblatt für Physiologie*, Bd. xxiv, Nu. 13, 1910) argued against any local nervous influence. He found in *Rana fusca* and *esculenta* that after castration in autumn the impulse to grasp the female persisted in some degrees and then disappeared, reappearing in a slight degree, however, every winter at the normal period of sexual activity. But when the testicular substance of actively sexual frogs was injected into the castrated frogs it exerted an elective action on the sexual reflex, sometimes in a few hours, but the action is, Steinach concludes, first central. The testicular secretion of frogs that were not sexually active had no stimulating action, but if the frogs were sexually active the injection of their central nervous substance was as effective as their testicular substance. In either case, Steinach concludes, there is the removal of an inhibition which is in operation at sexually quiescent periods.

Speaking generally, Steinach considers that there is a process of "erotisation" (Erotisieurung) of the nervous center under the influence of the internal testicular secretions, and that this persists even when the primary physical stimulus has been removed.

The experience of veterinary surgeons also shows that the sexual impulse tends to persist in animals after castration. Thus the ox and the gelding make frequent efforts to copulate with females in heat. In some cases, at all events in the case of the horse, castrated animals remain potent, and are even abnormally ardent, although impregnation cannot, of course, result.[8]

The results obtained by scientific experiment and veterinary experience on the lower animals are confirmed by observation of various groups of phenomena in the human species. There can be no doubt that castrated men may still possess sexual impulses. This has been noted by observers in various countries in which eunuchs are made and employed.[9]

It is important to remember that there are different degrees of castration, for in current language these are seldom distinguished. The Romans recognized four different degrees: 1. True *castrati*, from whom both the testicles and the penis had been removed. 2.*Spadones*, from whom the testicles only had been removed; this was the most common practice. 3. *Thlibiæ*, in whom the testicles had not been removed, but destroyed by crushing; this practice is referred to by Hippocrates. 4. *Thlasiæ*, in whom the spermatic cord had simply been cut. Millant, from whose Paris thesis (*Castration Criminelle et Maniaque*, 1902) I take these definitions, points out that it was recognized that *spadones*remained apt for coitus if the operation was performed after puberty, a fact appreciated by many Roman ladies, *ad seouras libidinationes*, as St. Jerome remarked, while Martial (lib. iv) said of a Roman lady who sought eunuchs: "Vult futui Gallia, non parere." (See also Millant, *Les Eunuques à Travers les Ages*, 1909, and articles by Lipa Bey and Zambaco, *Sexual-Probleme*, Oct. and Dec., 1911.)

In China, Matignon, formerly physician to the French legation in Pekin, tells us that eunuchs are by no means without sexual feeling, that they seek the company of women and, he believes, gratify their sexual desires by such methods as are left open to them, for the sexual organs are entirely removed. It would seem probable that, the earlier the age at which the operation is performed, the less marked are the sexual desires, for Matignon mentions that boys castrated before the age of 10 are regarded by the Chinese as peculiarly virginal and pure.[10] At Constantinople, where the eunuchs are of negro race, castration is usually complete and performed before puberty, in order to abolish sexual potency and desire as far as possible. Even when castration is effected in infancy, sexual desire is not necessarily rendered impossible. Thus Marie has recorded the case of an insane Egyptian eunuch whose penis and scrotum wereremoved in infancy; yet, he had frequent and intense sexual desire with ejaculation of mucus and believed that an invisible princess touched him and aroused voluptuous sensations. Although the body had a feminine appearance, the prostate was normal and the vesiculæ seminales not atrophied.[11] It may be added that Lancaster[12] quotes the following remark, made by a resident for many years in the land, concerning Nubian eunuchs: "As far as I can judge, sex feeling exists unmodified by absence of the sexual organs. The eunuch differs from the man not in the absence of sexual passion, but only in the fact that he cannot fully gratify it. As far as he can approach a gratification of it he does so." In this connection it may be noted that (as quoted by Moll) Jäger attributes the preference of some women—noted in ancient Rome and in the East—for castrated men as due not only to the freedom from risk of impregnation in such intercourse, but also to the longer duration of erection in the castrated.

When castration is performed without removal of the penis it is said that potency remains for at least ten years afterward, and Disselhorst, who in his *Die accessorischen Geschlechtsdrüsen der Wirbelthiere* takes the same view as has been here adopted, mentions that, according to Pelikan (*Das Skopzentum in Rüssland*), those castrated at puberty are fit for coitus long afterward. When castration is performed for surgical reasons at a later age it is still less likely to affect potency or to change the sexual feelings.[13] Guinard concludes that the sexual impulse after castration is relatively more persistent in man than in the lower animals, and is sometimes even heightened, being probably more dependent on external stimuli.[14]

Except in the East, castration is more often performed on women than on men, and then the evidence as to the influence of the removal of the ovaries on the sexual emotions shows varying results. It has been found that after castration sexual desire and sexual pleasure in coitus may either remain the same, be diminished or extinguished, or be increased. By some the diminution has been attributed to autosuggestion, the woman being convinced that she can no longer be like other women; the augmentation of desire and pleasure has been supposed to be due to the removal of the dread of impregnation. We have, of course, to take into account individual peculiarities, method of life, and the state of the health.

In France Jayle ("Effets physiologiques de la Castration chez la Femme," *Revue de Gynécologie*, 1897, pp. 403-57) found that, among 33 patients in whom ovariotomy had been performed, in 18 sexual desire remained the same, in 3 it was diminished, in 8 abolished, in 3 increased; while pleasure in coitus remained the same in 17, was diminished in 1, abolished in 4, and increased in 5, in 6 cases sexual intercourse was very painful. In two other groups of cases—one in which both ovaries and uterus were removed and another in which the uterus alone was removed—the results were not notably different.

In Germany Gläveke (*Archiv für Gynäkologie*, Bd. xxxv, 1889) found that desire remained in 6 cases, was diminished in 10, and disappeared in 11, while pleasure in intercourse remained in 8, was diminished in 10, and was lost in 8. Pfister, again (*Archiv für Gynäkologie*, Bd. lvi, 1898), examined this point in 99 castrated women; he remarks that sexual desire and sexual pleasure in intercourse were usually associated, and found the former unchanged in 19 cases, decreased in 24, lost in 35, never present in 21, while the latter was unchanged in 18 cases and diminished or lost in 60. Keppler (International Medical Congress, Berlin, 1890) found that among 46 castrated women sexual feeling was in no case abolished. Adler also, who discusses this question (*Die Mangelhafte Geschlechtsempfindung des Weibes*, 1904, p. 75 *et seq.*), criticises Gläveke's statements and concludes that there is no strict relation between the sexual organs and the sexual feelings. Kisch, who has known several cases in which the feelings remained the same as before the operation, brings together (*The Sexual Life of Women*) varying opinions of numerous authors regarding the effects of removal of the ovaries on the sexual appetite.

In America Bloom (as quoted in *Medical Standard*, 1896, p. 121) found that in none of the cases of women investigated, in which oöphorectomy had been performed before the age of 33, was the sexual appetite entirely lost; in most of them it had not materially diminished and in a few it was intensified. There was, however, a general consensus of opinion that the normal vaginal secretion during coitus was greatly lessened. In the cases of women over 33, including also hysterectomies, a gradual lessening of sexual feeling and desire was found to occur most generally. Dr. Isabel Davenport records 2 cases (reported in *Medical Standard*, 1895, p. 346) of women between 30 and 35 years of age whose erotic tendencies were extreme; the ovaries and tubes were removed, in one case for disease, in the other with a view of removing the sexual tendencies; in neither case was there any change. Lapthorn Smith (*Medical Record*, vol. xlviii) has reported the case of an unmarried woman of 24 whose ovaries and tubes had been removed seven years previously for pain and enlargement, and the periods had disappeared for six years; she had had experience of sexual intercourse, and declared that she had never felt such extreme sexual excitement and pleasure as during coitus at the end of this time.

In England Lawson Tait and Bantock (*British Medical Journal*, October 14, 1899, p. 975) have noted that sexual passion seems sometimes to be increased even after the removal of ovaries, tubes, and uterus. Lawson Tait also stated (*British Gynæcological Journal*, Feb., 1887, p. 534) that after systematic and extensive inquiry he had not found a single instance in which, provided that sexual appetite existed before the removal of the appendages, it was abolished by that operation. A Medical Inquiry Committee appointed by the Liverpool Medical Institute (*ibid.*, p. 617) had previously reported that a considerable number of patients stated that they had suffered a distinct loss of sexual feeling. Lawson Tait, however, throws doubts on the reliability of the Committee's results, which were based on the statements of unintelligent hospital patients.

I may quote the following remarks from a communication sent to me by an experienced physician in Australia: "No rule can be laid down in cases in which both ovaries have been extirpated. Some women say that, though formerly passionate, they have since become quite indifferent, but I am of opinion that the majority of women who have had prior sexual experience retain desire and gratification in an equal degree to that they had before operation. I know one case in which a young girl hardly 19 years old, who had been

7

accustomed to congress for some twelve months, had trouble which necessitated the removal of the ovaries and tubes on both sides. Far from losing all her desire or gratification, both were very materially increased in intensity. Menstruation has entirely ceased, without loss of femininity in either disposition or appearance. During intercourse, I am told, there is continuous spasmodic contraction of various parts of the vagina and vulva."

The independence of the sexual impulse from the distention of the sexual glands is further indicated by the great frequency with which sexual sensations, in a faint or even strong degree, are experienced in childhood and sometimes in infancy, and by the fact that they often persist in women long after the sexual glands have ceased their functions.

In the study of auto-erotism in another volume of these *Studies* I have brought together some of the evidence showing that even in very young children spontaneous self-induced sexual excitement, with orgasm, may occur. Indeed, from an early age sexual differences pervade the whole nervous tissue. I may here quote the remarks of an experienced gynecologist: "I venture to think," Braxton Hicks said many years ago, "that those who have much attended to children will agree with me in saying that, almost from the cradle, a difference can be seen in manner, habits of mind, and in illness, requiring variations in their treatment. The change is certainly hastened and intensified at the time of puberty; but there is, even to an average observer, a clear difference between the sexes from early infancy, gradually becoming more marked up to puberty. That sexual feelings exist [it would be better to say 'may exist'] from earliest infancy is well known, and therefore this function does not depend upon puberty, though intensified by it. Hence, may we not conclude that the progress toward development is not so abrupt as has been generally supposed?... The changes of puberty are all of them dependent on the primordial force which, gradually gathering in power, culminates in the perfection both of form and of the sexual system, primary and secondary."

There appear to have been but few systematic observations on the persistence of the sexual impulse in women after the menopause. It is regarded as a fairly frequent phenomenon by Kisch, and also by Löwenfeld (*Sexualleben und Nervenleiden*, p. 29). In America, Bloom (as quoted in *Medical Standard*, 1896), from an investigation of four hundred cases, found that in some cases the sexual impulse persisted to a very advanced age, and mentions a case of a woman of 70, twenty years past the menopause, who had been long a widow, but had recently married, and who declared that both desire and gratification were as great, if not greater, than before the menopause.

Reference may finally be made to those cases in which the sexual impulse has developed notwithstanding the absence, verified or probable, of any sexual glands at all. In such cases sexual desire and sexual gratification are sometimes even strongerthan normal. Colman has reported a case in which neither ovaries nor uterus could be detected, and the vagina was too small for coitus, but pleasurable intercourse took place by the rectum and sexual desire was at times so strong as to amount almost to nymphomania. Clara Barrus has reported the case of a woman in whom there was congenital absence of uterus and ovaries, as proved subsequently by autopsy, but the sexual impulse was very strong and she had had illicit intercourse with a lover. She suffered from recurrent mania, and then masturbated shamelessly; when sane she was attractively feminine. Macnaughton-Jones describes the case of a woman of 32 with normal sexual feelings and fully developed breasts, clitoris, and labia, but no vagina or internal genitalia could be detected even under the most thorough examination. In a case of Bridgman's, again, the womb and ovaries were absent, and the vagina small, but coitus was not painful, and the voluptuous sensations were complete and sexual passion was strong. In a case of Cotterill's, the ovaries and uterus were of minute size and functionless, and the vagina was absent, but the sexual feelings were normal, and the clitoris preserved its usual sensibility. Mundé had recorded two similar cases, of which he presents photographs. In all these cases not only was the sexual impulse present in full degree, but the subjects were feminine in disposition and of normal womanly conformation; in most cases the external sexual organs were properly developed.[15]

Féré (*L'Instinct sexuel*, p. 241) has sought to explain away some of these phenomena, in so far as they may be brought against the theory that the secretions and excretions of the sexual glands are the sole source of the sexual impulse. The persistence of sexual feelings after castration may be due, he argues, to the presence of the nerves in the cicatrices, just as the amputated have the illusion that the missing limb is still there. Exactly the same explanation has since been put forward by Moll, *Medizinische Klinik*, 1905, Nrs. 12 and 13. In the same way the presence of sexual feelings after the menopause may be due to similar irritation determined by degeneration during involution of the glands. The precocious appearance of the sexual impulse in childhood he would explain as due to an anomaly of development in the sexual organs. Féré makes no attempt to explain the presence of the sexual impulse in the congenital absence of the sexual glands; here, however, Mundé intervenes with the suggestion that it is possible that in most cases "an infinitesimal trace of ovary" may exist, and preserve femininity, though insufficient to produce ovulation or menstruation.

It is proper to mention these ingenious arguments. They are, however, purely hypothetical, obviously invented to support a theory. It can scarcely be said that they carry conviction. We may rather agree with Guinard that so great is the importance of reproduction that nature has multiplied the means by which preparation is made for the conjunction of the sexes and the roads by which sexual excitation may arrive. As Hirschfeld puts it, in a discussion of this subject (*Sexual-Probleme*, Feb., 1912), "Nature has several irons in the fire."

It will be seen that the conclusions we have reached indirectly involve the assumption that the spinal nervous centers, through which the sexual mechanism operates, are not sufficient to account for the whole of the phenomena of the sexual impulse. The nervous circuit tends to involve a cerebral element, which may sometimes be of dominant importance. Various investigators, from the time of Gall onward, have attempted to localize the sexual instinct centrally. Such attempts, however, cannot be said to have succeeded, although they tend to show that there is a real connection between the brain and the generative organs. Thus Ceni, of Modena, by experiments on chickens, claims to have proved the influence of the cortical centers of procreation on the faculty of generation, for he found that lesions of the cortex led to sterility corresponding in degree to the lesion; but as these results followed even independently of any disturbance of the sexual instinct, their significance is not altogether clear (Carlo Ceni, "L'Influenza dei Centri Corticali sui Fenomeni della Generazione," *Revista Sperimentale di Freniatria*, 1907, fasc. 2-3). At present, as Obici and Marchesini have well remarked, all that we can do is to assume the existence of cerebral as well as spinal sexual centers; a cerebral sexual center, in the strictest sense, remains purely hypothetical.

Although Gall's attempt to locate the sexual instinct in the cerebellum—well supported as it was by observations—is no longer considered to be tenable, his discussion of the sexual instinct was of great value, far in advance of his time, and accompanied by a mass of facts gathered from many fields. He maintained that the sexual instinct is a function of the brain, not of the sexual organs. He combated the view ruling in his day that the seat of erotic mania must be sought in the sexual organs. He fully dealt with the development of the sexual instinct in many children before maturity of the sexual glands, the prolongation of the instinct into old age, its existence in the castrated and in the congenital absence of the sexual glands; he pointed out that even with an apparently sound and normal sexual apparatus all sorts of psychic pathological deviations may yet occur. In fact, all the lines of argument I have briefly indicated in the foregoing pages—although when they were first written this fact was unknown to me—had been fully discussed by this remarkable man nearly a century ago. (The greater part of the third volume of Gall's *Sur les Fonctions du Cerveau*, in the edition of 1825, is devoted to this subject. For a good summary, sympathetic, though critical, of Gall's views on this matter, see Möbius, "Ueber Gall's Specielle Organologie," *Schmidt's Jahrbücher der Medicin*, 1900, vol. cclxvii; also *Ausgewahlte Werke*, vol. vii.)

It will be seen that the question of the nature of the sexual impulse has been slowly transformed. It is no longer a question of the formation of semen in the male, of the function of menstruation in the female. It has become largely a question of physiological chemistry. The chief parts in the drama of sex, alike on its psychic as on its physical sides, are thus supposed to be played by two mysterious protagonists, the hormones, or internal secretions, of the testes and of the ovary. Even the part played by the brain is now often

9

regarded as chemical, the brain being considered to be a great chemical laboratory. There is a tendency, moreover, to extend the sexual sphere so as to admit the influence of internal secretions from other glands. The thymus, the adrenals, the thyroid, the pituitary, even the kidneys: it is possible that internal secretions from all these glands may combine to fill in the complete picture of sexuality as we know it in men and women.[16] The subject is, however, so complex and at present so little known that it would be hazardous, and for the present purpose it is needless, to attempt to set forth any conclusions.

It is sufficiently clear that there is on the surface a striking analogy between sexual desire and the impulse to evacuate an excretion, and that this analogy is not only seen in the frog, but extends also to the highest vertebrates. It is quite another matter, however, to assert that the sexual impulse can be adequately defined as an impulse to evacuate. To show fully the inadequate nature of this conception would require a detailed consideration of the facts of sexual life. That is, however, unnecessary. It is enough to point out certain considerations which alone suffice to invalidate this view. In the first place, it must be remarked that the trifling amount of fluid emitted in sexual intercourse is altogether out of proportion to the emotions aroused by the act and to its after-effect on the organism; the ancient dictum *omne animal post coitum triste* may not be exact, but it is certain that the effect of coitus on the organism is far more profound than that produced by the far more extensive evacuation of the bladder or bowels. Again, this definition leaves unexplained all those elaborate preliminaries which, both in man and the lower animals, precede the sexual act, preliminaries which in civilized human beings sometimes themselves constitute a partial satisfaction to the sexual impulse. It must also be observed that, unlike the ordinary excretions, this discharge of the sexual glands is not always, or in every person, necessary at all. Moreover, the theory of evacuation at once becomes hopelessly inadequate when we apply it to women; no one will venture to claim that an adequate psychological explanation of the sexual impulse in a woman is to be found in the desire to expel a little bland mucus from the minute glands of the genital tract. We must undoubtedly reject this view of the sexual impulse. It has a certain element of truth and it permits an instructive and helpful analogy; but that is all. The sexual act presents many characters which are absent in an ordinary act of evacuation, and, on the other hand, it lacks thespecial characteristic of the evacuation proper, the elimination of waste material; the seminal fluid is not a waste material, and its retention is, to some extent perhaps, rather an advantage than a disadvantage to the organism.

Eduard von Hartmann long since remarked that the satisfaction of what we call the sexual instinct through an act carried out with a person of the opposite sex is a very wonderful phenomenon. It cannot be said, however, that the conception of the sexual act as a simple process of evacuation does anything to explain the wonder. We are, at most, in the same position as regards the stilling of normal sexual desire as we should be as regards the emptying of the bladder, supposing it were very difficult for either sex to effect this satisfactorily without the aid of a portion of the body of a person of the other sex acting as a catheter. In such a case our thoughts and ideals would center around persons of opposite sex, and we should court their attention and help precisely as we do now in the case of our sexual needs. Some such relationship does actually exist in the case of the suckling mother and her infant. The mother is indebted to the child for the pleasurable relief of her distended breasts; and, while in civilization more subtle pleasures and intelligent reflection render this massive physical satisfaction comparatively unessential to the act of suckling, in more primitive conditions and among animals the need of this pleasurable physical satisfaction is a real bond between the mother and her offspring. The analogy is indeed very close: the erectile nipple corresponds to the erectile penis, the eager watery mouth of the infant to the moist and throbbing vagina, the vitally albuminous milk to the vitally albuminous semen.[17] The complete mutual satisfaction, physical and psychic, of mother and child, in the transfer from one to the other of a precious organized fluid, is the one true physiological analogy to the relationship of a man and a woman at the climax of the sexual act. Even this close analogy, however, fails to cover all the facts of the sexual life.

A very different view is presented to us in the definition of the sexual instinct as a reproductive impulse, a desire for offspring. Hegar, Eulenburg, Näcke, and Löwenfeld have accepted this as, at all events, a partial definition.[18] No one, indeed, would argue that it is a complete definition, although a few writers appear to have asserted that it is so sometimes as regards the sexual impulse in women. There is, however, considerable mental confusion in the attempt to set up such a definition. If we define an instinct as an action adapted to an end which is not present to consciousness, then it is quite true that the sexual instinct is an instinct of reproduction. But we do not adequately define the sexual instinct by merely stating its ultimate object. We might as well say that the impulse by which young animals seize food is "an instinct of nutrition." The object of reproduction certainly constitutes no part of the sexual impulse whatever in any animal apart from man, and it reveals a lack of the most elementary sense of biological continuity to assert that in man so fundamental and involuntary a process can suddenly be revolutionized. That the sexual impulse is very often associated with a strong desire for offspring there can be no doubt, and in women the longing for a child—that is to say, the longing to fulfill those functions for which their bodies are constituted—may become so urgent and imperative that we may regard it as scarcely less imperative than the sexual impulse. But it is not the sexual impulse, though intimately associated with it, and though it explains it. A reproductive instinct might be found in parthenogenetic animals, but would be meaningless, because useless, in organisms propagating by sexual union. A woman may not want a lover, but may yet want a child. This merely means that her maternal instincts have been aroused, while her sexual instincts are still latent. A desire for reproduction, as soon as that desire becomes instinctive, necessarily takes on the form of the sexual impulse, for there is no other instinctive mechanism by which it can possibly express itself. A "reproductive instinct," apart from the sexual instinct and apart from the maternal instinct, cannot be admitted; it would be an absurdity. Even in women in whom the maternal instincts are strong, it may generally be observed that, although before a woman is in love, and also during the later stages of her love, the conscious desire for a child may be strong, during the time when sexual passion is at its highest the thought of offspring, under normally happy conditions, tends to recede into the background. Reproduction is the natural end and object of the sexual instinct, but the statement that it is part of the contents of the sexual impulse, or can in any way be used to define that impulse, must be dismissed as altogether inacceptable. Indeed, although the term "reproductive instinct" is frequently used, it is seldom used in a sense that we need take seriously; it is vaguely employed as a euphemism by those who wish to veil the facts of the sexual life; it is more precisely employed mainly by those who are unconsciously dominated by a superstitious repugnance to sex.

I now turn to a very much more serious and elaborate attempt to define the constitution of the sexual impulse, that of Moll. He finds that it is made up of two separate components, each of which may be looked upon as an uncontrollable impulse.[19] One of these is that by which the tension of the sexual organs is spasmodically relieved; this he calls the *impulse of detumescence*,[20] and he regards it as primary, resembling the impulse to empty a full bladder. The other impulse is the "instinct to approach, touch, and kiss another person, usually of the opposite sex"; this he terms the *impulse of contrectation*, and he includes under this head not only the tendency to general physical contact, but also the psychic inclination to become generally interested in a person of the opposite sex. Each of these primary impulses Moll regards as forming a constituent of the sexual instinct in both men and women. It seems to me undoubtedly true that these two impulses do correspond to the essential phenomena. The awkward and unsatisfactory part of Moll's analysis is the relation of the one to the other. It is true that he traces both impulses back to the sexual glands, that of detumescence directly, that of contrectation indirectly; but evidently he does not regard them as intimately related to each other; he insists on the fact that they may exist apart from each other, that they do not appear synchronously in youth: the contrectation impulse he regards as secondary; it is, he states, an indirect result of the sexual glands, "only to be understood by the developmental history of these glands and the object which they subserve"; that is to say, that it is connected with the rise of the sexual method of reproduction and the desirability of the mingling of the two sexes in procreation, while the impulse of detumescence arose before the sexual method of reproduction had appeared; thus the contrectation impulse was propagated by natural selection together with the sexual method of reproduction. The impulse of contrectation is secondary, and Moll even regards it as a secondary sexual character.

While, therefore, this analysis seems to include all the phenomena and to be worthy of very careful study as a serious and elaborate attempt to present an adequate psychological definition of the sexual impulse, it scarcely seems to me that we can accept it in precisely the form in which Moll presents it. I believe, however, that by analyzing the process a little more minutely we shall find that these two constituents of the sexual impulse are really much more intimately associated than at the first glance appears, and that we need by no means go back to the time when the sexual method of reproduction arose to explain the significance of the phenomena which Moll includes under the term contrectation.

To discover the true significance of the phenomena in men it is necessary to observe carefully the phenomena of love-making not only among men, but among animals, in which the impulse of contrectation plays a very large part, and involves an enormous expenditure of energy. Darwin was the first to present a comprehensive view of, at all events a certain group of, the phenomena of contrectation in animals; on his interpretation of those phenomena he founded his famous theory of sexual selection. We are not primarily concerned with that theory; but the facts on which Darwin based his theory lie at the very roots of our subject, and we are bound to consider their psychological significance. In the first place, since these phenomena are specially associated with Darwin's name, it may not be out of place to ask what Darwin himself considered to be their psychological significance. It is a somewhat important question, even for those who are mainly concerned with the validity of the theory which Darwin established on those facts, but so far as I know it has not hitherto been asked. I find that a careful perusal of the *Descent of Man* reveals the presence in Darwin's mind of two quite distinct theories, neither of them fully developed, as to the psychological meaning of the facts he was collecting. The two following groups of extracts will serve to show this very conclusively: "The lower animals have a sense of beauty," he declares, "powers of discrimination and taste on the part of the female" (p. 211[21]); "the females habitually or occasionally prefer the more beautiful males," "there is little improbability in the females of insects appreciating beauty in form or color" (p. 329); he speaks of birds as the most "esthetic" of all animals excepting man, and adds that they have "nearly the same taste for the beautiful as we have" (p. 359); he remarks that a change of any kind in the structure or color of the male bird "appears to have been admired by the female" (p. 385). He speaks of the female Argus pheasant as possessing "this almost human degree of taste." Birds, again, "seem to have some taste for the beautiful both in color and sound," and "we ought not to feel too sure that the female does not attend to each detail of beauty" (p. 421). Novelty, he says, is "admired by birds for its own sake" (p. 495). "Birds have fine powers of discrimination and in some few instances it can be shown that they have a taste for the beautiful" (p. 496). The "esthetic capacity" of female animals has been advanced by exercise just as our own taste has improved (p. 616). On the other hand, we find running throughout the book quite another idea. Of cicadas he tells us that it is probable that, "like female birds, they are excited or allured by the male with the most attractive voice" (p. 282); and, coming to *Locustidæ*, he states that "all observers agree that the sounds serve either to call or excite the mute females" (p. 283). Of birds he says, "I am led to believe that the females prefer or are most excited by the more brilliant males" (p. 316). Among birds also the males "endeavor to charm or excite their mates by love-notes," etc., and "the females are excited by certain males, and thus unconsciously prefer them" (p. 367), while ornaments of all kinds "apparently serve to excite, attract, or fascinate the female" (p. 394). In a supplemental note, also, written in 1876, five years after the first publication of the *Descent of Man*, and therefore a late statement of his views, Darwin remarks that "no supporter of the principle of sexual selection believes that the females select particular points of beauty in the males; they are merely excited or attracted in a greater degree by one male than by another, and this seems often to depend, especially with birds, on brilliant coloring" (p. 623). Thus, on the one hand, Darwin interprets the phenomena as involving a real esthetic element, a taste for the beautiful; on the other hand, he states, without apparently any clear perception that the two views are quite distinct, that the colors and sounds and other characteristics of the male are not an appeal to any esthetic sense of the female, but an appeal to her sexual emotions, a stimulus to sexual excitement, an allurement to sexual contact. According to the first theory, the female admires beauty, consciously or unconsciously, and selects the most beautiful partner[22]; according to the second theory, there is no esthetic question involved, but the female is unconsciously influenced by the most powerful or complex organic stimulus to which she is subjected. There can be no question that it is the second, and not the first, of these two views which we are justified in accepting. Darwin, it must be remembered, was not a psychologist, and he lived before the methods of comparative psychology had begun to be developed; had he written twenty years later we may be sure he would never have used so incautiously some of the vague and hazardous expressions I have quoted. He certainly injured his theory of sexual selection by stating it in too anthropomorphic language, by insisting on "choice," "preference," "esthetic sense," etc. There is no need whatever to burden any statement of the actual facts by such terms borrowed from human psychology. The female responds to the stimulation of the male at the right moment just as the tree responds to the stimulation of the warmest days in spring. We should but obscure this fact by stating that the tree "chooses" the most beautiful days on which to put forth its young sprouts. In explaining the correlation between responsive females and accomplished males the supposition of esthetic choice is equally unnecessary. It is, however, interesting to observe that, though Darwin failed to see that the love-combats, pursuits, dances, and parades of the males served as a method of stimulating the impulse of contrectation—or, as it would be better to term it, tumescence—in the male himself,[23] he to some extent realized the part thus played in exciting the equally necessary activity of tumescence in the female.

The justification for using the term "tumescence," which I here propose, is to be found in the fact that vascular congestion, more especially of the parts related to generation, is an essential preliminary to acute sexual desire. This is clearly brought out in Heape's careful study of the "sexual season" in mammals. Heape distinguishes between the "pro-estrum," or preliminary period of congestion, in female animals and the immediately following "estrus," or period of desire. The latter period is the result of the former, and, among the lower animals at all events, intercourse only takes place during the estrus, not during the pro-estrum. Tumescence must thus be obtained before desire can become acute, and courtship runs *pari passu* with physiological processes. "Normal estrus," Heape states, "occurs in conjunction with certain changes in the uterine tissue, and this is accompanied by congestion and stimulation or irritation of the copulatory organs.... Congestion is invariably present and is an essential condition.... The first sign of pro-estrum noticed in the lower mammals is a swollen and congested vulva and a general restlessness, excitement, or uneasiness. There are other signs familiar to breeders of various mammals, such as the congested conjunctiva of the rabbit's eye and the drooping ears of the pig. Many monkeys exhibit congestion of the face and nipples, as well as of the buttocks, thighs, and neighboring parts; sometimes they are congested to a very marked extent, and in some species a swelling, occasionally prodigious, of the soft tissues round the anal and generative openings, which is also at the time brilliantly congested, indicates the progress of the pro-estrum.... The growth of the stroma-tissue [in the uterus of monkeys during the pro-estrum] is rapidly followed by an increase in the number and size of the vessels of the stroma; the whole becomes richly supplied with blood, and the surface is flushed and highly vascular. This process goes on until the whole of the internal stroma becomes tense and brilliantly injected with blood.... In all essential points the menstruation or pro-estrum of the human female is identical with that of monkeys.... Estrus is possible only after the changes due to pro-estrum have taken place in the uterus. A wave of disturbance, at first evident in the external generative organs, extends to the uterus, and after the various phases of pro-estrum have gone through in that organ, and the excitement there is subsiding, it would seem as if the external organs gain renewed stimulus, and it is then that estrus takes place.... In all animals which have been investigated coition is not allowed by the female until some time after the swelling and congestion of the vulva and surrounding tissue are first demonstrated, and in those animals which suffer from a considerable discharge of blood the main portion of that discharge, if not the whole of it, will be evacuated before sexual intercourse is allowed." (W. Heape, "The 'Sexual Season' of Mammals," *Quarterly Journal of Microscopical Science*, vol. xliv, Part I, 1900.

Estrus has since been fully discussed in Marshall's *Physiology of Reproduction*.) This description clearly brings out the fundamentally vascular character of the process I have termed "tumescence"; it must be added, however, that in man the nervous elements in the process tend to become more conspicuous, and more or less obliterate these primitive limitations of sexual desire. (See "Sexual Periodicity" in the first volume of these *Studies*.)

Moll subsequently restated his position with reference to my somewhat different analysis of the sexual impulse, still maintaining his original view ("Analyse des Geschlechtstriebes,"*Medizinische Klinik*, Nos. 12 and 13, 1905; also *Geschlecht und Gesellschaft*, vol. ii, Nos. 9 and 10). Numa Praetorius (*Jahrbuch für Sexeuelle Zwischenstufen*, 1904, p. 592) accepts contrectation, tumescence, and detumescence as all being stages in the same process, contrectation, which he defines as the sexual craving for a definite individual, coming first. Robert Müller (*Sexualbiologie*, 1907, p. 37) criticises Moll much in the same sense as I have done and considers that contrectation and detumescence cannot be separated, but are two expressions of the same impulse; so also Max Katte, "Die Präliminarien des Geschlechtsaktes," *Zeitschrift für Sexualwissenschaft*, Oct., 1908, and G. Saint-Paul,*L'Homosexualité et les Types Homosexuels*, 1910, p. 390.

While I regard Moll's analysis as a valuable contribution to the elucidation of the sexual impulse, I must repeat that I cannot regard it as final or completely adequate. As I understand the process, contrectation is an incident in the development of tumescence, an extremely important incident indeed, but not an absolutely fundamental and primitive part of it. It is equally an incident, highly important though not primitive and fundamental, of detumescence. Contrectation, from first to last; furnishes the best conditions for the exercise of the sexual process, but it is not an absolutely essential part of the process and in the early stages of zoölogical development it had no existence at all. Tumescence and detumescence are alike fundamental, primitive, and essential; in resting the sexual impulse on these necessarily connected processes we are basing ourselves on the solid bedrock of nature.

Moreover, of the two processes, tumescence, which in time comes first, is by far the most important, and nearly the whole of sexual psychology is rooted in it. To assert, with Moll, that the sexual process may be analyzed into contrectation and detumescence alone is to omit the most essential part of the process. It is much the same as to analyze the mechanism of a gun into probable contact with the hand, and a more or less independent discharge, omitting all reference to the loading of the gun. The essential elements are the loading and the discharging. Contrectation is a part of loading, though not a necessary part, since the loading may be effected mechanically. But to understand the process of firing a gun and to comprehend the mechanism of the discharge, we must insist on the act of loading and not merely on the contact of the hand. So it is in analyzing the sexual impulse. Contrectation is indeed highly important, but it is important only in so far as it aids tumescence, and so may be subordinated to tumescence, exactly as it may also be subordinated to detumescence. It is tumescence which is the really essential part of the process, and we cannot afford, with Moll, to ignore it altogether.

Wallace opposed Darwin's theory of sexual selection, but it can scarcely be said that his attitude toward it bears critical examination. On the one hand, as has already been noted, he saw but one side of that theory and that the unessential side, and, on the other hand, his own view really coincided with the more essential elements in Darwin's theory. In his *Tropical Nature* he admitted that the male's "persistency and energy win the day," and also that this "vigor and liveliness" of the male are usually associated with intense coloration, while twenty years later (in his *Darwinism*) he admitted also that it is highly probable that the female is pleased or excited by the male's display. But all that is really essential in Darwin's theory is involved, directly or indirectly, in these admissions.

Espinas, in 1878, in his suggestive book, *Des Sociétés Animales*, described the odors, colors and forms, sounds, games, parades, and mock battles of animals, approaching the subject in a somewhat more psychological spirit than either Darwin or Wallace, and he somewhat more clearly apprehended the object of these phenomena in producing mutual excitement and stimulating tumescence. He noted the significance of the action of the hermaphroditic snails in inserting their darts into each other's flesh near the vulva in order to cause preliminary excitation. He remarks of this whole group of phenomena: "It is the preliminary of sexual union, it constitutes the first act of it. By it the image of the male is graven on the consciousness of the female, and in a manner impregnates it, so as to determine there, as the effects of this representation descend to the depths of the organism, the physiological modifications necessary to fecundation." Beaunis, again, in an analysis of the sexual sensations, was inclined to think that the dances and parades of the male are solely intended to excite the female, not perceiving, however, that they at the same time serve to further excite the male also.[24]

A better and more comprehensive statement was reached by Tillier, who, to some extent, may be said to have anticipated Groos. Darwin, Tillier pointed out, had not sufficiently taken into account the coexistence of combat and courtship, nor the order of the phenomena. Courtship without combat, Tillier argued, is rare; "there is a normal coexistence of combat and courtship."[25] Moreover, he proceeded, force is the chief factor in determining the possession of the female by the male, who in some species is even prepared to exert force on her; so that the female has little opportunity of sexual selection, though she is always present at these combats. He then emphasized the significant fact that courtship takes place long after pairing has ceased, and the question of selection thus been eliminated. The object of courtship, he concluded, is not sexual selection by the female, but the sexual excitement of both male and female, such excitement, he asserted, not only rendering coupling easier, but favoring fecundation. Modesty, also, Tillier further argued, again anticipating Groos, works toward the same end; it renders the male more ardent, and by retarding coupling may also increase the secretions of the sexual glands and favor the chances of reproduction.[26]

In a charming volume entitled *The Naturalist in La Plata* (1892) Mr. W. H. Hudson included a remarkable chapter on "Music and Dancing in Nature." In this chapter he described many of the dances, songs, and love-antics of birds, but regarded all such phenomena as merely "periodical fits of gladness." While, however, we may quite well agree with Mr. Hudson that conscious sexual gratification on the part of the female is not the cause of music and dancing performances in birds, nor of the brighter colors and ornaments that distinguish the male, such an opinion by no means excludes the conclusion that these phenomena are primarily sexual and intimately connected with the process of tumescence in both sexes. It is noteworthy that, according to H. E. Howard ("On Sexual Selection in Birds,"*Zoölogist*, Nov., 1903), color is most developed just before pairing, rapidly becoming less beautiful—even within a few hours—after this, and the most beautiful male is most successful in getting paired. The fact that, as Mr. Hudson himself points out, it is at the season of love that these manifestations mainly, if not exclusively, appear, and that it is the more brilliant and highly endowed males which play the chief part in them, only serves to confirm such a conclusion. To argue, with Mr. Hudson, that they cannot be sexual because they sometimes occur before the arrival of the females, is much the same as to argue that the antics of a kitten with a feather or a reel have no relationship whatever to mice. The birds that began earliest to practise their accomplishments would probably have most chance of success when the females arrived. Darwin himself said that nothing is commoner than for animals to take pleasure in practising whatever instinct they follow at other times for some real good. These manifestations are primarily for the sake of producing sexual tumescence, and could not well have been developed to the height they have reached unless they were connected closely with propagation. That they may incidentally serve to express "gladness" one need not feel called upon to question.

Another observer of birds, Mr. E. Selous, has made observations which are of interest in this connection. He finds that all bird-dances are not nuptial, but that some birds—the stone-curlew (or great plover), for example—have different kinds of dances. Among these birds he has made the observation, very significant from our present point of view, that the nuptial dances, taken part in by both of the pair, are immediately followed by intercourse. In spring "all such runnings and chasings are, at this time, but a part of the business of pairing, and one divines at once that such attitudes are of a sexual character.... Here we have a bird with distinct nuptial (sexual) and social (non-sexual) forms of display or antics, and the former as well as the latter are equally indulged in by both sexes." (E. Selous, *Bird Watching*, pp. 15-20.)

The same author (*ibid.*, pp. 79, 94) argues that in the fights of two males for one female—with violent emotion on one side and interested curiosity on the other—the attitude of the former "might gradually come to be a display made entirely for the female, and of the latter a greater or less degree of pleasurable excitement raised by it, with a choice in accordance." On this view the interest of the female would first have been directed, not to the plumage, but to the frenzied actions and antics of the male. From these antics in undecorated birds would gradually develop the interest in waving plumes and fluttering wings. Such a dance might come to be of a quite formal and non-courting nature.

Last, we owe to Professor Häcker what may fairly be regarded, in all main outlines, as an almost final statement of the matter. In his *Gesang der Vögel* (1900) he gives a very clear account of the evolution of bird-song, which he regards as the most essential element in all this group of manifestations, furnishing the key also to the dancing and other antics. Originally the song consists only of call-cries and recognition-notes. Under the parallel influence of natural selection and sexual selection they become at the pairing season reflexes of excitement and thus develop into methods of producing excitement, in the male by the muscular energy required, and in the female through the ear; finally they become play, though here also it is probable that use is not excluded. Thus, so far as the male bird is concerned, bird-song possesses a primary prenuptial significance in attracting the female, a secondary nuptial significance in producing excitement (p. 48). He holds also that the less-developed voices of the females aid in attaining the same end (p. 51). Finally, bird-song possesses a tertiary extranuptial significance (including exercise play, expression of gladness). Häcker points out, at the same time, that the maintenance of some degree of sexual excitement beyond pairing time may be of value for the preservation of the species, in case of disturbance during breeding and consequent necessity for commencing breeding over again.

Such a theory as this fairly coincides with the views brought forward in the preceding pages,—views which are believed to be in harmony with the general trend of thought today,—since it emphasizes the importance of tumescence and all that favors tumescence in the sexual process. The so-called esthetic element in sexual selection is only indirectly of importance. The male's beauty is really a symbol of his force.

It will be seen that this attitude toward the facts of tumescence among birds and other animals includes the recognition of dances, songs, etc., as expressions of "gladness." As such they are closely comparable to the art manifestations among human races. Here, as Weismann in his *Gedanken über Musik* has remarked, we may regard the artistic faculty as a by-product: "This [musical] faculty is, as it were, the mental hand with which we play on our own emotional nature, a hand not shaped for this purpose, not due to the necessity for the enjoyment of music, but owing its origin to entirely different requirements."

The psychological significance of these facts has been carefully studied and admirably developed by Groos in his classic works on the play instinct in animals and in men.[27] Going beyond Wallace, Groos denies *conscious* sexual selection, but, as he points out, this by no means involves the denial of unconscious selection in the sense that "the female is most easily won by the male who most strongly excites her sexual instincts." Groos further quotes a pregnant generalization of Ziegler: "In all animals a high degree of excitement of the nervous system is *necessary to procreation*, and thus we find an excited prelude to procreation widely spread."[28] Such a stage, indeed, as Groos points out, is usually necessary before any markedly passionate discharge of motor energy, as may be observed in angry dogs and the Homeric heroes. While, however, in other motor explosions the prelude may be reduced to a minimum, in courtship it is found in a highly marked degree. The primary object of courtship, Groos insists, is to produce sexual excitement.

It is true that Groos's main propositions were by no means novel. Thus, as I have pointed out, he was at most points anticipated by Tillier. But Groos developed the argument in so masterly a manner, and with so many wide-ranging illustrations, that he has carried conviction where the mere insight of others had passed unperceived. Since Darwin wrote the *Descent of Man* the chief step in the development of the theory of sexual selection has been taken by Groos, who has at the same time made it clear that sexual selection is largely a special case of natural selection.[29] The conjunction of the sexes is seen to be an end only to be obtained with much struggle; the difficulty of achieving sexual erethism in both sexes, the difficulty of so stimulating such erethism in the female that her instinctive coyness is overcome, these difficulties the best and most vigorous males,[30] those most adapted in other respects to carry on the race, may most easily overcome. In this connection we may note what Marro has said in another connection, when attempting to answer the question why it is that among savages courtship becomes so often a matter in which persuasion takes the form of force. The explanation, he remarks, is yet very simple. Force is the foundation of virility, and its psychic manifestation is courage. In the struggle for life violence is the first virtue. The modesty of women—in its primordial form consisting in physical resistance, active or passive, to the assaults of the male—aided selection by putting to the test man's most important quality, force. Thus it is that when choosing among rivals for her favors a woman attributes value to violence.[31] Marro thus independently confirms the result reached by Groos.

The debate which has for so many years been proceeding concerning the validity of the theory of sexual selection may now be said to be brought to an end. Those who supported Darwin and those who opposed him were, both alike, in part right and in part wrong, and it is now possible to combine the elements of truth on either side into a coherent whole. This is now beginning to be widely recognized; Lloyd Morgan,[32] for instance, has readjusted his position as regards the "pairing instinct" in the light of Groos's contribution to the subject. "The hypothesis of sexual selection," he concludes, "suggests that the accepted male is the one which adequately evokes the pairing impulse.... Courtship may thus be regarded from the physiological point of view as a means of producing the requisite amount of pairing hunger; of stimulating the whole system and facilitating general and special vascular changes; of creating that state of profound and explosive irritability which has for its psychological concomitant or antecedent an imperious and irresistible craving.... Courtship is thus the strong and steady bending of the bow that the arrow may find its mark in a biological end of the highest importance in the survival of a healthy and vigorous race."

Having thus viewed the matter broadly, we may consider in detail a few examples of the process of tumescence among the lower animals and man, for, as will be seen, the process in both is identical. As regards animal courtship, the best treasury of facts is Brehm's *Thierleben*, while Büchner's *Liebe und Liebes-Leben in der Thierwelt* is a useful summary; the admirable discussion of bird-dancing and other forms of courtship in Häcker's *Gesang der Vögel*, chapter iv, may also be consulted. As regards man, Wallaschek's *Primitive Music*, chapter vii, brings together much scattered material, and is all the more valuable since the author rejects any form of sexual selection; Hirn's *Origins of Art*, chapter xvii, is well worth reading, and Finck's *Primitive Love and Love-stories* contains a large amount of miscellaneous information. I have preferred not to draw on any of these easily accessible sources (except that in one or two cases I have utilized references they supplied), but here simply furnish illustrations met with in the course of my own reading.

Even in the hermaphroditic slugs (*Limax maximus*) the process of courtship is slow and elaborate. It has been described by James Bladon ("The Loves of the Slug [*Limax cinereus*]," *Zoölogist*, vol. xv, 1857, p. 6272). It begins toward midnight on sultry summer nights, one slug slowly following another, resting its mouth on what may be called the tail of the first, and following its every movement. Finally they stop and begin crawling around each other, emitting large quantities of mucus. When this has constituted a mass of sufficient size and consistence they suspend themselves from it by a cord of mucus from nine to fifteen inches in length, continuing to turn round each other till their bodies form a cone. Then the organs of generation are protruded from their orifice near the mouth and, hanging down a short distance, touch each other. They also then begin again the same spiral motion, twisting around each other, like a two-strand cord, assuming various and beautiful forms, sometimes like an inverted agaric, or a foliated murex, or a leaf of curled parsley, the light falling on the ever-varying surface of the generative organs sometimes producing iridescence. It is not until after a considerable time that the organs untwist and are withdrawn and the bodies separate, to crawl up the suspending cord and depart.

Some snails have a special organ for creating sexual excitement. A remarkable part of the reproductive system in many of the true Helicidæ is the so-called *dart, Liebespfeil,* or *telum*

Veneris. It consists of a straight or curved, sometimes slightly twisted, tubular shaft of carbonate of lime, tapering to a fine point above, and enlarging gradually, more often somewhat abruptly, to the base. The sides of the shaft are sometimes furnished with two or more blades; these are apparently not for cutting purposes, but simply to brace the stem. The dart is contained in a dart-sac, which is attached as a sort of pocket to the vagina, at no great distance from its orifice. In *Helix aspersa* the dart is about five-sixteenths of an inch in length, and one-eighth of an inch in breadth at its base. It appears most probable that the dart is employed as an adjunct for the sexual act. Besides the fact of the position of the dart-sac anatomically, we find that the darts are extended and become imbedded in the flesh, just before or during the act of copulation. It may be regarded, then, as an organ whose functions induce excitement preparatory to sexual union. It only occurs in well-grown specimens. (Rev. L. H. Cooke, "Molluscs," *Cambridge Natural History*, vol. iii, p. 143.)

Racovitza has shown that in the octopus (*Octopus vulgaris*) courtship is carried on with considerable delicacy, and not brutally, as had previously been supposed. The male gently stretches out his third arm on the right and caresses the female with its extremity, eventually passing it into the chamber formed by the mantle. The female contracts spasmodically, but does not attempt to move. They remain thus about an hour or more, and during this time the male shifts the arm from one oviduct to the other. Finally he withdraws his arm, caresses her with it for a few moments, and then replaces it with his other arm. (E. G. Racovitza, in *Archives de Zoölogie Expérimentale*, quoted in *Natural Science*, November, 1894.)

The phenomena of courtship are very well illustrated by spiders. Peckham, who has carefully studied them, tells us of *Saitis pulex*: "On May 24th we found a mature female, and placed her in one of the larger boxes, and the next day we put a male in with her. He saw her as she stood perfectly still, twelve inches away; the glance seemed to excite him, and he at once moved toward her; when some four inches from her he stood still, and then began the most remarkable performances that an amorous male could offer to an admiring female. She eyed him eagerly, changing her position from time to time so that he might be always in view. He, raising his whole body on one side by straightening out the legs, and lowering it on the other by folding the first two pairs of legs up and under, leaned so far over as to be in danger of losing his balance, which he only maintained by sliding rapidly toward the lowered side. The palpus, too, on this side was turned back to correspond to the direction of the legs nearest it. He moved in a semicircle for about two inches, and then instantly reversed the position of the legs and circled in the opposite direction, gradually approaching nearer and nearer to the female. Now she dashes toward him, while he, raising his first pair of legs, extends them upward and forward as if to hold her off, but withal slowly retreats. Again and again he circles from side to side, she gazing toward him in a softer mood, evidently admiring the grace of his antics. This is repeated until we have counted one hundred and eleven circles made by the ardent little male. Now he approaches nearer and nearer, and when almost within reach whirls madly around and around her, she joining and whirling with him in a giddy maze. Again he falls back and resumes his semicircular motions, with his body tilted over; she, all excitement, lowers her head and raises her body so that it is almost vertical; both draw nearer; she moves slowly under him, he crawling over her head, and the mating is accomplished."

The same author thus describes the courtship of *Dendryphantes elegans*: "While from three to five inches distant from her, he begins to wave his plumy first legs in a way that reminds one of a windmill. She eyes him fiercely, and he keeps at a proper distance for a long time. If he comes close she dashes at him, and he quickly retreats. Sometimes he becomes bolder, and when within an inch, pauses, with the first legs outstretched before him, not raised as is common in other species; the palpi also are held stiffly out in front with the points together. Again she drives him off, and so the play continues. Now the male grows excited as he approaches her, and while still several inches away, whirls completely around and around; pausing, he runs closer and begins to make his abdomen quiver as he stands on tiptoe in front of her. Prancing from side to side, he grows bolder and bolder, while she seems less fierce, and yielding to the excitement, lifts up her magnificently iridescent abdomen, holding it at one time vertical, and at another sideways to him. She no longer rushes at him, but retreats a little as he approaches. At last he comes close to her, lying flat, with his first legs stretched out and quivering. With the tips of his front legs he gently pats her; this seems to arouse the old demon of resistance, and she drives him back. Again and again he pats her with a caressing movement, gradually creeping nearer and nearer, which she now permits without resistance, until he crawls over her head to her abdomen, far enough to reach the epigynum with his palpus." (G. W. Peckham, "Sexual Selection of Spiders,"*Occasional Papers of the Natural History Society of Wisconsin*, 1889, quoted in *Nature*, August 21, 1890.)

The courtship of another spider, the *Agelena labyrinthica*, has been studied by Lécaillon ("Les Instincts et les Psychismes des Araignées," *Revue Scientifique*, Sept. 15, 1906.) The male enters the female's web and may be found there about the middle of July. When courtship has begun it is not interrupted by the closest observation, even under the magnifying glass. At first it is the male which seeks to couple and he pursues the female over her web till she consents. The pursuit may last some hours, the male agitating his abdomen in a peculiar way, while the female simply retreats a short distance without allowing herself to be approached. At last the female holds herself completely motionless, and then the male approaches, seizes her, places her on her side, sometimes carrying her to a more suitable part of the web. Then one of his copulative apparatus is applied to the female genital opening, and copulation begins. When completed (on an average in about two hours) the male withdraws his copulatory palpus and turns over the female, who is still inert, on to her other side, then brings his second copulatory apparatus to the female opening and starts afresh. When the process is definitely completed the male leaves the female, suddenly retiring to a little distance. The female, who had remained completely motionless for four hours, suddenly runs after the male. But she only pursues him for a short distance, and the two spiders remain together without any danger to either. Lécaillon disbelieves the statement of Romanes (in his *Animal Intelligence*) that the female eats the male after copulation. But this certainly seems to occur sometimes among insects, as illustrated by the following instance described by so careful an observer of insects as Fabre.

The *Mantis religiosa* is described by Fabre as contemplating the female for a long time in an attitude of ecstasy. She remains still and seems indifferent. He is small and she is large. At last he approaches; spreads his wings, which tremble convulsively; leaps on her back, and fixes himself there. The preludes are long and the coupling itself sometimes occupies five or six hours. Then they separate. But the same day or the following day she seizes him and eats him up in small mouthfuls. She will permit a whole series of males to have intercourse with her, always eating them up directly afterward. Fabre has even seen her eating the male while still on her back, his head and neck gone, but his body still firmly attached. (J. H. Fabre, *Souvenirs Entomologiques*, fifth series, p. 307.) Fabre also describes in great detail (*ibid.*, ninth series, chs. xxi-xxii) the sexual parades of the Languedoc scorpion (*Scorpio occitanus*), an arachnid. These parades are in public; for their subsequent intercourse the couple seek complete seclusion, and the female finally eats the male.

An insect (a species of *Empis*) has been described which excites the female by manipulating a large balloon. "This is of elliptical shape, about seven millimeters long (nearly twice as long as the fly), hollow, and composed entirely of a single layer of minute bubbles, nearly uniform in size, arranged in regular circles concentric with the axis of the structure. The beautiful, glistening whiteness of the object when the sun shines upon it makes it very conspicuous. The bubbles were slightly viscid, and in nearly every case there was a small fly pressed into the front end of the balloon, apparently as food for the *Empis*. In all cases they were dead. The balloon appears to be made while the insect is flying in the air. Those flying highest had the smallest balloons. The bubbles are probably produced by some modification of the anal organs. It is possible that the captured fly serves as a nucleus to begin the balloon on. One case of a captured fly but no balloon was observed. After commencing, it is probable that the rest of the structure is made by revolving the completed part between the hind legs and adding more bubbles somewhat spirally. The posterior end of the balloon is left more or less open. The purpose of this structure is to attract the female. When numerous males were flying up and down the road, it happened several times that a female was seen to approach them from some choke-cherry blossoms near by. The males immediately gathered in her path, and she with little hesitation selected for a mate the one with the largest balloon, taking a position *upon his back*. After copulation had begun, the pair would settle down toward the ground, select a quiet spot, and the female would alight by placing her front legs across a horizontal grass blade, her head resting against the blade so as to brace the body in position. Here she would continue to hold the male beneath her for a little time, until the process was finished. The male, meanwhile, would be rolling the balloon about in a variety of positions, juggling with it, one might almost say. After the male and female parted company, the male immediately dropped the balloon upon the ground, and it was greedily seized by ants. No illustration could properly show the beauty of the balloon." (Aldrich and Turley, "A Balloon-making Fly,"*American Naturalist*, October, 1899.)

"In many species of moths the males 'assemble' around the freshly emerged female, but no special advantage appears to attend on early arrival. The female sits apparently motionless, while the little crowd of suitors buzz around her for several minutes. Suddenly, and, as far as one can see, without any sign from the female, one of the males pairs with her and all the others immediately disappear. In these cases the males do not fight or struggle in any way, and as one watches the ceremony the wonder arises as to how the moment is determined, and why the pairing did not take place before. Proximity does not decide the point, for long beforehand the males often alight close to the female and brush against her with fluttering wings. I have watched the process exactly as I have described it in a common Northern *Noctua*, the antler moth (*Charæax graminis*), and I have seen the same thing among beetles." (E. B. Poulton, *The Colors of Animals*, 1890, p. 391.) This author mentions that among some butterflies the females take the active part. The example here quoted of courtship among moths illustrates how phenomena which are with difficulty explicable by the theory of sexual selection in its original form become at once intelligible when we realize the importance of tumescence in courtship.

Of the Argentine cow-bird (*Molothrus bonariensis*) Hudson says (*Argentine Ornithology*, vol. i, p. 73): "The song of the male, particularly when making love, is accompanied with gestures and actions somewhat like those of the domestic pigeon. He swells himself out, beating the ground with his wings, and uttering a series of deep internal notes, followed by others loud and clear; and occasionally, when uttering them, he suddenly takes wing and flies directly away from the female to a distance of fifty yards, and performs a wide circuit about her in the air, singing all the time. The homely object of his passion always appears utterly indifferent to this curious and pretty performance; yet she must be even more impressionable than most female birds, since she continues scattering about her parasitical and often wasted eggs during four months in every year."

Of a tyrant-bird (*Pitangus Bolivianus*) Hudson writes (*Argentine Ornithology*, vol. i, p. 148): "Though the male and female are greatly attached, they do not go afield to hunt in company, but separate to meet again at intervals during the day. One of a couple (say, the female) returns to the trees where they are accustomed to meet, and after a time, becoming impatient or anxious at the delay of her consort, utters a very long, clear call-note. He is perhaps a quarter of a mile away, watching for a frog beside a pool, or beating over a thistle-bed, but he hears the note and presently responds with one of equal power. Then, perhaps, for half an hour, at intervals of half a minute, the birds answer each other, though the powerful call of the one must interfere with his hunting. At length he returns; then the two birds, perched close together, with their yellow bosoms almost touching, crests elevated, and beating the branch with their wings, scream their loudest notes in concert—a confused jubilant noise that rings through the whole plantation. Their joy at meeting is patent, and their action corresponds to the warm embrace of a loving human couple."

Of the red-breasted marsh-bird (*Leistes superciliaris*) Hudson (*Argentine Ornithology*, vol. i, p. 100) writes: "These birds are migratory, and appear everywhere in the eastern part of the Argentine country early in October, arriving singly, after which each male takes up a position in a field or open space abounding with coarse grass and herbage, where he spends most of his time perched on the summit of a tall stalk or weed, his glowing crimson bosom showing at a distance like some splendid flower above the herbage. At intervals of two or three minutes he soars vertically up to a height of twenty or twenty-five yards to utter his song, composed of a single long, powerful and rather musical note, ending with an attempt at a flourish, during which the bird flutters and turns about in the air; then, as if discouraged at his failure, he drops down, emitting harsh, guttural chirps, to resume his stand. Meanwhile the female is invisible, keeping closely concealed under the long grass. But at length, attracted perhaps by the bright bosom and aërial music of the male, she occasionally exhibits herself for a few moments, starting up with a wild zigzag flight, and, darting this way and that, presently drops into the grass once more. The moment she appears above the grass the male gives chase, and they vanish from sight together."

"Courtship with the mallard," says J. G. Millais (*Natural History of British Ducks*, p. 6), "appears to be carried on by both sexes, though generally three or four drakes are seen showing themselves off to attract the attention of a single duck. Swimming round her, in a coy and semi-self-conscious manner, they now and again all stop quite still, nod, bow, and throw their necks out in token of their admiration and their desire of a favorable response. But the most interesting display is when all the drakes simultaneously stand up in the water and rapidly pass their bills down their breasts, uttering at the same time a low single note somewhat like the first half of the call that teal and pintail make when 'showing off.' At other times the love-making of the drake seems to be rather passive than active. While graciously allowing himself to be courted, he holds his head high with conscious pride, and accepts as a matter of course any attention that may be paid to him. A proud bird is he when three or four ducks come swimming along beside and around him, uttering a curious guttural note, and at the same time dipping their bills in quick succession to right and left. He knows what that means, and carries himself with even greater dignity than before. In the end, however, he must give in. As a last appeal, one of his lady lovers may coyly lower herself in the water till only the top of her back, head, and neck is seen, and so fascinating an advance as this no drake of any sensibility can withstand."

The courting of the Argus pheasant, noted for the extreme beauty of the male's plumage, was observed by H. O. Forbes in Sumatra. It is the habit of this bird to make "a large circus, some ten or twelve feet in diameter, in the forest, which it clears of every leaf and twig and branch, till the ground is perfectly swept and garnished. On the margin of this circus there is invariably a projecting branch or high-arched root, at a few feet elevation above the ground, on which the female bird takes its place, while in the ring the male—the male birds alone possess great decoration—shows off all its magnificence for the gratification and pleasure of his consort and to exalt himself in her eyes." (H. O. Forbes, *A. Naturalist's Wanderings*, 1885, p. 131.)

"All ostriches, adults as well as chicks, have a strange habit known as 'waltzing.' After running for a few hundred yards they will also stop, and, with raised wings, spin around rapidly for some time after until quite giddy, when a broken leg occasionally occurs.... Vicious cocks 'roll' when challenging to fight or when wooing the hen. The cock will suddenly bump down on to his knees (the ankle-joint), open his wings, and then swing them alternately backward and forward, as if on a pivot.... While rolling, every feather over the whole body is on end, and the plumes are open, like a large white fan. At such a time the bird sees very imperfectly, if at all; in fact, he seems so preoccupied that, if pursued, one may often approach unnoticed. Just before rolling, a cock, especially if courting the hen, will often run slowly and daintily on the points of his toes, with neck slightly inflated, upright, and rigid, the tail half-drooped, and all his body-feathers fluffed up; the wings raised and expanded, the inside edges touching the sides of the neck for nearly the whole of its length, and the plumes showing separately, like an open fan. In no other attitude is the splendid beauty of his plumage displayed to such advantage." (S. C. Cronwright Schreiner, "The Ostrich,"*Zoölogist*, March, 1897.)

As may be seen from the foregoing fairly typical examples, the phenomena of courtship are highly developed, and have been most carefully studied, in animals outside the mammal series. It may seem a long leap from birds to man; yet, as will be seen, the phenomena among primitive human peoples, if not, indeed, among many civilized peoples also, closely resemble those found among birds, though, unfortunately, they have not usually been so carefully studied.

In Australia, where dancing is carried to a high pitch of elaboration, its association with the sexual impulse is close and unmistakable. Thus, Mr. Samuel Gason (of whom it has been said that "no man living has been more among blacks or knows more of their ways") remarks concerning a dance of the Dieyerie tribe: "This dance men and women only take part in, in regular form and position, keeping splendid time to the rattle of the beat of two boomerangs; some of the women keep time by clapping their hands between their thighs; promiscuous sexual intercourse follows after the dance; jealousy is forbidden." Again, at the Mobierrie, or rat-harvest, "many weeks' preparation before the dance comes off; no quarreling is allowed; promiscuous sexual intercourse during the ceremony." The fact that jealousy is forbidden at these festivals clearly indicates that sexual intercourse is a recognized and probably essential element in the ceremonies. This is further emphasized by the fact that at other festivals open sexual intercourse is not allowed. Thus, at the Mindarie, or dance at a peace festival (when a number of tribes comes together), "there is great rejoicing at the coming festival, which is generally held at the full of the moon, and kept up all night. The men are artistically decorated with down and feathers, with all kinds of designs. The down and feathers are stuck on their bodies with blood freshly taken from their penis; they are also nicely painted with various colors; tufts of boughs are tied on their ankles to make a noise while dancing. Promiscuous sexual intercourse is carried on *secretly*; many quarrels occur at this time." (*Journal of the Anthropological Institute*, vol. xxiv, November, 1894, p. 174.)

In Australian dances, sometimes men and women dance together, sometimes the men dance alone, sometimes the women. In one dance described by Eyre: "Women are the chief performers; their bodies are painted with white streaks, and their hair adorned with cockatoo feathers. They carry large sticks in their hands, and place themselves in a row in front, while the men with their spears stand in a row behind them. They then all commence their movements, but without intermingling, the males and females dancing by themselves. The women have occasionally another mode of dancing, by joining the hands together over the head, closing the feet, and bringing the knees into contact. The legs are then thrown outward from the knee, while the feet and hands are kept in their original position, and, being drawn quickly in again, a sharp sound is produced by the collision. This is also practised alone by young girls or by several together for their own amusement. It is adopted also when a single woman is placed in front of a row of male dancers to excite their passions." (E. J. Eyre, *Journals of Expeditions into Central Australia*, vol. ii, p. 235.)

A charming Australian folk-tale concerning two sisters with wings, who disliked men, and their wooing by a man, clearly indicates, even among the Australians (whose love-making is commonly supposed to be somewhat brutal in character), the consciousness that it is by his beauty, charm, and skill in courtship that a man wins a woman. Unahanach, the lover, stole unperceived to the river where the girls were bathing and at last showed himself carelessly sitting on a high tree. The girls were startled, but thought it would be safe to amuse themselves by looking at the intruder. "Young and with the most active figure, yet of a strength that defied the strongest emu, and even enabled him to resist an 'old man' kangaroo, he had no equal in the chase, and conscious power gave a dignity to his expression that at one glance calmed the fears of the two girls. His large brilliant eyes, shaded by a deep fringe of soft black eyelashes, gazed down upon them admiringly, and his rich black hair hung around his well-formed face, smooth and shining from the emu-oil with which it was abundantly covered." At last he persuaded them to talk and by and by induced them to call him husband. Then they went off with him, with no thought of flight in their hearts. ("Australian Folklore Stories," collected by W. Dunlop, *Journal of the Anthropological Institute*, new series, vol. i, 1898, p. 33.)

Of the people of Torres Straits Haddon states (*Reports Anthropological Expedition to Torres Straits*, vol. v, p. 222): "It was during the secular dance, or *Kap*, that the girls usually lost their hearts to the young men. A young man who was a good dancer would find favor in the sight of the girls. This can be readily understood by anyone who has seen the active, skilful, and fatiguing dances of these people. A young man who could acquit himself well in these dances must be possessed of no mean strength and agility, qualities which everywhere appeal to the opposite sex. Further, he was decorated, according to local custom, with all that would render him more imposing in the eyes of the spectators. As the former chief of Mabuiag put it, 'In England if a man has plenty of money, women want to marry him; so here, if a man dances well they too want him.' In olden days the war-dance, which was performed after a successful foray, would be the most powerful excitement to a marriageable girl, especially if a young man had distinguished himself sufficiently to bring home the head of someone he had killed."

Among the tribes inhabiting the mouth of the Wanigela River, New Guinea, "when a boy admires a girl, he will not look at her, speak to her, or go near her. He, however, shows his love by athletic bounds, posing, and pursuit, and by the spearing of imaginary enemies, etc., before her, to attract her attention. If the girl reciprocates his love she will employ a small girl to give to him an *ugauga gauna*, or love invitation, consisting of an areca-nut whose skin has been marked with different designs, significant of her wish to *ugauga*. After dark he is apprised of the place where the girl awaits him; repairing thither, he seats himself beside her as close as possible, and they mutually share in the consumption of the betel-nut." This constitutes betrothal; henceforth he is free to visit the girl's house and sleep there. Marriages usually take place at the most important festival of the year, the *kapa*, preparations for which are made during the three previous months, so that there may be a bountiful and unfailing supply of bananas. Much dancing takes place among the unmarried girls, who, also, are tattooed at this time over the whole of the front of the body, special attention being paid to the lower parts, as a girl who is not properly tattooed there possesses no attraction in the eyes of young men. Married women and widows and divorced women are not forbidden to take part in these dances, but it would be considered ridiculous for them to do so. (R. E. Guise, "On the Tribes of the Wanigela River," *Journal of the Anthropological Institute*, new series, vol. i, 1899, pp. 209, 214 *et seq.*)

In the island of Nias in the Malay Archipelago, Modigliani (mainly on the excellent authority of Sundermann, the missionary) states, at a wedding "dancing and singing go on throughout the day. The women, two or three at a time, a little apart from the men, take part in the dancing, which is very well adapted to emphasize the curves of the flanks and the breasts, though at the same time the defects of their legs are exhibited in this series of rhythmic contortions which constitute a Nias dance. The most graceful movement they execute is a lascivious undulation of the flanks while the face and breast are slowly wound round by the *sarong* [a sort of skirt] held in the hands, and then again revealed. These movements are executed with jerks of the wrist and contortions of the flanks, not always graceful, but which excite the admiration of the spectators, even of the women, who form in groups to sing in chorus a compliment, more or less sincere, in which they say: 'They dance with the grace of birds when they fly. They dance as the hawk flies; it is lovely to see.' They sing and dance both at weddings and at other festivals." (Elio Modigliani, *Un Viaggio a Nias*, 1890, p. 549.)

In Sumatra Marsden states that chastity prevails more, perhaps, than among any other people: "But little apparent courtship precedes their marriages. Their manners do not admit of it, the *boojong* and *geddas* (youths of each sex) being carefully kept asunder and the latter seldom trusted from under the wings of their mothers.... The opportunities which the young people have of seeing and conversing with each other are at the *birnbangs*, or public festivals. On these occasions the young people meet together and dance and sing in company. The men, when determined in their regard, generally employ an old woman as their agent, by whom they make known their sentiments, and send presents to the female of their choice. The parents then interfere, and the preliminaries being settled, a *birnbang* takes place. The young women proceed in a body to the upper end of the *balli* (hall), where there is a part divided off for them by a curtain. They do not always make their appearance before dinner, that time, previous to a second or third meal, being appropriated to cock-fighting or other diversions peculiar to men. In the evening their other amusements take place, of which the dances are the principal. These are performed either singly or by two women, two men, or with both mixed. Their motions and attitudes are usually slow, approaching often to the lascivious. They bend forward as they dance, and usually carry a fan, which they close and strike smartly against their elbows at particular cadences.... The assembly seldom breaks up before daylight and these *birnbangs* are often continued for several days together. The young men frequent them in order to look out for wives, and the lasses of course set themselves off to the best advantage. They wear their best silken dresses, of their own weaving, as many ornaments of filigree as they possess, silver rings upon their arms and legs, and ear-rings of a particular construction. Their hair is variously adorned with flowers, and perfumed with oil of benjamin. Civet is also in repute, but more used by the men. To render their skin fine, smooth, and soft they make use of a white cosmetic called *poopoor* [a mixture of ginger, patch-leaf, maize, sandal-wood, fairy-cotton, and mush-seed with a basis of fine rice]." (W. Marsden, *History of Sumatra*, 1783, p. 230.)

The Alfurus of Seram in the Moluccas, who have not yet been spoilt by foreign influences, are very fond of music and dancing. Their *maku* dances, which take place at night, have been described by Joest: "Great torches of dry bamboos and piles of burning resinous leaves light up the giant trees to their very summits and reveal in the distance the little huts which the Alfuras have built in the virgin forests, as well as the skulls of the slain. The women squat together by the fire, making a deafening noise with the gongs and the drums, while the young girls, richly adorned with pearls and fragrant flowers, await the beginning of the dance. Then appear the men and youths without weapons, but in full war-costume, the girdle freshly marked with the number of slain enemies. [Among the Alfuras it is the man who has the largest number of heads to show who has most chance of winning the object of his love.] They hold each other's arms and form a circle, which is not, however, completely closed. A song is started, and with small, slow steps this ring of bodies, like a winding snake, moves sideways, backward, closes, opens again, the steps become heavier, the songs and drums louder, the girls enter the circle and with closed eyes grasp the girdle of their chosen youths, who clasp them by the hips and necks, the chain becomes longer and longer, the dance and song more ardent, until the dancers grow tired and disappear in the gloom of the forest." (W. Joest, *Welt-Fahrten*, 1895, Bd. ii, p. 159.)

The women of the New Hebrides dance, or rather sway, to and fro in the midst of a circle formed by the men, with whom they do not directly mingle. They leap, show their genital parts to the men, and imitate the movements of coitus. Meanwhile the men unfasten the *manou* (penis-wrap) from their girdles with one hand, with the other imitating the action of seizing a woman, and, excited by the women, also go through a mock copulation. Sometimes, it is said, the dancers masturbate. This takes place amid plaintive songs, interrupted from time to time by loud cries and howls. (*Untrodden Fields of Anthropology*, by a French army-surgeon, 1898, vol. ii, p. 341.)

Among the hill tribes of the Central Indian Hills may be traced a desire to secure communion with the spirit of fertility embodied in vegetation. This appears, for instance, in a tree-dance, which is carried out on a date associated not only with the growths of the crops or with harvest, but also with the seasonal period for marriage and the annual Saturnalia. (W. Crooke, "The Hill Tribes," *Journal of the Anthropological Institute*, new series, vol. i, 1899, p. 243.) The association of dancing with seasonal ritual festivals of a generative character—of which the above is a fairly typical instance—leads us to another aspect of these phenomena on which I have elsewhere touched in these *Studies* (vol. i) when discussing the "Phenomena of Periodicity."

The Tahitians, when first discovered by Europeans, appear to have been highly civilized on the sexual side and very licentious. Yet even at Tahiti, when visited by Cook, the strict primitive relationship between dancing and courtship still remained traceable. Cook found "a dance called Timorodee, which is performed by young girls, whenever eight or ten of them can be collected together, consisting of motions and gestures beyond imagination wanton, in the practice of which they are brought up from their earliest childhood, accompanied by words which, if it were possible, would more explicitly convey the same ideas. But the practice which is allowed to the virgin is prohibited to the woman from the moment that she has put these hopeful lessons in practice and realized the symbols of the dance." He added, however, that among the specially privileged class of the Areoi these limitations were not observed, for he had heard that this dance was sometimes performed by them as a preliminary to sexual intercourse. (Hawkesworth, *An Account of the Voyages*, etc., 1775, vol. ii, p. 54.)

Among the Marquesans at the marriage of a woman, even of high rank, she lies with her head at the bridegroom's knees and all the male guests come in single file, singing and dancing—those of lower class first and the great chiefs last—and have connection with the woman. There are often a very large number of guests and the bride is sometimes so exhausted at the end that she has to spend several days in bed. (Tautain, "Etude sur le

Mariage chez les Polynésiens," *L'Anthropologie*, November-December, 1895, p. 642.) The interesting point for us here is that singing and dancing are still regarded as a preliminary to a sexual act. It has been noted that in sexual matters the Polynesians, when first discovered by Europeans, had largely gone beyond the primitive stage, and that this applies also to some of their dances. Thus the *hula-hula* dance, while primitive in origin, may probably be compared more to a civilized than to a primitive dance, since it has become divorced from real life. In the same way, while the sexual pantomime dance of the Azimba girls of central Africa has a direct and recognized relationship to the demands of real life, the somewhat allied *danses du ventre* of the Hamitic peoples of northern Africa are merely an amusement, a play more or less based on the sexual instinct. At the same time it is important to bear in mind that there is no rigid distinction between dances that are, and those that are not, primitive. As Haddon truly points out in a book containing valuable detailed descriptions of dances, even among savages dances are so developed that it is difficult to trace their origin, and at Torres Straits, he remarks, "there are certainly play or secular dances, dances for pure amusement without any ulterior design." (A. C. Haddon, *Head Hunters*, p. 233.) When we remember that dancing had probably become highly developed long before man appeared on the earth, this difficulty in determining the precise origin of human dancing cannot cause surprise.

Spix and Martius described how the Muras of Brazil by moonlight would engage all night in a Bacchantic dance in a great circle, hand in hand, the men on one side, the women on the other, shouting out all the time, the men "Who will marry me?" the women, "You are a beautiful devil; all women will marry you," (Spix and Martius, *Reise in Brasilien*, 1831, vol. iii, p. 1117.) They also described in detail the dance of the Brazilian Puris, performed in a state of complete nakedness, the men in a row, the women in another row behind them. They danced backward and forward, stamping and singing, at first in a slow and melancholy style, but gradually with increasing vigor and excitement. Then the women began to rotate the pelvis backward and forward, and the men to thrust their bodies forward, the dance becoming a pantomimic representation of sexual intercourse (*ibid.*, vol. i, 1823, pp. 373-5).

Among the Apinages of Brazil, also, the women stand in a row, almost motionless, while the men dance and leap in front of them, both men and women at the same time singing. (Buscalioni, "Reise zu den Apinages," *Zeitschrift für Ethnologie*, 1899, ht. 6, p. 650.)

Among the Gilas of New Mexico, "when a young man sees a girl whom he desires for a wife, he first endeavors to gain the good-will of the parents; this accomplished, he proceeds to serenade his lady-love, and will often sit for hours, day after day, near her home, playing on his flute. Should the girl not appear, it is a sign she rejects him; but if, on the other hand, she comes out to meet him, he knows that his suit is accepted, and he takes her to his home. No marriage ceremony is performed."[33] (H. H. Bancroft, *Native Races of the Pacific*, vol. i, p. 549.)

"Among the Minnetarees a singular night-dance is, it is said, sometimes held. During this amusement an opportunity is given to the squaws to select their favorites. A squaw, as she dances, will advance to a person with whom she is captivated, either for his personal attractions or for his renown in arms; she taps him on the shoulder and immediately runs out of the lodge and betakes herself to the bushes, followed by the favorite. But if it should happen that he has a particular preference for another from whom he expects the same favor, or if he is restrained by a vow, or is already satiated with indulgence, he politely declines her offer by placing his hand in her bosom, on which they return to the assembly and rejoin the dance." It is worthy of remark that in the language of the Omahas the word *watche* applies equally to the amusement of dancing and to sexual intercourse. (S. H. Long, *Expedition to the Rocky Mountains*, 1823, vol. i, p. 337.)

At a Kaffir marriage "singing and dancing last until midnight. Each party [the bride's and the bridegroom's] dances in front of the other, but they do not mingle together. As the evening advances, the spirits and passions of all become greatly excited; and the power of song, the display of muscular action, and the gesticulations of the dancers and leapers are something extraordinary. The manner in which, at certain times, one man or woman, more excited than the rest, bounds from the ranks, leaps into the air, bounces forward, and darts backward beggars all description. These violent exercises usually close about midnight, when each party retires; generally, each man selects a paramour, and, indulging in sexual

25

gratification, spends the remainder of the night." (W. C. Holden, *The Kaffir Race*, 1866, p. 192.)

At the initiation of Kaffir boys into manhood, as described by Holden, they were circumcised. "Cattle are then slaughtered by the parents, and the boys are plentifully supplied with flesh meat; a good deal of dancing also ensues at this stage of the proceedings. The *ukut-shila* consists in attiring themselves with the leaves of the wild date in the most fantastic manner; thus attired they visit each of the kraals to which they belong in rotation, for the purpose of dancing. These dances are the most licentious which can be imagined. The women act a prominent part in them, and endeavor to excite the passions of the novices by performing all sorts of obscene gesticulations. As soon as the soreness occasioned by the act of circumcision is healed the boys are, as it were, let loose upon society, and exempted from nearly all the restraints of law; so that should they even steal and slaughter their neighbor's cattle they would not be punished; and they have the special privilege of seizing by force, if force be necessary, every unmarried woman they choose, for the purpose of gratifying their passions." Similar festivals take place at the initiation of girls. (W. C. Holden, *The Kaffir Race*, 1866, p. 185.)

The Rev. J. Macdonald has described the ceremonies and customs attending and following the initiation-rites of a young girl on her first menstruation among the Zulus between the Tugela and Delagoa Bay. At this time the girl is called an *intonjane*. A beast is killed as a thank-offering to the ancestral spirits, high revel is held for several days, and dancing and music take place every night till those engaged in it are all exhausted or daylight arrives. "After a few days and when dancing has been discontinued, young men and girls congregate in the outer apartment of the hut, and begin singing, clapping their hands, and making a grunting noise to show their joy. At nightfall most of the young girls who were the intonjane's attendants, leave for their own homes for the night, to return the following morning. Thereafter the young men and girls who gathered into the hut in the afternoon separate into pairs and sleep together *in puris naturalibus*, for that is strictly ordained by custom. Sexual intercourse is not allowed, but what is known as *metsha* or *ukumetsha* is the sole purpose of the novel arrangement. *Ukumetsha* may be defined as partial intercourse. Every man who sleeps thus with a girl has to send to the father of the intonjane an assegai; should he have formed an attachment for his partner of the night and wish to pay her his addresses, he sends two assegais." (Rev. J. Macdonald, "Manners, etc., of South African Tribes," *Journal of the Anthropological Institute*, vol. xx, November, 1890, p. 117.)

Goncourt reports the account given him by a French officer from Senegal of the dances of the women, "a dance which is a gentle oscillation of the body, with gradually increasing excitement, from time to time a woman darting forward from the group to stand in front of her lover, contorting herself as though in a passionate embrace, and, on passing her hand between her thighs, showing it covered with the moisture of amorous enjoyment." (*Journal*, vol. ix, p. 79.) The dance here referred to is probably the Bamboula dance of the Wolofs, a spring festival which has been described by Pierre Loti in his *Roman d'un Spahi*, and concerning which various details are furnished by a French army-surgeon, acquainted with Senegal, in his *Untrodden Fields of Anthropology*. The dance, as described by the latter, takes place at night during full moon, the dancers, male and female, beginning timidly, but, as the beat of the tam-tams and the encouraging cries of the spectators become louder, the dance becomes more furious. The native name of the dance is *anamalis fobil*, "the dance of the treading drake." "The dancer in his movements imitates the copulation of the great Indian duck. This drake has a member of a corkscrew shape, and a peculiar movement is required to introduce it into the duck. The woman tucks up her clothes and convulsively agitates the lower part of her body; she alternately shows her partner her vulva and hides it from him by a regular movement, backward and forward, of the body." (*Untrodden Fields of Anthropology*, Paris, 1898, vol. ii, p. 112.)

Among the Gurus of the Ivory Coast (Gulf of Guinea), Eysséric observes, dancing is usually carried on at night and more especially by the men, and on certain occasions women must not appear, for if they assisted at fetichistic dances "they would die." Under other circumstances men and women dance together with ardor, not forming couples but often *vis-à-vis*: their movements are lascivious. Even the dances following a funeral tend to become

26

sexual in character. At the end of the rites attending the funeral of a chief's son the entire population began to dance with ever-growing ardor; there was nothing ritualistic or sad in these contortions, which took on the character of a lascivious dance. Men and women, boys and girls, young and old, sought to rival each other in suppleness, and the festival became joyous and general, as if in celebration of a marriage or a victory. (Eysséric, "La Côte d'Ivoire," *Nouvelles Archives des Missions Scientifiques*, tome ix, 1890, pp. 241-49.)

Mrs. French-Sheldon has described the marriage-rites she observed at Taveta in East Africa. "During this time the young people dance and carouse and make themselves generally merry and promiscuously drunk, carrying the excess of their dissipation to such an extent that they dance until they fall down in a species of epileptic fit." It is the privilege of the bridegroom's four groomsmen to enjoy the bride first, and she is then handed over to her legitimate husband. This people, both men and women, are "great dancers and merry-makers; the young fellows will collect in groups and dance as though in competition one with the other; one lad will dash out from the circle of his companions, rush into the middle of a circumscribed space, and scream out 'Wow, wow!' Another follows him and screams; then a third does the same. These men will dance with their knees almost rigid, jumping into the air until their excitement becomes very great and their energy almost spasmodic, leaving the ground frequently three feet as they spring into the air. At some of their festivals their dancing is carried to such an extent that I have seen a young fellow's muscles quiver from head to foot and his jaws tremble without any apparent ability on his part to control them, until, foaming at the mouth and with his eyes rolling, he falls in a paroxysm upon the ground, to be carried off by his companions." The writer adds significantly that this dancing "would seem to emanate from a species of voluptuousness." (Mrs. French-Sheldon, "Customs among the Natives of East Africa," *Journal of the Anthropological Institute*, vol. xxi, May, 1892, pp. 366-67.) It may be added that among the Suaheli dances are intimately associated with weddings; the Suaheli dances have been minutely described by Velten (*Sitten und Gebraüche der Suaheli*, pp. 144-175). Among the Akamba of British East Africa, also, according to H. R. Tate (*Journal of the Anthropological Institute*, Jan.-June, 1904, p. 137), the dances are followed by connection between the young men and girls, approved of by the parents.

The dances of the Faroe Islanders have been described by Raymond Pilet ("Rapport sur une Mission en Islande et aux Iles Féroë," *Nouvelles Archives des Missions Scientifiques*, tome vii, 1897, p. 285). These dances, which are entirely decorous, include poetry, music, and much mimicry, especially of battle. They sometimes last for two consecutive days and nights. "The dance is simply a permitted and discreet method by which the young men may court the young girls. The islander enters the circle and places himself beside the girl to whom he desires to show his affection; if he meets with her approval she stays and continues to dance at his side; if not, she leaves the circle and appears later at another spot."

Pitre (*Usi, etc., del Popolo Siciliano*, vol. ii, p. 24, as quoted in Marro's *Pubertà*) states that in Sicily the youth who wishes to marry seeks to give some public proof of his valor and to show himself off. In Chiaramonte, in evidence of his virile force, he bears in procession the standard of some confraternity, a high and richly adorned standard which makes its staff bend to a semicircle, of such enormous weight that the bearer must walk in a painfully bent position, his head thrown back and his feet forward. On reaching the house of his betrothed he makes proof of his boldness and skill in wielding this extremely heavy standard which at this moment seems a plaything in his hands, but may yet prove fatal to him through injury to the loins or other parts.

This same tendency, which we find in so highly developed a degree among animals and primitive human peoples, is also universal among the children of even the most civilized human races, although in a less organized and more confused way. It manifests itself as "showing-off." Sanford Bell, in his study of the emotion of love in children, finds that "showing-off" is an essential element in the love of children in what he terms the second stage (from the eighth to the twelfth year in girls and the fourteenth in boys). "It constitutes one of the chief numbers in the boy's repertory of love charms, and is not totally absent from the girl's. It is a most common sight to see the boys taxing theirresources in devising means of exposing their own excellencies, and often doing the most ridiculous and extravagant things. Running, jumping, dancing, prancing, sparring, wrestling, turning handsprings, somersaults, climbing, walking fences, swinging, giving yodels and yells, whistling, imitating the movements of animals, 'taking people off,' courting danger, affecting courage are some of its common forms.... This 'showing-off' in the boy lover is the forerunner of the skilful, purposive, and elaborate means of self-exhibition in the adult male and the charming coquetry in the adult female, in their love-relations." (Sanford Bell, "The Emotion of Love Between the Sexes," *American Journal Psychology*, July, 1902; *cf.* "Showing-off and Bashfulness," *Pedagogical Seminary*, June, 1903.)

If, in the light of the previous discussion, we examine such facts as those here collected, we may easily trace throughout the perpetual operations of the same instinct. It is everywhere the instinctive object of the male, who is very rarely passive in the process of courtship, to assure by his activity in display, his energy or skill or beauty, both his own passion and the passion of the female. Throughout nature sexual conjugation only takes place after much expenditure of energy.[34] We are deceived by what we see among highly fed domesticated animals, and among the lazy classes of human society, whose sexual instincts are at once both unnaturally stimulated and unnaturally repressed, when we imagine that the instinct of detumescence is normally ever craving to be satisfied, and that throughout nature it can always be set off at a touch whenever the stimulus is applied. So far from the instinct of tumescence naturally needing to be crushed, it needs, on the contrary, in either sex to be submitted to the most elaborate and prolonged processes in order to bring about those conditions which detumescence relieves. A state of tumescence is not normally constant, and tumescence must be obtained before detumescence is possible.[35] The whole object of courtship, of the mutual approximation and caresses of two persons of the opposite sex, is to create the state of sexual tumescence.

It will be seen that the most usual method of attaining tumescence—a method found among the most various kinds of animals, from insects and birds to man—is some form of the dance. Among the Negritos of the Philippines dancing is described by A. B. Meyer as "jumping in a circle around a girl and stamping with the feet"; as we have seen, such a dance is, essentially, a form of courtship that is widespread among animals. "The true cake-walk," again, Stanley Hall remarks, "as seen in the South is perhaps the purest expression of this impulse to courtship antics seen in man."[36]Muscular movement of which the dance is the highest and most complex expression, is undoubtedly a method of auto-intoxication of the very greatest potency. All energetic movement, indeed, tends to produce active congestion. In its influence on the brain violent exercise may thus result in a state of intoxication even resembling insanity. As Lagrange remarks, the visible effects of exercise—heightened color, bright eyes, resolute air and walk—are those of slight intoxication, and a girl who has waltzed for a quarter of an hour is in the same condition as if she had drunk champagne.[37] Groos regards the dance as, above all, an intoxicating play of movement, possessing, like other methods of intoxication,—and even apart from its relationship to combat and love,—the charm of being able to draw us out of our everyday life and lead us into a self-created dream-world.[38] That the dance is not only a narcotic, but also a powerful stimulant, we may clearly realize from the experiments which show that this effect is produced even by much less complex kinds of muscular movement. This has been clearly determined, for instance, by Féré, in the course of a long and elaborate series of experiments dealing with the various influences that modify work as measured by Mosso's ergograph. This investigator found that muscular movement is the most efficacious of all stimulants in increasing muscular power.[39] It is easy to trace these pleasurable effects of combined narcotic and stimulant motion in everyday life and it is unnecessary to enumerate its manifestations.[40]

Dancing is so powerful an agent on the organism, as Sergi truly remarks (*Les Emotions*, p. 288), because its excitation is general, because it touches every vital organ, the higher centers no longer dominating. Primitive dancing differs very widely from that civilized kind of dancing—finding its extreme type in the ballet—in which energy is concentrated into the muscles below the knee. In the finest kinds of primitive dancing all the limbs, the whole body, take part. For instance, "the Marquisan girls," Herman Melville remarked in *Typee*, "dance all over, as it were; not only do their feet dance, but their arms, hands, fingers,—ay, their very eyes seem to dance in their heads. In good sooth, they so sway their floating forms, arch their necks, toss aloft their naked arms, and glide, and swim, and whirl," etc.

If we turn to a very different people, we find this characteristic of primitive dancing admirably illustrated by the missionary, Holden, in the case of Kaffir dances. "So far as I have observed," he states, "the perfection of the art or science consists in their *being able to put every part of the body into motion at the same time*. And as they are naked, the bystander has a good opportunity of observing the whole process, which presents a remarkably odd and grotesque appearance,—the head, the trunk, the arms, the legs, the hands, the feet, bones, muscles, sinews, skin, scalp, and hair, each and all in motion at the same time, with feathers waving, tails of monkeys and wild beasts dangling, and shields beating, accompanied with whistling, shouting, and leaping. It would appear as though the whole frame was hung on springing wires or cords. Dances are held in high repute, being the natural expression of joyous emotion, or creating it when absent. There is, perhaps, no exercise in greater accordance with the sentiments or feelings of a barbarous people, or more fully calculated to gratify their wild and ungoverned passions." (W. C. Holden, *The Kaffir Race*, 1866, p. 274.)

Dancing, as the highest and most complex form of muscular movement, is the most potent method of obtaining the organic excitement muscular movement yields, and thus we understand how from the earliest zoölogical ages it has been brought to the service of the sexual instinct as a mode of attaining tumescence. Among savages this use of dancing works harmoniously with the various other uses which dancing possesses in primitive times and which cause it to occupy so large and vital a part in savage life that it may possibly even affect the organism to such an extent as to mold the bones; so that some authorities have associated platycnemia with dancing. As civilization advances, the other uses of dancing fall away, but it still remains a sexual stimulant. Burton, in his *Anatomy of Melancholy*, brings forward a number of quotations from old authors showing that dancing is an incitement to love.[41]

The Catholic theologians (Debreyne, *Mœchialogie*, pp. 190-199) for the most part condemn dancing with much severity. In Protestant Germany, also, it is held that dance meetings and musical gatherings are frequent occasions of unchastity. Thus in the Leipzig district when a girl is asked "How did you fall?" she nearly always replies "At the dance." (*Die Geschlechtlich-Sittliche Verhältnisse im Deutschen Reiche*, vol. i, p. 196.) It leads quite as often, and no doubt oftener, to marriage. Rousseau defended it on this account (*Nouvelle Heloïse*, bk. iv, letter x); dancing is, he held, an admirable preliminary to courtship, and the best way for young people to reveal themselves to each other, in their grace and decorum, their qualities and defects, while its publicity is its safeguard. An International Congress of Dancing Masters was held at Barcelona in 1907. In connection with this Congress, Giraudet, president of the International Academy of Dancing Masters, issued an inquiry to over 3000 teachers of dancing throughout the world in order to ascertain the frequency with which dancing led to marriage. Of over one million pupils of dancing, either married or engaged to be married, it was found that in most countries more than 50 per cent. met their conjugal partners at dances. The smallest proportion was in Norway, with only 39 per cent., and the highest, Germany, with 97 per cent. Intermediate are France, 83 per cent.; America, 80 per cent.; Italy, 70 per cent.; Spain, 68 per cent.; Holland, Bulgaria, and England, 65 per cent.; Australia and Roumania, 60 per cent., etc. Of the teachers themselves 92 per cent. met their partners at dances. (Quoted from the *Figaro* in Beiblatt "Sexualreform" to *Geschlecht und Gesellschaft*, 1907, p. 175.)

In civilization, however, dancing is not only an incitement to love and a preliminary to courtship, but it is often a substitute for the normal gratification of the sexual instinct, procuring something of the pleasure and relief of gratified love. In occasional abnormal cases this may be consciously realized. Thus Sadger, who regards the joy of dancing as a manifestation of "muscular eroticism," gives the case of a married hysterical woman of 21, with genital anesthesia, but otherwise strongly developed skin eroticism, who was a passionate dancer: "I often felt as though I was giving myself to my partner in dancing," she said, "and was actually having coitus with him. I have the feeling that in me dancing takes the place of coitus."[42] Normally something of the same feeling is experienced by many young women, who will expend a prodigious amount of energy in dancing, thus procuring, not fatigue, but happiness and relief.[43] It is significant that, after sexual relations have begun, girls generally lose much of their ardor in dancing. Even our modern dances, it is worthy of note, are often of sexual origin; thus, the most typical of all, the waltz, was originally (as Schaller, quoted by Groos, states) the close of a complicated dance which "represented the romance of love, the seeking and the fleeing, the playful sulking and shunning, and finally the jubilation of the wedding."[44]

Not only is movement itself a source of tumescence, but even the spectacle of movement tends to produce the same effect. The pleasure of witnessing movement, as represented by its stimulating effect on the muscular system,—for states of well-being are accompanied by an increase of power,—has been found susceptible of exact measurement by Féré. He has shown that to watch a colored disk when in motion produced stronger muscular contractions, as measured by the dynamometer, than to watch the same disk when motionless. Even in the absence of color a similar influence of movement was noted, and watching a modified metronome produced a greater increase of work with the ergograph than when working to the rhythm of the metronome without watching it.[45] This psychological fact has been independently discovered by advertisers, who seek to impress the value of their wares on the public by the device of announcing them by moving colored lights. The pleasure given by the ballet largely depends on the same fact. Not only is dancing an excitation, but the spectacle of dancing is itself exciting, and even among savages dances have a public which becomes almost as passionately excited as the dancers themselves.[46] It is in virtue of this effect of dancing and similar movements that we so frequently find, both among the lower animals and savage man, that to obtain tumescence in both sexes, it is sufficient for one sex alone, usually the male, to take the active part. This point attracted the attention of Kulischer many years ago, and he showed how the dances of the men, among savages, excite the women, who watch them intently though unobtrusively, and are thus influenced in choosing their lovers. He was probably the first to insist that in man sexual selection has taken place mainly through the agency of dances, games, and festivals.[47]

It is now clear, therefore, why the evacuation theory of the sexual impulse must necessarily be partial and inadequate. It leaves out of account the whole of the phenomena connected with tumescence, and those phenomena constitute the most prolonged, the most important, the most significant stage of the sexual process. It is during tumescence that the whole psychology of the sexual impulse is built up; it is as an incident arising during tumescence and influencing its course that we must probably regard nearly every sexual aberration. It is with the second stage of the sexual process, when the instinct of detumescence arises, that the analogy of evacuation can alone be called in. Even here, that analogy, though real, is not complete, the nervous element involved in detumescence being out of all proportion to the extent of the evacuation. The typical act of evacuation, however, is a nervous process, and when we bear this in mind we may see whatever truth the evacuation theory possesses. Beaunis classes the sexual impulse with the "needs of activity," but under this head he coordinates it with the "need of urination." That is to say, that both alike are nervous explosions. Micturition, like detumescence, is a convulsive act, and, like detumescence also, it is certainly connected with cerebral processes; thus in epilepsy the passage of urine which may occur (as in a girl described by Gowers with minor attacks during which it was emitted consciously, but involuntarily) is really a part of the process.[48]

There appears, indeed, to be a special and intimate connection between the explosion of sexual detumescence and the explosive energy of the bladder; so that they may reinforce each other and to a limited extent act vicariously in relieving each other's tension. It is noteworthy that nocturnal and diurnal incontinence of urine, as well as "stammering" of the bladder, are all specially liable to begin or to cease at puberty. In men and even infants, distention of the bladder favors tumescence by producing venous congestion, though at the same time it acts as a physical hindrance to sexual detumescence[49]; in women—probably not from pressure alone, but from reflex nervous action—a full bladder increases both sexual excitement and pleasure, and I have been informed by several women that they have independently discovered this fact for themselves and acted in accordance with it. Conversely, sexual excitement increases the explosive force of the bladder, the desire to urinate is aroused, and in women the sexual orgasm, when very acute and occurring with a full bladder, is occasionally accompanied, alike in savage and civilized life, by an involuntary and sometimes full and forcible expulsion of urine.[50] The desire to urinate may possibly be, as has been said, the normal accompaniment of sexual excitement in women (just as it is said to be in mares; so that the Arabs judge that the mare is ready for the stallion when she urinates immediately on hearing him neigh). The association may even form the basis of sexual obsessions.[51] I have elsewhere shown that, of all the influences which increase the expulsive force of the bladder, sexual excitement is the most powerful.[52] It may also have a reverse influence and inhibit contraction of the bladder, sometimes in association with shyness, but also independently of shyness. There is also reason to suppose that the nervous energy expended in an explosion of the tension of the sexual organs may sometimes relieve the bladder; it is well recognized that a full bladder is a factor in producing sexual emissions during sleep, the explosive energy of the bladder being inhibited and passing over into the sexual sphere. Conversely, it appears that explosion of the bladder relieves sexual tension. An explosion of the nervous centers connected with the contraction of the bladder will relieve nervous tension generally; there are forms of epilepsy in which the act of urination constitutes the climax, and Gowers, in dealing with minor epilepsy, emphasizes the frequency of micturition, which "may occur with spasmodic energy when there is only the slightest general stiffness," especially in women. He adds the significant remark that it "sometimes seems to relieve the cerebral tension,"[53] and gives the case of a girl in whom the aura consisted mainly of a desire to urinate; if she could satisfy this the fit was arrested; if not she lost consciousness and a severe fit followed.

If micturition may thus relieve nervous tension generally, it is not surprising that it should relieve the tension of the centers with which it is most intimately connected. Sérieux records the case of a girl of 12, possessed by an impulse to masturbation which she was unable to control, although anxious to conquer it, who only found relief in the act of urination; this soothed her and to some extent satisfied the sexual excitement; when the impulse to masturbate was restrained the impulse to urinate became imperative; she would rise four or five times in the night for this purpose, and even urinate in bed or in her clothes to obtain the desired sexual relief.[54] I am acquainted with a lady who had a similar, but less intense, experience during childhood. Sometimes, especially in children, the act of urination becomes an act of gratification at the climax of sexual pleasure, the imitative symbol of detumescence. Thus Schultze-Malkowsky describes a little girl of 7 who would bribe her girl companions with little presents to play the part of horses on all fours while she would ride on their necks with naked thighs in order to obtain the pleasurable sensation of close contact. With one special friend she would ride facing backward, and leaning forward to embrace her body impulsively, and at the same time pressing the neck closely between her thighs, would urinate.[55] Féré has recorded the interesting case of a man who, having all his life after puberty been subject to monthly attacks of sexual excitement, after the age of 45 completely lost the liability to these manifestations, but found himself subject, in place of them, to monthly attacks of frequent and copious urination, accompanied by sexual day-dreams, but by no genital excitement.[56] Such a case admirably illustrates the compensatory relation of sexual and vesical excitation. This mutual interaction is easily comprehensible when we recall the very close nervous connection which exists between the mechanisms of the sexual organs and the bladder.

Nor are such relationships found to be confined to these two centers; in a lesser degree the more remote explosive centers are also affected; all motor influences may spread to related muscles; the convulsion of laughter, for instance, seems to be often in relation with the sexual center, and Groos has suggested that the laughter which, especially in the sexually minded, often follows allusions to the genital sphere is merely an effort to dispel nascent sexual excitement by liberating an explosion of nervous energy in another direction.[57] Nervous discharges tend to spread, or to act vicariously, because the motor centers are more or less connected.[58] Of all the physiological motor explosions, the sexual orgasm, or detumescence, is the most massive, powerful, and overwhelming. So volcanic is it that to the ancient Greek philosophers it seemed to be a minor kind of epilepsy. The relief of detumescence is not merely the relief of an evacuation; it is the discharge, by the most powerful apparatus for nervous explosion in the body, of the energy accumulated and stored up in the slow process of tumescence, and that discharge reverberates through all the nervous centers in the organism.

"The sophist of Abdera said that coitus is a slight fit of epilepsy, judging it to be an incurable disease." (Clement of Alexandria,*Pædagogus*, bk. ii, chapter x.) And Cœlius Aurelianus, one of the chief physicians of antiquity, said that "coitus is a brief epilepsy." Féré has pointed out that both these forms of nervous storm are sometimes accompanied by similar phenomena, by subjective sensations of sight or smell, for example; and that the two kinds of discharge may even be combined. (Féré, *Les Epileptiques*, pp. 283-84; also "Exces Vénériens et Epilepsie," *Comptes-rendus de la Société de Biologie*, April 3, 1897, and the same author's*Instinct Sexuel*, pp. 209, 221, and his "Priapisme Epileptique," *La Médecine Moderne*, February 4, 1899.) The epileptic convulsion in some cases involves the sexual mechanism, and it is noteworthy that epilepsy tends to appear at puberty. In modern times even so great a physician as Boerhaave said that coitus is a "true epilepsy," and more recently Roubaud, Hammond, and Kowalevsky have emphasized the resemblance between coitus and epilepsy, though without identifying the two states. Some authorities have considered that coitus is a cause of epilepsy, but this is denied by Christian, Strümpell, and Löwenfeld. (Löwenfeld, *Sexualleben und Nervenleiden*, 1899, p. 68.) Féré has recorded the case of a youth in whom the adoption of the practice of masturbation, several times a day, was followed by epileptic attacks which ceased when masturbation was abandoned. (Féré, *Comptes-rendus de la Socitété de Biologie*, April 3, 1897.)

It seems unprofitable at present to attempt any more fundamental analysis of the sexual impulse. Beaunis, in the work already quoted, vaguely suggests that we ought possibly to connect the sexual excitation which leads the male to seek the female with chemical action, either exercised directly on the protoplasm of the organism or indirectly by the intermediary of the nervous system, and especially by smell in the higher animals. Clevenger, Spitzka, Kiernan, and others have also regarded the sexual impulse as protoplasmic hunger, tracing it back to the presexual times when one protozoal form absorbed another. In the same way Joanny Roux, insisting that the sexual need is a need of the whole organism, and that "we love with the whole of our body," compares the sexual instinct to hunger, and distinguishes between "sexual hunger" affecting the whole system and "sexual appetite" as a more localized desire; he concludes that the sexual need is an aspect of the nutritive need.[59] Useful as these views are as a protest against too crude and narrow a conception of the part played by the sexual impulse, they carry us into a speculative region where proof is difficult.

We are now, however, at all events, in a better position to define the contents of the sexual impulse. We see that there are certainly, as Moll has indicated, two constituents in that impulse; but, instead of being unrelated, or only distantly related, we see that they are really so intimately connected as to form two distinct stages in the same process: a first stage, in which—usually under the parallel influence of internal and external stimuli—images, desires, and ideals grow up within the mind, while the organism generally is charged with energy and the sexual apparatus congested with blood; and a second stage, in which the sexual apparatus is discharged amid profound sexual excitement, followed by deep organic relief. By the first process is constituted the tension which the second process relieves. It seems best to call the first impulse the*process of tumescence*; the second the *process of detumescence*.[60] The first, taking on usually a more active form in the male, has the double object of bringing the male himself into the condition in which discharge becomes imperative, and at the same time arousing in the female a similar ardent state of emotional excitement and sexual turgescence. The second process has the object, directly, of discharging the tension thus produced and, indirectly, of effecting the act by which the race is propagated.

It seems to me that this is at present the most satisfactory way in which we can attempt to define the sexual impulse.

[1]
C. Lloyd Morgan, "Instinct and Intelligence in Animals," *Nature*, February 3, 1898.
[2]
Essais, livre iii, ch. v.

[3]
Féré, "La Prédisposition dans l'étiologie des perversions sexuelles," *Revue de médecine*, 1898. In his more recent work on the evolution and dissolution of the sexual instinct Féré perhaps slightly modified his position by stating that "the sexual appetite is, above all, a general need of the organism based on a sensation of fullness, a sort of need of evacuation," *L'Instinct sexuel*, 1899, p. 6. Löwenfeld (*Ueber die Sexuelle Konstitution*, p. 30) gives a qualified acceptance to the excretory theory, as also Rohleder (*Die Zeugung beim Menschen*, p. 25).

[4]
Goltz, *Centralblatt für die med. Wissenschaften*, 1865, No. 19, and 1866, No. 18; also *Beiträge zur Lehre von den Funktionen des Frosches*, Berlin, 1869, p. 20.

[5]
J. Tarchanoff, "Zur Physiologie des Geschlechtsapparatus des Frosches,"*Archiv für die Gesammte Physiologie*, 1887, vol. xl, p. 330.

[6]
E. Steinach, "Untersuchungen zur vergleichenden Physiologie der männlicher Geschlechtsorgane insbesondere der accessorischen Geschlechtsdrüsen," *Archiv für die Gesammte Physiologie*, vol. lvi, 1894, pp. 304-338.

[7]
See, *e.g.*, Shattock and Seligmann, "The Acquirement of Secondary Sexual Characters," *Proceedings of the Royal Society*, vol. lxxiii, 1904, p. 49.

[8]
For facts bearing on this point, see Guinard, art. "Castration," Richet's*Dictionnaire de Physiologie*. The general results of castration are summarized by Robert Müller in ch. vii of his *Sexualbiologie*; also by F. H. A. Marshall, *The Physiology of Reproduction*, ch, ix; see also E. Pittard, "Les Skoptzy," *L'Anthropologie*, 1903, p. 463.

[9]
For an ancient discussion of this point, see Schurig, *Spermatologia*, 1720, cap. ix.

[10]
J. J. Matignon, *Superstition, Crime, et Misère en Chine*, "Les Eunuques du Palais Impérial de Pékin," 1901.

[11]
P. Marie, "Eunuchisme et Erotisme," *Nouvelle Iconographie de la Salpêtrière*, 1906, No. 5, and *Progrès médical*, Jan. 26, 1907.

[12]
Pedagogical Seminary, July, 1897, p. 121.

[13]
See, for instance, the case reported in another volume of these *Studies*("Sexual Inversion"), in which castration was performed on a sexual invert without effecting any change.

[14]
Guinard, art. "Castration," *Dictionnaire de Physiologie*.

[15]
M. A. Colman, *Medical Standard*, August, 1895; Clara Barrus, *American Journal of Insanity*, April, 1895; Macnaughton-Jones, *British Gynæcological Journal*, August, 1902; W. G. Bridgman, *Medical Standard*, 1896; J. M. Cotterill, *British Medical Journal*, April 7, 1900 (also private communication); Paul F. Mundé, *American Journal of Obstetrics*, March, 1899.

[16]
See Swale Vincent, *Internal Secretion and the Ductless Glands*, 1912; F. H. A. Marshall, *The Physiology of Reproduction*, 1910, ch. ix; Munzer,*Berliner klinische Wochenschrift*, Nov., 1910; C. Sajous, *The Internal Secretions*, vol. i, 1911. The adrenal glands have been fully and interestingly studied by Glynn,*Quarterly Journal of Medicine*, Jan., 1912; the thyroid, by Ewan Waller, *Practitioner*, Aug., 1912; the internal secretion of the ovary, by A. Louise McIlroy, *Proceedings Royal Society Medicine*, July, 1912. For a discussion at the Neurology Section of the British Medical Association Meeting, 1912, see *British Medical Journal*, Nov. 16, 1912.

[17]

Since this was written I have come across a passage in *Hampa* (p. 228), by Rafael Salillas, the Spanish sociologist, which shows that the analogy has been detected by the popular mind and been embodied in popular language: "A significant anatomico-physiological concordance supposes a resemblance between the mouth and the sexual organs of a woman, between coitus and the ingestion of food, and between foods which do not require mastication and the spermatic ejaculation; these representations find expression in the popular name *papo* given to women's genital organs. 'Papo' is the crop of birds, and is derived from 'papar' (Latin, *papare*), to eat soft food such as we call pap. With this representation of infantile food is connected the term *leche* [milk] as applied to the ejaculated genital fluid." Cleland, it may be added, in the most remarkable of English erotic novels,*The Memoirs of Fanny Hill*, refers to "the compressive exsuction with which the sensitive mechanism of that part [the vagina] thirstily draws and drains the nipple of Love," and proceeds to compare it to the action of the child at the breast. It appears that, in some parts of the animal world at least, there is a real analogy of formation between the oral and vaginal ends of the trunk. This is notably the case in some insects, and the point has been elaborately discussed by Walter Wesché, "The Genitalia of Both the Sexes in Diptera, and their Relation to the Armature of the Mouth," *Transactions of the Linnean Society*, second series, vol. ix, Zoölogy, 1906.

[18]

Näcke now expresses himself very dubiously on the point; see, *e.g.*, *Archiv für Kriminal-Anthropologie*, 1905, p. 186.

[19]

Untersuchungen über die Libido Sexualis, Berlin, 1897-98.

[20]

Moll adopts the term "impulse of detumescence" (*Detumescenztrieb*) instead of "impulse of ejaculation," because in women there is either no ejaculation or it cannot be regarded as essential.

[21]

I quote from the second edition, as issued in 1881.

[22]

This is the theory which by many has alone been seen in Darwin's *Descent of Man*. Thus even his friend Wallace states unconditionally (*Tropical Nature*, p. 193) that Darwin accepted a "voluntary or conscious sexual selection," and seems to repeat the same statement in *Darwinism* (1889), p. 283. Lloyd Morgan, in his discussion of the pairing instinct in *Habit and Instinct* (1896), seems also only to see this side of Darwin's statement.

[23]

In his *Variation of Animals and Plants under Domestication*, Darwin was puzzled by the fact that, in captivity, animals often copulate without conceiving and failed to connect that fact with the processes behind his own theory of sexual selection.

[24]

Beaunis, *Sensations Internes*, ch. v, "Besoins Sexuels," 1889. It may be noted that many years earlier Burdach (in his *Physiologie als Erfahrungswissenschaft*, 1826) had recognized that the activity of the male favored procreation, and that mental and physical excitement seemed to have the same effect in the female also.

[25]

It is scarcely necessary to point out that this is too extreme a position. As J. G. Millais remarks of ducks (*Natural History of British Ducks*, p. 45), in courtship "success in winning the admiration of the female is rather a matter of persistent and active attention than physical force," though the males occasionally fight over the female. The ruff (*Machetes pugnax*) is a pugnacious bird, as his name indicates. Yet, the reeve, the female of this species, is, as E. Selous shows ("Sexual Selection in Birds," *Zoölogist*, Feb. and May, 1907), completely mistress of the situation. "She seems the plain and unconcerned little mistress of a numerous and handsome seraglio, each member of which, however he flounce and bounce, can only wait to be chosen." Any fighting among the males is only incidental and is not a factor in selection. Moreover, as R. Müller points out (*loc. cit.*, p. 290), fighting would not usually attain

34

the end desired, for if the males expend their time and strength in a serious combat they merely afford a third less pugnacious male a better opportunity of running off with the prize.

[26]

L. Tillier, *L'Instinct Sexuel*, 1889, pp. 74, 118, 119, 124 *et seq.*, 289.

[27]

K. Groos, *Die Spiele der Thiere*, 1896; *Die Spiele der Menschen*, 1899; both are translated into English.

[28]

Prof. H. E. Ziegler, in a private letter to Professor Groos, *Spiele der Thiere*, p. 202.

[29]

Die Spiele der Thiere, p. 244. This had been briefly pointed out by earlier writers. Thus, Haeckel (*Gen. Morph.*, ii, p. 244) remarked that fighting for females is a special or modified kind of struggle for existence, and that it acts on both sexes.

[30]

It may be added that in the human species, as Bray remarks ("Le Beau dans la Nature," *Revue Philosophique*, October, 1901, p. 403), "the hymen would seem to tend to the same end, as if nature had wished to reinforce by a natural obstacle the moral restraint of modesty, so that only the vigorous male could insure his reproduction." There can be no doubt that among many animals pairing is delayed so far as possible until maturity is reached. "It is a strict rule amongst birds," remarks J. G. Millais (*op. cit.*, p. 46), "that they do not breed until both sexes have attained the perfect adult plumage." Until that happens, it seems probable, the conditions for sexual excitation are not fully established. We know little, says Howard (*Zoölogist*, 1903, p. 407), of the age at which birds begin to breed, but it is known that "there are yearly great numbers of individuals who do not breed, and the evidence seems to show that such individuals are immature."

[31]

A. Marro, *La Puberté*, 1901, p. 464.

[32]

Lloyd Morgan, *Animal Behavior*, 1900, pp. 264-5. It may be added that, on the esthetic side, Hirn, in his study (*The Origins of Art*, 1900), reaches conclusions which likewise, in the main, concord with those of Groos.

[33]

It may be noted that the marriage ceremony itself is often of the nature of a courtship, a symbolic courtship, embodying a method of attaining tumescence. As Crawley, who has brought out this point, puts it, "Marriage-rites of union are essentially identical with love charms," and he refers in illustration to the custom of the Australian Arunta, among whom the man or woman by making music on the bull-roarer compels a person of the opposite sex to court him or her, the marriage being thus completed. (E. Crawley, *The Mystic Rose*, p. 318.)

[34]

The more carefully animals are observed, the more often this is found to be the case, even with respect to species which possess no obvious and elaborate process for obtaining tumescence. See, for instance, the detailed and very instructive account—too long to quote here—given by E. Selous of the preliminaries to intercourse practised by a pair of great crested grebes, while nest-building. Intercourse only took place with much difficulty, after many fruitless invitations, more usually given by the female. ("Observational Diary of the Habits of the Great Crested Grebe," *Zoölogist*, September, 1901.) It is exactly the same with savages. The observation of Foley (*Bulletin de la Société d'Anthropologie de Paris*, November 6, 1879) that in savages "sexual erethism is very difficult" is of great significance and certainly in accordance with the facts. This difficulty of erethism is the real cause of many savage practices which to the civilized person often seem perverse; the women of the Caroline Islands, for instance, as described by Finsch, require the tongue or even the teeth to be applied to the clitoris, or a great ant to be applied to bite the parts, in order to stimulate orgasm. Westermarck, after quoting a remark of Mariner's concerning the women of Tonga,—"it must not be supposed that these women are always easily won; the greatest attentions and the most fervent solicitations are sometimes requisite, even though there be

35

no other lover in the way,"—adds that these words "hold true for a great many, not to say all, savage and barbarous races now existing." (*Human Marriage*, p. 163.) The old notions, however, as to the sexual licentiousness of peoples living in natural conditions have scarcely yet disappeared. See Appendix A; "The Sexual Instinct in Savages."

[35]

In men a certain degree of tumescence is essential before coitus can be effected at all; in women, though tumescence is not essential to coitus, it is essential to orgasm and the accompanying physical and psychic relief. The preference which women often experience for prolonged coitus is not, as might possibly be imagined, due to sensuality, but has a profound physiological basis.

[36]

Stanley Hall, *Adolescence*, vol. i, p. 223.

[37]

See Lagrange's *Physiology of Bodily Exercise*, especially chapter ii. It is a significant fact that, as Sergi remarks (*Les Emotions*, p. 330), the physiological results of dancing are identical with the physiological results of pleasure.

[38]

Groos, *Spiele der Menschen*, p. 112. Zmigrodzki (*Die Mutter bei den Volkern des Arischen Stammes*, p. 414 *et seq.*) has an interesting passage describing the dance—especially the Russian dance—in its orgiastic aspects.

[39]

Féré, "L'Influence sur le Travail Volontaire d'un muscle de l'activité d'autres muscles," *Nouvelles Iconographie de la Salpêtrière*, 1901.

[40]

"The sensation of motion," Kline remarks ("The Migratory Impulse,"*American Journal of Psychology*, October, 1898, p. 62), "as yet but little studied from a pleasure-pain standpoint, is undoubtedly a pleasure-giving sensation. For Aristippus the end of life is pleasure, which he defines as gentle motion. Motherhood long ago discovered its virtue as furnished by the cradle. Galloping to town on the parental knee is a pleasing pastime in every nursery. The several varieties of swings, the hammock, see-saw, flying-jenny, merry-go-round, shooting the chutes, sailing, coasting, rowing, and skating, together with the fondness of children for rotating rapidly in one spot until dizzy and for jumping from high places, are all devices and sports for stimulating the sense of motion. In most of these modes of motion the body is passive or semipassive, save in such motions as skating and rotating on the feet. The passiveness of the body precludes any important contribution of stimuli from kinesthetic sources. The stimuli are probably furnished, as Dr. Hall and others have suggested, by a redistribution of fluid pressure (due to the unusual motions and positions of the body) to the inner walls of the several vascular systems of the body."

[41]

Anatomy of Melancholy, part iii., sect. ii, mem. ii, subs. iv.

[42]

Sadger, "Haut-, Schleimhaut-, und Muskel-erotik," *Jahrbuch für psychoanalytische Forschungen*, Bd. iii, 1912, p. 556.

[43]

Marro (*Pubertà*, p. 367 *et seq.*) has some observations on this point. It was an insight into this action of dancing which led the Spanish clergy of the eighteenth century to encourage the national enthusiasm for dancing (as Baretti informs us) in the interests of morality.

[44]

It is scarcely necessary to remark that a primitive dance, even when associated with courtship, is not necessarily a sexual pantomime; as Wallaschek, in his comprehensive survey of primitive dances, observes, it is more usually an animal pantomime, but nonetheless connected with the sexual instinct, separation of the sexes, also, being no proof to the contrary. (Wallaschek, *Primitive Music*, pp. 211-13.) Grosse (*Anfänge der Kunst*, English translation, p. 228) has pointed out that the best dancer would be the best fighter and hunter, and that sexual selection and natural selection would thus work in harmony.

[45]

Féré, "Le plaisir de la vue du Mouvement," *Comptes-rendus de la Société de Biologie*, November 2, 1901; also *Travail et Plaisir*, ch. xxix.

[46]

Groos repeatedly emphasizes the significance of this fact (*Spiele der Menschen*, pp. 81-9, 460 *et seq*.); Grosse (*Anfänge der Kunst*, p. 215) had previously made some remarks on this point.

[47]

M. Kulischer, "Die Geschlechtliche Zuchtwahl bei den Menschen in der Urzeit," *Zeitschrift für Ethnologie*, 1876, p. 140 *et seq.*

[48]

Sir W. R. Gowers, *Epilepsy*, 2d ed., 1901, pp. 61, 138.

[49]

Guyon, *Leçons Cliniques sur les Maladies des Voies Urinaires*, 3d ed., 1896, vol. ii, p. 397.

[50]

See, *e.g.*, Féré, *L'Instinct Sexuel*, pp. 222-23: Brantôme was probably the first writer in modern times who referred to this phenomenon. MacGillicuddy (*Functional Disorders of the Nervous System in Women*, p. 110) refers to the case of a lady who always had sudden and uncontrollable expulsion of urine whenever her husband even began to perform the marital act, on which account he finally ceased intercourse with her. Kubary states that in Ponape (Western Carolines) the men are accustomed to titillate the vulva of their women with the tongue until the excitement is so intense that involuntary emission of urine takes place; this is regarded as the proper moment for intercourse.

[51]

Thus Pitres and Régis (*Transactions of the International Medical Congress, Moscow*, vol. iv, p. 19) record the case of a young girl whose life was for some years tormented by a groundless fear of experiencing an irresistible desire to urinate. This obsession arose from once seeing at a theater a man whom she liked, and being overcome by sexual feeling accompanied by so strong a desire to urinate that she had to leave the theater. An exactly similar case in a young woman of erotic temperament, but prudish, has been recorded by Freud (*Zur Neurosenlehre*, Bd. i, p. 54). Morbid obsessions of modesty involving the urinary sphere and appearing at puberty are evidently based on transformed sexual emotion. Such a case has been recorded by Marandon de Montyel (*Archives de Neurologie*, vol. xii, 1901, p. 36); this lady, who was of somewhat neuropathic temperament, from puberty onward, in order to be able to urinate found it necessary not only to be absolutely alone, but to feel assured that no one even knew what was taking place.

[52]

H. Ellis, "The Bladder as a Dynamometer," *American Journal of Dermatology*, May, 1902.

[53]

Sir W. Gowers, "Minor Epilepsy," *British Medical Journal*, January 6, 1900; *ib.*, *Epilepsy*, 2d ed., 1901, p. 106; see also H. Ellis, art. "Urinary Bladder, Influence of the Mind on the," in Tuke's *Dictionary of Psychological Medicine*.

[54]

Sérieux, *Recherches Cliniques sur les Anomalies de l'Instinct Sexuel*, p. 22.

[55]

Emil Schultze-Malkowsky, "Der Sexuelle Trieb in Kindesalter," *Geschlecht und Gesellschaft*, vol. ii, part 8, p. 372.

[56]

Féré, "Note sur un Cas de Periodicité Sexuelle chez l'Homme," *Comptes-rendus Société de Biologie*, July 23, 1904.

[57]

It is a familiar fact that, in women, occasionally, a violent explosion of laughter may be propagated to the bladder-center and produce urination. "She laughed till she nearly wetted the floor," I have heard a young woman in the country say, evidently using without thought a familiar locution. Professor Bechterew has recorded the case of a young married lady who, from childhood, wherever she might be—in friends' houses, in the street, in her own drawing-room—had always experienced an involuntary and forcible emission of urine, which could not be stopped or controlled, whenever she laughed; the bladder was quite sound and no muscular effort produced the same result. (W. Bechterew, *Neurologisches Centralblatt*, 1899.) In women these relationships are most easily observed, partly because in them the explosive centers are more easily discharged, and partly, it is probable, so far as the bladder is concerned, because, although after death the resistance to the emission of urine is notably less in women, during life about the same amount of force is necessary in both sexes; so that a greater amount of energy flows to the bladder in women, and any nervous storm or disturbance is thus specially apt to affect the bladder.

[58]

"Every pain," remarks Marie de Manacéine, "produces a number of movements which are apparently useless: we cry out, we groan, we move our limbs, we throw ourselves from one side to the other, and at bottom all these movements are logical because by interrupting and breaking our attention they render us less sensitive to the pain. In the days before chloroform, skillful surgeons requested their patients to cry out during the operation, as we are told by Gratiolet, who could not explain so strange a fact, for in his time the antagonism of movements and attention was not recognized." (Marie de Manacéine, *Archives Italiennes de Biologie*, 1894, p. 250.) This antagonism of attention by movement is but another way of expressing the vicarious relationship of motor discharges.

[59]

Joanny Roux, *Psychologie de l'Instinct Sexuel*, 1899, pp. 22-23. It is disputed whether hunger is located in the whole organism, and powerful arguments have been brought against the view. (W. Cannon, "The Nature of Hunger," *Popular Science Monthly*, Sept., 1912.) Thirst is usually regarded as organic (A. Mayer, *La Soif*, 1901).

[60]

If there is any objection to these terms it is chiefly because they have reference to vascular congestion rather than to the underlying nervous charging and discharging, which is equally fundamental, and in man more prominent than the vascular phenomena.

LOVE AND PAIN.
I.

The Chief Key to the Relationship between Love and Pain to be Found in Animal Courtship—Courtship a Source of Combativity and of Cruelty—Human Play in the Light of Animal Courtship—The Frequency of Crimes Against the Person in Adolescence—Marriage by Capture and its Psychological Basis—Man's Pleasure in Exerting Force and Woman's Pleasure in Experiencing it—Resemblance of Love to Pain even in Outward Expression—The Love-bite—In what Sense Pain may be Pleasurable—The Natural Contradiction in the Emotional Attitude of Women Toward Men—Relative Insensibility to Pain of the Organic Sexual Sphere in Women—The Significance of the Use of the Ampallang and Similar Appliances in Coitus—The Sexual Subjection of Women to Men in Part Explainable as the Necessary Condition for Sexual Pleasure.

The relation of love to pain is one of the most difficult problems, and yet one of the most fundamental, in the whole range of sexual psychology. Why is it that love inflicts, and even seeks to inflict, pain? Why is it that love suffers pain, and even seeks to suffer it? In answering that question, it seems to me, we have to take an apparently circuitous route, sometimes going beyond the ostensible limits of sex altogether; but if we can succeed in answering it we shall have come very near one of the great mysteries of love. At the same time we shall have made clear the normal basis on which rest the extreme aberrations of love.

The chief key to the relationship of love to pain is to be found by returning to the consideration of the essential phenomena of courtship in the animal world generally. Courtship is a play, a game; even its combats are often, to a large extent, mock-combats; but the process behind it is one of terrible earnestness, and the play may at any moment become deadly. Courtship tends to involve a mock-combat between males for the possession of the female which may at any time become a real combat; it is a pursuit of the female by the male which may at any time become a kind of persecution; so that, as Colin Scott remarks, "Courting may be looked upon as a refined and delicate form of combat." The note of courtship, more especially among mammals, is very easily forced, and as soon as we force it we reach pain.[61] The intimate and inevitable association in the animal world of combat—of the fighting and hunting impulses—with the process of courtship alone suffices to bring love into close connection with pain.

Among mammals the male wins the female very largely by the display of force. The infliction of pain must inevitably be a frequent indirect result of the exertion of power. It is even more than this; the infliction of pain by the male on the female may itself be a gratification of the impulse to exert force. This tendency has always to be held in check, for it is of the essence of courtship that the male should win the female, and she can only be won by the promise of pleasure. The tendency of the male to inflict pain must be restrained, so far as the female is concerned, by the consideration of what is pleasing to her. Yet, the more carefully we study the essential elements of courtship, the clearer it becomes that, playful as these manifestations may seem on the surface, in every direction they are verging on pain. It is so among animals generally; it is so in man among savages. "It is precisely the alliance of pleasure and pain," wrote the physiologist Burdach, "which constitutes the voluptuous emotion."

Nor is this emotional attitude entirely confined to the male. The female also in courtship delights to arouse to the highest degree in the male the desire for her favors and to withhold those favors from him, thus finding on her part also the enjoyment of power in cruelty. "One's cruelty is one's power," Millament says in Congreve's *Way of the World*, "and when one parts with one's cruelty one parts with one's power."

At the outset, then, the impulse to inflict pain is brought into courtship, and at the same time rendered a pleasurable idea to the female, because with primitive man, as well as among his immediate ancestors, the victor in love has been the bravest and strongest rather than the most beautiful or the most skilful. Until he can fight he is not reckoned a man and he cannot hope to win a woman. Among the African Masai a man is not supposed to marry until he has blooded his spear, and in a very different part of the world, among the Dyaks of Borneo, there can be little doubt that the chief incentive to head-hunting is the desire to please the women, the possession of a head decapitated by himself being an excellent way of winning a maiden's favor.[62] Such instances are too well known to need multiplication here, and they survive in civilization, for, even among ourselves, although courtship is now chiefly ruled by quite other considerations, most women are in some degree emotionally affected by strength and courage. But the direct result of this is that a group of phenomena with which cruelty and the infliction of pain must inevitably be more or less allied is brought within the sphere of courtship and rendered agreeable to women. Here, indeed, we have the source of that love of cruelty which some have found so marked in women. This is a phase of courtship which helps us to understand how it is that, as we shall see, the idea of pain, having become associated with sexual emotion, may be pleasurable to women.

Thus, in order to understand the connection between love and pain, we have once more to return to the consideration, under a somewhat new aspect, of the fundamental elements in the sexual impulse. In discussing the "Evolution of Modesty" we found that the primary part of the female in courtship is the playful, yet serious, assumption of the rôle of a hunted animal who lures on the pursuer, not with the object of escaping, but with the object of being finally caught. In considering the "Analysis of the Sexual Impulse" we found that the primary part of the male in courtship is by the display of his energy and skill to capture the female or to arouse in her an emotional condition which leads her to surrender herself to him, this process itself at the same time heightening his own excitement. In the playing of these two different parts is attained in both male and female that charging of nervous energy, that degree of vascular tumescence, necessary for adequate discharge and detumescence in an explosion by which sperm-cells and germ-cells are brought together for the propagation of the race. We are now concerned with the necessary interplay of the differing male and female rôles in courtship, and with their accidental emotional by-products. Both male and female are instinctively seeking the same end of sexual union at the moment of highest excitement. There cannot, therefore, be real conflict.[63] But there is the semblance of a conflict, an apparent clash of aim, an appearance of cruelty. Moreover,—and this is a significant moment in the process from our present point of view,—when there are rivals for the possession of one female there is always a possibility of actual combat, so tending to introduce an element of real violence, of undisguised cruelty, which the male inflicts on his rival and which the female views with satisfaction and delight in the prowess of the successful claimant. Here we are brought close to the zoölogical root of the connection between love and pain.[64]

In his admirable work on play in man Groos has fully discussed the plays of combat (*Kampfspiele*), which begin to develop even in childhood and assume full activity during adolescence; and he points out that, while the impulse to such play certainly has a wider biological significance, it still possesses a relationship to the sexual life and to the rivalries of animals in courtship which must not be forgotten.[65]

Nor is it only in play that the connection between love and combativity may still be traced. With the epoch of the first sexual relationship, Marro points out, awakes the instinct of cruelty, which prompts the youth to acts which are sometimes in absolute contrast to his previous conduct, and leads him to be careless of the lives of others as well as of his own life.[66] Marro presents a diagram showing how crimes against the person in Italy rise rapidly from the age of 16 to 20 and reach a climax between 21 and 25. In Paris, Gamier states, crimes of blood are six times more frequent in adolescents (aged 16 to 20) than in adults. It is the same elsewhere.[67] This tendency to criminal violence during the age-period of courtship is a by-product of the sexual impulse, a kind of tertiary sexual character.

In the process of what is commonly termed "marriage by capture" we have a method of courtship which closely resembles the most typical form of animal courtship, and is yet found in all but the highest and most artificial stages of human society. It may not be true that, as MacLennan and others have argued, almost every race of man has passed through an actual stage of marriage by capture, but the phenomena in question have certainly been extremely widespread and exist in popular custom even among the highest races today. George Sand has presented a charming picture of such a custom, existing in France, in her *Mare au Diable*. Farther away, among the Kirghiz, the young woman is pursued by all her lovers, but she is armed with a formidable whip, which she does not hesitate to use if overtaken by a lover to whom she is not favorable. Among the Malays, according to early travelers, courtship is carried on in the water in canoes with double-bladed paddles; or, if no water is near, the damsel, stripped naked of all but a waistband, is given a certain start and runs off on foot followed by her lover. Vaughan Stevens in 1896 reported that this performance is merely a sport; but Skeat and Blagden, in their more recent and very elaborate investigations in the Malay States, find that it is a rite.

Even if we regard "marriage by capture" as simply a primitive human institution stimulated by tribal exigencies and early social conditions, yet, when we recall its widespread and persistent character, its close resemblance to the most general method of courtship among animals, and the emotional tendencies which still persist even in the most civilized men and women, we have to recognize that we are in presence of a real psychological impulse which cannot fail in its exercise to introduce some element of pain into love.

There are, however, two fundamentally different theories concerning "marriage by capture." According to the first, that of MacLennan, which, until recently, has been very widely accepted, and to which Professor Tylor has given the weight of his authority, there has really been in primitive society a recognized stage in which marriages were effected by the capture of the wife. Such a state of things MacLennan regarded as once world-wide. There can be no doubt that women very frequently have been captured in this way among primitive peoples. Nor, indeed, has the custom been confined to savages. In Europe we find that even up to comparatively recent times the abduction of women was not only very common, but was often more or less recognized. In England it was not until Henry VII's time that the violent seizure of a woman was made a criminal offense, and even then the statute was limited to women possessed of lands and goods. A man might still carry off a girl provided she was not an heiress; but even the abduction of heiresses continued to be common, and in Ireland remained so until the end of the eighteenth century. But it is not so clear that such raids and abductions, even when not of a genuinely hostile character, have ever been a recognized and constant method of marriage.

According to the second set of theories, the capture is not real, but simulated, and may be accounted for by psychological reasons. Fustel de Coulanges, in *La Cité Antique*,[68] discussing simulated marriage by capture among the Romans, mentioned the view that it was "a symbol of the young girl's modesty," but himself regarded it as an act of force to symbolize the husband's power. He was possibly alluding to Herbert Spencer, who suggested a psychological explanation of the apparent prevalence of marriage by capture based on the supposition that, capturing a wife being a proof of bravery, such a method of obtaining a wife would be practised by the strongest men and be admired, while, on the other hand, he considered that "female coyness" was "an important factor" in constituting the more formal kinds of marriage by capture ceremonial.[69]Westermarck, while accepting true marriage by capture, considers that Spencer's statement "can scarcely be disproved."[70] In his valuable study of certain aspects of primitive marriage Crawley, developing the explanation rejected by Fustel de Coulanges, regards the fundamental fact to be the modesty of women, which has to be neutralized, and this is done by "a ceremonial use of force, which is half real and half make-believe." Thus the manifestations are not survivals, but "arising in a natural way from normal human feelings. It is not the tribe from which the bride is abducted, nor, primarily, her family and kindred, but her *sex*"; and her "sexual characters of timidity, bashfulness, and passivity are sympathetically overcome by make-believe representations of male characteristic actions."[71]

It is not necessary for the present purpose that either of these two opposing theories concerning the origin of the customs and feelings we are here concerned with should be definitely rejected. Whichever theory is adopted, the fundamental psychic element which here alone concerns us still exists intact.[72] It may be pointed out, however, that we probably have to accept two groups of such phenomena: one, seldom or never existing as the sole form of marriage, in which the capture is real; and another in which the "capture" is more or less ceremonial or playful. The two groups coexist among the Turcomans, as described by Vambery, who are constantly capturing and enslaving the Persians of both sexes, and, side by side with this, have a marriage ceremonial of mock-capture of entirely playful character. At the same time the two groups sometimes overlap, as is indicated by cases in which, while the "capture" appears to be ceremonial, the girl is still allowed to escape altogether if she wishes. The difficulty of disentangling the two groups is shown by the fact that so careful an investigator as Westermarck cites cases of real capture and mock-capture together without attempting to distinguish between them. From our present point of view it is quite unnecessary to attempt such a distinction. Whether the capture is simulated or real, the man is still playing the masculine and aggressive part proper to the male; the woman is still playing the feminine and defensive part proper to the female. The universal prevalence of these phenomena is due to the fact that manifestations of this kind, real or pretended, afford each sex the very best opportunity for playing its proper part in courtship, and so, even when the force is real, must always gratify a profound instinct.

It is not necessary to quote examples of marriage by capture from the numerous and easily accessible books on the evolution of marriage. (Sir A. B. Ellis, adopting MacLennan's standpoint, presented a concise statement of the facts in an article on "Survivals from Marriage by Capture," *Popular Science Monthly*, 1891, p. 207.) It may, however, be worth while to bring together from scattered sources a few of the facts concerning the phenomena in this group and their accompanying emotional state, more especially as they bear on the association of love with force, inflicted or suffered.

In New Caledonia, Foley remarks, the successful coquette goes off with her lover into the bush. "It usually happens that, when she is successful, she returns from her expedition, tumbled, beaten, scratched, even bitten on the nape and shoulders, her wounds thus bearing witness to the quadrupedal attitude she has assumed amid the foliage." (Foley, *Bulletin de la Société d'Anthropologie*, Paris, November 6, 1879.)

Of the natives of New South Wales, Turnbull remarked at the beginning of the nineteenth century that "their mode of courtship is not without its singularity. When a young man sees a female to his fancy he informs her she must accompany him home; the lady

41

refuses; he not only enforces compliance with threats but blows; thus the gallant, according to the custom, never fails to gain the victory, and bears off the willing, though struggling pugilist. The colonists for some time entertained the idea that the women were compelled and forced away against their inclinations; but the young ladies informed them that this mode of gallantry was the custom, and perfectly to their taste," (J. Turnbull, *A Voyage Round the World*, 1813, p. 98; *cf.* Brough Smyth, *Aborigines of Victoria*, 1878, vol. i, p. 81.)

As regards capture of women among Central Australian tribes, Spencer and Gillen remark: "We have never in any of these central tribes met with any such thing, and the clubbing part of the story may be dismissed, so far as the central area of the continent is concerned. To the casual observer what looks like a capture (we are, of course, only speaking of these tribes) is in reality an elopement, in which the woman is an aiding and abetting party." (*Northern Tribes of Central Australia.* p. 32.)

"The New Zealand method of courtship and matrimony is a most extraordinary one. A man sees a woman whom he fancies he should like for a wife; he asks the consent of her father, or, if an orphan, of her nearest relative, which, if he obtain, he carries his intended off by force, she resisting with all her strength, and, as the New Zealand girls are generally fairly robust, sometimes a dreadful struggle takes place; both are soon stripped to the skin and it is sometimes the work of hours to remove the fair prize a hundred yards. It sometimes happens that she secures her retreat into her father's house, and the lover loses all chance of ever obtaining her." (A. Earle, *Narratives of Residence in New Zealand*, 1832, p. 244.)

Among the Eskimos (probably near Smith Sound) "there is no marriage ceremony further than that the boy is required to carry off his bride by main force, for even among these blubber-eating people the woman only saves her modesty by a show of resistance, although she knows years beforehand that her destiny is sealed and that she is to become the wife of the man from whose embraces, when the nuptial day comes, she is obliged by the inexorable law of public opinion to free herself, if possible, by kicking and screaming with might and main until she is safely landed in the hut of her future lord, when she gives up the combat very cheerfully and takes possession of her new abode. The betrothal often takes place at a very early period of life and at very dissimilar ages." Marriage only takes place when the lover has killed his first seal; this is the test of manhood and maturity. (J. J. Hayes, *Open Polar Sea*, 1867, p. 432.)

Marriage by "capture" is common in war and raiding in central Africa. "The women, as a rule," Johnston says, "make no very great resistance on these occasions. It is almost like playing a game. A woman is surprised as she goes to get water at the stream, or when she is on the way to or from the plantation. The man has only got to show her she is cornered and that escape is not easy or pleasant and she submits to be carried off. As a general rule, they seem to accept very cheerfully these abrupt changes in their matrimonial existence." (Sir H. H. Johnston, *British Central Africa*, p. 412.)

Among the wild tribes of the Malay Peninsula in one form of wedding rite the bridegroom is required to run seven times around an artificial mound decorated with flowers and the emblem of the people's religion. In the event of the bridegroom failing to catch the bride the marriage has to be postponed. Among the Orang Laut, or sea-gipsies, the pursuit sometimes takes the form of a canoe-race; the woman is given a good start and must be overtaken before she has gone a certain distance. (W. W. Skeat, *Journal Anthropological Institute*, Jan.-June, 1902, p. 134; Skeat and Blagden, *Pagan Races of the Malay*, vol. ii, p. 69 *et seq.*, fully discuss the ceremony around the mound.)

"Calmuck women ride better than the men. A male Calmuck on horseback looks as if he was intoxicated, and likely to fall off every instant, though he never loses his seat; but the women sit with more ease, and ride with extraordinary skill. The ceremony of marriage among the Calmucks is performed on horseback. A girl is first mounted, who rides off at full speed. Her lover pursues, and if he overtakes her she becomes his wife and the marriage is consummated upon the spot, after which she returns with him to his tent. But it sometimes happens that the woman does not wish to marry the person by whom she is pursued, in which case she will not suffer him to overtake her; and we were assured that no instance occurs of a Calmuck girl being thus caught, unless she has a partiality for her pursuer. If she dislikes him, she rides, to use the language of English sportsmen, 'neck or nothing,' until she

42

has completely escaped or until the pursuer's horse is tired out, leaving her at liberty to return, to be afterward chased by some more favored admirer." (E. D. Clarke, *Travels*, 1810, vol. i, p. 333.)

Among the Bedouins marriage is arranged between the lover and the girl's father, often without consulting the girl herself. "Among the Arabs of Sinai the young maid comes home in the evening with the cattle. At a short distance from the camp she is met by the future spouse and a couple of his young friends and carried off by force to her father's tent. If she entertains any suspicion of their designs she defends herself with stones, and often inflicts wounds on the young men, even though she does not dislike the lover, for, according to custom, the more she struggles, bites, kicks, cries, and strikes, the more she is applauded ever after by her own companions." After being taken to her father's tent, where a man's cloak is thrown over her by one of the bridegroom's relations, she is dressed in garments provided by her future husband, and placed on a camel, "still continuing to struggle in a most unruly manner, and held by the bridegroom's friends on both sides." She is then placed in a recess of the husband's tent. Here the marriage is finally consummated, "the bride still continuing to cry very loudly. It sometimes happens that the husband is obliged to tie his bride, and even to beat her, before she can be induced to comply with his desires." If, however, she really does not like her husband, she is perfectly free to leave him next morning, and her father is obliged to receive her back whether he wishes to or not. It is not considered proper for a widow or divorced woman to make any resistance on being married. (J. L. Burckhardt, *Notes on the Bedouins and Wahábys*, 1830, p. 149 *et seq.*)

Among the Turcomans forays for capturing and enslaving their Persian neighbors were once habitual. Vambery describes their "marriage ceremonial when the young maiden, attired in bridal costume, mounts a high-bred courser, taking on her lap the carcass of a lamb or goat, and setting off at full gallop, followed by the bridegroom and other young men of the party, also on horseback; she is always to strive, by adroit turns, etc., to avoid her pursuers, that no one approach near enough to snatch from her the burden on her lap. This game, called *kökbüri* (green wolf), is in use among all the nomads of central Asia." (A. Vambery, *Travels in Central Asia*, 1864, p. 323.)

In China, a missionary describes how, when he was called upon to marry the daughter of a Chinese Christian brought up in native customs, he was compelled to wait several hours, as the bride refused to get up and dress until long after the time appointed for the wedding ceremony, and then only by force. "Extreme reluctance and dislike and fear are the true marks of a happy and lively wedding." (A. E. Moule, *New China and Old*, p. 128.)

It is interesting to find that in the Indian art of love a kind of mock-combat, accompanied by striking, is a recognized and normalmethod of heightening tumescence. Vatsyayana has a chapter "On Various Manners of Striking," and he approves of the man striking the woman on the back, belly, flanks, and buttocks, before and during coitus, as a kind of play, increasing as sexual excitement increases, which the woman, with cries and groans, pretends to bid the man to stop. It is mentioned that, especially in southern India, various instruments (scissors, needles, etc.) are used in striking, but this practice is condemned as barbarous and dangerous. (*Kama Sutra*, French translation, iii, chapter v.)

In the story of Aladdin, in the *Arabian Nights*, the bride is undressed by the mother and the other women, who place her in the bridegroom's bed "as if by force, and, according to the custom of the newly married, she pretends to resist, twisting herself in every direction, and seeking to escape from their hands." (*Les Mille Nuits*, tr. Mardrus, vol. xi, p. 253.)

It is said that in those parts of Germany where preliminary*Probenächte* before formal marriage are the rule it is not uncommon for a young woman before finally giving herself to a man to provoke him to a physical struggle. If she proves stronger she dismisses him; if he is stronger she yields herself willingly. (W. Henz, "Probenächte," *Sexual-Probleme*, Oct., 1910, p. 743.)

Among the South Slavs of Servia and Bulgaria, according to Krauss, it is the custom to win a woman by seizing her by the ankle and bringing her to the ground by force. This method of wooing is to the taste of the woman, and they are refractory to any other method.

The custom of beating or being beaten before coitus is also found among the South Slavs. (Κρυπτάδια, vol. vi, p. 209.)

In earlier days violent courtship was viewed with approval in the European world, even among aristocratic circles. Thus in the medieval *Lai de Graélent* of Marie de France this Breton knight is represented as very chaste, possessing a high ideal of love and able to withstand the wiles of women. One day when he is hunting in a forest he comes upon a naked damsel bathing, together with her handmaidens. Overcome by her beauty, he seizes her clothes in case she should be alarmed, but is persuaded to hand them to her; then he proceeds to make love to her. She replies that his love is an insult to a woman of her high lineage. Finding her so proud, Graélent sees that his prayers are in vain. He drags her by force into the depth of the forest, has his will of her, and begs her very gently not to be angry, promising to love her loyally and never to leave her. The damsel saw that he was a good knight, courteous, and wise. She thought within herself that if she were to leave him she would never find a better friend.

Brantôme mentions a lady who confessed that she liked to be "half-forced" by her husband, and he remarks that a woman who is "a little difficult and resists" gives more pleasure also to her lover than one who yields at once, just as a hard-fought battle is a more notable triumph than an easily won victory. (Brantôme, *Vie des Dames Galantes*, discours i.) Restif de la Bretonne, again, whose experience was extensive, wrote in his *Anti-Justine* that "all women of strong temperament like a sort of brutality in sexual intercourse and its accessories."

Ovid had said that a little force is pleasing to a woman, and that she is grateful to the ravisher against whom she struggles (*Ars Amatoria*, lib. i). One of Janet's patients (Raymond and Janet, *Les Obsessions et la Psychasthénie*, vol. ii, p. 406) complained that her husband was too good, too devoted. "He does not know how to make me suffer a little. One cannot love anyone who does not make one suffer a little." Another hysterical woman (a silk fetichist, frigid with men) had dreams of men and animals abusing her: "I cried with pain and was happy at the same time." (Clérambault, *Archives d'Anthropologie Criminelle*, June, 1908, p. 442.)

It has been said that among Slavs of the lower class the wives feel hurt if they are not beaten by their husbands. Paullinus, in the seventeenth century, remarked that Russian women are never more pleased and happy than when beaten by their husbands, and regard such treatment as proof of love. (See, *e.g.*, C. F. von Schlichtegroll, *Sacher-Masoch und der Masochismus*, p. 69.) Krafft-Ebing believes that this is true at the present day, and adds that it is the same in Hungary, a Hungarian official having informed him that the peasant women of the Somogyer Comitate do not think they are loved by their husbands until they have received the first box on the ear. (Krafft-Ebing, *Psychopathia Sexualis*, English translation of the tenth edition, p. 188.) I may add that a Russian proverb says "Love your wife like your soul and beat her like your *shuba*" (overcoat); and, according to another Russian proverb, "a dear one's blows hurt not long." At the same time it has been remarked that the domination of men by women is peculiarly frequent among the Slav peoples. (V. Schlichtegroll, *op. cit.*, p. 23.) Cellini, in an interesting passage in his *Life* (book ii, chapters xxxiv-xxxv), describes his own brutal treatment of his model Caterina, who was also his mistress, and the pleasure which, to his surprise, she took in it. Dr. Simon Forman, also, the astrologer, tells in his *Autobiography* (p. 7) how, as a young and puny apprentice to a hosier, he was beaten, scolded, and badly treated by the servant girl, but after some years of this treatment he turned on her, beat her black and blue, and ever after "Mary would do for him all that she could."

That it is a sign of love for a man to beat his sweetheart, and a sign much appreciated by women, is illustrated by the episode of Cariharta and Repolido, in "Rinconete and Cortadillo," one of Cervantes's *Exemplary Novels*. The Indian women of South America feel in the same way, and Mantegazza when traveling in Bolivia found that they complained when they were not beaten by their husbands, and that a girl was proud when she could say "He loves me greatly, for he often beats me." (*Fisiologia della Donna*, chapter xiii.) The same feeling evidently existed in classic antiquity, for we find Lucian, in his "Dialogues of Courtesans," makes a woman say: "He who has not rained blows on his mistress and torn her hair and her garments is not yet in love," while Ovid advises lovers sometimes to be angry with their sweethearts and to tear their dresses.

Among the Italian Camorrista, according to Russo, wives are very badly treated. Expression is given to this fact in the popular songs. But the women only feel themselves tenderly loved when they are badly treated by their husbands; the man who does not beat them they look upon as a fool. It is the same in the east end of London. "If anyone has doubts as to the brutalities practised on women by men," writes a London magistrate, "let him visit the London Hospital on a Saturday night. Very terrible sights will meet his eye. Sometimes as many as twelve or fourteen women may be seen seated in the receiving room, waiting for their bruised and bleeding faces and bodies to be attended to. In nine cases out of ten the injuries have been inflicted by brutal and perhaps drunken husbands. The nurses tell me, however, that any remarks they may make reflecting on the aggressors are received with great indignation by the wretched sufferers. They positively will not hear a single word against the cowardly ruffians. 'Sometimes,' said a nurse to me, 'when I have told a woman that her husband is a brute, she has drawn herself up and replied: "You mind your own business, miss. We find the rates and taxes, and the likes of you are paid out of 'em to wait on us."'" (Montagu Williams, *Round London*, p. 79.)

"The prostitute really loves her *souteneur*, notwithstanding all the persecutions he inflicts on her. Their torments only increase the devotion of the poor slaves to their 'Alphonses.' Parent-Duchâtelet wrote that he had seen them come to the hospital with their eyes out of their heads, faces bleeding, and bodies torn by the blows of their drunken lovers, but as soon as they were healed they went back to them. Police-officers tell us that it is very difficult to make a prostitute confess anything concerning her *souteneur*. Thus, Rosa L., whom her 'Alphonse' had often threatened to kill, even putting the knife to her throat, would say nothing, and denied everything when the magistrate questioned her. Maria R., with her face marked by a terrible scar produced by her *souteneur*, still carefully preserved many years afterward the portrait of the aggressor, and when we asked her to explain her affection she replied: 'But he wounded me because he loved me.' The *souteneur's* brutality only increases the ill-treated woman's love; the humiliation and slavery in which the woman's soul is drowned feed her love." (Niceforo, *Il Gergo*, etc., 1897, p. 128.)

In a modern novel written in autobiographic form by a young Australian lady the heroine is represented as striking her betrothed with a whip when he merely attempts to kiss her. Later on her behavior so stings him that his self-control breaks down and he seizes her fiercely by the arms. For the first time she realizes that he loves her. "I laughed a joyous little laugh, saying 'Hal, we are quits'; when on disrobing for the night I discovered on my soft white shoulders and arms—so susceptible to bruises—many marks, and black. It had been a very happy day for me." (Miles Franklin, *My Brilliant Career*.)

It is in large measure the existence of this feeling of attraction for violence which accounts for the love-letters received by men who are accused of crimes of violence. Thus in one instance, in Chicago (as Dr. Kiernan writes to me), "a man arrested for conspiracy to commit abortion, and also suspected of being a sadist, received many proposals of marriage and other less modest expressions of affection from unknown women. To judge by the signatures, these women belonged to the Germans and Slavs rather than to the Anglo-Celts."

Neuropathic or degenerative conditions sometimes serve to accentuate or reveal ancestral traits that are very ancient in the race. Under such conditions the tendency to find pleasure in subjection and pain, which is often faintly traceable even in normal civilized women, may become more pronounced. This may be seen in a case described in some detail in the *Archivio di Psichiatria*. The subject was a young lady of 19, of noble Italian birth, but born in Tunis. On the maternal side there is a somewhat neurotic heredity, and she is herself subject to attacks of hystero-epileptoid character. She was very carefully, but strictly, educated; she knows several languages, possesses marked intellectual aptitudes, and is greatly interested in social and political questions, in which she takes the socialistic and revolutionary side. She has an attractive and sympathetic personality; in complexion she is dark, with dark eyes and very dark and abundant hair; the fine down on the upper lip and lower parts of the cheeks is also much developed; the jaw is large, the head acrocephalic, and the external genital organs of normal size, but rather asymmetric. Ever since she was a child she has loved to work and dream in solitude. Her dreams have always been of love, since menstruation began as early as the age of 10, and accompanied by strong sexual feelings, though at that age these feelings remained vague and indefinite; but in them the desire for pleasure was always accompanied by the desire for pain, the desire to bite and destroy something, and, as it were, to annihilate herself. She experienced great relief after periods of "erotic rumination," and if this rumination took place at night she would sometimes masturbate, the contact of the bedclothes, she said, giving her the illusion of a man. In time this vague longing for the male gave place to more definite desires for a man who would love her, and, as she imagined, strike her. Eventually she formed secret relationships with two or three lovers in succession, each of these relationships being, however, discovered by her family and leading to ineffectual attempts at suicide. But the association of pain with love, which had developed spontaneously in her solitary dreams, continued in her actual relations with her lovers. During coitus she would bite and squeeze her arms until the nails penetrated the flesh. When her lover asked her why at the moment of coitus she would vigorously repel him, she replied: "Because I want to be possessed by force, to be hurt, suffocated, to be thrown down in a struggle." At another time she said: "I want a man with all his vitality, so that he can torture and kill my body." We seem to see here clearly the ancient biological character of animal courtship, the desire of the female to be violently subjugated by the male. In this case it was united to sensitiveness to the sexual domination of an intellectual man, and the subject also sought to stimulate her lovers' intellectual tastes. (*Archivio di Psichiatria*, vol. xx, fasc. 5-6, p. 528.)

This association between love and pain still persists even among the most normal civilized men and women possessing well-developed sexual impulses. The masculine tendency to delight in domination, the feminine tendency to delight in submission, still maintain the ancient traditions when the male animal pursued the female. The phenomena of "marriage by capture," in its real and its simulated forms, have been traced to various causes. But it has to be remembered that these causes could only have been operative in the presence of a favorable emotional aptitude, constituted by the zoölogical history of our race and still traceable even today. To exert power, as psychologists well recognize, is one of our most primary impulses, and it always tends to be manifested in the attitude of a man toward the woman he loves.[73]

It might be possible to maintain that the primitive element of more or less latent cruelty in courtship tends to be more rather than less marked in civilized man. In civilization the opportunity of dissipating the surplus energy of the courtship process by inflicting pain on rivals usually has to be inhibited; thus the woman to be wooed tends to become the recipient of the whole of this energy, both in its pleasure-giving and its pain-giving aspects. Moreover, the natural process of courtship, as it exists among animals and usually among the lower human races, tends to become disguised and distorted in civilization, as well by economic conditions as by conventional social conditions and even ethical prescription. It becomes forgotten that the woman's pleasure is an essential element in the process of courtship. A woman is often reduced to seek a man for the sake of maintenance; she is taught that pleasure is sinful or shameful, that sex-matters are disgusting, and that it is a woman's duty, and also her best policy, to be in subjection to her husband. Thus, various external checks which normally inhibit any passing over of masculine sexual energy into cruelty are liable to be removed.

We have to admit that a certain pleasure in manifesting his power over a woman by inflicting pain upon her is an outcome and survival of the primitive process of courtship, and an almost or quite normal constituent of the sexual impulse in man. But it must be at once added that in the normal well-balanced and well-conditioned man this constituent of the sexual impulse, when present, is always held in check. When the normal man inflicts, or feels the impulse to inflict, some degree of physical pain on the woman he loves he can scarcely be said to be moved by cruelty. He feels, more or less obscurely, that the pain he inflicts, or desires to inflict, is really a part of his love, and that, moreover, it is not really resented by the woman on whom it is exercised. His feeling is by no means always according to knowledge, but it has to be taken into account as an essential part of his emotional state. The physical force, the teasing and bullying, which he may be moved to exert under the stress of sexual excitement, are, he usually more or less unconsciously persuades himself, not really unwelcome to the object of his love.[74] Moreover, we have to bear in mind the fact—a very significant fact from more than one point of view—that the normal manifestations of a woman's sexual pleasure are exceedingly like those of pain. "The outward expressions of pain," as a lady very truly writes,—"tears, cries, etc.,—which are laid stress on to prove the cruelty of the person who inflicts it, are not so different from those of a woman in the ecstasy of passion, when she implores the man to desist, though that is really the last thing she desires."[75] If a man is convinced that he is causing real and unmitigated pain, he becomes repentant at once. If this is not the case he must either be regarded as a radically abnormal person or as carried away by passion to a point of temporary insanity.

The intimate connection of love with pain, its tendency to approach cruelty, is seen in one of the most widespread of the occasional and non-essential manifestations of strong sexual emotion, especially in women, the tendency to bite. We may find references to love-bites in the literature of ancient as well as of modern times, in the East as well as in the West. Plautus, Catullus, Propertius, Horace, Ovid, Petronius, and other Latin writers refer to bites as associated with kisses and usually on the lips. Plutarch says that Flora, the mistress of Cnæus Pompey, in commending her lover remarked that he was so lovable that she could never leave him without giving him a bite. In the Arabic *Perfumed Garden* there are many references to love-bites, while in the Indian *Kama Sutra* of Vatsyayana a chapter is devoted to this subject. Biting in love is also common among the South Slavs.[76] The phenomenon is indeed sufficiently familiar to enable Heine, in one of his *Romancero*, to describe those marks by which the ancient chronicler states that Edith Swanneck recognized Harold, after the Battle of Hastings, as the scars of the bites she had once given him.

It would be fanciful to trace this tendency back to that process of devouring to which sexual congress has, in the primitive stages of its evolution, been reduced. But we may probably find one of the germs of the love-bite in the attitude of many mammals during or before coitus; in attaining a firm grip of the female it is not uncommon (as may be observed in the donkey) for the male to seize the female's neck between his teeth. The horse sometimes bites the mare before coitus and it is said that among the Arabs when a mare is not apt for coitus she is sent to pasture with a small ardent horse, who excites her by playing with her and biting her.[77] It may be noted, also, that dogs often show their affection for their masters by gentle bites. Children also, as Stanley Hall has pointed out, are similarly fond of biting.

Perhaps a still more important factor is the element of combat in tumescence, since the primitive conditions associated with tumescence provide a reservoir of emotions which are constantly drawn on even in the sexual excitement of individuals belonging to civilization. The tendency to show affection by biting is, indeed, commoner among women than among men and not only in civilization. It has been noted among idiot girls as well as among the women of various savage races. It may thus be that the conservative instincts of women have preserved a primitive tendency that at its origin marked the male more than the female. But in any case the tendency to bite at the climax of sexual excitement is so common and widespread that it must be regarded, when occurring in women, as coming within the normal range of variation in such manifestations. The gradations are of wide extent; while in its slight forms it is more or less normal and is one of the origins of the kiss,[78] in its extreme forms it tends to become one of the most violent and antisocial of sexual aberrations.

A correspondent writes regarding his experience of biting and being bitten: "I have often felt inclination to bite a woman I love, even when not in coitus or even excited. (I like doing so also with my little boy, playfully, as a cat and kittens.) There seem to be several reasons for this: (1) the muscular effect relieves me; (2) I imagine I am giving the woman pleasure; (3) I seem to attain to a more intimate possession of the loved one. I cannot remember when I first felt desire to be bitten in coitus, or whether the idea was first suggested to me. I was initiated into pinching by a French prostitute who once pinched my nates in coitus, no doubt as a matter of business; it heightened my pleasure, perhaps by stimulating muscular movement. It does not occur to me to ask to be pinched when I am very much excited already, but only at an earlier stage, no doubt with the object of promoting excitement. Apart altogether from sexual excitement, being pinched is unpleasant to me. It has not seemed to me that women usually like to be bitten. One or two women have bitten and sucked my flesh. (The latter does not affect me.) I like being bitten, partly for the same reason as I like being pinched, because if spontaneous it is a sign of my partner's amorousness and the biting never seems too hard. Women do not usually seem to like being bitten, though there are exceptions; 'I should like to bite you and I should like you to bite me,' said one woman; I did so hard, in coitus, and she did not flinch." "She is particularly anxious to eat me alive," another correspondent writes, "and nothing gives her greater satisfaction than to tear open my clothes and fasten her teeth into my flesh until I yell for mercy. My experience has generally been, however," the same correspondent continues, "that the cruelty is *unconscious*. A woman just grows mad with the desire to squeeze or bite something, with a complete unconsciousness of what result it will produce in the victim. She is astonished when she sees the result and will hardly believe she has done it." It is unnecessary to accumulate evidence of a tendency which is sufficiently common to be fairly well known, but one or two quotations may be presented to show its wide distribution. In the *Kama Sutra* we read: "If she is very exalted, and if in the exaltation of her passionate transports she begins a sort of combat, then she takes her lover by the hair, draws his head to hers, kisses his lower lip, and then in her delirium bites him all over his body, shutting her eyes"; it is added that with the marks of such bites lovers can remind each other of their affections, and that such love will last for ages. In Japan the maiden of Ainu race feels the same impulse. A. H. Savage Landor (*Alone with the Hairy Ainu*, 1893, p. 140) says of an Ainu girl: "Loving and biting went together with her. She could not do the one without the other. As we sat on a stone in the twilight she began by gently biting my fingers without hurting me, as affectionate dogs do to their masters. She then bit my arm, then my shoulder, and when she had worked herself up into a passion she put her arms around my neck and bit my cheeks. It was undoubtedly a curious way of making love, and, when I had been bitten all over, and was pretty tired of the new sensation, we retired to our respective homes. Kissing, apparently, was an unknown art to her."

The significance of biting, and the close relationship which, as will have to be pointed out later, it reveals to other phenomena, may be illustrated by some observations which have been made by Alonzi on the peasant women of Sicily. "The women of the people," he remarks, "especially in the districts where crimes of blood are prevalent, give vent to their affection for their little ones by kissing and sucking them on the neck and arms till they make them cry convulsively; all the while they say: 'How sweet you are! I will bite you, I will gnaw you all over,' exhibiting every appearance of great pleasure. If a child commits some slight fault they do not resort to simple blows, but pursue it through the street and bite it on the face, ears, and arms until the blood flows. At such moments the face of even a beautiful woman is transformed, with injected eyes, gnashing teeth, and convulsive tremors. Among both men and women a very common threat is 'I will drink your blood.' It is told on ocular evidence that a man who had murdered another in a quarrel licked the hot blood from the victim's hand." (G. Alonzi, *Archivio di Psichiatria*, vol. vi, fasc. 4.) A few years ago a nurse girl in New York was sentenced to prison for cruelty to the baby in her charge. The mother had frequently noticed that the child was in pain and at last discovered the marks of teeth on its legs. The girl admitted that she had bitten the child because that action gave her intense pleasure. (*Alienist and Neurologist*, August, 1901, p. 558.) In the light of such observations as these we may understand a morbid perversion of affection such as was recorded in the London police news some years ago (1894). A man of 30 was charged with ill-treating his wife's illegitimate daughter, aged 3, during a period of many months; her lips, eyes, and hands were bitten and bruised from sucking, and sometimes her pinafore was covered with blood. "Defendant admitted he had bitten the child because he loved it."

It is not surprising that such phenomena as these should sometimes be the stimulant and accompaniment to the sexual act. Ferriani thus reports such a case in the words of the young man's mistress: "Certainly he is a strange, maddish youth, though he is fond of me and spends money on me when he has any. He likes much sexual intercourse, but, to tell the truth, he has worn out my patience, for before our embraces there are always struggles which become assaults. He tells me he has no pleasure except when he sees me crying on account of his bites and vigorous pinching. Lately, just before going with me, when I was groaning

48

with pleasure, he threw himself on me and at the moment of emission furiously bit my right cheek till the blood came. Then he kissed me and begged my pardon, but would do it again if the wish took him." (L. Ferriani, *Archivio di Psicopatie Sessuale*, vol. i, fasc. 7 and 8, 1896, p. 107.)

In morbid cases biting may even become a substitute for coitus. Thus, Moll (*Die Konträre Sexualempfindung*, second edition, p. 323) records the case of a hysterical woman who was sexually anesthetic, though she greatly loved her husband. It was her chief delight to bite him till the blood flowed, and she was content if, instead of coitus, he bit her and she him, though she was grieved if she inflicted much pain. In other still more morbid cases the fear of inflicting pain is more or less abolished.

An idealized view of the impulse of love to bite and devour is presented in the following passage from a letter by a lady who associates this impulse with the idea of the Last Supper: "Your remarks about the Lord's Supper in 'Whitman' make it natural to me to tell you my thoughts about that 'central sacrament of Christianity.' I cannot tell many people because they misunderstand, and a clergyman, a very great friend of mine, when I once told what I thought and felt, said I was carnal. He did not understand the divinity and intensity of human love as I understand it. Well, when one loves anyone very much,—a child, a woman, or a man,—one loves everything belonging to him: the things he wears, still more his hands, and his face, every bit of his body. We always want to have all, or part, of him as part of ourselves. Hence the expression: I could *devour* you, I love you so. In some such warm, devouring way Jesus Christ, I have always felt, loved each and every human creature. So it was that he took this mystery of food, which by eating became part of ourselves, as the symbol of the most intense human love, the most intense Divine love. Some day, perhaps, love will be so understood by all that this sacrament will cease to be a superstition, a bone of contention, an 'article' of the church, and become, in all simplicity, a symbol of pure love."

While in men it is possible to trace a tendency to inflict pain, or the simulacrum of pain, on the women they love, it is still easier to trace in women a delight in experiencing physical pain when inflicted by a lover, and an eagerness to accept subjection to his will. Such a tendency is certainly normal. To abandon herself to her lover, to be able to rely on his physical strength and mental resourcefulness, to be swept out of herself and beyond the control of her own will, to drift idly in delicious submission to another and stronger will— this is one of the commonest aspirations in a young woman's intimate love-dreams. In our own age these aspirations most often only find their expression in such dreams. In ages when life was more nakedly lived, and emotion more openly expressed, it was easier to trace this impulse. In the thirteenth century we have found Marie de France—a French poetess living in England who has been credited with "an exquisite sense of the generosities and delicacy of the heart," and whose work was certainly highly appreciated in the best circles and among the most cultivated class of her day—describing as a perfect, wise, and courteous knight a man who practically commits a rape on a woman who has refused to have anything to do with him, and, in so acting, he wins her entire love. The savage beauty of New Caledonia furnishes no better illustration of the fascination of force, for she, at all events, has done her best to court the violence she undergoes. In Middleton's *Spanish Gypsy* we find exactly the same episode, and the unhappy Portuguese nun wrote: "Love me for ever and make me suffer still more." To find in literature more attenuated examples of the same tendency is easy. Shakespeare, whose observation so little escaped, has seldom depicted the adult passion of a grown woman, but in the play which he has mainly devoted to this subject he makes Cleopatra refer to "amorous pinches," and she says in the end: "The stroke of death is as a lover's pinch, which hurts and is desired." "I think the Sabine woman enjoyed being carried off like that," a woman remarked in front of Rubens's "Rape of the Sabines," confessing that such a method of love-making appealed strongly to herself, and it is probable that the majority of women would be prepared to echo that remark.

It may be argued that pain cannot give pleasure, and that when what would usually be pain is felt as pleasure it cannot be regarded as pain at all. It must be admitted that the emotional state is often somewhat complex. Moreover, women by no means always agree in the statement of their experience. It is noteworthy, however, that even when the pleasurableness of pain in love is denied it is still admitted that, under some circumstances, pain, or the idea of pain, is felt as pleasurable. I am indebted to a lady for a somewhat elaborate discussion of this subject, which I may here quote at length: "As regards physical pain, though the idea of it is sometimes exciting, I think the reality is the reverse. A very slight amount of pain destroys my pleasure completely. This was the case with me for fully a month after marriage, and since. When pain has occasionally been associated with passion, pleasure has been sensibly diminished. I can imagine that, when there is a want of sensitiveness so that the tender kiss or caress might fail to give pleasure, more forcible methods are desired; but in that case what would be pain to a sensitive person would be only a pleasant excitement, and it could not be truly said that such obtuse persons liked pain, though they might appear to do so. I cannot think that anyone enjoys what is pain *to them*, if only from the fact that it detracts and divides the attention. This, however, is only my own idea drawn from my own negative experience. No woman has ever told me that she would like to have pain inflicted on her. On the other hand, the desire to inflict pain seems almost universal among men. I have only met one man in whom I have never at any time been able to detect it. At the same time most men shrink from putting their ideas into practice. A friend of my husband finds his chief pleasure in imagining women hurt and ill-treated, but is too tender-hearted ever to inflict pain on them in reality, even when they are willing to submit to it. Perhaps a woman's readiness to submit to pain to please a man may sometimes be taken for pleasure in it. Even when women like the idea of pain, I fancy it is only because it implies subjection to the man, from association with the fact that physical pleasure must necessarily be preceded by submission to his will."

In a subsequent communication this lady enlarged and perhaps somewhat modified her statements on this point:—

"I don't think that what I said to you was quite correct. *Actual* pain gives me no pleasure, yet the *idea* of pain does, *if inflicted by way of discipline and for the ultimate good of the person suffering it*. This is essential. For instance, I once read a poem in which the devil and the lost souls in hell were represented as recognizing that they could not be good except under torture, but that while suffering the purifying actions of the flames of hell they so realized the beauty of holiness that they submitted willingly to their agony and praised God for the sternness of his judgment. This poem gave me decided physical pleasure, yet I know that if my hand were held in a fire for five minutes I should feel nothing but the pain of the burning. To get the feeling of pleasure, too, I must, for the moment, revert to my old religious beliefs and my old notion that mere suffering has an elevating influence; one's emotions are greatly modified by one's beliefs. When I was about fifteen I invented a game which I played with a younger sister, in which we were supposed to be going through a process of discipline and preparation for heaven after death. Each person was supposed to enter this state on dying and to pass successively into the charge of different angels named after the special virtues it was their function to instill. The last angel was that of Love, who governed solely by the quality whose name he bore. In the lower stages, we were under an angel called Severity who prepared us by extreme harshness and by exacting implicit obedience to arbitrary orders for the acquirement of later virtues. Our duties were to superintend the weather, paint the sunrise and sunset, etc., the constant work involved exercising us in patience and submission. The physical pleasure came in in inventing and recounting to each other our day's work and the penalties and hardships we had been subjected to. We never told each other that we got any physical pleasure out of this, and I cannot therefore be sure that my sister did so; I only imagine she did because she entered so heartily into the spirit of the game. I could get as much pleasure by imagining myself the angel and inflicting the pain, under the conditions mentioned; but my sister did not like this so much, as she then had no companion in subjection. I could not, however, thus reverse my feelings in regard to a man, as it would appear to me unnatural, and, besides, the greater physical strength is essential in the superior position. I can, however, by imagining myself a man, sometimes get pleasure in conceiving myself as educating and disciplining a woman by severe measures. There is, however, no real cruelty in this idea, as I always imagine her liking it.

"I only get pleasure in the idea of a woman submitting herself to pain and harshness from the man she loves when the following conditions are fulfilled: 1. She must be absolutely sure of the man's love. 2. She must have perfect confidence in his judgment. 3. The pain must be deliberately inflicted, not accidental. 4. It must be inflicted in kindness and for her own improvement, not in anger or with any revengeful feelings, as that would spoil one's ideal of the man. 5. The pain must not be excessive and must be what when we were children we used to call a 'tidy' pain; *i.e.*, there must be no mutilation, cutting, etc. 6. Last, one would have to feel very sure of one's own influence over the man. So much for the idea. As I have never suffered pain under a combination of all these conditions, I have no right to say that I should or should not experience pleasure from its infliction in reality."

Another lady writes: "I quite agree that the idea of pain may be pleasurable, but must be associated with something to be gained by it. My experience is that it [coitus] does often hurt for a few moments, but that passes and the rest is easy; so that the little hurt is nothing terrible, but all the same annoying if only for the sake of a few minutes' pleasure, which is not long enough. I do not know how my experience compares with other women's, but I feel sure that in my case the time needed is longer than usual, and the longer the better, always, with me. As to liking pain—no, I do not really like it, although I can tolerate pain very well, of any kind; but I like to feel force and strength; this is usual, I think, women being—or supposed to be—passive in love. I have not found that 'pain at once kills pleasure.'"

Again, another lady briefly states that, for her, pain has a mental fascination, and that such pain as she has had she has liked, but that, if it had been any stronger, pleasure would have been destroyed.

The evidence thus seems to point, with various shades of gradation, to the conclusion that the idea or even the reality of pain in sexual emotion is welcomed by women, provided that this element of pain is of small amount and subordinate to the pleasure which is to follow it. Unless coitus is fundamentally pleasure the element of pain must necessarily be unmitigated pain, and a craving for pain unassociated with a greater satisfaction to follow it cannot be regarded as normal.

In this connection I may refer to a suggestive chapter on "The Enjoyment of Pain" in Hirn's *Origins of Art.* "If we take into account," says Hirn, "the powerful stimulating effect which is produced by acute pain, we may easily understand why people submit to momentary unpleasantness for the sake of enjoying the subsequent excitement. This motive leads to the deliberate creation, not only of pain-sensations, but also of emotions in which pain enters as an element. The violent activity which is involved in the reaction against fear, and still more in that against anger, affords us a sensation of pleasurable excitement which is well worth the cost of the passing unpleasantness. It is, moreover, notorious that some persons have developed a peculiar art of making the initial pain of anger so transient that they can enjoy the active elements in it with almost undivided delight. Such an accomplishment is far more difficult in the case of sorrow.... The creation of pain-sensations may be explained as a desperate device for enhancing the intensity of the emotional state."

The relation of pain and pleasure to emotion has been thoroughly discussed, I may add, by H. R. Marshall in his *Pain, Pleasure, and Æsthetics.* He contends that pleasure and pain are "general qualities, one of which must, and either of which may, belong to any fixed element of consciousness." "Pleasure," he considers, "is experienced whenever the physical activity coincident with the psychic state to which the pleasure is attached involves the use of surplus stored force." We can see, therefore, how, if pain acts as a stimulant to emotion, it becomes the servant of pleasure by supplying it with surplus stored force.

This problem of pain is thus one of psychic dynamics. If we realize this we shall begin to understand the place of cruelty in life. "One ought to learn anew about cruelty," said Nietzsche (*Beyond Good and Evil*, 229), "and open one's eyes. Almost everything that we call 'higher culture' is based upon the spiritualizing and intensifying of *cruelty*.... Then, to be sure, we must put aside teaching the blundering psychology of former times, which could only teach with regard to cruelty that it originated at the sight of the suffering of *others*; there is an abundant, superabundant enjoyment even in one's own suffering, in causing one's own suffering." The element of paradox disappears from this statement if we realize that it is not a question of "cruelty," but of the dynamics of pain.

Camille Bos in a suggestive essay ("Du Plaisir de la Douleur,"*Revue Philosophique*, July, 1902) finds the explanation of the mystery in that complexity of the phenomena to which I have already referred. Both pain and pleasure are complex feelings, the resultant of various components, and we name that resultant in accordance with the nature of the strongest component. "Thus we give to a complexus a name which strictly belongs only to one of its factors, *and in pain all is not painful.*" When pain becomes a desired end Camille Bos regards the desire as due to three causes: (1) the pain contrasts with and revives a pleasure which custom threatens to dull; (2) the pain by preceding the pleasure accentuates the positive character of the latter; (3) pain momentarily raises the lowered level of sensibility and restores to the organism for a brief period the faculty of enjoyment it had lost.

It must therefore be said that, in so far as pain is pleasurable, it is so only in so far as it is recognized as a prelude to pleasure, or else when it is an actual stimulus to the nerves conveying the sensation of pleasure. The nymphomaniac who experienced an orgasm at the moment when the knife passed through her clitoris (as recorded by Mantegazza) and the prostitute who experienced keen pleasure when the surgeon removed vegetations from her vulva (as recorded by Féré) took no pleasure in pain, but in one case the intense craving for strong sexual emotion, and in the other the long-blunted nerves of pleasure, welcomed the abnormally strong impulse; and the pain of the incision, if felt at all, was immediately swallowed up in the sensation of pleasure. Moll remarks (*Konträre Sexualempfindung*, third edition, p. 278) that even in man a trace of physical pain may be normally combined withsexual pleasure, when the vagina contracts on the penis at the moment of ejaculation, the pain, when not too severe, being almost immediately felt as pleasure. That there is no pleasure in the actual pain, even in masochism, is indicated by the following statement which Krafft-Ebing gives as representing the experiences of a masochist (*Psychopathia Sexualis* English translation, p. 201): "The relation is not of such a nature that what causes physical pain is simply perceived as physical pleasure, for the person in a state of masochistic ecstasy feels no pain, either because by reason of his emotional state (like that of the soldier in battle) the physical effect on his cutaneous nerves is not apperceived, or because (as with religious martyrs and enthusiasts) in the preoccupation of consciousness with sexual emotion the idea of maltreatment remains merely a symbol, without its quality of pain. To a certain extent there is overcompensation of physical pain in psychic pleasure, and only the excess remains in consciousness as psychic lust. This also undergoes an increase, since, either through reflex spinal influence or through a peculiar coloring in the sensorium of sensory impressions, a kind of hallucination of bodily pleasure takes place, with a vague localization of the objectively projected sensation. In the self-torture of religious enthusiasts (fakirs, howling dervishes, religious flagellants) there is an analogous state, only with a difference in the quality of pleasurable feeling. Here the conception of martyrdom is also apperceived without its pain, for consciousness is filled with the pleasurably colored idea of serving God, atoning for sins, deserving Heaven, etc., through martyrdom." This statement cannot be said to clear up the matter entirely; but it is fairly evident that, when a woman says that she finds pleasure in the pain inflicted by a lover, she means that under the special circumstances she finds pleasure in treatment which would at other times be felt as pain, or else that the slight real pain experienced is so quickly followed by overwhelming pleasure that in memory the pain itself seems to have been pleasure and may even be regarded as the symbol of pleasure.

There is a special peculiarity of physical pain, which may be well borne in mind in considering the phenomena now before us, for it helps to account for the tolerance with which the idea of pain is regarded. I refer to the great ease with which physical pain is forgotten, a fact well known to all mothers, or to all who have been present at the birth of a child. As Professor von Tschisch points out ("Der Schmerz," *Zeitschrift für Psychologie und Physiologie der Sinnesorgane*, Bd. xxvi, ht. 1 and 2, 1901), memory can only preserve impressions as a whole; physical pain consists of a sensation and of a feeling. But memory cannot easily reproduce the definite sensation of the pain, and thus the whole memory is disintegrated and speedily forgotten. It is quite otherwise with moral suffering, which persists in memory and has far more influence on conduct. No one wishes to suffer moral pain or has any pleasure even in the idea of suffering it.

It is the presence of this essential tendency which leads to a certain apparent contradiction in a woman's emotions. On the one hand, rooted in the maternal instinct, we find pity, tenderness, and compassion; on the other hand, rooted in the sexual instinct, we find a delight in roughness, violence, pain, and danger, sometimes in herself, sometimes also in others. The one impulse craves something innocent and helpless, to cherish and protect; the other delights in the spectacle of recklessness, audacity, sometimes even effrontery.[79] A woman is not perfectly happy in her lover unless he can give at least some satisfaction to each of these two opposite longings.

The psychological satisfaction which women tend to feel in a certain degree of pain in love is strictly co-ordinated with a physical fact. Women possess a minor degree of sensibility in the sexual region. This fact must not be misunderstood. On the one hand, it by no means begs the question as to whether women's sensibility generally is greater or less than that of men; this is a disputed question and the evidence is still somewhat conflicting.[80] On the other hand, it also by no means involves a less degree of specific sexual pleasure in women, for the tactile sensibility of the sexual organs is no index to the specific sexual sensibility of those organs when in a state of tumescence. The real significance of the less tactile sensibility of the genital region in women is to be found in parturition and the special liability of the sexual region in women to injury.[81] The women who are less sensitive in this respect would be better able and more willing to endure the risks of childbirth, and would therefore tend to supplant those who were more sensitive. But, as a by-product of this less degree of sensibility, we have a condition in which physical irritation amounting even to pain may become to normal women in the state of extreme tumescence a source of pleasurable excitement, such as it would rarely be to normal men.

To Calmann appear to be due the first carefully made observations showing the minor sensibility of the genital tract in women. (Adolf Calmann, "Sensibilitütsprufungen am weiblicken Genitale nach forensichen Gesichtspunkten," *Archiv für Gynäkologie*, 1898, p. 454.) He investigated the vagina, urethra, and anus in eighteen women and found a great lack of sensibility, least marked in anus, and most marked in vagina. [This distribution of the insensitiveness alone indicates that it is due, as I have suggested, to natural selection.] Sometimes a finger in the vagina could not be felt at all. One woman, when a catheter was introduced into the anus, said it might be the vagina or urethra, but was certainly not the anus. (Calmann remarks that he was careful to put his questions in an intelligible form.) The women were only conscious of the urine being drawn off when they heard the familiar sound of the stream or when the bladder was very full; if the sound of the stream was deadened by a towel they were quite unconscious that the bladder had been emptied. [In confirmation of this statement I have noticed that in a lady whose distended bladder it was necessary to empty by the catheter shortly before the birth of her first child—but who had, indeed, been partly under the influence of chloroform—there was no consciousness of the artificial relief; she merely remarked that she thought she could now relieve herself.] There was some sense of temperature, but sense of locality, tactile sense, and judgment of size were often widely erroneous. It is significant that virgins were just as insensitive as married women or those who had had children. Calmann's experiments appear to be confirmed by the experiments of Marco Treves, of Turin, on the thermoesthesiometry of mucous membranes, as reported to the Turin International Congress of Physiology (and briefly noted in *Nature*, November 21, 1901). Treves found that the sensitivity of mucous membranes is always less than that of the skin. The mucosa of the urethra and of the cervix uteri was quite incapable of heat and cold sensations, and even the cautery excited only slight, and that painful, sensation.

In further illustration of this point reference may be made to the not infrequent cases in which the whole process of parturition and the enormous distention of tissues which it involves proceed throughout in an almost or quite painless manner. It is sufficient to refer to two cases reported in Paris by Macé and briefly summarized in the *British Medical Journal*, May 25, 1901. In the first the patient was a primipara 20 years of age, and, until the dilatation of the cervix was complete and efforts at expulsion had commenced, the uterine contractions were quite painless. In the second case, the mother, aged 25, a tripara, had previously had very rapid labors; she awoke in the middle of the night without pains, but during micturition the fetal head appeared at the vulva, and was soon born.

Further illustration may be found in those cases in which severe inflammatory processes may take place in the genital canal without being noticed. Thus, Maxwell reports the case of a young Chinese woman, certainly quite normal, in whom after the birth of her first child the vagina became almost obliterated, yet beyond slight occasional pain she noticed nothing wrong until the husband found that penetration was impossible (*British Medical Journal*, January 11, 1902, p. 78). The insensitiveness of the vagina and its contrast, in this respect, with the penis—though we are justified in regarding the penis as being, like organs of special sense, relatively deficient in general sensibility—are vividly presented in such an incident as the following, reported a few years ago in America by Dr. G. W. Allen in the *Boston Medical and Surgical Journal*: A man came under observation with an edematous, inflamed penis. The wife, the night previous, on advice of friends, had injected pure carbolic acid into the vagina just previous to coitus. The husband, ignorant of the fact, experienced untoward burning and smarting during and after coitus, but thought little of it, and soon fell asleep. The next morning there were large blisters on the penis, but it was no longer painful. When seen by Dr. Allen the prepuce was retracted and edematous, the whole penis was much swollen, and there were large, perfectly raw surfaces on either side of the glans.

In this connection we may well bring into line a remarkable group of phenomena concerning which much evidence has now accumulated. I refer to the use of various appliances, fixed in or around the penis, whether permanently or temporarily during coitus, such appliance being employed at the woman's instigation and solely in order to heighten her excitement in congress. These appliances have their great center among the Indonesian peoples (in Borneo, Java, Sumatra, the Malay peninsula, the Philippines, etc.), thence extending in a modified form through China, to become, it appears, considerably prevalent in Russia; I have also a note of their appearance in India. They have another widely diffused center, through which, however, they are more sparsely scattered, among the American Indians of the northern and more especially of the southern continents. Amerigo Vespucci and other early travelers noted the existence of some of these appliances, and since Miklucho-Macleay carefully described them as used in Borneo[82] their existence has been generally recognized. They are usually regarded merely as ethnological curiosities. As such they would not concern us here. Their real significance for us is that they illustrate the comparative insensitiveness of the genital canal in women, while at the same time they show that a certain amount of what we cannot but regard as painful stimulation is craved by women, in order to heighten tumescence and increase sexual pleasure, even though it can only be procured by artificial methods. It is, of course, possible to argue that in these cases we are not concerned with pain at all, but with a strong stimulation that is felt as purely pleasurable. There can be no doubt, however, that in the absence of sexual excitement this stimulation would be felt as purely painful, and—in the light of our previous discussion—we may, perhaps, fairly regard it as a painful stimulation which is craved, not because it is itself pleasurable, but because it heightens the highly pleasurable state of tumescence.

Borneo, the geographical center of the Indonesian world, appears also to be the district in which these instruments are most popular. The *ampallang, palang, kambion*, or *sprit-sail yard*, as it is variously termed, is a little rod of bone or metal nearly two inches in length, rounded at the ends, and used by the Kyans and Dyaks of Borneo. Before coitus it is inserted into a transverse orifice in the penis, made by a painful and somewhat dangerous operation and kept open by a quill. Two or more of these instruments are occasionally worn. Sometimes little brushes are attached to each end of the instrument. Another instrument, used by the Dyaks, but said to have been borrowed from the Malays, is the *palang anus*, which is a ring or collar of plaited palm-fiber, furnished with a pair of stiffish horns of the same wiry material; it is worn on the neck of the glans and fits tight to the skin so as not to slip off. (Brooke Low, "The Natives of Borneo," *Journal of the Anthropological Institute*, August and November, 1892, p. 45; the *ampallang* and similar instruments are described by Ploss and Bartels, *Das Weib*, Bd. i, chapter xvii; also in *Untrodden Fields of Anthropology*, by a French army surgeon, 1898, vol. ii, pp. 135-141; also Mantegazza, *Gli Amori degli Uomini*, French translation, p. 83 *et seq.*) Riedel informed Miklucho-Macleay that in the Celebes the Alfurus fasten the eyelids of goats with the eyelashes round the corona of the glans penis, and in Java a piece of goatskin is used in a similar way, so as to form a hairy sheath (*Zeitschrift für Ethnologie*, 1876, pp. 22-25), while among the Batta, of Sumatra, Hagen found that small stones are inserted by an incision under the skin of the penis (*Zeitschrift für Ethnologie*, 1891, ht. 3, p. 351).

In the Malay peninsula Stevens found instruments somewhat similar to the *ampallang* still in use among some tribes, and among others formerly in use. He thinks they were brought from Borneo. (H. V. Stevens, *Zeitschrift für Ethnologie*, 1896, ht. 4, p. 181.) Bloch, who brings forward other examples of similar devices (*Beiträge zur Ætiologie der Psychopathia Sexualis*, pp. 56-58), considers that the Australian mica operation may thus in part be explained.

Such instruments are not, however, entirely unknown in Europe. In France, in the eighteenth century, it appears that rings, sometimes set with hard knobs, and called "aides," were occasionally used by men to heighten the pleasure of women in intercourse. (Dühren, *Marquis de Sade*, 1901, p. 130.) In Russia, according to Weissenberg, of Elizabethsgrad, it is not uncommon to use elastic rings set with little teeth; these rings are fastened around the base of the glans. (Weissenberg, *Zeitschrift für Ethnologie*, 1893, ht. 2, p. 135.) This instrument must have been brought to Russia from the East, for Burton (in the notes to his *Arabian Nights*) mentions a precisely similar instrument as in use in China. Somewhat similar is the "Chinese hedgehog," a wreath of fine, soft feathers with the quills solidly fastened by silver wire to a ring of the same metal, which is slipped over the glans. In South America the Araucanians of Argentina use a little horsehair brush fastened around the penis; one of these is in the museum at La Plata; it is said the custom may have been borrowed from the Patagonians; these instruments, called *geskels*, are made by the women and the workmanship is very delicate. (Lehmann-Nitsche, *Zeitschrift für Ethnologie*, 1900, ht. 6, p. 491.) It is noteworthy that a somewhat similar tuft of horsehair is also worn in Borneo. (Breitenstein, *21 Jahre in India*, 1899, pt. i, p. 227.) Most of the accounts state that the women attach great importance to the gratification afforded by such instruments. In Borneo a modest woman symbolically indicates to her lover the exact length of the ampallang she would prefer by leaving at a particular spot a cigarette of that length. Miklucho-Macleay considers that these instruments were invented by women. Brooke Low remarks that "no woman once habituated to its use will ever dream of permitting her bedfellow to discontinue the practice of wearing it," and Stevens states that at one time no woman would marry a man who was not furnished with such an apparatus. It may be added that a very similar appliance may be found in European countries (especially Germany) in the use of a condom furnished with irregularities, or a frill, in order to increase the woman's excitement. It is not impossible to find evidence that, in European countries, even in the absence of such instruments, the craving which they gratify still exists in women. Thus, Mauriac tells of a patient with vegetations on the glans who delayed treatment because his mistress liked him so best (art. "Végétations," *Dictionnaire de Médecine et Chirurgie pratique*).

It may seem that such impulses and such devices to gratify them are altogether unnatural. This is not so. They have a zoölogical basis and in many animals are embodied in the anatomical structure. Many rodents, ruminants, and some of the carnivora show natural developments of the penis closely resembling some of those artificially adopted by man. Thus the guinea-pigs possess two horny styles attached to the penis, while the glans of the penis is covered with sharp spines. Some of the Caviidæ also have two sharp, horny saws at the side of the penis. The cat, the rhinoceros, the tapir, and other animals possess projecting structures on the penis, and some species of ruminants, such as the sheep, the giraffe, and many antelopes, have, attached to the penis, long filiform processes through which the urethra passes. (F. H. A. Marshall, *The Physiology of Reproduction*, pp. 246-248.)

We find, even in creatures so delicate and ethereal as the butterflies, a whole armory of keen weapons for use in coitus. These were described in detail in an elaborate and fully illustrated memoir by P. H. Gosse ("On the Clasping Organs Ancillary to Generation in Certain Groups of the Lepidoptera," *Transactions of the Linnæan Society*, second series, vol. ii, Zoölogy, 1882). These organs, which Gosse terms *harpes* (or grappling irons), are found in the Papilionidæ and are very beautiful and varied, taking the forms of projecting claws, hooks, pikes, swords, knobs, and strange combinations of these, commonly brought to a keen edge and then cut into sharp teeth.

It is probable that all these structures serve to excite the sexual apparatus of the female and to promote tumescence.

To the careless observer there may seem to be something vicious or perverted in such manifestations in man. That opinion becomesvery doubtful when we consider how these tendencies occur in people living under natural conditions in widely separated parts of the world. It becomes still further untenable if we are justified in believing that the ancestors of men possessed projecting epithelial appendages attached to the penis, and if we accept the discovery by Friedenthal of the rudiment of these appendages on the penis of the human fetus at an early stage (Friedenthal, "Sonderformen der menschlichen Leibesbildung," *Sexual-Probleme*, Feb., 1912, p. 129). In this case human ingenuity would merely be seeking to supply an organ which nature has ceased to furnish, although it is still in some cases needed, especially among peoples whose aptitude for erethism has remained at, or fallen to, a subhuman level.

At first sight the connection between love and pain—the tendency of men to delight in inflicting it and women in suffering it—seems strange and inexplicable. It seems amazing that a tender and even independent woman should maintain a passionate attachment to a man who subjects her to physical and moral insults, and that a strong man, often intelligent, reasonable, and even kind-hearted, should desire to subject to such insults a woman whom he loves passionately and who has given him every final proof of her own passion. In understanding such cases we have to remember that it is only within limits that a woman really enjoys the pain, discomfort, or subjection to which she submits. A little pain which the man knows he can himself soothe, a little pain which the woman gladly accepts as the sign and forerunner of pleasure—this degree of pain comes within the normal limits of love and is rooted, as we have seen, in the experience of the race. But when it is carried beyond these limits, though it may still be tolerated because of the support it receives from its biological basis, it is no longer enjoyed. The natural note has been too violently struck, and the rhythm of love has ceased to be perfect. A woman may desire to be forced, to be roughly forced, to be ravished away beyond her own will. But all the time she only desires to be forced toward those things which are essentially and profoundly agreeable to her. A man who fails to realize this has made little progress in the art of love. "I like being knocked about and made to do things I don't want to do," a woman said, but she admitted, on being questioned, that she would not like to have *much* pain inflicted, and that she might not care to be made to do important things she did not want to do. The story of Griselda's unbounded submissiveness can scarcely be said to be psychologically right, though it has its artistic rightness as an elaborate fantasia on this theme justified by its conclusion.

This point is further illustrated by the following passage from a letter written by a lady: "Submission to the man's will is still, and always must be, the prelude to pleasure, and the association of ideas will probably always produce this much misunderstood instinct. Now, I find, indirectly from other women and directly from my own experience, that, when the point in dispute is very important and the man exerts his authority, the desire to get one's own way completely obliterates the sexual feeling, while, conversely, in small things the sexual feeling obliterates the desire to have one's own way. Where the two are nearly equal a conflict between them ensues, and I can stand aside and wonder which will get the best of it, though I encourage the sexual feeling when possible, as, if the other conquers, it leaves a sense of great mental irritation and physical discomfort. A man should command in small things, as in nine cases out of ten this will produce excitement. He should *advise* in large matters, or he may find either that he is unable to enforce his orders or that he produces a feeling of dislike and annoyance he was far from intending. Women imagine men must be stronger than themselves to excite their passion. I disagree. A passionate man has the best chance, for in him the primitive instincts are strong. The wish to subdue the female is one of them, and in small things he will exert his authority to make her feel his power, while she knows that on a question of real importance she has a good chance of getting her own way by working on his greater susceptibility. Perhaps an illustration will show what I mean. I was listening to the band and a girl and her *fiancé* came up to occupy two seats near me. The girl sank into one seat, but for some reason the man wished her to take the other. She refused. He repeated his order twice, the second time so peremptorily that she changed places, and I heard him say: 'I don't think you heard what I said. I don't expect to give an order three times.'

"This little scene interested me, and I afterward asked the girl the following questions:—

"'Had you any reason for taking one chair more than the other?'

"'No.'

"'Did Mr. ——'s insistence on your changing give you any pleasure?'

"'Yes' (after a little hesitation).

"'Why?'

"'I don't know.'

"'Would it have done so if you had particularly wished to sit in that chair; if, for instance, you had had a boil on your cheek and wished to turn that side away from him?'

"'No; certainly not. The worry of thinking he was looking at it would have made me too cross to feel pleased.'

"'Does this explain what I mean? The occasion, by the way, need not be really important, but, as in this imaginary case of the boil, if it *seems important* to the woman, irritation will outweigh the physical sensation."

I am well aware that in thus asserting a certain tendency in women to delight in suffering pain—however careful and qualified the position I have taken—many estimable people will cry out that I am degrading a whole sex and generally supporting the "subjection of women." But the day for academic discussion concerning the "subjection of women" has gone by. The tendency I have sought to make clear is too well established by the experience of normal and typical women—however numerous the exceptions may be—to be called in question. I would point out to those who would deprecate the influence of such facts in relation to social progress that nothing is gained by regarding women as simply men of smaller growth. They are not so; they have the laws of their own nature; their development must be along their own lines, and not along masculine lines. It is as true now as in Bacon's day that we only learn to command nature by obeying her. To ignore facts is to court disappointment in our measure of progress. The particular fact with which we have here come in contact is very vital and radical, and most subtle in its influence. It is foolish to ignore it; we must allow for its existence. We can neither attain a sane view of life nor a sane social legislation of life unless we possess a just and accurate knowledge of the fundamental instincts upon which life is built.

[61]

Various mammals, carried away by the reckless fury of the sexual impulse, are apt to ill-treat their females (R. Müller, *Sexualbiologie*, p. 123). This treatment is, however, usually only an incident of courtship, the result of excess of ardor. "The chaffinches and saffron-finches (*Fringella* and *Sycalis*) are very rough wooers," says A. G. Butler (*Zoölogist*, 1902, p. 241); "they sing vociferously, and chase their hens violently, knocking them over in their flight, pursuing and savagely pecking them even on the ground; but when once the hens become submissive, the males change their tactics, and become for the time model husbands, feeding their wives from their crop, and assisting in rearing the young."

[62]

Cf. A. C. Haddon, *Head Hunters*, p. 107.

[63]

Marro considers that there may be transference of emotion,—the impulse of violence generated in the male by his rivals being turned against his partner,—according to a tendency noted by Sully and illustrated by Ribot in his *Psychology of the Emotions*, part i, chapter xii.

[64]

Several writers have found in the facts of primitive animal courtship the explanation of the connection between love and pain. Thus, Krafft-Ebing (*Psychopathia Sexualis*, English translation of tenth German edition, p. 80) briefly notes that outbreaks of sadism are possibly atavistic. Marro (*La Pubertà*, 1898, p. 219 *et seq.*) has some suggestive pages on this subject. It would appear that this explanation was vaguely outlined by Jäger. Laserre, in a Bordeaux thesis mentioned by Féré, has argued in the same sense. Féré (*L'Instinct Sexuel*, p. 134), on grounds that are scarcely sufficient, regards this explanation as merely a superficial analogy. But it is certainly not a complete explanation.

[65]

Schäfer (*Jahrbücher für Psychologie*, Bd. ii, p. 128, and quoted by Krafft-Ebing in *Psychopathia Sexualis*), in connection with a case in which sexual excitement was produced by the sight of battles or of paintings of them, remarks: "The pleasure of battle and murder is so predominantly an attribute of the male sex throughout the animal kingdom that there can be no question about the close connection between this side of the masculine character and male sexuality. I believe that I can show by observation that in men who are absolutely normal, mentally and physically, the first indefinite and incomprehensible precursors of sexual excitement may be induced by reading exciting scenes of chase and war. These give rise to unconscious longings for a kind of satisfaction in warlike games (wrestling, etc.) which express the fundamental sexual impulse to close and complete contact with a companion, with a secondary more or less clearly defined thought of conquest." Groos (*Spiele der Menschen*, 1899, p. 232) also thinks there is more or less truth in this suggestion of a subconscious sexual element in the playful wrestling combats of boys. Freud considers (*Drei Abhandlungen zur Sexualtheorie*, p. 49) that the tendency to sexual excitement through muscular activity in wrestling, etc., is one of the roots of sadism. I have been told of normal men who feel a conscious pleasure of this kind when lifted in games, as may happen, for instance, in football. It may be added that in some parts of the world the suitor has to throw the girl in a wrestling-bout in order to secure her hand.

[66]

A minor manifestation of this tendency, appearing even in quite normal and well-conditioned individuals, is the impulse among boys at and after puberty to take pleasure in persecuting and hurting lower animals or their own young companions. Some youths display a diabolical enjoyment and ingenuity in torturing sensitive juniors, and even a boy who is otherwise kindly and considerate may find enjoyment in deliberately mutilating a frog. In some cases, in boys and youths who have no true sadistic impulse and are not usually cruel, this infliction of torture on a lower animal produces an erection, though not necessarily any pleasant sexual sensations.

[67]

Marro, *La Pubertà*, 1898, p. 223; Garnier, "La Criminalité Juvenile,"*Comptes-rendus Congrès Internationale d'Anthropologie Criminelle*, Amsterdam, 1901, p. 296; *Archivio di Psichiatria*, 1899, fasc. v-vi, p. 572.

[68]

Bk. ii, ch. ii.

[69]

Herbert Spencer, *Principles of Sociology*, 1876, vol. i, p. 651.

[70]

Westermarck, *Human Marriage*, p. 388. Grosse is of the same opinion; he considers also that the mock-capture is often an imitation, due to admiration, of real capture; he does not believe that the latter has ever been a form of marriage recognized by custom and law, but only "an occasional and punishable act of violence." (*Die Formen der Familie*, pp. 105-7.) This position is too extreme.

[71]

Ernest Crawley, *The Mystic Rose*, 1902, p. 350 *et seq*. Van Gennep rightly remarks that we cannot correctly say that the woman is abducted from "her sex," but only from her "sexual society."

[72]

A. Van Gennep (*Rites de Passage*, 1909, pp. 175-186) has put forward a third theory, though also of a psychological character, according to which the "capture" is a rite indicating the separation of the young girl from the special societies of her childhood. Gennep regards this rite as one of a vast group of "rites of passage," which come into action whenever a person changes his social or natural environment.

[73]

Féré (*L'Instinct Sexuel*, p. 133) appears to regard the satisfaction, based on the sentiment of personal power, which may be experienced in the suffering and subjection of a victim as an adequate explanation of the association of pain with love. This I can scarcely admit. It is a factor in the emotional attitude, but when it only exists in the sexual sphere it is reasonable to base this attitude largely on the still more fundamental biological attitude of the male toward the female in the process of courtship. Féré regards this biological element as merely a superficial analogy, on the ground that an act of cruelty may become an equivalent of coitus. But a sexual perversion is quite commonly constituted by the selection and magnification of a single moment in the normal sexual process.

[74]

The process may, however, be quite conscious. Thus, a correspondent tells me that he not only finds sexual pleasure in cruelty toward the woman he loves, but that he regards this as an essential element. He is convinced that it gives the woman pleasure, and that it is possible to distinguish by gesture, inflection of voice, etc., an hysterical, assumed, or imagined feeling of pain from real pain. He would not wish to give real pain, and would regard that as sadism.

[75]

De Sade had already made the same remark, while Duchenne, of Boulogne, pointed out that the facial expressions of sexual passion and of cruelty are similar.

[76]

Κρυπτάδια, vol. vi, p. 208.

[77]

Daumas, *Chevaux de Sahara*, p. 49.

[78]

See in vol. iv of these *Studies* ("Sexual Selection in Man"), Appendix A, on "The Origins of the Kiss."

[79]

De Stendhal (*De l'Amour*) mentions that when in London he was on terms of friendship with an English actress who was the mistress of a wealthy colonel, but privately had another lover. One day the colonel arrived when the other man was present. "This gentleman has called about the pony I want to sell," said the actress. "I have come for a very different purpose," said the little man, and thus aroused a love which was beginning to languish.

[80]

See Havelock Ellis, *Man and Woman*, chapter vi, "The Senses."

[81]

This liability is emphasized by Adler, *Die Mangelhafte Geschlechtsempfindung des Weibes*, p. 125.

[82]

Zeitschrift für Ethnologie, Bd. viii, 1876, pp. 22-28.

II.

The Definition of Sadism—De Sade—Masochism to some Extent Normal—Sacher-Masoch—No Real Line of Demarcation between Sadism and Masochism—Algolagnia includes both Groups of Manifestations—The Love-bite as a Bridge from Normal Phenomena to Algolagnia—The Fascination of Blood—The Most Extreme Perversions are Linked on to Normal Phenomena.

We thus see that there are here two separate groups of feelings: one, in the masculine line, which delights in displaying force and often inflicts pain or the simulacrum of pain; the other, in the feminine line, which delights in submitting to that force, and even finds pleasure in a slight amount of pain, or the idea of pain, when associated with the experiences of love. We see, also, that these two groups of feelings are complementary. Within the limits consistent with normal and healthy life, what men are impelled to give women love to receive. So that we need not unduly deprecate the "cruelty" of men within these limits, nor unduly commiserate the women who are subjected to it.

Such a conclusion, however, as we have also seen, only holds good within those normal limits which an attempt has here been made to determine. The phenomena we have been considering are strictly normal phenomena, having their basis in the conditions of tumescence and detumescence in animal and primitive human courtship. At one point, however, when discussing the phenomena of the love-bite, I referred to the facts which indicate how this purely normal manifestation yet insensibly passes over into the region of the morbid. It is an instance that enables us to realize how even the most terrible and repugnant sexual perversions are still demonstrably linked on to phenomena that are fundamentally normal. The love-bite may be said to give us the key to that perverse impulse which has been commonly called sadism.

There is some difference of opinion as to how "sadism" may be best defined. Perhaps the simplest and most usual definition is that of Krafft-Ebing, as sexual emotion associated with the wish to inflict pain and use violence, or, as he elsewhere expresses it, "the impulse to cruel and violent treatment of the opposite sex, and the coloring of the idea of such acts with lustful feeling."[183] A more complete definition is that of Moll, who describes sadism as a condition in which "the sexual impulse consists in the tendency to strike, ill-use, and humiliate the beloved person."[184] This definition has the advantage of bringing in the element of moral pain. A further extension is made in Féré's definition as "the need of association of violence and cruelty with sexual enjoyment, such violence or cruelty not being necessarily exerted by the person himself who seeks sexual pleasure in this association."[185] Garnier's definition, while comprising all these points, further allows for the fact that a certain degree of sadism may be regarded as normal. "Pathological sadism," he states, "is an impulsive and obsessing sexual perversion characterized by a close connection between suffering inflicted or mentally represented and the sexual orgasm, without this necessary and sufficing condition frigidity usually remaining absolute."[186] It must be added that these definitions are very incomplete if by "sadism" we are to understand the special sexual perversions which are displayed in De Sade's novels. Iwan Bloch ("Eugen Dühren"), in the course of his book on De Sade, has attempted a definition strictly on this basis, and, as will be seen, it is necessary to make it very elaborate: "A connection, whether intentionally sought or offered by chance, of sexual excitement and sexual enjoyment with the real or only symbolic (ideal, illusionary) appearance of frightful and shocking events, destructive occurrences and practices, which threaten or destroy the life, health, and property of man and other living creatures, and threaten and interrupt the continuity of inanimate objects, whereby the person who from such occurrences obtains sexual enjoyment may either himself be the direct cause, or cause them to take place by means of other persons, or merely be the spectator, or, finally, be, voluntarily or involuntarily, the object against which these processes are directed."[187] This definition of sadism as found in De Sade's works is thus, more especially by its final clause, a very much wider conception than the usual definition.

Donatien Alphonse François, Marquis De Sade, was born in 1740 at Paris in the house of the great Condé. He belonged to a very noble, ancient, and distinguished Provençal family; Petrarch's Laura, who married a De Sade, was one of his ancestors, and the family had cultivated both arms and letters with success. He was, according to Lacroix, "an adorable youth whose delicately pale and dusky face, lighted up by two large black [according to another account blue] eyes, already bore the languorous imprint of the vice which was to corrupt his whole being"; his voice was "drawling and caressing"; his gait had "a softly feminine grace." Unfortunately there is no authentic portrait of him. His early life is sketched in letter iv of his *Aline et Valcourt*. On leaving the Collège-Louis-le-Grand he became a cavalry officer and went through the Seven Years' War in Germany. There can be little doubt that the experiences of his military life, working on a femininely vicious temperament, had much to do with the development of his perversion. He appears to have got into numerous scrapes, of which the details are unknown, and his father sought to marry him to the daughter of an aristocratic friend of his own, a noble and amiable girl of 20. It so chanced that when young De Sade first went to the house of his future wife only her younger sister, a girl of 13, was at home; with her he at once fell in love and his love was reciprocated; they were both musical enthusiasts, and she had a beautiful voice. The parents insisted on carrying out the original scheme of marriage. De Sade's wife loved him, and, in spite of everything, served his interests with Griselda-like devotion; she was, Ginisty remarks, a saint, a saint of conjugal life; but her love was from the first only requited with repulsion, contempt, and suspicion. There were, however, children of the marriage; the career of the eldest—an estimable young man who went into the army and also had artistic ability, but otherwise had no community of tastes with his father—has been sketched by Paul Ginisty, who has also edited the letters of the Marquise. De Sade's passion for the younger sister continued (he idealized her as Juliette), though she was placed in a convent beyond his reach, and at a much later period he eloped with her and spent perhaps the happiest period of his life, soon terminated by her death. It is evident that this unhappy marriage was decisive in determining De Sade's career; he at once threw himself recklessly into every form of dissipation, spending his health and his substance sometimes among refinedly debauched nobles and sometimes among coarsely debauched lackeys. He was, however, always something of an artist, something of a student, something of a philosopher, and at an early period he began to write, apparently at the age of 23. It was at this age, and only a few months after his marriage, that on account of some excess he was for a time confined in Vincennes. He was destined to spend 27 years of his life in prisons, if we include the 13 years which in old age he passed in the asylum at Charenton. His actual offenses were by no means so terrible as those he loved to dwell on in imagination, and for the most part they have been greatly exaggerated. His most extreme offenses were the indecent and forcible flagellation in 1768 of a young woman, Rosa Keller, who had accosted him in the street for alms, and whom he induced by false pretenses to come to his house, and the administration of aphrodisiacal bonbons to some prostitutes at Marseilles. It is owing to the fact that the prime of his manhood was spent in prisons that De Sade fell back on dreaming, study, and novel-writing. Shut out from real life, he solaced his imagination with the perverted visions—to a very large extent, however, founded on knowledge of the real facts of perverted life in his time—which he has recorded in *Justine* (1781); *Les 120 Journées de Sodome ou l'Ecole du Libertinage* (1785); *Aline et Valcour ou le Roman Philosophique* (1788); *Juliette* (1796); *La Philosophie dans le Boudoir* (1795). These books constitute a sort of encyclopedia of sexual perversions, an eighteenth century *Psychopathia Sexualis*, and embody, at the same time, a philosophy. He was the first, Bloch remarks, who realized the immense importance of the sexual question. His general attitude may be illustrated by the following passage (as quoted by Lacassagne): "If there are beings in the world whose acts shock all accepted prejudices, we must not preach at nor punish them ... because their bizarre tastes no more depend upon themselves than it depends on you whether you are witty or stupid, well made or hump-backed.... What would become of your laws, your morality, your religion, your gallows, your Paradise, your gods, your hell, if it were shown that such and such fluids, such fibers, or a certain acridity in the blood, or in the animal spirits, alone suffice to make a man the object of your punishments or your rewards?" He was enormously well read, Bloch points out, and his interest extended to every field of literature: *belles lettres*, philosophy, theology, politics, sociology, ethnology, mythology, and history. Perhaps his favorite reading was travels. He was minutely familiar with the bible, though his attitude was extremely critical. His favorite philosopher was Lamettrie, whom he very frequently quotes, and he had carefully studied Machiavelli.

De Sade had foreseen the Revolution; he was an ardent admirer of Marat, and at this period he entered into public life as a mild, gentle, rather bald and gray-haired person. Many scenes of the Revolution were the embodiment in real life of De Sade's imagination; such, for instance, were the barbaric tortures inflicted, at the instigation of Théroigne de Méricourt, on La Belle Bouquetière. Yet De Sade played a very peaceful part in the events of that time, chiefly as a philanthropist, spending much of his time in the hospitals. He saved his parents-in-law from the scaffold, although they had always been hostile to him, and by his moderation aroused the suspicions of the revolutionary party, and was again imprisoned. Later he wrote a pamphlet against Napoleon, who never forgave him and had him shut up in Charenton as a lunatic; it was a not unusual method at that time of disposing of persons

61

whom it was wished to put out of the way, and, notwithstanding De Sade's organically abnormal temperament, there is no reason to regard him as actually insane. Royer-Collard, an eminent alienist of that period, then at the head of Charenton, declared De Sade to be sane, and his detailed report is still extant. Other specialists were of the same opinion. Bloch, who quotes these opinions (*Neue Forschungen*, etc., p. 370), says that the only possible conclusion is that De Sade was sane, but neurasthenic, and Eulenburg also concludes that he cannot be regarded as insane, although he was highly degenerate. In the asylum he amused himself by organizing a theater. Lacroix, many years later, questioning old people who had known him, was surprised to find that even in the memory of most virtuous and respectable persons he lived merely as an "*aimable mauvais sujet.*" It is noteworthy that De Sade aroused, in a singular degree, the love and devotion of women,—whether or not we may regard this as evidence of the fascination exerted on women by cruelty. Janin remarks that he had seen many pretty little letters written by young and charming women of the great world, begging for the release of the "*pauvre marquis.*"

Sardou, the dramatist, has stated that in 1855 he visited the Bicêtre and met an old gardener who had known De Sade during hisreclusion there. He told that one of the marquis's amusements was to procure baskets of the most beautiful and expensive roses; he would then sit on a footstool by a dirty streamlet which ran through the courtyard, and would take the roses, one by one, gaze at them, smell them with a voluptuous expression, soak them in the muddy water, and fling them away, laughing as he did so. He died on the 2d of December, 1814, at the age of 74. He was almost blind, and had long been a martyr to gout, asthma, and an affection of the stomach. It was his wish that acorns should be planted over his grave and his memory effaced. At a later period his skull was examined by a phrenologist, who found it small and well formed; "one would take it at first for a woman's head." The skull belonged to Dr. Londe, but about the middle of the century it was stolen by a doctor who conveyed it to England, where it may possibly yet be found. [The foregoing account is mainly founded on Paul Lacroix, *Revue de Paris*, 1837, and *Curiosités de l'Histoire de France*, second series, *Procès Célèbres*, p. 225; Janin, *Revue de Paris*, 1834; Eugen Dühren (Iwan Bloch), *Der Marquis de Sade und Seine Zeit*, third edition, 1901; *id.*, *Neue Forschungen über den Marquis de Sade und Seine Zeit*, 1904; Lacassagne, *Vacher l'Eventreur et les Crimes Sadiques*, 1899; Paul Ginisty, *La Marquise de Sade*, 1901.]

The attempt to define sadism strictly and penetrate to its roots in De Sade's personal temperament reveals a certain weakness in the current conception of this sexual perversion. It is not, as we might infer, both from the definition usually given and from its probable biological heredity from primitive times, a perversion due to excessive masculinity. The strong man is more apt to be tender than cruel, or at all events knows how to restrain within bounds any impulse to cruelty; the most extreme and elaborate forms of sadism (putting aside such as are associated with a considerable degree of imbecility) are more apt to be allied with a somewhat feminine organization. Montaigne, indeed, observed long ago that cruelty is usually accompanied by feminine softness.

In the same way it is a mistake to suppose that the very feminine woman is not capable of sadistic tendencies. Even if we take into account the primitive animal conditions of combat, the male must suffer as well as inflict pain, and the female must not only experience subjection to the male, but also share in the emotions of her partner's victory over his rivals. As bearing on these points, I may quote the following remarks written by a lady: "It is said that, the weaker and more feminine a woman is, the greater the subjection she likes. I don't think it has anything at all to do with the general character, but depends entirely on whether the feeling of constraint and helplessness affects her sexually. In men I have several times noticed that those who were most desirous of subjection to the women they loved had, in ordinary life, very strong and determined characters. I know of others, too, who with very weak characters are very imperious toward the women they care for. Among women I have often been surprised to see how a strong, determined woman will give way to a man she loves, and how tenacious of her own will may be some fragile, clinging creature who in daily life seems quite unable to act on her own responsibility. A certain amount of passivity, a desire to have their emotions worked on, seems to me, so far as my small experience goes, very common among ordinary, presumably normal men. A good deal of stress is laid on femininity as an attraction in a woman, and this may be so to very strong natures, but, so far as I have seen, the women who obtain extraordinary empire over men are those with a certain *virility* in their character and passions. If with this virility they combine a fragility or childishness of appearance which appeals to a man in another way at the same time, they appear to be irresistible."

I have noted some of the feminine traits in De Sade's temperament and appearance. The same may often be noted in sadists whose crimes were very much more serious and brutal than those of De Sade. A man who stabbed women in the streets at St. Louis was a waiter with a high-pitched, effeminate voice and boyish appearance. Reidel, the sadistic murderer, was timid, modest, and delicate; he was too shy to urinate in the presence of other people. A sadistic zoöphilist, described by A. Marie, who attempted to strangle a woman fellow-worker, had always been very timid, blushed with much facility, could not look even children in the eyes, or urinate in the presence of another person, or make sexual advances to women.

Kiernan and Moyer are inclined to connect the modesty and timidity of sadists with a disgust for normal coitus. They were called upon to examine an inverted married woman who had inflicted several hundred wounds, mostly superficial, with forks, scissors, etc., on the genital organs and other parts of a girl whom she had adopted from a "Home." This woman was very prominent in church and social matters in the city in which she lived, so that many clergymen and local persons of importance testified to her chaste, modest, and even prudish character; she was found to be sane at the time of the acts. (Moyer, *Alienist and Neurologist*, May, 1907, and private letter from Dr. Kiernan.)

We are thus led to another sexual perversion, which is usually considered the opposite of sadism. Masochism is commonly regarded as a peculiarly feminine sexual perversion, in women, indeed, as normal in some degree, and in man as a sort of inversion of the normal masculine emotional attitude, but this view of the matter is not altogether justified, for definite and pronounced masochism seems to be much rarer in women than sadism.[88] Krafft-Ebing, whose treatment of this phenomenon is, perhaps, his most valuable and original contribution to sexual psychology, has dealt very fully with the matter and brought forward many cases. He thus defines this perversion: "By masochism I understand a peculiar perversion of the psychical *vita sexualis* in which the individual affected, in sexual feeling and thought, is controlled by the idea of being completely and unconditionally subject to the will of a person of the opposite sex, of being treated by this person as by a master, humiliated and abused. This idea is colored by sexual feeling; the masochist lives in fancies in which he creates situations of this kind, and he often attempts to realize them."[89]

In a minor degree, not amounting to a complete perversion of the sexual instinct, this sentiment of abnegation, the desire to be even physically subjected to the adored woman, cannot be regarded as abnormal. More than two centuries before Krafft-Ebing appeared, Robert Burton, who was no mean psychologist, dilated on the fact that love is a kind of slavery. "They are commonly slaves," he wrote of lovers, "captives, voluntary servants; *amator amicæ mancipium*, as Castilio terms him; his mistress's servant, her drudge, prisoner, bondman, what not?"[90] Before Burton's time the legend of the erotic servitude of Aristotle was widely spread in Europe, and pictures exist of the venerable philosopher on all fours ridden by a woman with a whip.[91] In classic times various masochistic phenomena are noted with approval by Ovid. It has been pointed out by Moll[92] that there are traces of masochistic feeling in some of Goethe's poems, especially "Lilis Park" and "Erwin und Elmire." Similar traces have been found in the poems of Heine, Platen, Hamerling, and many other poets.[93] The poetry of the people is also said to contain many such traces. It may, indeed, be said that passion in its more lyric exaltations almost necessarily involves some resort to masochistic expression. A popular lady novelist in a novel written many years ago represents her hero, a robust soldier, imploring the lady of his love, in a moment of passionate exaltation, to trample on him, certainly without any wish to suggest sexual perversion. If it is true that the Antonio of Otway's *Venice Preserved* is a caricature of Shaftesbury, then it would appear that one of the greatest of English statesmen was supposed to exhibit very pronounced and characteristic masochistic tendencies; and in more recent days masochistic expressions have been noted as occurring in the love-letters of so emphatically virile a statesman as Bismarck.

Thus a minor degree of the masochistic tendency may be said to be fairly common, while its more pronounced manifestations are more common than pronounced sadism.[94] It very frequently affects persons of a sensitive, refined, and artistic temperament. It may even be said that this tendency is in the line of civilization. Krafft-Ebing points out that some of the most delicate and romantic love-episodes of the Middle Ages are distinctly colored by masochistic emotion.[95] The increasing tendency to masochism with increasing civilization becomes explicable if we accept Colin Scott's "secondary law of courting" as accessory to the primary law that the male is active, and the female passive and imaginatively attentive to the states of the excited male. According to the secondary law, "the female develops a superadded activity, the male becoming relatively passive and imaginatively attentive to the psychical and bodily states of the female."[96] We may probably agree that this "secondary law of courting" does really represent a tendency of love in individuals of complex and sensitive nature, and the outcome of such a receptive attitude on the part of the male is undoubtedly in well-marked cases a desire of submission to the female's will, and a craving to experience in some physical or psychic form, not necessarily painful, the manifestations of her activity.

When we turn from vague and unpronounced forms of the masochistic tendency to the more definite forms in which it becomes an unquestionable sexual perversion, we find a very eminent and fairly typical example in Rousseau, an example all the more interesting because here the subject has himself portrayed his perversion in his famous *Confessions.* It is, however, the name of a less eminent author, the Austrian novelist, Sacher-Masoch, which has become identified with the perversion through the fact that Krafft-Ebing fixed upon it as furnishing a convenient counterpart to the term "sadism." It is on the strength of a considerable number of his novels and stories, more especially of *Die Venus im Pelz,* that Krafft-Ebing took the scarcely warrantable liberty of identifying his name, while yet living, with a sexual perversion.

Sacher-Masoch's biography has been written with intimate knowledge and much candor by C. F. von Schlichtegroll (*Sacher-Masoch und der Masochismus,* 1901) and, more indirectly, by his first wife Wanda von Sacher-Masoch in her autobiography (*Meine Lebensbeichte,* 1906; French translation, *Confession de ma Vie,* 1907). Schlichtegroll's book is written with a somewhat undue attempt to exalt his hero and to attribute his misfortunes to his first wife. The autobiography of the latter, however, enables us to form a more complete picture of Sacher-Masoch's life, for, while his wife by no means spares herself, she clearly shows that Sacher-Masoch was the victim of his own abnormal temperament, and she presents both the sensitive, refined, exalted, and generous aspects of his nature, and his morbid, imaginative, vain aspects.

Leopold von Sacher-Masoch was born in 1836 at Lemberg in Galicia. He was of Spanish, German, and more especially Slavonic race. The founder of the family may be said to be a certain Don Matthias Sacher, a young Spanish nobleman, in the sixteenth century, who settled in Prague. The novelist's father was director of police in Lemberg and married Charlotte von Masoch, a Little Russian lady of noble birth. The novelist, the eldest child of this union, was not born until after nine years of marriage, and in infancy was so delicate that he was not expected to survive. He began to improve, however, when his mother gave him to be suckled to a robust Russian peasant woman, from whom, as he said later, he gained not only health, but "his soul"; from her he learned all the strange and melancholy legends of her people and a love of the Little Russians which never left him. While still a child young Sacher-Masoch was in the midst of the bloody scenes of the revolution which culminated in 1848. When he was 12 the family migrated to Prague, and the boy, though precocious in his development, then first learned the German language, of which he attained so fine a mastery. At a very early age he had found the atmosphere, and even some of the most characteristic elements, of the peculiar types which mark his work as a novelist.

It is interesting to trace the germinal elements of those peculiarities which so strongly affected his imagination on the sexual side. As a child, he was greatly attracted by representations of cruelty; he loved to gaze at pictures of executions, the legends of martyrs were his favorite reading, and with the onset of puberty he regularly dreamed that he was fettered and in the power of a cruel woman who tortured him. It has been said by an anonymous author that the women of Galicia either rule their husbands entirely and make them their slaves or themselves sink to be the wretchedest of slaves. At the age of 10, according to Schlichtegroll's narrative, the child Leopold witnessed a scene in which a woman of the former kind, a certain Countess XenobiaX., a relative of his own on the paternal side, played the chief part, and this scene left an undying impress on his imagination. The Countess was a beautiful but wanton creature, and the child adored her, impressed alike by her beauty and the costly furs she wore. She accepted his devotion and little services and would sometimes allow him to assist her in dressing; on one occasion, as he was kneeling before her to put on her ermine slippers, he kissed her feet; she smiled and gave him a kick which filled him with pleasure. Not long afterward occurred the episode which so profoundly affected his imagination. He was playing with his sisters at hide-and-seek and had carefully hidden himself behind the dresses on a clothes-rail in the Countess's bedroom. At this moment the Countess suddenly entered the house and ascended the stairs, followed by a lover, and the child, who dared not betray his presence, saw the countess sink down on a sofa and begin to caress her lover. But a few moments later the husband, accompanied by two friends, dashed into the room. Before, however, he could decide which of the lovers to turn against the Countess had risen and struck him so powerful a blow in the face with her fist that he fell back streaming with blood. She then seized a whip, drove all three men out of the room, and in the confusion the lover slipped away. At this moment the clothes-rail fell and the child, the involuntary witness of the scene, was revealed to the Countess, who now fell on him in anger, threw him to the ground, pressed her knee on his shoulder, and struck him unmercifully. The pain was great, and yet he was conscious of a strange pleasure. While this castigation was proceeding the Count returned, no longer in a rage, but meek and humble as a slave, and kneeled down before her to beg forgiveness. As the boy escaped he saw her kick her husband. The child could not resist the temptation to return to the spot; the door was closed and he could see nothing, but he heard the sound of the whip and the groans of the Count beneath his wife's blows.

It is unnecessary to insist that in this scene, acting on a highly sensitive and somewhat peculiar child, we have the key to the emotional attitude which affected so much of Sacher-Masoch's work. As his biographer remarks, woman became to him, during a considerable part of his life, a creature at once to be loved and hated, a being whose beauty and brutality enabled her to set her foot at will on the necks of men, and in the heroine of his first important novel, the *Emissär*, dealing with the Polish Revolution, he embodied the contradictory personality of Countess Xenobia. Even the whip and the fur garments, Sacher-Masoch's favorite emotional symbols, find their explanation in this early episode. He was accustomed to say of an attractive woman: "I should like to see her in furs," and, of an unattractive woman: "I could not imagine her in furs." His writing-paper at one time was adorned with the figure of a woman in Russian Boyar costume, her cloak lined with ermine, and brandishing a scourge. On his walls he liked to have pictures of women in furs, of the kind of which there is so magnificent an example by Rubens in the gallery at Munich. He would even keep a woman's fur cloak on an ottoman in his study and stroke it from time to time, finding that his brain thus received the same kind of stimulation as Schiller found in the odor of rotten apples.[97]

At the age of 13, in the revolution of 1848, young Sacher-Masoch received his baptism of fire; carried away in the popular movement, he helped to defend the barricades together with a young lady, a relative of his family, an amazon with a pistol in her girdle, such as later he loved to depict. This episode was, however, but a brief interruption of his education; he pursued his studies with brilliance, and on the higher side his education was aided by his father's esthetic tastes. Amateur theatricals were in special favor at his home, and here even the serious plays of Goethe and Gogol were performed, thus helping to train and direct the boy's taste. It is, perhaps, however, significant that it was a tragic event which, at the age of 16, first brought to him the full realization of life and the consciousness of his own power. This was the sudden death of his favorite sister. He became serious and quiet, and always regarded this grief as a turning-point in his life.

At the Universities of Prague and Graz he studied with such zeal that when only 19 he took his doctor's degree in law and shortly afterward became a *privatdocent* for German history at Graz. Gradually, however, the charms of literature asserted themselves definitely, and he soon abandoned teaching. He took part, however, in the war of 1866 in Italy, and at the battle of Solferino he was decorated on the field for bravery in action by the Austrian field-marshal. These incidents, however, had little disturbing influence on Sacher-Masoch's literary career, and he was gradually acquiring a European reputation by his novels and stories.

A far more seriously disturbing influence had already begun to be exerted on his life by a series of love-episodes. Some of these were of slight and ephemeral character; some were a source of unalloyed happiness, all the more so if there was an element of extravagance to appeal to his Quixotic nature. He always longed to give a dramatic and romantic character to his life, his wife says, and he spent some blissful days on an occasion when he ran away to Florence with a Russian princess as her private secretary. Most often these episodes culminated in deception and misery. It was after a relationship of this kind from which he could not free himself for four years that he wrote *Die Geschiedene Frau, Passionsgeschichte eines Idealisten*, putting into it much of his own personal history. At one time he was engaged to a sweet and charming young girl. Then it was that he met a young woman at Graz, Laura Rümelin, 27 years of age, engaged as a glove-maker, and living with her mother. Though of poor parentage, with little or no knowledge of the world, she had great natural ability and intelligence. Schlichtegroll represents her as spontaneously engaging in a mysterious intrigue with the novelist. Her own detailed narrative renders the circumstances more intelligible. She approached Sacher-Masoch by letter, adopting for disguise the name of his heroine Wanda von Dunajev, in order to recover possession of some compromising letters which had been written to him, as a joke, by a friend of hers. Sacher-Masoch insisted on seeing his correspondent before returning the letters, and with his eager thirst for romantic adventure he imagined that she was a married woman of the aristocratic world, probably a Russian countess, whose simple costume was a disguise. Most anxious to reveal the prosaic facts, she humored him in his imaginations and a web of mystification was thus formed. A strong attraction grew up on both sides and, though for some time Laura Rümelin maintained the mystery and held herself aloof from him, a relationship was formed and a child born. Thereupon, in 1893, they married. Before long, however, there was disillusion on both sides. She began to detect the morbid, chimerical, and unpractical aspects of his character, and he realized that not only was his wife not an aristocrat, but, what was of more importance to him, she was by no means the domineering heroine of his dreams. Soon after marriage, in the course of an innocent romp in which the whole of the small household took part, he asked his wife to inflict a whipping on him. She refused, and he thereupon suggested that the servant should do it; the wife failed to take this idea seriously; but he had it carried out, with great satisfaction at the severity of the castigation he received. When, however, his wife explained to him that, after this incident, it was impossible for the servant to stay, Sacher-Masoch quite agreed and she was at once discharged. But he constantly found pleasure in placing his wife in awkward or compromising circumstances, a pleasure she was too normal to share. This necessarily led to much domestic wretchedness. He had persuaded her, against her wish, to whip him nearly every day, with whips which he devised, having nails attached to them. He found this a stimulant to his literary work, and it enabled him to dispense in his novels with his stereotyped heroine who is always engaged in subjugating men, for, as he explained to his wife, when he had the reality in his life he was no longer obsessed by it in his imaginative dreams. Not content with this, however, he was constantly desirous for his wife to be unfaithful. He even put an advertisement in a newspaper to the effect that a young and beautiful woman desired to make the acquaintance of an energetic man. The wife, however, though she wished to please her husband, was not anxious to do so to this extent. She went to an hotel by appointment to meet a stranger who had answered this advertisement, but when she had explained to him the state of affairs he chivalrously conducted her home. It was some time before Sacher-Masoch eventually succeeded in rendering his wife unfaithful. He attended to the minutest details of her toilette on this occasion, and as he bade her farewell at the door he exclaimed: "How I envy him!" This episode thoroughly humiliated the wife, and from that moment her love for her husband turned to hate. A final separation was only a question of time. Sacher-Masoch formed a relationship with Hulda Meister, who had come to act as secretary and translator to him, while his wife became attached to Rosenthal, a clever journalist later known to readers of the *Figaro* as "Jacques St.-Cère," who realized her painful position and felt sympathy and affection for her. She went to live with him in Paris and, having refused to divorce her husband, he eventually obtained a divorce from her; she states, however, that she never at any time had physical relationships with Rosenthal, who was a man of fragile organization and health. Sacher-Masoch united himself to Hulda Meister, who is described by the first wife as a prim and faded but coquettish old maid, and by the biographer as a highly accomplished and gentle woman, who cared for him with almost maternal devotion. No doubt there is truth in both descriptions. It must be noted that, as Wanda clearly shows, apart from his abnormal sexual temperament, Sacher-Masoch was kind and sympathetic, and he was strongly attached to his eldest child. Eulenburg also quotes the statement of a distinguished Austrian woman writer acquainted with him that, "apart from his sexual eccentricities, he was an amiable, simple, and sympathetic man with a touchingly tender love for his children." He had very few needs, did not drink or smoke, and though he liked to put the woman he was attached to in rich furs and fantastically gorgeous raiment he dressed himself with extreme simplicity. His wife quotes the saying of another woman that he was as simple as a child and as naughty as a monkey.

In 1883 Sacher-Masoch and Hulda Meister settled in Lindheim, a village in Germany near the Taunus, a spot to which the novelist seems to have been attached because in the grounds of his little estate was a haunted and ruined tower associated with a tragic medieval episode. Here, after many legal delays, Sacher-Masoch was able to render his union with Hulda Meister legitimate; here two children were in due course born, and here the novelist spent the remaining years of his life in comparative peace. At first, as is usual, treated with suspicion by the peasants, Sacher-Masoch gradually acquired great influence over them; he became a kind of Tolstoy in the rural life around him, the friend and confidant of all the villagers (something of Tolstoy's communism is also, it appears, to be seen in the books he wrote at this time), while the theatrical performances which he inaugurated, and in which his wife took an active part, spread the fame of the household in many neighboring villages. Meanwhile his health began to break up; a visit to Nauheim in 1894 was of no benefit, and he died March 9, 1895.

A careful consideration of the phenomena of sadism and masochism may be said to lead us to the conclusion that there is no real line of demarcation. Even De Sade himself was not a pure sadist, as Bloch's careful definition is alone sufficient to indicate; it might even be argued that De Sade was really a masochist; the investigation of histories of sadism and masochism, even those given by Krafft-Ebing (as, indeed, Colin Scott and Féré have already pointed out), constantly reveals traces of both groups of phenomena in the same individual. They cannot, therefore, be regarded as opposed manifestations. This has been felt by some writers, who have, in consequence, proposed other names more clearly indicating the relationship of the phenomena. Féré speaks of sexual algophily[98]; he only applies the term to masochism; it might equally well be applied to sadism. Schrenck-Notzing, to cover both sadism and masochism, has invented the term algolagnia ($\check{\alpha}\lambda\gamma o\varsigma$, pain, and $\lambda\acute{\alpha}\gamma\nu o\varsigma$ sexually excited), and calls the former active, the latter passive, algolagnia.[99] Eulenburg has also emphasized the close connection between these groups of perverted sexual manifestations, and has adopted the same terms, adding the further group of ideal (illusionary) algolagnia, to cover the cases in which the mere autosuggestive representation of pain, inflicted or suffered, suffices to give sexual gratification.[100]

A brief discussion of the terms "sadism" and "masochism" has imposed itself upon us at this point because as soon as, in any study of the relationship between love and pain, we pass over the limits of normal manifestations into a region which is more or less abnormal, these two conceptions are always brought before us, and it was necessary to show on what grounds they are here rejected as the pivots on which the discussion ought to turn. We may accept them as useful terms to indicate two groups of clinical phenomena; but we cannot regard them as of any real scientific value. Having reached this result, we may continue our consideration of the love-bite, as the normal manifestation of the connection between love and pain which most naturally leads us across the frontier of the abnormal.

The result of the love-bite in its extreme degree is to shed blood. This cannot be regarded as the direct aim of the bite in its normal manifestations, for the mingled feelings of close contact, of passionate gripping, of symbolic devouring, which constitute the emotional accompaniments of the bite would be too violently discomposed by actual wounding and real shedding of blood. With some persons, however, perhaps more especially women, the love-bite is really associated with a conscious desire, even if more or less restrained, to draw blood, a real delight in this process, a love of blood. Probably this only occurs in persons who are not absolutely normal, but on the borderland of the abnormal. We have to admit that this craving has, however, a perfectly normal basis. There is scarcely any natural object with so profoundly emotional an effect as blood, and it is very easy to understand why this should be so.[101] Moreover, blood enters into the sphere of courtship by virtue of the same conditions by which cruelty enters into it; they are both accidents of combat, and combat is of the very essence of animal and primitive human courtship, certainly its most frequent accompaniment. So that the repelling or attracting fascination of blood may be regarded as a by-product of normal courtship, which, like other such by-products, may become an essential element of abnormal courtship.[102]

Normally the fascination of blood, if present at all during sexual excitement, remains more or less latent, either because it is weak or because the checks that inhibit it are inevitably very powerful. Occasionally it becomes more clearly manifest, and this may happen early in life. Féré records the case of a man of Anglo-Saxon origin, of sound heredity so far as could be ascertained and presenting no obvious stigmata of degeneration, who first experienced sexual manifestations at the age of 5 when a boy cousin was attacked by bleeding at the nose. It was the first time he had seen such a thing and he experienced erection and much pleasure at the sight. This was repeated the next time the cousin's nose bled and also whenever he witnessed any injuries or wounds, especially when occurring in males. A few years later he began to find pleasure in pinching and otherwise inflicting slight suffering. This sadism was not, however, further developed, although a tendency to inversion persisted.[103]

Somewhat similar may have been the origin of the attraction of blood in a case which has been reported to me of a youth of 17, the youngest of a large family who are all very strong and entirely normal. He is himself, however, delicate, overgrown, with a narrow chest, a small head, and babyish features, while mentally he is backward, with very defective memory and scant powers of assimilation. He is intensely nervous, peevish, and subject to fits of childish rage. He takes violent fancies to persons of his own sex. But he appears to have only one way of obtaining sexual excitement and gratification. It is his custom to get into a hot bath and there to produce erection and emission, not by masturbation, but by thinking of flowing blood. He does not associate himself with the causation of this imaginary flow of blood; he is merely the passive but pleased spectator. He is aware of his peculiarity and endeavors to shake it off, but his efforts to obtain normal pleasure by thinking of a girl are vain.

I may here narrate a case which has been communicated to me of algolagnia in a woman, combined with sexual hyperesthesia.

R. D., aged 25, married, and of good social position; she is a small and dark woman, restless and alert in manner. She has one child.

She has practised masturbation from an early age—ever since she can remember—by the method of external friction and pressure. From the age of 17 she was able (and is still) to produce the orgasm almost without effort, by calling up the image of any man who had struck her fancy. She has often done so while seated talking to such a man, even when he is almost a stranger; in doing it, she says, a tightening of the muscles of the thighs and the slightest movement are sufficient. Ugly men (if not deformed), as well as men with the reputation of being *roués*, greatly excite her sexually, more especially if of good social position, though this is not essential.

At the age of 18 she became hysterical, probably, she herself believes, in consequence of a great increase at that time of indulgence in masturbation. The doctors, apparently suspecting her habits, urged her parents to get her married early. She married, at the age of 20, a man about twice her own age.

As a child (and in a less degree still) she was very fond of watching dog-fights. This spectacle produced strong sexual feelings and usually orgasm, especially if much blood was shed during the fight. Clean cuts and wounds greatly attract her, whether on herself or a man. She has frequently slightly cut or scratched herself "to see the blood," and likes to suck the wound, thinking the taste "delicious." This produces strong sexual feelings and often orgasm, especially if at the time she thinks of some attractive man and imagines that she is sucking his blood. The sight of injury to a woman only very slightly affects her, and that, she thinks, only because of an involuntary association of ideas. Nor has the sight of suffering in illness any exciting effects, only that which is due to violence, and when there is a visible cause for the suffering, such as cuts and wounds. (Bruises, from the absence of blood, have only a slight effect.) The excitement is intensified if she imagines that she has herself inflicted the injury. She likes to imagine that the man wished to rape her, and that she fought him in order to make him more greatly value her favor, so wounding him.

Impersonal ideas of torture also excite her. She thinks Fox's *Book of Martyrs* "lovely," and the more horrible and bloody the tortures described the greater is the sexual excitement produced. The book excites her from the point of view of the torturer, not that of the victim. She has frequently masturbated while reading it.

So far as practicable she has sought to carry out these ideas in her relations with her husband. She has several times bitten him till the blood came and sucked the bite during coitus. She likes to bite him enough to make him wince. The pleasure is greatly heightened by thinking of various tortures, chiefly by cutting. She likes to have her husband talk to her, and she to him, of all the tortures they could inflict on each other. She has, however, never actually tried to carry out these tortures. She would like to, but dares not, as she is sure he could not endure them. She has no desire for her husband to try them on her, although she likes to hear him talk about it.

She is at the same time fond of normal coitus, even to excess. She likes her husband to remain entirely passive during connection, so that he can continue in a state of strong erection for a long time. She can thus, she says, procure for herself the orgasm a number of times in succession, even nine or ten, quite easily. On one occasion she even had the orgasm twenty-six times within about one and a quarter hours, her husband during this time having two orgasms. (She is quite certain about the accuracy of this statement.) During this feat much talk about torture was indulged in, and it took place after a month's separation from her husband, during which she was careful not to masturbate, so that she might have "a real good time" when he came back. She acknowledges that on this occasion she was a "complete wreck" for a couple of days afterward, but states that usually ten or a dozen orgasms (or spasms, as she terms them) only make her "feel lively." She becomes frenzied with excitement during intercourse and insensible to everything but the pleasure of it.

She has never hitherto allowed anyone (except her husband after marriage) to know of her sadistic impulses, nor has she carried them out with anyone, though she would like to, if she dared. Nor has she allowed any man but her husband to have connection with her or to take any liberties.

Outbursts of sadism may occur episodically in fairly normal persons. Thus, Coutagne describes the case of a lad of 17—always regarded as quite normal, and without any signs of degeneracy, even on careful examination, or any traces of hysteria or alcoholism, though there was insanity among his cousins—who had had occasional sexual relations for a year or two, and on one occasion, being in a state of erection, struck the girl three times on the breast and abdomen with a kitchen knife bought for the purpose. He was much ashamed of his act immediately afterward, and, all the circumstances being taken into consideration, he was acquitted by the court.[104] Here we seem to have the obscure and latent fascination of blood, which is almost normal, germinating momentarily into an active impulse which is distinctly abnormal, though it produced little beyond those incisions which Vatsyayana disapproved of, but still regarded as a part of courtship. One step more and we are amid the most outrageous and extreme of all forms of sexual perversion: with the heroes of De Sade's novels, who, in exemplification of their author's most cherished ideals, plan scenes of debauchery in which the flowing of blood is an essential element of coitus; with the Marshall Gilles de Rais and the Hungarian Countess Bathory, whose lust could only be satiated by the death of innumerable victims.

This impulse to stab—with no desire to kill, or even in most cases to give pain, but only to draw blood and so either stimulate or altogether gratify the sexual impulse—is no doubt the commonest form of sanguinary sadism. These women-stabbers have been known in France as *piqueurs* for nearly a century, and in Germany are termed *Stecher* or *Messerstecher* (they have been studied by Näcke, "Zur Psychologie der sadistischen Messerstecher," *Archiv für Kriminal-Anthropologie*, Bd. 35, 1909). A case of this kind where a man stabbed girls in the abdomen occurred in Paris in the middle of the eighteenth century, and in 1819 or 1820 there seems to have been an epidemic of *piqueurs* in Paris; as we learn from a letter of Charlotte von Schiller's to Knebel; the offenders (though perhaps there was only one) frequented the Boulevards and the Palais Royal and stabbed women in the buttocks or thighs; they were never caught. About the same time similar cases of a slighter kind occurred in London, Brussels, Hamburg, and Munich.

Stabbers are nearly always men, but cases of the same perversion in women are not unknown. Thus Dr. Kiernan informs me of an Irish woman, aged 40, and at the beginning of the menopause, who, in New York in 1909, stabbed five men with a hatpin. The motive was sexual and she told one of the men that she stabbed him because she "loved" him.

Gilles de Rais, who had fought beside Joan of Arc, is the classic example of sadism in its extreme form, involving the murder of youths and maidens. Bernelle considers that there is some truth in the contention of Huysmans that the association with Joan of Arc was a predisposing cause in unbalancing Gilles de Rais. Another cause was his luxurious habit of life. He himself, no doubt rightly, attached importance to the suggestions received in reading Suetonius. He appears to have been a sexually precocious child, judging from an obscure passage in his confessions. He was artistic and scholarly, fond of books, of the society of learned men, and of music. Bernelle sums him up as "a pious warrior, a cruel and keen artist, a voluptuous assassin, an exalted mystic," who was at the same time unbalanced, a superior degenerate, and morbidly impulsive. (The best books on Gilles de Rais are the Abbé Bossard's *Gilles de Rais*, in which, however, the author, being a priest, treats his subject as quite sane and abnormally wicked; Huysmans's novel, *La-Bas*, which embodies a detailed study of Gilles de Rais, and F. H. Bernelle's Thèse de Paris, *La Psychose de Gilles de Rais*, 1910.)

The opinion has been hazarded that the history of Gilles de Rais is merely a legend. This view is not accepted, but there can be no doubt that the sadistic manifestations which occurred in the Middle Ages were mixed up with legendary and folk-lore elements. These elements centered on the conception of the *werwolf*, supposed to be a man temporarily transformed into a wolf with blood-thirsty impulses. (See, *e.g.*, articles "Werwolf" and "Lycanthropy" in *Encyclopædia Britannica*.) France, especially, was infested with werwolves in the sixteenth century. In 1603, however, it was decided at Bordeaux, in a trial involving a werwolf, that lycanthropy was only an insane delusion. Dumas ("Les Loup-Garous," *Journal de Psychologie Normale et Pathologique*, May-June, 1907) argues that the medieval werwolves were sadists whose crimes were largely imaginative, though sometimes real, the predecessor of the modern Jack the Ripper. The complex nature of the elements making up the belief in the werwolf is emphasized by Ernest Jones, *Der Alptraum*, 1912.

Related to the werwolf, but distinct, was the *vampire*, supposed to be a dead person who rose from the dead to suck the blood of the living during sleep. By way of reprisal the living dug up, exorcised, and mutilated the supposed vampires. This was called vampirism. The name vampire was then transferred to the living person who had so treated a corpse. All profanation of the corpse, whatever its origin, is now frequently called vampirism (Epaulow, *Vampirisme*, Thèse de Lyon, 1901; *id.*, "Le Vampire du Muy," *Archives d'Anthropologie Criminelle*, Sept., 1903). The earliest definite reference to necrophily is in Herodotus, who tells (bk. ii, ch. lxxxix) of an Egyptian who had connection with the corpse of a woman recently dead. Epaulow gives various old cases and, at full length, the case which he himself investigated, of Ardisson, the "Vampire du Muy." W. A. F. Browne also has an interesting article on "Necrophilism" (*Journal of Mental Science*, Jan., 1875) which he regards as atavistic. When there is, in addition, mutilation of the corpse, the condition is termed necrosadism. There seems usually to be no true sadism in either necrosadism or necrophilism. (See, however, Bloch, *Beiträge*, vol. ii, p. 284 *et seq.*)

It must be said also that cases of rape followed by murder are quite commonly not sadistic. The type of such cases is represented by Soleilland, who raped and then murdered children. He showed no sadistic perversion. He merely killed to prevent discovery, as a burglar who is interrupted may commit murder in order to escape. (E. Dupré, "L'Affaire Soleilland," *Archives d'Anthropologie Criminelle*, Jan.-Feb., 1910.)

A careful and elaborate study of a completely developed sadist has been furnished by Lacassagne, Rousset, and Papillon ("L'Affaire Reidal," *Archives d'Anthropologie Criminelle*, Oct.-Nov., 1907). Reidal, a youth of 18, a seminarist, was a congenital sanguinary sadist who killed another youth and was finally sent to an asylum. From the age of 4 he had voluptuous ideas connected with blood and killing, and liked to play at killing with other children. He was of infantile physical development, with a pleasant, childish expression of face, very religious, and hated obscenity and immorality. But the love of blood and murder was an irresistible obsession and its gratification produced immense emotional relief.

Sadism generally has been especially studied by Lacassagne, *Vacher l'Eventreur et les Crimes Sadiques*, 1899. Zoösadism, or sadism toward animals, has been dealt with by P. Thomas, "Le Sadisme sur les Animaux," *Archives d'Anthropologie Criminelle*, Sept., 1903. Auto-sadism, or "auto-erotic cruelty," that is to say, injuries inflicted on a person by himself with a sexual motive, has been investigated by G. Bach (*Sexuelle Verrirungen des Menschen und der Nature*, p. 427); this condition seems, however, a form of algolagnia more masochistic than sadistic in character.

With regard to the medico-legal aspects, Kiernan ("Responsibility in Active Algophily," *Medicine*, April, 1903) sets forth the reasons in favor of the full and complete responsibility of sadists, and Harold Moyer comes to the same conclusion ("Is Sexual Perversion Insanity?" *Alienist and Neurologist*, May, 1907). See also Thoinot's *Medico-legal Aspects of Moral Offenses* (edited by Weysse, 1911), ch. xviii. While we are probably justified in considering the sadist as morally not insane in the technical sense, we must remember that he is, for the most part, highly abnormal from the outset. As Gaupp points out (*Sexual-Probleme*, Oct., 1909, p. 797), we cannot measure the influences which create the sadist and we must not therefore attempt to "punish" him, but we are bound to place him in a position where he will not injure society.

It is enough here to emphasize the fact that there is no solution of continuity in the links that bind the absolutely normal manifestations of sex with the most extreme violations of all human law. This is so true that in saying that these manifestations are violations of all human law we cannot go on to add, what would seem fairly obvious, that they are violations also of all natural law. We have but to go sufficiently far back, or sufficiently far afield, in the various zoölogical series to find that manifestations which, from the human point of view, are in the extreme degree abnormally sadistic here become actually normal. Among very various species wounding and rending normally take place at or immediately after coitus; if we go back to the beginning of animal life in the protozoa sexual conjugation itself is sometimes found to present the similitude, if not the actuality, of the complete devouring of one organism by another. Over a very large part of nature, as it has been truly said, "but a thin veil divides love from death."[105]

There is, indeed, on the whole, a point of difference. In that abnormal sadism which appears from time to time among civilized human beings it is nearly always the female who becomes the victim of the male. But in the normal sadism which occurs throughout a large part of nature it is nearly always the male who is the victim of the female. It is the male spider who impregnates the female at the risk of his life and sometimes perishes in the attempt; it is the male bee who, after intercourse with the queen, falls dead from that fatal embrace, leaving her to fling aside his entrails and calmly pursue her course.[106] If it may seem to some that the course of our inquiry leads us to contemplate with equanimity, as a natural phenomenon, a certain semblance of cruelty in man in his relations with woman, they may, if they will, reflect that this phenomenon is but a very slight counterpoise to that cruelty which has been naturally exerted by the female on the male long even before man began to be.

[83]
Krafft-Ebing, *Psychopathia Sexualis*, English translation of tenth German edition, pp. 80, 209. It should be added that the object of the sadistic impulse is not necessarily a person of the opposite sex.

[84]
A. Moll, *Die Konträre Sexualempfindung*, third edition, 1899, p. 309.

[85]
Féré, *L'Instinct Sexuel*, p. 133.

[86]
P. Garnier, "Des Perversions Sexuelles," Thirteenth International Congress of Medicine, Section of Psychiatry, Paris, 1900.

[87]
E. Dühren, *Der Marquis de Sade und Seine Zeit*, third edition, 1901, p. 449.

[88]
See, for instance, Bloch's *Beiträge zur Ætiologie der Psychopathia Sexualis*, part ii, p. 178.

[89]
Krafft-Ebing, *Psychopathia Sexualis*, English translation of tenth German edition, p. 115. Stefanowsky, who also discussed this condition (*Archives de l'Anthropologie Criminelle*, May, 1892, and translation, with notes by Kiernan, *Alienist and Neurologist*, Oct., 1892), termed it passivism.

[90]
Anatomy of Melancholy, part iii, section 2, mem. iii, subs, 1.

[91]
"Aristoteles als Masochist," *Geschlecht und Gesellschaft*, Bd. ii, ht. 2.

[92]
Die Konträre Sexualempfindung, third edition, p. 277. *Cf.* C. F. von Schlichtegroll, *Sacher-Masoch und der Masochismus*, p. 120.

[93]
See C. F. von Schlichtegroll, *loc. cit.*, p. 124 *et seq.*

[94]
Iwan Bloch considers that it is the commonest of all sexual perversions, more prevalent even than homosexuality.

[95]
It has no doubt been prominent in earlier civilization. A very pronounced masochist utterance may be found in an ancient Egyptian love-song written about 1200 B.C.: "Oh! were I made her porter, I should cause her to be wrathful with me. Then when I did but hear her voice, the voice of her anger, a child shall I be for fear." (Wiedemann, *Popular Literature in Ancient Egypt*, p. 9.) The activity and independence of the Egyptian women at the time may well have offered many opportunities to the ancient Egyptian masochist.

[96]
Colin Scott, "Sex and Art," *American Journal of Psychology*, vol. vii, No. 2, p. 208.

[97]
It must not be supposed that the attraction of fur or of the whip is altogether accounted for by such a casual early experience as in Sacher-Masoch's case served to evoke it. The whip we shall have to consider briefly later on. The fascination exerted by fur, whether manifesting itself as love or fear, would appear to be very common in many children, and almost instinctive. Stanley Hall, in his "Study of Fears" (*American Journal of Psychology*, vol. viii, p. 213) has obtained as many as 111 well-developed cases of fear of fur, or, as he terms it, doraphobia, in some cases appearing as early as the age of 6 months, and he gives many examples. He remarks that the love of fur is still more common, and concludes that "both this love and fear are so strong and instinctive that they can hardly be fully accounted for without recourse to a time when association with animals was far closer

than now, or perhaps when our remote ancestors were hairy." (*Cf.* "Erotic Symbolism," iv, in the fifth volume of these *Studies*.)

[98]

Féré, *L'Instinct Sexuel*, p. 138.

[99]

Schrenck-Notzing, *Zeitschrift für Hypnotismus*, Bd. ix, ht. 2, 1899.

[100]

Eulenburg, *Sadismus und Masochismus*, second edition, 1911, p. 5.

[101]

I have elsewhere dealt with this point in discussing the special emotional tone of red (Havelock Ellis, "The Psychology of Red," *Popular Science Monthly*, August and September, 1900).

[102]

It is probable that the motive of sexual murders is nearly always to shed blood, and not to cause death. Leppmann (*Bulletin Internationale de Droit Pénal*, vol. vi, 1896, p. 115) points out that such murders are generally produced by wounds in the neck or mutilation of the abdomen, never by wounds of the head. T. Claye Shaw, who terms the lust for blood hemothymia, has written an interesting and suggestive paper ("A Prominent Motive in Murder," *Lancet*, June 19, 1909) on the natural fascination of blood. Blumröder, in 1830, seems to have been the first who definitely called attention to the connection between lust and blood.

[103]

Féré, *Revue de Chirurgie*, March 10, 1905.

[104]

H. Coutagne, "Cas de Perversion Sanguinaire de l'Instinct Sexuel," *Annales Médico-Psychologiques*, July and August, 1893. D. S. Booth (*Alienist and Neurologist*, Aug., 1906) describes the case of a man of neurotic heredity who slightly stabbed a woman with a penknife when on his way to a prostitute.

[105]

Kiernan appears to have been the first to suggest the bearing of these facts on sadism, which he would regard as the abnormal human form of phenomena which may be found at the very beginning of animal life, as, indeed, the survival or atavistic reappearance of a primitive sexual cannibalism. See his "Psychological Aspects of the Sexual Appetite,"*Alienist and Neurologist*, April, 1891, and "Responsibility in Sexual Perversion," *Chicago Medical Recorder*, March, 1892. Penta has also independently developed the conception of the biological basis of sadism and other sexual perversions (*I Pervertimenti Sessuali*, 1893). It must be added that, as Remy de Gourmont points out (*Promenades Philosophiques*, 2d series, p. 273), this sexual cannibalism exerted by the female may have, primarily, no erotic significance: "She eats him because she is hungry and because when exhausted he is an easy prey."

[106]

In the chapter entitled "Le Vol Nuptial" of his charming book on the life of bees Maeterlinck has given an incomparable picture of the tragic courtship of these insects.

III.

Flagellation as a Typical Illustration of Algolagnia—Causes of Connection between Sexual Emotion and Whipping—Physical Causes—Psychic Causes probably more Important—The Varied Emotional Associations of Whipping—Its Wide Prevalence.

The whole problem of love and pain, in its complementary sadistic and masochistic aspects, is presented to us in connection with the pleasure sometimes experienced in whipping, or in being whipped, or in witnessing or thinking about scenes of whipping. The association of sexual emotion with bloodshed is so extreme a perversion, it so swiftly sinks to phases that are obviously cruel, repulsive, and monstrous in an extreme degree, that it is necessarily rare, and those who are afflicted by it are often more or less imbecile. With whipping it is otherwise. Whipping has always been a recognized religious penance; it is still regarded as a beneficial and harmless method of chastisement; there is nothing necessarily cruel, repulsive, or monstrous in the idea or the reality of whipping, and it is perfectly easy and natural for an interest in the subject to arise in an innocent and even normal child, and thus to furnish a germ around which, temporarily at all events, sexual ideas may crystallize. For these reasons the connection between love and pain may be more clearly brought out in connection with whipping than with blood.

There is, by no means, any necessary connection between flagellation and the sexual emotions. If there were, this form of penance would not have been so long approved or at all events tolerated by the Church.[107]

As a matter of fact, indeed, it was not always approved or even tolerated. Pope Adrian IV in the eighth century forbade priests to beat their penitents, and at the time of the epidemic of flagellation in the thirteenth century, which was highly approved by many holy men, the abuses were yet so frequent that Clement VI issued a bull against these processions. All such papal prohibitions remained without effect. The association of religious flagellation with perverted sexual motives is shown by its condemnation in later ages by the Inquisition, which was accustomed to prosecute the priests who, in prescribing flagellation as a penance, exerted it personally, or caused it to be inflicted on the stripped penitent in his presence, or made a woman penitent discipline him, such offences being regarded as forms of "solicitation."[108] There seems even to be some reason to suppose that the religious flagellation mania which was so prevalent in the later Middle Ages, when processions of penitents, male and female, eagerly flogged themselves and each other, may have had something to do with the discovery of erotic flagellation,[109] which, at all events in Europe, seems scarcely to have been known before the sixteenth century. It must, in any case, have assisted to create a predisposition. The introduction of flagellation as a definitely recognized sexual stimulant is by Eulenburg, in his interesting book, *Sadismus und Masochismus*, attributed to the Arabian physicians. It would appear to have been by the advice of an Arabian physician that the Duchess Leonora Gonzaga, of Mantua, was whipped by her mother to aid her in responding more warmly to her husband's embraces and to conceive.

Whatever the precise origin of sexual flagellation in Europe, there can be no doubt that it soon became extremely common, and so it remains at the present day. Those who possess a special knowledge of such matters declare that sexual flagellation is the most frequent of all sexual perversions in England.[110] This belief is, I know, shared by many people both inside and outside England. However this may be, the tendency is certainly common. I doubt if it is any or at all less common in Germany, judging by the large number of books on the subject of flagellation which have been published in German. In a catalogue of "interesting books" on this and allied subjects issued by a German publisher and bookseller, I find that, of fifty-five volumes, as many as seventeen or eighteen, all in German, deal solely with the question of flagellation, while many of the other books appear to deal in part with the same subject.[111] It is, no doubt, true that the large part which the rod has played in the past history of our civilization justifies a considerable amount of scientific interest in the subject of flagellation, but it is clear that the interest in these books is by no means scientific, but very frequently sexual.

It is remarkable that, while the sexual associations of whipping, whether in slight or in marked degrees, are so frequent in modern times, they appear to be by no means easy to trace in ancient times. "Flagellation," I find it stated by a modern editor of the *Priapeia*, "so extensively practised in England as a provocation to venery, is almost entirely unnoticed by the Latin erotic writers, although, in the *Satyricon* of Petronius (ch. cxxxviii), Encolpius, in describing the steps taken by Œnothea to undo the temporary impotence to which he was subjected, says: 'Next she mixed nasturtium-juice with southern wood, and, having bathed my foreparts, she took a bunch of green nettles, and gently whipped my belly all over below the navel.'" It appears also that many ancient courtesans dedicated to Venus as ex-votos a whip, a bridle, or a spur as tokens of their skill in riding their lovers. The whip was sometimes used in antiquity, but if it aroused sexual emotions they seem to have passed unregarded. "We naturally know nothing," Eulenburg remarks (*Sadismus und Masochismus*, p. 72), "of the feelings of the priestess of Artemis at the flagellation of Spartan youths; or what emotions inspired the priestess of the Syrian goddess under similar circumstances; or what

74

the Roman Pontifex Maximus felt when he castigated the exposed body of a negligent vestal (as described by Plutarch) behind a curtain, and the 'plagosus Orbilius' only practised on children."

It was at the Renaissance that cases of abnormal sexual pleasure in flagellation began to be recorded. The earliest distinct reference to a masochistic flagellant seems to have been made by Pico della Mirandola, toward the end of the fifteenth century, in his *Disputationes Adversus Astrologiam Divinatricem*, bk. iii, ch. xxvii. Cœlius Rhodiginus in 1516, again, narrated the case of a man he knew who liked to be severely whipped, and found this a stimulant to coitus. Otto Brunfels, in his *Onomasticon* (1534), art. "Coitus," refers to another case of a man who could not have intercourse with his wife until he had been whipped. Then, a century later, in 1643, Meibomius wrote *De Usu Flagrorum in re Venerea*, the earliest treatise on this subject, narrating various cases. Numerous old cases of pleasure in flagellation and urtication were brought together by Schurig in 1720 in his *Spermatologia*, pp. 253-258.

The earliest definitely described medical case of sadistic pleasure in the sight of active whipping which I have myself come across belongs to the year 1672, and occurs in a letter in which Nesterus seeks the opinion of Garmann. He knows intimately, he states, a very learned man—whose name, for the honor he bears him, he refrains from mentioning—who, whenever in a school or elsewhere he sees a boy unbreeched and birched, and hears him crying out, at once emits semen copiously without any erection, but with great mental commotion. The same accident frequently happens to him during sleep, accompanied by dreams of whipping. Nesterus proceeds to mention that this "*laudatus vir*" was also extremely sensitive to the odor of strawberries and other fruits, which produced nausea. He was evidently a neurotic subject. (L. C. F. Garmanni et Aliorum Virorum Clarissimorum, *Epistolarum Centuria*, Rostochi et Lipsiæ, 1714.)

In England we find that toward the end of the sixteenth century one of Marlowe's epigrams deals with a certain Francus who before intercourse with his mistress "sends for rods and strips himself stark naked," and by the middle of the seventeenth century the existence of an association between flagellation and sexual pleasure seems to have been popularly recognized. In 1661, in a vulgar "tragicomedy" entitled *The Presbyterian Lash*, we find: "I warrant he thought that the tickling of the wench's buttocks with the rod would provoke her to lechery." That whipping was well known as a sexual stimulant in England in the eighteenth century is sufficiently indicated by the fact that in one of Hogarth's series representing the "Harlot's Progress" a birch rod hangs over the bed. The prevalence of sexual flagellation in England at the end of that century and the beginning of the nineteenth is discussed by Dühren (Iwan Bloch) in his *Geschlechtsleben in England* (1901-3), especially vol. ii, ch. vi.

While, however, the evidence regarding sexual flagellation is rare, until recent times whipping as a punishment was extremely common. It is even possible that its very prevalence, and the consequent familiarity with which it was regarded, were unfavorable to the development of any mysterious emotional state likely to act on the sexual sphere, except in markedly neurotic subjects. Thus, the corporal chastisement of wives by husbands was common and permitted. Not only was this so to a proverbial extent in eastern Europe, but also in the extreme west and among a people whose women enjoyed much freedom and honor. Cymric law allowed a husband to chastise his wife for angry speaking, such as calling him a cur; for giving away property she was not entitled to give away; or for being found in hiding with another man. For the first two offenses she had the option of paying him three kine. When she accepted the chastisement she was to receive "three strokes with a rod of the length of her husband's forearm and the thickness of his long finger, and that wheresoever he might will, excepting on the head"; so that she was to suffer pain only, and not injury. (R. B. Holt, "Marriage Laws and Customs of the Cymri," *Journal of the Anthropological Institute*, August-November, 1898, p. 162.)

"The Cymric law," writes a correspondent, "seems to have survived in popular belief in the Eastern and Middle States of the United States. In police-courts in New York, for example, it has been unsuccessfully pleaded that a man is entitled to beat his wife with a stick no thicker than his thumb. In Pennsylvania actual acquittals have been rendered."

Among all classes children were severely whipped by their parents and others in authority over them. It may be recalled that in the twelfth century when Abelard became tutor to Heloise, then about 18 years of age, her uncle authorized him to beat her, if negligent in her studies. Even in the sixteenth century Jeanne d'Albert, who became the mother of Henry IV of France, at the age of 13½ was married to the Duke of Cleves, and to overcome her resistance to this union the Queen, her mother, had her whipped to such an extent that she thought she would die of it. The whip on this occasion was, however, only partially successful, for the Duke never succeeded in consummating the marriage, which was, in consequence, annulled. (Cabanès brings together numerous facts regarding the prevalence of flagellation as a chastisement in ancient France in the interesting chapter on "La Flagellation a la Cour et à la Ville" in his *Indiscretions de l'Histoire*, 1903.)

As to the prevalence of whipping in England evidence is furnished by Andrews, in the chapter on "Whipping and Whipping Posts," in his book on ancient punishments. It existed from the earliest times and was administered for a great variety of offenses, to men and women alike, for vagrancy, for theft, to the fathers and mothers of illegitimate children, for drunkenness, for insanity, even sometimes for small-pox. At one time both sexes were whipped naked, but from Queen Elizabeth's time only from the waist upward. In 1791 the whipping of female vagrants ceased by law. (W. Andrews, *Bygone Punishments*, 1899.)

It must, however, be remarked that law always lags far behind social feeling and custom, and flagellation as a common punishment had fallen into disuse or become very perfunctory long before any change was made in the law, though it is not absolutely extinct, even by law, today. There is even an ignorant and retrograde tendency to revive it. Thus, even in severe Commonwealth days, the alleged whipping with rods of a servant-girl by her master, though with no serious physical injury, produced a great public outcry, as we see by the case of the Rev. Zachary Crofton, a distinguished London clergyman, who was prosecuted in 1657 on the charge of whipping his servant-girl, Mary Cadman, because she lay in bed late in the morning and stole sugar. This incident led to several pamphlets. In *The Presbyterian, Lash or Noctroff's Maid Whipt* (1661), a satire on Crofton, we read: "It is not only contrary to Gospel but good manners to take up a wench's petticoats, smock and all"; and in the doggerel ballad of "Bo-Peep," which was also written on the same subject, it is said that Crofton should have left his wife to chastise the maid. Crofton published two pamphlets, one under his own name and one under that of Alethes Noctroff (1657), in which he elaborately dealt with the charge as both false and frivolous. In one passage he offers a qualified defense of such an act: "I cannot but bewail the exceeding rudeness of our times to suffer such foolery to be prosecuted as of some high and notorious crime. Suppose it were (as it is not) true, may not some eminent congregational brother be found guilty of the same act? Is it notmuch short of drinking an health naked on a signpost? May it not be as theologically defended as the husband's correction of his wife?" This passage, and the whole episode, show that feeling in regard to this matter was at that time in a state of transition.

Flagellation as a penance, whether inflicted by the penitent himself or by another person, was also extremely common in medieval and later days. According to Walsingham ("Master of the Rolls' Collection," vol. i, p. 275), in England, in the middle of the fourteenth century, penitents, sometimes men of noble birth, would severely flagellate themselves, even to the shedding of blood, weeping or singing as they did so; they used cords with knots containing nails.

At a later time the custom of religious flagellation was more especially preserved in Spain. The Countess d'Aulnoy, who visited Spain in 1685, has described the flagellations practised in public at Madrid. After giving an account of the dress worn by these flagellants, which corresponds to that worn in Spain in Holy Week at the present time by the members of the *Cofradias*, the face concealed by the high sugar-loaf head-covering, she continues: "They attach ribbons to their scourges, and usually their mistresses honor them with their favors. In gaining public admiration they must not gesticulate with the arm, but only move the wrist and hand; the blows must be given without haste, and the blood must not spoil the costume. They make terrible wounds on their shoulders, from which the blood flows in streams; they march through the streets with measured steps; they pass before the windows of their mistresses, where they flagellate themselves with marvelous patience. The lady gazes at this fine sight through the blinds of her room, and by a sign she encourages him to flog himself, and lets him understand how much she likes this sort of gallantry. When they meet a good-looking woman they strike themselves in such a way that the blood goes on to her; this is a great honor, and the grateful lady thanks them.... All this is true to the letter."

The Countess proceeds to describe other and more genuine penitents, often of high birth, who may be seen in the street naked above the waist, and with naked feet on the rough and sharp pavement; some had swords passed through the skin of their body and arms, others heavy crosses that weighed them down. She remarks that she was told by the Papal Nuncio that he had forbidden confessors to impose such penances, and that they were due to the devotion of the penitents themselves. (*Relation du Voyage d'Espagne*, 1692, vol. ii, pp. 158-164.)

The practice of public self-flagellation in church during Lent existed in Spain and Portugal up to the early years of the nineteenth century. Descriptions of it will often be met with in old volumes of travel. Thus, I find a traveler through Spain in 1786 describing how, at Barcelona, he was present when, in Lent, at a Miserere in the Convent Church of San Felipe Neri on Friday evening the doors were shut, the lights put out, and in perfect darkness all bared their backs and applied the discipline, singing while they scourged themselves, ever louder and harsher and with ever greater vehemence until in twenty minutes' time the whole ended in a deep groan. It is mentioned that at Malaga, after such a scene, the whole church was in the morning sprinkled with blood. (Joseph Townsend, *A Journey through Spain in 1786*, vol. i, p. 122; vol. iii, p. 15.)

Even to our own day religious self-flagellation is practised by Spaniards in the Azores, in the darkened churches during Lent, and the walls are often spotted and smeared with blood at this time. (O. H. Howarth, "The Survival of Corporal Punishment,"*Journal Anthropological Institute*, Feb., 1889.) In remote districts of Spain (as near Haro in Rioja) there are also brotherhoods who will flagellate themselves on Good Friday, but not within the church. (Dario de Regoyos, *España Negra*, 1899, p. 72.)

When we glance over the history of flagellation and realize that, though whipping as a punishment has been very widespread and common, there have been periods and lands showing no clear knowledge of any sexual association of whipping, it becomes clear that whipping is not necessarily an algolagnic manifestation. It seems evident that there must be special circumstances, and perhaps a congenital predisposition, to bring out definitely the relationship of flagellation to the sexual impulse. Thus, Löwenfeld considers that only about 1 per cent, of people can be sexually excited by flagellation of the buttocks,[112] and Näcke also is decidedly of opinion that there can be no sexual pleasure in flagellation without predisposition, which is rare.[113] On these grounds many are of opinion that physical chastisement, provided it is moderate, seldom applied, and only to children who are quite healthy and vigorous, need not be absolutely prohibited.[114] But, however rare and abnormal a sexual response to actual flagellation may be in adults, we shall see that the general sexual association of whipping in the minds of children, and frequently of their elders, is by; no means rare and scarcely abnormal.

What is the cause of the connection between sexual emotion and whipping? A very simple physical cause has been believed by some to account fully for the phenomena. It is known that strong stimulation of the gluteal region may, especially under predisposing conditions, produce or heighten sexual excitement, by virtue of the fact that both regions are supplied by branches of the same nerve.

There is another reason why whipping should exert a sexual influence. As Féré especially has pointed out, in moderate amount it has a tonic effect, and as such has a general beneficial result in stimulating the whole body. This fact was, indeed, recognized by the classic physicians, and Galen regarded flagellation as a tonic.[115]Thus, not only must it be said that whipping, when applied to the gluteal region, has a direct influence in stimulating the sexual organs, but its general tonic influence must naturally extend to the sexual system.

It is possible that we must take into account here a biological factor, such as we have found involved in other forms of sadism and masochism. In this connection a lady writes to me: "With regard to the theory which connects the desire for whipping with the way in which animals make love, where blows or pressure on the hindquarters are almost a

77

necessary preliminary to pleasure, have you ever noticed the way in which stags behave? Their does seem as timid as the males are excitable, and the blows inflicted on them by the horns of their mates to reduce them to submission must be, I should think, an exact equivalent to being beaten with a stick."

It is remarkable that in some cases the whip would even appear to have a psychic influence in producing sexual excitement in animals accustomed to its application as a stimulant to action. Thus, Professor Cornevin, of Lyons, describes the case of a Hungarian stallion, otherwise quite potent, in whom erection could only be produced in the presence of a mare in heat when a whip was cracked near him, and occasionally applied gently to his legs. (Cornevin, *Archives d'Anthropologie Criminelle*, January, 1896.)

Here, undoubtedly, we have a definite anatomical and physiological relationship which often serves as a starting-point for the turning of the sexual feelings in this direction, and will sometimes support the perversion when it has otherwise arisen. But this relationship, even if we regard it as a fairly frequent channel by which sexual emotion is aroused, will not suffice to account for most, or even many, of the cases in which whipping exerts a sexual fascination. In many, if not most, cases it is found that the idea of whipping asserts its sexual significance quite apart from any personal experience, even in persons who have never been whipped;[116] not seldom also in persons who have been whipped and who feel nothing but repugnance for the actual performance, attractive as it may be in imagination.

It is evident that we have to seek the explanation of this phenomenon largely in psychic causes. Whipping, whether inflicted or suffered, tends to arouse, vaguely but massively, the very fundamental and primitive emotions of anger and fear, which, as we have seen, have always been associated with courtship, and it tends to arouse them at an age when the sexual emotions have not become clearly defined, and under circumstances which are likely to introduce sexual associations. From their earliest years children have been trained to fear whipping, even when not actually submitted to it, and an unjust punishment of this kind, whether inflicted on themselves or others, frequently arouses intense anger, nervous excitement, or terror in the sensitive minds of children.[117] Moreover, as has been pointed out to me by a lady who herself in early life was affected by the sexual associations of whipping, a child only sees the naked body of elder children when uncovered for whipping, and its sexual charm may in part be due to this cause. We further have to remark that the spectacle of suffering itself is, to some extent and under some circumstances, a stimulant of sexual emotion. It is evident that a number of factors contribute to surround whipping at a very early age with powerful emotional associations, and that these associations are of such a character that in predisposed subjects they are very easily led into a sexual channel.[118] Various lines of evidence support this conclusion. Thus, from several reliable quarters I learn that the sight of a boy being caned at school may produce sexual excitement in the boys who look on. The association of sexual emotion with whipping is, again, very liable to show itself in schoolmasters, and many cases have been recorded in which the flogging of boys, under the stress of this impulse, has been carried to extreme lengths. An early and eminent example is furnished by Udall, the humanist, at one time headmaster of Eton, who was noted for his habit of inflicting frequent corporal punishment for little or no cause, and who confessed to sexual practices with the boys under his care.[119]

Sanitchenko has called attention to the case of a Russian functionary, a school inspector, who every day had some fifty pupils flogged in his presence, as evidence of a morbid pleasure in such scenes. Even when no sexual element can be distinctly traced, scenes of whipping sometimes exert a singular fascination on some persons of sensitive emotional temperament. A friend, a clergyman, who has read many novels tells me that he has been struck by the frequency with which novelists describe such scenes with much luxury of detail; his list includes novels by well-known religious writers of both sexes. In some of these cases there is reason to believe that the writers felt this sexual association of whipping.

It is natural that an interest in whipping should be developed very early in childhood, and, indeed, it enters very frequently into the games of young children, and constitutes a much relished element of such games, more especially among girls. I know of many cases in which young girls between 6 and 12 years of age took great pleasure in games in which the chief point consisted in unfastening each other's drawers and smacking each other, and some of these girls, when they grew older, realized that there was an element of sexual enjoyment in their games. It has indeed, it seems, always been a child's game, and even an amusement of older persons, to play at smacking each other's nates. In *The Presbyter's Lash* in 1661 a young woman is represented as stating that she had done this as a child, and in ancient France it was a privileged custom on Innocents' Day (December 28th) to smack all the young people found lying late in bed; it was a custom which, as Clement Marot bears witness, was attractive to lovers.

If we turn to the histories I have brought together in Appendix B we find various references to whipping more or less clearly connected with the rudimentary sexual feelings of childhood.

I am acquainted with numerous cases in which the idea of whipping, or the impulse to whip or be whipped, distinctly exists, though usually, when persisting to adult life, only in a rudimentary form. History I in the Appendix B presents a well-marked instance. I may quote the remarks in another case of a lady regarding her early feelings: "As a child the idea of being whipped excited me, but only in connection with a person I loved, and, moreover, one who had the right to correct me. On one occasion I was beaten with the back of a brush, and the pain was sufficient to overcome any excitement; so that, ever after, this particular form of whipping left me unaffected, though the excitement still remained connected with forms of which I had no experience."

Another lady states that when a little girl of 4 or 5 the servants used to smack her nates with a soft brush to amuse themselves (undoubtedly, as she now believes, this gave them a kind of sexual pleasure); it did not hurt her, but she disliked it. Her father used to whip her severely on the nates at this age and onward to the age of 13, but this never gave her any pleasure. When, however, she was about 9 she began in waking dreams to imagine that she was whipping somebody, and would finish by imagining that she was herself being whipped. She would make up stories of which the climax was a whipping, and felt at the same time a pleasurable burning sensation in her sexual parts; she used to prolong the preliminaries of the story to heighten the climax; she felt more pleasure in the idea of being whipped than of whipping, although she never experienced any pleasure from an actual whipping. These day-dreams were most vivid when she was at school, between the ages of 11 and 14. They began to fade with the growth of affection for real persons. But in dreams, even in adult life, she occasionally experienced sexual excitement accompanied by images of smacking.

Another correspondent, this time a man, writes: "I experienced the connection between sexual excitement and whipping long before I knew what sexuality meant or had any notion regarding the functions of the sexual organs. What I now know to be distinct sexual feeling used to occur whenever the idea of whipping arose or the mention of whipping was made in a way to arrest my attention. I well remember the strange, mysterious fascination it had, even apart from any actual physical excitement. I have been told by many men and a few women that it was the same with them. Even now the feeling exists sometimes, especially when reading about whipping."

The following confession, which I find recorded by a German manufacturer's wife, corresponds with those I have obtained in England: "When about 5 years old I was playing with a little girl friend in the park. Our governesses sat on a bench talking. For some reason—perhaps because we had wandered away too far and failed to hear a call to return— my friend aroused the anger of the governess in charge of her. That young lady, therefore, took her aside, raised her dress, and vigorously smacked her with the flat hand. I looked on fascinated, and possessed by an inexplicable feeling to which I naïvely gave myself up. The impression was so deep that the scene and the persons concerned are still clearly present to my mind, and I can even recall the little details of my companion's underclothing." When sexual associations are permanently brought into play through such an early incident it is possible that a special predisposition exists. (*Gesellschaft und Geschlecht*, Bd. ii, ht. 4, p. 120.)

It would certainly seem that we must look upon this association as coming well within the normal range of emotional life in childhood, although after puberty, when the sexual feelings become clearly defined, the attraction of whipping normally tends to be left behind as a piece of childishness, only surviving in the background of consciousness, if at all, to furnish a vaguely sexual emotional tone to the subject of whipping, but not affecting conduct, sometimes only emerging in erotic dreams.

This, however, is not invariably the case in persons who are organically abnormal. In such cases, and especially, it would seem, in highly sensitive and emotional children, the impress left by the fact or the image of whipping may be so strong that it affects not only definitely, but permanently, the whole subsequent course of development of the sexual impulse. Régis has recorded a case which well illustrates the circumstances and hereditary conditions under which the idea of whipping may take such firm root in the sexual emotional nature of a child as to persist into adult life; at the same time the case shows how a sexual perversion may, in an intelligent person, take on an intellectual character, and it also indicates a rational method of treatment.

Jules P., aged 22, of good heredity on father's side, but bad on that of mother, who is highly hysterical, while his grandmother was very impulsive and sometimes pursued other women with a knife. He has one brother and one sister, who are somewhat morbid and original. He is himself healthy, intelligent, good looking, and agreeable, though with slightly morbid peculiarities. At the age of 4 or 5 he suddenly opened a door and saw his sister, then a girl of 14 or 15, kneeling, with her clothes raised and her head on her governess's lap, at the moment of being whipped for some offense. This trivial incident left a profound impression on his mind, and he recalls every detail of it, especially the sight of his sister's buttocks,—round, white, and enormous as they seemed to his childish eyes,—and that momentary vision gave a permanent direction to the whole of his sexual life. Always after that he desired to touch and pat his sister's gluteal regions. He shared her bed, and, though only a child, acquired great skill in attaining his ends without attracting her attention, lifting her night-gown when she slept and gently caressing the buttocks, also contriving to turn her over on to her stomach and then make a pillow of her hips. This went on until the age of 7, when he began to play with two little girls of the neighborhood, the eldest of whom was 10; he liked to take the part of the father and whip them. The older girl was big for her age, and he would separate her drawers and smack her with much voluptuous emotion; so that he frequently sought opportunities to repeat the experience, to which the girl willingly lent herself, and they were constantly together in dark corners, the girl herself opening her drawers to enable him to caress her thighs and buttocks with his hand until he became conscious of an erection. Sometimes he would gently use a whip. On one occasion she asked him if he would not now like to see her in front, but he declined.

One day, when 8 or 9 years old, being with a boy companion, he came upon a picture of a monk being flagellated, and thereupon persuaded his companion to let himself be whipped; the boy enjoyed the experience, which was therefore often repeated. Jules P. himself, however, never took the slightest pleasure in playing the passive part. These practices were continued even after the friend became a conscript, when, however, they became very rare. Only once or twice has he ever done anything of this kind to girls who were strangers to him. Nor has he ever masturbated or had any desire for sexual intercourse. He contents himself with the pleasure of being occasionally able to witness scenes of whipping in public places—parks and gardens—or of catching glimpses of the thighs and buttocks of young girls or, if possible, women.

His principal enjoyment is in imagination. From the first he has loved to invent stories in which whippings were the climax, and at 13 such stories produced the first spontaneous emission. Thus, he imagines, for instance, a young girl from the country who comes up to Paris by train; on the way a lady is attracted by her, takes an interest in her, brings her home to dinner, and at last can no longer resist the temptation to take the girl in her arms and whip her amorously. He writes out these scenes and illustrates them with drawings, many of which Régis reproduces. He has even written comedies in which whipping plays a prominent part. He has, moreover, searched public libraries for references to flagellation, inserted queries in the *Intermédiare des Chercheurs et des Curieux*, and thus obtained a complete bibliography of flagellation which is of considerable value. Régis is acquainted with these *Archives de la Fessée*, and states that they are carried on with great method and care. He is especially interested in the whipping of women by women. He considers that the pleasure of whippings should always be shared by the person whipped, and he is somewhat concerned to find that he has an increasing inclination to imagine an element of cruelty in the whipping. Emissions are somewhat frequent. According to the latest information, he is much better; he has entered into sexual relationship with a woman who is much in love with him, and to whom he has confided his peculiarities. With her aid and suggestions he has been able to have intercourse with her, at the moment of coitus whipping her with a harmless India-rubber tube. (E. Régis, "Un Cas de Perversion Sexuelle, a forme Sadique," *Archives d'Anthropologie Criminelles*, July, 1899.)

In a case also occurring in a highly educated man (narrated by Marandon de Montyel) a doctor of laws, brilliantly intellectual and belonging to a family in which there had been some insanity, when at school at the age of 11, saw for the first time a schoolfellow whipped on the nates, and experienced a new pleasure and emotion. He was never himself whipped at school, but would invent games with his sisters and playfellows in which whipping formed an essential part. At the age of 13 he teased a young woman, a cook, until she seized him and whipped him. He put his arms around her and experienced his first voluptuous spasm of sex. The love of flagellation temporarily died out, however, and gave place to masturbation and later to a normal attraction to women. But at the age of 32 the old ideas were aroused anew by a story his mistress told him. He suffered from various obsessions and finally committed suicide. (Marandon de Montyel, "Obsessions et Vie Sexuelle," *Archives de Neurologie*, Oct., 1904.)

In a case that has been reported to me, somewhat similar ideas played a part. The subject is a tall, well-developed man, aged 28, delicate in childhood, but now normal in health and physical condition, though not fond of athletics. His mental ability is much above the average, especially in scientific directions; he was brought up in narrow and strict religious views, but at an early age developed agnostic views of his own.

From the age of 6, and perhaps earlier, he practised masturbation almost every night. This was a habit which he carried on in all innocence. It was as invariable a preliminary, he states, to going to sleep as was lying down, and at this period he would have felt no hesitation in telling all about it had the question been asked. At the age of 12 or 13 he recognized the habit as abnormal, and fear of ridicule then caused him to keep silence and to avoid observation. In carrying it out he would lie on his stomach with the penis directed downward, and not up, and the thumb resting on the region above the root of the penis. There was desire for micturition after the act, and when that was satisfied sound sleep followed. When he realized that the habit was abnormal he began to make efforts to discontinue it, and these efforts have been continued up to the present. The chief obstacle has been the difficulty of sleep without carrying out the practice. Emissions first began to occur at the age of 13 and at first caused some alarm. During the six following years indulgence was irregular, sometimes occurring every other night and sometimes with a week's intermission. Then at the age of 19 the habit was broken for a year, during which nocturnal emissions took place during sleep about every three weeks. Since this, shorter periods of non-indulgence have occurred, these periods always coinciding with unusual mental or physical strain, as of examinations. He has some degree of attraction for women; this is strongest during cessation from masturbation and tends to disappear when the habit is resumed. He has never had sexual intercourse because he prefers his own method of gratification and feels great abhorrence for professional prostitutes; he could not afford to marry. Any indecency or immorality, except (he observes) his own variety, disgusts him.

At the earliest period no mental images accompanied the act of masturbation. At about the age of 8, however, sexual excitement began to be constantly associated with ideas of being whipped. At or soon after this age only the fear of disgrace prevented him from committing serious childish offenses likely to be punished by a good whipping. Parents and masters, however, seem to have used corporal punishment very sparingly.

At first this desire was for whipping in general, without reference to the operator. Soon after the age of 10, however, he began to wish that certain boy friends should be the operators. At about the same time definite desire arose for closer contact with these friends and later for definite indecent acts which, however, the subject failed to specify; he probably meant mutual masturbation. These desires were under control, and the fear of ridicule seems to have been the chief restraining cause. At about the age of 15 he began to realize that such acts might be considered morally bad and wrong, and this led to reticence and careful concealment. Up to the age of 20 there were four definite attachments to persons of his own sex. There was a tendency, sometimes, to regard women as possible whippers, and this became stronger at 22, the images of the two sexes then mingling in his thoughts of flagellation. Latterly the mental accompaniments of masturbation have been less personal, lapsing into the mental picture of being whipped by an unknown and vague somebody. When definite it has always been a man, and preferably of the type of a schoolmaster. His desire has been for punishment by whips, canes, or birches, especially upon the buttocks. He has always shrunk from the thought of the production of blood or bruises. He wishes, in mental contemplation, for a punishment sufficiently severe to make him anxious to stop it, and yet not able to stop it. He also takes pleasure in the idea of being tied up so as to be unable to move.

He has at times indulged in self-whipping, of no great severity.

In the preceding case we see a tendency to erotic self-flagellation which in a minor degree is not uncommon. Occasionally it becomes highly developed. Max Marcuse has presented such a case in elaborate detail (*Zeitschrift für die Gesamte Neurologie*, 1912, ht. 3, fully summarized in *Sexual-Probleme*, Nov., 1912, pp. 815-820). This is the case of a Catholic priest of highly neurotic heredity, who spontaneously began to whip himself at the age of 12, this self-flagellation being continued and accompanied by masturbation after the age of 15. Other associated perversions were Narcissism and nates fetichism, as well as homosexual phantasies. He experienced a certain pleasure (with erection, not ejaculation) in punishing his boy pupils. It is not uncommon for all forms of erotic flagellation to be associated with a homosexual element. I have elsewhere brought forward a case of this kind (the case of A. F., vol. ii of these *Studies*).

Significant is Rousseau's account of the origin of his own masochistic pleasure in whipping at the age of 8: "Mademoiselle Lambercier showed toward me a mother's affection and also a mother's authority, which she sometimes carried so far as to inflict on us the usual punishment of children when we had deserved it. For a long time she was content with the threat, and that threat of a chastisement which for me was quite new seemed very terrible; but after it had been executed I found the experience less terrible than the expectation had been; and, strangely enough, this punishment increased my affection for her who had inflicted it. It needed all my affection and all my natural gentleness to prevent me from seeking a renewal of the same treatment by deserving it, for I had found in the pain and even in the shame of it an element of sensuality which left more desire than fear of receiving the experience again from the same hand. It is true that, as in all this a precocious sexual element was doubtless mixed, the same chastisement if inflicted by her brother would not have seemed so pleasant." He goes on to say that the punishment was inflicted a second time, but that that time was the last, Mademoiselle Lambercier having apparently noted the effects it produced, and, henceforth, instead of sleeping in her room, he was placed in another room and treated by her as a big boy. "Who would have believed," he adds, "that this childish punishment, received at the age of 8 from the hand of a young woman of 30, would have determined my tastes, my desires, my passions, for the rest of my life?" He remarks that this strange taste drove him almost to madness, but maintained the purity of his morals, and the joys of love existed for him chiefly in imagination. (J. J. Rousseau, *Les Confessions*, partie i, livre i.) It will be seen how all the favoring conditions of fear, shame, and precocious sexuality were here present in an extremely sensitive child destined to become thegreatest emotional force of his century, and receptive to influences which would have had no permanent effect on any ordinary child. (When, as occasionally happens, the first sexual feelings are experienced under the stimulation of whipping in normal children, no permanent perversion necessarily follows; Moll mentions that he knows such cases, *Zeitschrift für Pädagogie, Psychiatrie, und Pathologie*, 1901.) It may be added that it is, perhaps, not fanciful to see a certain inevitableness in the fact that on Rousseau's highly sensitive and receptive temperament it was a masochistic germ that fell and fructified, while on Régis's subject, with his more impulsive ancestral antecedents, a sadistic germ found favorable soil.

It may be noted that in Régis's sadistic case the little girl who was the boy's playmate found scarcely less pleasure in the passive part of whipping than he found in the active. There is ample evidence to show that this is very often the case, and that the attractiveness of the idea of being whipped often even arises spontaneously in children. Lombroso (*La Donna Delinquente*, p. 404) refers to a girl of 7 who had voluptuous pleasure in being whipped, and Hammer (*Monatschrift für Harnkrankheiten*, 1906, p. 398) speaks of a young girl who similarly experienced pleasure in punishment by whipping. Krafft-Ebing records the case of a girl of between 6 and 8 years of age, never at that time having been whipped or seen anyone else whipped, who spontaneously acquired—how she did not know—the desire to be castigated in this manner. It gave her very great pleasure to imagine a woman friend doing this to her. She never desired to be whipped by a man, though there was no trace of inversion, and she never masturbated until the age of 24, when a marriage engagement was broken off. At the age of 10 this longing passed away before it was ever actually realized. (Krafft-Ebing, *Psychopathia Sexualis*, eighth edition, p. 136.)

In the case of another young woman described by Krafft-Ebing—where there was neurasthenia with other minor morbid conditions in the family, but the girl herself appears to have been sound—the desire to be whipped existed from a very early age. She traced it to the fact that when she was 5 years old a friend of her father's playfully placed her across his knees and pretended to whip her. Since then she has always longed to be caned, but to her great regret the wish has never been realized. She longs to be the slave of a man whom she loves: "Lying in fancy before him, he puts one foot on my neck while I kiss the other. I revel in the idea of being whipped by him and imagine different scenes in which he beats me. I take the blows as so many tokens of love; he is at first extremely kind and tender, but then in the excess of his love he beats me. I fancy that to beat me for love's sake gives him the highest pleasure." Sometimes she imagines that she is his slave, but not his female slave, for every woman may be her husband's slave. She is of proud and independent nature in all other matters, and to imagine herself a man who consents to be a slave gives her a more satisfying sense of humiliation. She does not understand that these manifestations are of a sexual nature. (Krafft-Ebing,*Psychopathia Sexualis*, English translation of tenth edition, p. 189.)

Sometimes a woman desires to take the active part in whipping. Thus Marandon de Montyel records the case of a girl of 19, hereditarily neuropathic (her father was alcoholic), but very intelligent and good-hearted, who had never been whipped or seen anyone whipped. At this age, however, she happened to visit a married friend who was just about to punish her boy of 9 by whipping him with a wet towel. The girl spectator was much interested, and though the boy screamed and struggled she experienced a new sensation she could not define. "At every stroke," she said, "a strange shiver went through all my body from my brain to my heels." She would like to have whipped him herself and felt sorry when it was over. She could not forget the scene and would dream of herself whipping a boy. At last the desire became irresistible and she persuaded a boy of 12, whom she was very fond of, and who was much attached to her, to let her whip him on the naked nates. She did this so ferociously that he at last fainted. She was overcome by grief and remorse. (Marandon de Montyel, *Archives d'Anthropologie Criminelle*, Jan., 1906, p. 30.)

Although masochism in a pronounced degree may be said to be rare in women, the love of active flagellation, and sadistic impulses generally are not uncommon among them. Bloch believes they are especially common among English women. Cases occur from time to time of extreme harshness, cruelty, degrading punishment, and semi-starvation inflicted upon children. The accused are most usually women, and when a man and woman in conjunction are accused it appears generally to have been the woman who played the more active part. But it is rarely demonstrated in these cases that the cruelty exercised had a definite sexual origin. There is nothing, for instance, to indicate true sadism in the famous English case in the eighteenth century of Mrs. Brownrigg (Bloch, *Geschlechtsleben in England*, vol. ii, p. 425). It may well be, however, in many of these cases that the real motive is sexual, although latent and unconscious. The normal sexual impulse in women is often obscured and disguised, and it would not be surprising if the perverse instinct is so likewise.

It is noteworthy that a passion for whipping may be aroused by contact with a person who desires to be whipped. This is illustrated by the following case which has been communicated to me: "K. is a Jew, about 40 years of age, apparently normal. Nothing is known of his antecedents. He is a manufacturer with several shops. S., an Englishwoman, aged 25, entered his service; she is illegitimate, believed to have been reared in a brothel kept by her mother, is prepossessing in appearance. On entering K.'s service S. was continually negligent and careless. This so provoked K. that on one occasion he struck her. She showed great pleasure and confessed that her blunder had been deliberately intended to arouse him to physical violence. At her suggestion K. ultimately consented to thrash her. This operation took place in K.'s office, S. stripping for the purpose, and the leather driving band from a sewing-machine was used. S. manifested unmistakable pleasure during the flagellation, and connection occurred after it. These thrashings were repeated at frequent intervals, and K. found a growing liking for the operation on his own part. Once, at the suggestion of S., a girl of 13 employed by K. was thrashed by both K. and S. alternately. The child complained to her parents and K. made a money payment to them to avoid scandal, the parents agreeing to keep silence. Other women (Jewish tailoresses) employed by K. were subsequently thrashed by him. He asserts that they enjoyed the experience. Mrs. K., discovering her husband's infatuation for S., commenced divorce proceedings. S. consented to leave the country at K.'s request, but returned almost immediately and was kept in hiding until the decree was granted. The mutual infatuation of K. and S. continues, though K. asserts that he cares less for her than formerly. Flagellation has, however, now become a passion with him, though he declares that the practice was unknown to him before he met S. His great fear is that he will kill S. during one of these operations. He is convinced that S. is not an isolated case, and that all women enjoy flagellation. He claims that the experiences of the numerous women whom he has now thrashed bear out this opinion; one of them is a wealthy woman separated from her husband, and is now infatuated with K."

Flagellation, more especially in its masochistic form, is sometimes associated with true inversion. Moll presents the case of a young inverted woman of 26, showing, indeed, many other minor sexual anomalies, who is sexually excited when beaten with a switch. A whip would not do, and the blows must only be on the nates; she cannot imagine being beaten by a small woman. She has often in this way been beaten by a friend, who should be naked at the time, and must submit afterward to cunnilinctus. (Moll, *Konträre Sexualempfindung* third edition, p. 568.)

In the preceding case there were no masochistic ideas; it is likely that in such a case beating is desired largely on account of that purely physical effect to which attention has already been called. In the same way self-beating with a switch or whip has sometimes been spontaneously discovered as a method of self-excitement preliminary to masturbation. I am acquainted with a lady of much intellectual ability, sexually normal, who made this discovery at the age of 18, and practised it for a time. Professor Reverdin, also, speaks of the case of a young girl under his care who, after having exhausted all the resources of her intelligence, finally discovered that the climax of enjoyment was best reached by violently whipping her own buttocks and thighs. She had invented for this purpose a whip composed of twelve cords each of which terminated in a large chestnut-burr provided with its spines. (A. Reverdin, *Revue Médicale de la Suisse Romande*, January 20, 1888, p. 17.)

[107]
The discipline or scourge was classed with fasting as a method of mastering the flesh and of penance. See, *e.g.*, Lea, *History of Auricular Confession*, vol. ii, p. 122. For many centuries bishops and priests used themselves to apply the discipline to their penitents. At first it was applied to the back; later, especially in the case of female penitents, it was frequently applied to the nates. Moreover, partial or complete nudity came to be frequently demanded, the humiliation thereby caused being pleasant in the sight of God.

[108]
Dulaure, *Des Divinités Génératrices*, ch. xv; Lea, *History of Sacerdotal Celibacy*, 3d ed., vol. ii, p. 278; Kiernan, "Asceticism as an Auto-erotism,"*Alienist and Neurologist*, Aug., 1911.

[109]
This is the opinion of Löwenfeld, *Ueber die Sexuelle Konstitution*, p. 43.

[110]

Thus, Dühren (Iwan Bloch) remarks (*Der Marquis de Sade und Seine Zeit*, 1901, p. 211): "It is well known that England is today the classic land of sexual flagellation." See the same author's *Geschlechtsleben in England*, vol. ii, ch. vi. In America it appears also to be common, and Kiernan mentions that in advertisements of Chicago "massage shops" there often appears the announcement: "Flagellation a Specialty." The reports of police inspectors in eighteenth century France show how common flagellation then was in Paris. It may be added that various men of distinguished intellectual ability of recent times and earlier are reported as addicted to passive flagellation; this was the case with Helvétius.

[111]
A full bibliography of flagellation would include many hundred items. The more important works on this subject, in connection with the sexual impulse, are enumerated by Eulenburg, in his *Sadismus und Masochismus*. An elaborate history of flagellation generally is now being written by Georg Collas, *Geschichte des Flagellantismus*, vol. i, 1912.

[112]
Löwenfeld, *Ueber die Sexuelle Konstitution*, p. 43.

[113]
Archiv für Kriminal-Anthropologie, 1909, p. 361. He brings forward the evidence of a reliable and cultured man who at one time sought to obtain the pleasures of passive sexual flagellation. But in spite of his expectation and good will the only result was to disperse every trace of sexual desire.

[114]
E.g., Kiefer, *Zeitschrift für Sexualwissenschaft*, Aug., 1908.

[115]
Féré, *Revue de Médecine*, August, 1900. In this paper Féré brings together many interesting facts concerning flagellation in ancient times.

[116]
Schmidt-Heuert (*Monatschrift für Harnkrankheiten*, 1906, ht. 7) argues that it is not so much the actual use of the rod as playful, threatening and mysterious suggestions playing around it which nowadays gives it sexual fascination.

[117]
Moll (*Untersuchungen über die Libido Sexualis*, Bd. 1, p. 18) points out that these emotions frequently suffice to cause sexual emissions in schoolboys.

[118]
As Eulenburg truly points out, the circumstances attending the whipping of a woman may be sexually attractive, even in the absence of any morbid impulse. Such circumstances are "the sight of naked feminine charms and especially—in the usual mode of flagellation—of those parts which possess for the sexual epicure a peculiar esthetic attraction; the idea of treating a loved, or at all events desired, person as a child, of having her in complete subjection and being able to dispose of her despotically; and finally the immediate results of whipping: the changes in skin-color, the to and fro movements which simulate or anticipate the initial phenomena of coitus." (Eulenburg, *Sexuale Neuropathie*, p. 121.)

[119]
See the article on Udall in the *Dictionary of National Biography*.

IV.

The Impulse to Strangle the Object of Sexual Desire—The Wish to be Strangled—Respiratory Disturbance the Essential Element in this Group of Phenomena—The Part Played by Respiratory Excitement in the Process of Courtship—Swinging and Suspension—The Attraction Exerted by the Idea of being Chained and Fettered.

There is another impulse which it may be worth while to consider briefly here, for the sake of the light it throws on the relationship between love and pain. I allude to the impulse to strangle the object of sexual desire, and to the corresponding craving to be strangled. Cases have been recorded in which this impulse was so powerful that men have actually strangled women at the moment of coitus.[120] Such cases are rare; but, as a mere idea, the thought of strangling a woman appears to be not infrequently associated with sexual emotion. We must probably regard it as, in the main,—with whatever subsidiary elements,— an aspect of that physical seizure, domination, and forcible embrace of the female which is one of the primitive elements of courtship.[121]

The corresponding idea—the pleasurable connection of the thought of being strangled with sexual emotion—appears to occur still more frequently, perhaps especially in women. Here we seem to have, as in the case of whipping, a combination of a physical with a psychic element. Not only is the idea attractive, but, as a matter of fact, strangulation, suffocation, or any arrest of respiration, even when carried to the extent of producing death, may actually provoke emission, as is observed after death by hanging.[122] It is noteworthy that, as Eulenburg remarks, the method of treating diseases of the spinal cord by suspension—a method much in vogue a few years ago—often produced sexual excitement.[123] In brothels, it is said, some of the clients desire to be suspended vertically by a cord furnished with pads.[124] A playful attempt to throttle her on the part of her lover is often felt by a woman as pleasurable, though it may not necessarily produce definite sexual excitement. Sometimes, however, this feeling becomes so strong that it must be regarded as an actual perversion, and I have been told of a woman who is indifferent to the ordinary sexual embrace; her chief longing is to be throttled, and she will do anything to have her neck squeezed by her lover till her eyeballs bulge.[125]

"I think if I could be left my present feelings," a lady writes, "and be changed into a male imbecile,—that is, given a man's strength, but deprived, to a large extent, of reasoning power,—I might very likely act in the apparently cruel way they do. And this partly because many of their actions appeal to me on the passive side. The idea of being *strangled* by a person I love does. The great sensitiveness of one's throat and neck come in here as well as the loss of breath. Once when I was about to be separated from a man I cared for I put his hands on my throat and implored him to kill me. It was a moment of madness, which helps me to understand the feelings of a person always insane. Even now that I am cool and collected I know that if I were deeply in love with a man who I thought was going to kill me, especially in that way, I would make no effort to save myself beforehand, though, of course, in the final moments nature would assert herself without my volition. What makes the horror of such cases in insanity is the fact of the love being left out. But I think I find no greater difficulty in picturing the mental attitude of a sadistic lunatic than that of a normal man who gets pleasure out of women for whom he has no love."

The imagined pleasure of being strangled by a lover brings us to a group of feelings which would seem to be not unconnected with respiratory elements. I refer to the pleasurable excitement experienced by some in suspension, swinging, restraint, and fetters. Strangulation is the extreme and most decided type of this group of imagined or real situations, in all of which a respiratory disturbance seems to be an essential element.[126]

In explaining these phenomena we have to remark that respiratory excitement has always been a conspicuous part of the whole process of tumescence and detumescence, of the struggles of courtship and of its climax, and that any restraint upon respiration, or, indeed, any restraint upon muscular and emotional activity generally, tends to heighten the state of sexual excitement associated with such activity.

I have elsewhere, when studying the spontaneous solitary manifestation of the sexual instinct (*Auto-erotism*, in vol. i of these *Studies*), referred to the pleasurably emotional, and sometimes sexual, effects of swinging and similar kinds of movement. It is possible that there is a certain significance in the frequency with which the eighteenth-century French painters, who lived at a time when the refinements of sexual emotion were carefully sought out, have painted women in the act of swinging. Fragonard mentions that in 1763 a gentleman invited him into the country, with the request to paint his mistress, especially stipulating that she should be depicted in a swing. The same motive was common among the leading artists of that time. It may be said that this attitude was merely a pretext to secure a vision of ankles, but that result could easily have been attained without the aid of the swing.

I may here quote, as bearing on this and allied questions, a somewhat lengthy communication from a lady to whom I am indebted for many subtle and suggestive remarks on the whole of this group of manifestations:—

86

"With regard to the connection between swinging and suspension, perhaps the physical basis of it is the loss of breath. Temporary loss of breath with me produces excitement. Swinging at a height or a fall from a height would cause loss of breath; in a state of suspension the imagination would suggest the idea of falling and the attendant loss of breath. People suffering from lung disease are often erotically inclined, and anesthetics affect the breathing. Men also seem to like the idea of suspension, but from the active side. One man used to put his wife on a high swinging shelf when she displeased him, and my husband told me once he would like to suspend me to a crane we were watching at work, though I have never mentioned my own feeling on this point to him. Suspension is often mentioned in descriptions of torture. Beatrice Cenci was hung up by her hair and the recently murdered Queen of Korea was similarly treated. In Tolstoi's *My Husband and I* the girl says she would like her husband to hold her over a precipice. That passage gave me great pleasure.[127]

"The idea of slipping off an inclined plane gives me the same sensation. I always feel it on seeing Michael Angelo's 'Night,' though the slipping look displeases me artistically. I remember that when I saw the 'Night' first I did feel excited and was annoyed, and it seemed to me it was the slipping-off look that gave it; but I think I am now less affected by that idea. Certain general ideas seem to excite one, but the particular forms under which they are presented lose their effect and have to be varied. The sentence mentioned in Tolstoi leaves me now quite cold, but if I came across the same idea elsewhere, expressed differently, then it would excite me. I am very capricious in the small things, and I think women are so more than men. The idea of slipping down a plank formerly produced excitement with me; now it has a less vivid effect, though the idea of loss of breath still produces excitement. The idea of the plank does not now affect me unless there is a certain amount of drapery. I think, therefore, that the feeling must come in part from the possibility of the drapery catching on some roughness of the surface of the slope, and so producing pressure on the sexual organs. The effect is still produced, however, even without any clothing, if the slope is supposed to end in a deep drop, so that the idea of falling is strongly presented. I cannot recollect any early associations that would tend to explain these feelings, except that jumping from a height, which I used frequently to do as a child, has a tendency to create excitement.

"With me, I may add, it is when I cannot express myself, or am trying to understand what I feel is beyond my grasp, that the first stage of sexual excitement results. For instance, I never get excited in thinking over sexual questions, because my ideas, correct or incorrect, are fairly clear and definite. But I often feel sexually excited over that question of the inheritance of acquired characteristics, not because I can't decide between the two sets of evidence, but because I don't feel confident of having fully grasped the true significance of either. This feeling of want of power, mental or physical, always has the same effect. I feel it if my eyes are blindfolded or my hands tied. I don't like to see the Washington Post dance, in which the man stands behind the woman and holds her hands, on that account. If he held her wrists the feeling would be stronger, as her apparent helplessness would be increased. The nervous irritability that is caused by being under restraint seems to manifest itself in that way, while in the case of mental disability the excitement, which should flow down a mental channel, being checked, seems to take a physical course instead.

"Possibly this would help to explain masochistic sexual feelings. A physical cause working in the present would be preferable as an explanation to a psychological cause to be traced back through heredity to primitive conditions. I believe such feelings are very common in men as well as in women, only people do not care to admit them, as a rule."

The idea of being chained and fettered appears to be not uncommonly associated with pleasurable sexual feelings, for I have met with numerous cases in both men and women, and it not infrequently coexists with a tendency to inversion. It often arises at a very early age, and it is of considerable interest because we cannot account for its frequency by any chance association nor by any actual experiences. It would appear to be a purely psychic fantasia founded on the elementary physical fact that restraint of emotion, like suspension, produces a heightening of emotion. In any case the spontaneous character of such ideas and emotions in children of both sexes suffices to show that they must possess a very definite organic basis.

In one of the histories (X) contained in Appendix B at the end of the present volume a lady describes how, as a child, she reveled in the idea of being chained and tortured, these ideas appearing to rise spontaneously. In another case, that of A. N. (for the most part reproduced in "Erotic Symbolism," in vol. v of these *Studies*), whose ideals are inverted and who is also affected by boot-fetichism, the idea of fetters is very attractive. In this case self-excitement was produced at a very early age, without the use of the hands, by strapping the legs together. We can, however, scarcely explain away the idea of fetters in this case as merely the result of an early association, for it may well be argued that the idea led to this method of self-excitement. "The mere idea of fetters," this subject writes, "produces the greatest excitement, and the sight of pictures representing such things is a temptation. The reading of books dealing with prison life, etc., anywhere where physical restraint is treated of, is a temptation. The temptation is aggravated when the picture represents the person booted. I suppose all this will have been intensified in my case by my practices as a child. But why should a child of 6 do such things unless it were a natural instinct in him? Nobody showed me; I have never mentioned such things to anyone. I used to read historical romances for the pleasure of reading of people being put in prison, in fetters, and tortured, and always envied them. I feel now that I should like to undergo the sensation. If I could get anyone to humor me without losing their self-respect, I should jump at the opportunity. I have been most powerfully excited by visiting an old Australian convict-ship, where all the means of restraint are shown; I have been attracted to it night after night, wanting, but not daring to ask, to be allowed to have a practical experience."

Stcherbak, of Warsaw, has recorded a case which resembles that of A. N., but there was no inversion and the attraction of fetters was active rather than passive; the subject desired to fetter and not to be fettered. It is possible that this difference is not fundamental, though Stcherbak regards the case as one of fetichism of sadistic origin ("Contribution à l'Etude des Perversions Sexuelles,"*Archives de Neurologie*, Oct., 1907). The subject was a highly intelligent though neurasthenic youth, who from the age of 5 had been deeply interested in criminals who were fettered and sent to prison. The fate of Siberian prisoners was a frequent source of prolonged meditations. It was the fettering which alone interested him, and he spent much time in trying to imagine the feelings of the fettered prisoners, and he often imagined that he was himself a prisoner in fetters. (This seems to indicate that the impulse was in its origin masochistic as much as sadistic, and better described as algolagnia than as sadism.) He delighted in stories and pictures of fettered persons. At the age of 15 the sex of the fettered person became important and he was interested chiefly in fettered women. A new element also appeared; he was attracted to well-dressed women and especially to those wearing elegant shoes, delighting to imagine them fettered. He fastened his own feet together with chains, attempting to walk about his room in this condition, but experienced comparatively little pleasure in this way. At the age of 15 he met a lady 10 years older than himself and of great intelligence. As he began to know her more intimately she allowed him to take liberties with her; he fastened her hands behind her back, and this caused him a violent but delicious emotion which he had never experienced before. Next time he fastened her feet together as well as her hands; as he did so her shoes slightly touched his sexual organs; this caused erection and ejaculation, accompanied by the most acute sexual pleasure he had ever felt. He had no wish to see her naked or to uncover himself, and as long as this relationship lasted he had no abnormal thoughts at other times, or in connection with other people. He never masturbated, and his sexual dreams were of fettered men or women. Stcherbak discusses the case at length and considers that it is essentially an example of sadism, on the ground that the impulse of fettering was prompted by the desire to humiliate. There is, however, no evidence of any such desire, and, as a matter of fact, no humiliation was effected. The primary and fundamental element in this and similar cases is an almost abstract sexual fascination in the idea of restraint, whether endured, inflicted, or merely witnessed or imagined; the feet become the chief focus of this fascination, and the basis on which a foot-fetichism or shoe-fetichism tends to arise, because restraint of the feet produces a more marked effect than restraint of the hands.

[120]

88

An attenuated and symbolic form of this impulse is seen in the desire to strangle birds with the object of stimulating or even satisfying sexual desire. Prostitutes are sometimes acquainted with men who bring a live pigeon with them to be strangled just before intercourse. Lanphear, of St. Louis (*Alienist and Neurologist*, May, 1907, p. 204) knew a woman, having learned masturbation in a convent school, who was only excited and not satisfied by coitus with her husband, and had to rise from bed, catch and caress a chicken, and finally wring its neck, whereupon orgasm occurred.

[121]

Even young girls, however, may experience pleasure in the playful attempt to strangle. Thus a lady speaking of herself at the time of puberty, when she was in the habit of masturbating, writes (*Sexual-Probleme*, Aug., 1909, p. 636): "I acquired a desire to seize people, especially girls, by the throat, and I enjoyed their way of screaming out."

[122]

Godard observed that when animals are bled, or felled, as well as strangled, there is often abundant emission, rich in spermatozoa, but without erection, though accompanied by the same movements of the tail as during copulation. Robin (art. "Fécondation," *Dictionnaire Encyclopédique des Sciences Médicales*), who quotes this observation, has the following remarks on this subject: "Ejaculation occurring at the moment when the circulation, maintained artificially, stops is a fact of significance. It shows how congestive conditions—or inversely anemic conditions—constitute organic states sufficient to set in movement the activity of the nerve-centers, as is the case for muscular contractility.... Everything leads us to believe that at the moment when the motor nervous action takes place the corresponding sensitive centers also come into play." It must be added that Minovici, in his elaborate study of death by hanging ("Etude sur la Pendaison," *Archives d'Anthropologie Criminelle*, 1905, especially p. 791 *et seq.*), concludes that the turgescence of penis and flow of spermatic fluid (sometimes only prostatic secretion) usually observed in these cases is purely passive and generally, though not always, of post-mortem occurrence. There is, therefore, no sexual pleasure in death by hanging, and persons who have been rescued at the last moment have experienced no voluptuous sensations. This was so even in the case, referred to by Minovici, of a man who hanged himself solely with the object of producing sexual pleasure.

[123]

Eulenburg, *Sexuale Neuropathie*, p. 114.

[124]

Bernaldo de Quirós and Llanos Aguilaniedo (*La Mala Vida en Madrid*, p. 294) knew the case of a man who found pleasure in lying back on an inclined couch while a prostitute behind him pulled at a slipknot until he was nearly suffocated; it was the only way in which he could attain sexual gratification.

[125]

Arrest of respiration, it may be noted, may accompany strong sexual excitement, as it may some other emotional states; one recalls passages in the *Arabian Nights* in which we are told of ladies who at the sight of a very beautiful youth "felt their reason leave them, yearned to embrace the marvelous youth, and *ceased breathing*." Inhibited respiration is indeed, as Stevens shows ("Study of Attention," *American Journal of Psychology*, Oct., 1905), a characteristic of all active attention.

[126]

The exact part played by the respiration and even the circulation in constituting emotional states is still not clear, although various experiments have been made; see, *e.g.*, Angell and Thompson, "A Study of the Relations between Certain Organic Processes and Consciousness," *Psychological Review*, January, 1899. A summary statement of the relations of the respiration and circulation to emotional states will be found in Külpe's *Outlines of Psychology*, part i, section 2, § 37.

[127]

The words alluded to by my correspondent are as follows: "I needed a struggle; what I needed was that feeling should guide life, and not that life should guide feeling. I wanted to go with him to the edge of an abyss and say: 'Here a step and I will throw myself over; and here a motion and I have gone to destruction'; and for him, turning pale, to seize me in his strong arms, hold me back over it till my heart grew cold within me, and then carry me away wherever he pleased." The whole of the passage in which these lines occur is of considerable psychological interest. In one English translation the story is entitled *Family Happiness.*

V.

Pain, and Not Cruelty, the Essential Element in Sadism and Masochism—Pain Felt as Pleasure—Does the Sadist Identify Himself with the Feelings of his Victim?—The Sadist often a Masochist in Disguise—The Spectacle of Pain or Struggle as a Sexual Stimulant.

In the foregoing rapid survey of the great group of manifestations in which the sexual emotions come into intimate relationship with pain, it has become fairly clear that the ordinary division between "sadism" and "masochism," convenient as these terms may be, has a very slight correspondence with facts. Sadism and masochism may be regarded as complementary emotional states; they cannot be regarded as opposed states.[128] Even De Sade himself, we have seen, can scarcely be regarded as a pure sadist. A passage in one of his works expressing regret that sadistic feeling is rare among women, as well as his definite recognition of the fact that the suffering of pain may call forth voluptuous emotions, shows that he was not insensitive to the charm of masochistic experience, and it is evident that a merely blood-thirsty vampire, sane or insane, could never have retained, as De Sade retained, the undying devotion of two women so superior in heart and intelligence as his wife and sister-in-law. Had De Sade possessed any wanton love of cruelty, it would have appeared during the days of the Revolution, when it was safer for a man to simulate blood-thirstiness, even if he did not feel it, than to show humanity. But De Sade distinguished himself at that time not merely by his general philanthropic activities, but by saving from the scaffold, at great risk to himself, those who had injured him. It is clear that, apart from the organically morbid twist by which he obtained sexual satisfaction in his partner's pain,—a cravingwhich was, for the most part, only gratified in imaginary visions developed to an inhuman extent under the influence of solitude,—De Sade was simply, to those who knew him, "*un aimable mauvais sujet*" gifted with exceptional intellectual powers. Unless we realize this we run the risk of confounding De Sade and his like with men of whom Judge Jeffreys was the sinister type.

It is necessary to emphasize this point because there can be no doubt that De Sade is really a typical instance of the group of perversions he represents, and when we understand that it is pain only, and not cruelty, that is the essential in this group of manifestations we begin to come nearer to their explanation. The masochist desires to experience pain, but he generally desires that it should be inflicted in love; the sadist desires to inflict pain, but in some cases, if not in most, he desires that it should be felt as love. How far De Sade consciously desired that the pain he sought to inflict should be felt as pleasure it may not now be possible to discover, except by indirect inference, but the confessions of sadists show that such a desire is quite commonly essential.

I am indebted to a lady for the following communication on the foregoing aspect of this question: "I believe that, when a person takes pleasure in inflicting pain, he or she imagines himself or herself in the victim's place. This would account for the transmutability of the two sets of feelings. This might be particularly so in the case of men. A man may not care to lower his dignity and vanity by putting himself in subjection to a woman, and he might fear she would feel contempt for him. By subduing her and subjecting her to passive restraint he would preserve, even enhance, his own power and dignity, while at the same time obtaining a reflected pleasure from what he imagined she was feeling.

"I think that when I get pleasure out of the idea of subduing another it is this reflected pleasure I get. And if this is so one could thus feel more kindly to persons guilty of cruelty, which has hitherto always seemed the one unpardonable sin. Even criminals, if it is true that they are themselves often very insensitive, may, in the excitement of the moment, imagine that they are only inflicting trifling pain, as it would be to them, and that their victim's feelings are really pleasurable. The men I have known most given to inflicting pain are all particularly tender-hearted when their passions are not in question. I cannot understand how (as in a case mentioned by Krafft-Ebing) a man could find any pleasure in binding a girl's hands except by imagining what he supposed were her feelings, though he would probably be unconscious that he put himself in her place.

"As a child I exercised a good deal of authority and influence over my youngest sister. It used to give me considerable pleasure to be somewhat arbitrary and severe with her, but, though I never admitted it to myself or to her, I knew instinctively that she took pleasure in my treatment. I used to give her childish lessons, over which I was very strict. I invented catechisms and chapters of the Bible in which elder sisters were exhorted to keep their juniors under discipline, and younger sisters were commanded to give implicit submission and obedience. Some parts of the *Imitation* lent themselves to this sort of parody, which never struck me as in any way irreverent. I used to give her arbitrary orders to 'exercise her in obedience,' as I told her, and I used to punish her if she disobeyed me. In all this I was, *though only half consciously*, guided through my own feelings as to what I should have liked in her place. For instance, I would make her put down her playthings and come and repeat a lesson; but, though she was in appearance having her will subdued to mine, I always chose a moment when I foresaw she would soon be tired of play. There was sufficient resistance to make restraint pleasurable, not enough to render it irksome. In my punishments I acted on a similar principle. I used to tie her hands behind her (like the man in Krafft-Ebing's case), but only for a few moments; I once shut her in a sort of cupboard-room, also for a very short time. On two or three occasions I completely undressed her, made her lie down on the bed, tied her hands and feet to the bedstead, and gave her a slight whipping. I did not wish to hurt her, only to inflict just enough pain to produce the desire to move or resist. *My pleasure, a very keen one, came from the imagined excitement produced by the thwarting of this desire.* (Are not your own words—that 'emotion' is 'motion in a more or less arrested form'—an epigrammatic summary of all this, though in a somewhat different connection?) I did not undress her from any connection of nakedness with sexual feeling, but simply to enhance her feeling of helplessness and defenselessness under my hands. If I were a man and the woman I loved were refractory I should undress her before finding fault with her. A woman's dress symbolizes to her the protection civilization affords to the weak and gives her a fictitious strength. Naked, she is face to face with primitive conditions, her weakness opposed to the man's power. Besides, the sense of shame at being naked under the eyes of a man who regarded her with displeasure would extend itself to her offense and give him a distinct, though perhaps unfair, advantage. I used the bristle side of a brush to chastise her with, as suggesting the greatest amount of severity with the least possible pain. In fact, my idea was to produce the maximum of emotion with the minimum of actual discomfort.

"You must not, however, suppose that at the time I reasoned about it at all in this way. I was very fond of her, and honestly believed I was doing it for her good. Had I realized then, as I do now, that my sole aim and object was physical pleasure, I believe my pleasure would have ceased; in any case I should not have felt justified in so treating her. Do I at all persuade you that my pleasure was a reflection of hers? That it was, I think, is clear from the fact that I only obtained it when she was willing to submit. Any *real* resistance or signs that I was overpassing the boundary of pleasure in her and urging on pain without excitement caused me to desist and my own pleasure to cease.

"I disclaim all altruism in my dealings with my sister. What occurs appears to me to be this: A situation appeals to one in imagination and one at once desires to transfer it to the realms of fact, being one's self one of the principal actors. If it is the passive side which appeals to one, one would prefer to be passive; but if that is not obtainable then one takes the active part as next best. In either case, however, it is *the realization of the imagined situation* that gives the pleasure, not the other person's pleasure as such, although his or her supposed pleasure creates the situation. If I were a man it would afford me great delight to hold a woman over a precipice, even if she disliked it. The idea appeals to me so strongly that I could not help *imagining* her pleasure, though I might *know* she got none, and even though she made every demonstration of fear and dislike of it. The situation so often imagined would have become a fact. It seems to me I have to say a thing is and is not in the same breath, but the confusion is only in the words.

"Let me give you another example: I have a tame pigeon which has a great affection for me. It sits on my shoulder and squats down with its wings out as birds do when courting, pecking me to make me take notice of it, and flickering its wings. I like to hold it so that it can't move its wings, because I imagine this increases its excitement. If it struggles, or seems to dislike my holding it, I let it go.

"In an early engagement (afterward broken off) my *fiancé* used to take an evident pleasure in telling me how he would punish me if I disobeyed him when we were married. Though we had but little in common mentally, I was frequently struck with the similarity between his ideas and what my own had been in regard to my sister. He used his authority over me most capriciously. On one occasion he would not let me have any supper at a dance. On another he objected to my drinking black coffee. No day passed without a command or prohibition on some trifling point. Whenever he saw, though, that I really disliked the interference or made any decided resistance, which happened very seldom, he let me have my own way at once. I cannot but think, when I recall the various circumstances, that he got a certain pleasure, as I had done with my sister, by an almost unconscious transference of my feelings to himself.

"I find, too, that, when I want a man to say or do to me what would cause me pleasure and he does not gratify me, I feel an intense longing to change places, to be the man and make him, as the woman, feel what I want to feel. Combined with this is a sense of irritation at not being gratified and a desire to punish him for my deprivation, for his stupidity in not saying or doing the right thing. I don't feel any anger at a man not caring for me, but only for not divining my feelings when he does care.

"Now let me take another case: that of the man who used to experience pleasure when surprising a woman making water. (*Cf. Archives d'Anthropologie Criminelle*, Nov. 15, 1900.) Here the woman's embarrassment appears to be a factor; but it seems to me there must be more than this, as confusion might be produced in so many other ways, as if she were found bathing, or undressed, though it might not be so acute. In reality, I fancy she would be checked in what she was doing, and that the man, perhaps unconsciously, imagined this check and a resulting excitement. That such a check does sometimes produce excitement I know from experience in traveling. If the bladder is not emptied before connection the pleasure is often more intense. Long before I understood these things at all I was struck by this quotation: 'Cette volupté que ressentent les bords de la mer, d'être toujours pleins sans jamais déborder?' What would be the effect on a man of a sudden check at the supreme moment of sexual pleasure? In reality, I suppose, pain, as the nerves would be at their full tension and unable to respond to any further stimulus; but, in imagination, one's nerves are *not* at their highest tension, and one imagines an increase or, at any rate, a prolongation of the pleasurable sensations. Something of all this, some vague *reflection* of the woman's possible sensations, seems to enter in the man's feelings in surprising the woman. In any case his pleasure in her confusion seems to me a reflection of her feelings, for the sense of shame and embarrassment before a man is very exciting, and doubly so if one realizes that the man enjoys it. Ouida speaks of the 'delicious shame' experienced by 'Folle Farine.'

"It seems to me that whenever we are affected by another's emotion we do practically, though unconsciously, put ourselves in his place; but we are not always able to gauge accurately its intensity or to allow for differences between ourselves and another, and, in the case of pain, it is doubly difficult, as we can never recall the pain itself, but only the mental effects upon us of the pain. We cannot even recall the feeling of heat when we are cold, or *vice versâ*, with any degree of vividness.

"A woman tells me of a man who frequently asks her if she would not like him to whip her. He is greatly disappointed when she says she gets no pleasure from it, as it would give him so much to do it. He cannot believe she experiences none, because he would enjoy being whipped so keenly if he were a girl. In another case the man thinks the woman *must* enjoy suffering, *because* he would get intense pleasure from inflicting it! Why is this, unless he would like it if a woman, and confuses in his mind the two personalities? All the men I know who are sadistically inclined admit that if they were women they would like to be harshly treated.

"Of course, I quite see there may be many complications; a man's natural anger at resistance may come in, and also simple, not sexual, pleasure in acts of crushing, etc. I always feel inclined to crush anything very soft or a person with very pretty thick hair, to rub together two shining surfaces, two bits of satin, etc., apart from any feelings of excitement. My explanation only refers to that part of sadism which is sexual enjoyment of another's pain."

That the foregoing view holds good as regards the traces of sadism found within the normal limits of sexual emotion has already been stated. We may also believe that it is true in many genuinely perverse cases. In this connection reference may be made to an interesting case, reported by Moll, of a married lady 23 years of age, with pronounced sadistic feelings. She belongs to a normal family and is herself apparently quite healthy, a tall and strongly built person, of feminine aspect, fond of music and dancing, of more than average intelligence. Her perverse inclinations commenced obscurely about the age of 14, when she began to be dominated by the thought of the pleasure it would be to strike and torture a man, but were not clearly defined until the age of 18, while at an early age she was fond of teasing and contradicting men, though she never experienced the same impulse toward women. She has never, except in a very slight degree, actually carried her ideas into practice, either with her husband or anyone else, being restrained, she says, by a feeling of shame. Coitus, though frequently practised, gives her no pleasure, seems, indeed, somewhat disgusting to her, and has never produced orgasm. Her own ideas, also, though very pleasurable to her, have not produced definite sexual excitement, except on two or three occasions, when they had been combined with the influence of alcohol. She frankly regrets that modern social relationship makes it impossible for her to find sexual satisfaction in the only way in which such satisfaction would be possible to her.

Her chief delight would be to torture the man she was attached to in every possible way; to inflict physical pain and mental pain would give her equal pleasure. "I would bite him till the blood came, as I have often done to my husband. At that moment all sympathy for him would disappear." She frequently identifies her imaginary lover with a real man to whom she feels that she could be much more attracted than she is to her husband. She imagines to herself that she makes appointments with this lover, and that she reaches the rendezvous in her carriage, but only after her lover has been waiting for her a very long time in the cold. Then he must feel all her power, he must be her slave with no will of his own, and she would torture him with various implements as seemed good to her. She would use a rod, a riding-whip, bind him and chain him, and so on. But it is to be noted that she declares "*this could, in general, only give me enjoyment if the man concerned endured such torture with a certain pleasure. He must, indeed, writhe with pain, but at the same time in a state of sexual ecstasy, followed by satisfaction.*" His pleasure must not, however, be so great that it overwhelms his pain; if it did, her own pleasure would vanish, and she has found witty her husband that when in kissing him her bites have given him much pleasure she has at once refrained.

It is further noteworthy that only the pain she herself had inflicted would give her pleasure. If the lover suffered pain from an accident or a wound she is convinced that she would be full of sympathy for him. Outside her special sexual perversion she is sympathetic and very generous. (Moll, *Konträre Sexualempfindung*, 1899, pp. 507-510.)

This case is interesting as an uncomplicated example of almost purely ideal sadism. It is interesting to note the feelings of the sadist subject toward her imaginary lover's feelings. It is probably significant that, while his pleasure is regarded as essential, his pain is regarded as even more essential, and the resulting apparent confusion may well be of the very essence of the whole phenomenon. The pleasure of the imaginary lover must be secured or the manifestation passes out of the sexual sphere; but his pleasure must, at all costs, be conciliated with his pain, for in the sadist's eyes the victim's pain has become a vicarious form of sexual emotion. That, at the same time, the sadist desires to give pleasure rather than pain finds confirmation in the fact that he often insists on pleasure being feigned even though it is not felt. Some years ago a rich Jewish merchant became notorious for torturing girls with whom he had intercourse; his performances acquired for him the title of "*l'homme qui pique*," and led to his prosecution. It was his custom to spend some hours in sticking pins into various parts of the girl's body, but it was essential that she should wear a smiling face throughout the proceedings. (Hamon, *La France Sociale et Politique*, 1891, p. 445 *et seq.*)

We have thus to recognize that sadism by no means involves any love of inflicting pain outside the sphere of sexual emotion, and is even compatible with a high degree of general tender-heartedness. We have also to recognize that even within the sexual sphere the sadist by no means wishes to exclude the victim's pleasure, and may even regard that pleasure as essential to his own satisfaction. We have, further, to recognize that, in view of the close connection between sadism and masochism, it is highly probable that in some cases the sadist is really a disguised masochist and enjoys his victim's pain because he identifies himself with that pain.

But there is a further group of cases, and a very important group, on account of the light it throws on the essential nature of these phenomena, and that is the group in which the thought or the spectacle of pain acts as a sexual stimulant, without the subject identifying himself clearly either with the inflicter or the sufferer of the pain. Such cases are sometimes classed as sadistic; but this is incorrect, for they might just as truly be called masochistic. The term algolagnia might properly be applied to them (and Eulenburg now classes them as "ideal algolagnia"), for they reveal an undifferentiated connection between sexual excitement and pain not developed into either active or passive participation. Such feelings may arise sporadically in persons in whom no sadistic or masochistic perversion can be said to exist, though they usually appear in individuals of neurotic temperament. Casanova describes an instance of this association which came immediately under his own eyes at the torture and execution of Damiens in 1757.[129] W. G. Stearns knew a man (having masturbated and had intercourse to excess) who desired to see his wife delivered of a child, and finally became impotent without this idea. He witnessed many deliveries and especially obtained voluptuous gratification at the delivery of a primipara when the suffering was greatest.[130] A very trifling episode may, however, suffice. In one case known to me a man, neither sadistic nor masochistic in his tendencies, when sitting looking out of his window saw a spider come out of its hole to capture and infold a fly which had just been caught in its web; as he watched the process he became conscious of a powerful erection, an occurrence which had never taken place under such circumstances before.[131] Under favoring conditions some incident of this kind at an early age may exert a decisive influence on the sexual life. Tambroni, of Ferrara, records the case of a boy of 11 who first felt voluptuous emotions on seeing in an illustrated journal the picture of a man trampling on his daughter; ever afterward he was obliged to evoke this image in masturbation or coitus.[132] An instructive case has been recorded by Féré. In this case a lady of neurotic heredity on one side, and herself liable to hysteria, experienced her first sexual crisis at the age of 13, not long after menstruation had become established, and when she had just recovered from an attack of chorea. Her old nurse, who had remained in the service of the family, had a ne'er-do-well son who had disappeared for some years and had just now suddenly returned and thrown himself, crying and sobbing, at the knees of his mother, who thrust him away. The young girl accidentally witnessed this scene. The cries and the sobs provoked in her a sexual excitement she had never experienced before. She rushed away in surprise to the next room, where, however, she could still hear the sobs, and soon she was overcome by a sexual orgasm. She was much troubled at this occurrence, and at the attraction which she now experienced for a man she had never seen before and whom she had always looked upon as a worthless vagabond. Shortly afterward she had an erotic dream concerning a man who sobbed at her knees. Later she again saw the nurse's son, but was agreeably surprised to find that, though a good-looking youth, he no longer caused her any emotion, and he disappeared from her mind, though the erotic dreams concerning an unknown sobbing man still occurred rather frequently. During the next ten years she suffered from various disorders of more or less hysterical character, and, although not disinclined to the idea of marriage, she refused all offers, for no man attracted her. At the age of 23, when staying in the Pyrenees, she made an excursion into Spain, and was present at a bull-fight. She was greatly excited by the charges of the bull, especially when the charge was suddenly arrested.[133] She felt no interest in any of the men who took part in the performance or were present; no man was occupying her imagination. But she experienced sexual sensations and accompanying general exhilaration, which were highly agreeable. After one bull had charged successively several times the orgasm took place. She considered the whole performance barbarous, but could not resist the desire to be present at subsequent bull-fights, a desire several times gratified, always with the same results, which were often afterward repeated in dreams. From that time she began to take an interest in horse-races, which she now found produced the same effect, though not to the same degree, especially when there was a fall. She subsequently married, but never experienced sexual satisfaction except under these abnormal circumstances or in dreams.[134]

As the foregoing case indicates, horses, and especially running or struggling horses, sometimes have the same effect in stimulating the sexual emotions, especially on persons predisposed by neurotic heredity, as we have found that the spectacle of pain possesses. A medical correspondent in New Zealand tells me of a patient of his own, a young carpenter of 26, not in good health, who had never masturbated or had connection with a woman. He lived in a room overlooking a livery-stable yard where was kept, among other animals, a large black horse. Nearly every night he had a dream in which he seemed to be pursuing this large black horse, and when he caught it, which he invariably did, there was a copious emission. A holiday in the country and tonic treatment dispelled the dreams and reduced the nocturnal emissions to normal frequency. Féré has recorded a case of a boy, of neuropathic heredity, who, when 14 years of age, was one day about to practise mutual masturbation with another boy of his own age. They were seated on a hillside overlooking a steep road, and at this moment a heavy wagon came up the road drawn by four horses, which struggled painfully up, encouraged by the cries and the whip of the driver. This sight increased the boy's sexual excitement, which reached its climax when one of the horses suddenly fell. He had never before experienced such intense excitement, and always afterward a similar spectacle of struggling horses produced a similar effect.[135]

In this connection reference may be made to the frequency with which dreams of struggling horses occur in connection with disturbance or disease of the heart. In such cases it is clear that the struggling horses seem to dream-consciousness to embody and explain the panting struggles to which the heart is subjected. They become, as it were, a visual symbol of the cardiac oppression. In much the same way, it would appear, under the influence of sexual excitement, in which cardiac disturbance is one of the chief constituent elements, the struggling horses became a sexual symbol, and, having attained that position, they are henceforth alone adequate to produce sexual excitement.

[128]
This opinion appears to be in harmony with the conclusions of Eulenburg, who has devoted special study to De Sade, and points out that the ordinary conception of "sadism" is much too narrow. (Eulenburg, *Sexuale Neuropathie*, 1895, p. 110 *et seq.*)

[129]
Casanova, *Mémoires*, vol. viii, pp. 74-76. Goncourt in his *Journal*, under date of April, 1862 (vol. ii, p. 27), tells a story of an Englishman who engaged a room overlooking a scaffold where a murderer was to be hanged, proposing to take a woman with him and to avail himself of the excitement aroused by the scene. This scheme was frustrated by the remission of the death penalty.

[130]
Alienist and Neurologist, May, 1907, p. 204.

[131]
This spectacle of the spider and the fly seems indeed to be specially apt to exert a sexual influence. I have heard of a precisely similar case in a man of intellectual distinction, and another in a lady who acknowledged to a feeling of "exquisite pleasure," on one occasion, at the mere sound of the death agony of a fly in a spider's web.

[132]
Quoted by Obici and Marchesini, *Le Amicizie di Collegio*, p. 245.

[133]
It may be noted that we have already several times encountered this increase of excitement produced by arrest of movement. The effect is produced whether the arrest is witnessed or is actually experienced. "A man can increase a woman's excitement," a lady

writes, "by forbidding her to respond in any way to his caresses. It is impossible to remain quite passive for more than a few seconds, but, during these few, excitement is considerably augmented." In a similar way I have been told of a man of brilliant intellectual ability who very seldom has connection with a woman without getting her to compress with her hand the base of the urethral canal to such an extent as to impede the passage of the semen. On withdrawal of the hand copious emission occurs, but it is the shock of the arrest caused by the constriction which gives him supreme pleasure. He has practised this method for years without evil results.

[134]
Féré, "Le Sadisme aux Courses de Taureaux," *Revue de médecine*, August, 1900.

[135]
Féré, *L'Instinct sexuel*, p. 255.

VI.

Why is Pain a Sexual Stimulant?—It is the Most Effective Method of Arousing Emotion—Anger and Fear the Most Powerful Emotions—Their Biological Significance in Courtship—Their General and Special Effects in Stimulating the Organism—Grief as a Sexual Stimulant—The Physiological Mechanism of Fatigue Renders Pain Pleasurable.

We have seen that the distinction between "sadism" and "masochism" cannot be maintained; not only was even De Sade himself something of a masochist and Sacher-Masoch something of a sadist, but between these two extreme groups of phenomena there is a central group in which the algolagnia is neither active nor passive. "Sadism" and "masochism" are simply convenient clinical terms for classes of manifestations which quite commonly occur in the same person. We have further found that—as might have been anticipated in view of the foregoing result—it is scarcely correct to use the word "cruelty" in connection with the phenomena we have been considering. The persons who experience these impulses usually show no love of cruelty outside the sphere of sexual emotion; they may even be very intolerant of cruelty. Even when their sexual impulses come into play they may still desire to secure the pleasure of the persons who arouse their sexual emotions, even though it may not be often true that those who desire to inflict pain at these moments identify themselves with the feelings of those on whom they inflict it. We have thus seen that when we take a comprehensive survey of all these phenomena a somewhat general formula will alone cover them. Our conclusion so far must be that under certain abnormal circumstances pain, more especially the mental representation of pain, acts as a powerful sexual stimulant.

The reader, however, who has followed the discussion to this point will be prepared to take the next and final step in our discussion and to reach a more definite conclusion. The question naturally arises: By what process does pain or its mental representation thus act as a sexual stimulant? The answer has over and over again been suggested by the facts brought forward in this study. Pain acts as a sexual stimulant because it is the most powerful of all methods for arousing emotion.

The two emotions most intimately associated with pain are anger and fear. The more masculine and sthenic emotion of anger, the more passive and asthenic emotion of fear, are the fundamental animal emotions through which, on the psychic side, the process of natural selection largely works. Every animal in some degree owes its survival to the emotional reaction of anger against weaker rivals, to the emotional reaction of fear against stronger rivals. To this cause we owe it that these two emotions are so powerfully and deeply rooted in the whole zoölogical series to which we belong. But anger and fear are not less fundamental in the sexual life. Courtship on the male's part is largely a display of combativity, and even the very gestures by which the male seeks to appeal to the female are often those gestures of angry hostility by which he seeks to intimidate enemies. On the female's part courtship is a skillful manipulation of her own fears, and, as we have seen elsewhere, when studying the phenomena of modesty, that fundamental attitude of the female in courtship is nothing but an agglomeration of fears.

The biological significance of the emotions is now well recognized. "In general," remarks one of the shrewdest writers on animal psychology, "we may say that emotional states are, under natural conditions, closely associated with behavior of biological value— with tendencies that are beneficial in self-preservation and race preservation—with actions that promote survival, and especially with the behavior which clusters round the pairing and parental instincts. The value of the emotions in animals is that they are an indirect means of furthering survival." (Lloyd Morgan, *Animal Behavior*, p. 293.) Emotional aptitudes persist not only by virtue of the fact that they are still beneficial, but because they once were; that is to say, they may exist as survivals. In this connection I may quote from a suggestive paper on "Teasing and Bullying," by F. L. Burk; at the conclusion of this study, which is founded on a large body of data concerning American children, the author asks: "Accepting for the moment the theories of Spencer and Ribot upon the transmission of rudimentary instincts, is it possible that the movements which comprise the chief elements of bullying, teasing, and the egotistic impulses in general of the classes cited—pursuing, throwing down, punching, striking, throwing missiles, etc.—are, from the standpoint of consciousness, broken neurological fragments, which are parts of old chains of activity involved in the pursuit, combat, capture, torture, and killing of men and enemies?... Is not this hypothesis of transmitted fragments of instincts in accord with the strangely anomalous fact that children are at one moment seemingly cruel and at the next affectionate and kind, vibrating, as it were, between two worlds, egotistic and altruistic, without conscious sense of incongruity?" (F. L. Burk, "Teasing and Bullying," *Pedagogical Seminary*, April, 1897.)

The primitive connection of the special emotions of anger and fear with the sexual impulse has been well expressed by Colin Scott in his remarkable study of "Sex and Art": "If the higher forms of courting are based on combat, among the males at least anger must be intimately associated with love. And below both of these lies the possibility of fear. In combat the animal is defeated who is first afraid. Competitive exhibition of prowess will inspire the less able birds with a deterring fear. Young grouse and woodcock do not enter the lists with the older birds, and sing very quietly. It is the same with the very oldest birds. Audubon says that the old maids and bachelors of the Canada goose move off by themselves during the courting of the younger birds. In order to succeed in love, fear must be overcome in the male as well as in the female. Courage is the essential male virtue, love is its outcome and reward. The strutting, crowing, dancing, and singing of male birds and the preliminary movements generally of animals must gorge the neuromotor and muscular systems with blood and put them in better fighting trim. The effects of this upon the feelings of the animal himself must be very great. Hereditary tendencies swell his heart. He has 'the joy that warriors feel.' He becomes regardless of danger, and sometimes almost oblivious of his surroundings. This intense passionateness must react powerfully on the whole system, and more particularly on those parts which are capable, such as the brain, of using up a great surplus of blood, and on the naturally erethic functions of sex. The flood of anger or fighting instinct is drained off by the sexual desires, the antipathy of the female is overcome, and sexual union successfully ensues.... Courting and combat shade into one another, courting tending to take the place of the more basal form of combat. The passions which thus come to be associated with love are those of fear and anger, both of which, by arousing the whole nature and stimulating the nutritive sources from which they flow, come to increase the force of the sexual passion to which they lead up and in which they culminate and are absorbed," (Colin Scott, "Sex and Art," *American Journal of Psychology*, vol. vii, No. 2, pp. 170 and 215.)

It must be remembered that fear is an element liable to arise in all courtship on one side or the other. It is usually on the side of the female, but not invariably. Among spiders, for instance, it is usually the male who feels fear, and very reasonably, for he is much weaker than the female. "Courtship by the male spider" says T. H. Montgomery ("The Courtship of Araneads," *American Naturalist*, March, 1910, p. 166), "results from a combination of the state of desire for and fear of the female." It is by his movements of fear that he advertises himself to the female as a male, and it is by the same movements that he is unconsciously impelled to display prominently his own ornamentation.

We are thus brought to those essential facts of primitive courtship with which we started. But we are now able to understand more clearly how it is that alien emotional states became abnormally associated with the sexual life. Normally the sexual impulse is sufficiently reinforced by the ordinary active energies of the organism which courtship itself arouses, energies which, while they may be ultimately in part founded on anger and fear, rarely allow these emotions to be otherwise than latent. Motion, it may be said, is more prominent than emotion.

Even normally a stimulant to emotional activities is pleasurable, just as motion itself is pleasurable. It may even be useful, as was noted long ago by Erasmus Darwin; he tells of a friend of his who, when painfully fatigued by riding, would call up ideas arousing indignation, and thus relieve the fatigue, the indignation, as Darwin pointed out, increasing muscular activity.[136]

It is owing to this stimulating action that discomfort, even pain, may be welcomed on account of the emotional waves they call up, because they "lash into movement the dreary calm of the sea's soul," and produce that alternation of pain and enjoyment for which Faust longed. Groos, who recalls this passage in his very thorough and profound discussion of the region wherein tragedy has its psychological roots, points out that it is the overwhelming might of the storm itself, and not the peace of calm after the storm, which appeals to us. In the same way, he observes, even surprise and shock may also be pleasurable, and fear, though the most depressing of emotional states, by virtue of the joy produced by strong stimuli is felt as attractive; we not only experience an impulse of pleasure in dominating our environment, but also have pleasure in being dominated and rendered helpless by a higher power.[137] Hirn, again, in his work on the origins of art, has an interesting chapter on "The Enjoyment of Pain," a phenomenon which he explains by its resultant reactions in increase of outward activity, of motor excitement. Anger, he observes elsewhere, is "in its active stage a decidedly pleasurable emotion. Fear, which in its initial stage is paralyzing and depressing, often changes in time when the first shock has been relieved by motor reaction.... Anger, fear, sorrow, notwithstanding their distinctly painful initial stage, are often not only not avoided, but even deliberately sought."[138]

In the ordinary healthy organism, however, although the stimulants of strong emotion may be vaguely pleasurable, they do not have more than a general action on the sexual sphere, nor are they required for the due action of the sexual mechanism. But in a slightly abnormal organism—whether the anomaly is due to a congenital neuropathic condition, or to a possibly acquired neurasthenic condition, or merely to the physiological inadequacy of childhood or old age—the balance of nervous energy is less favorable for the adequate play of the ordinary energies in courtship. The sexual impulse is itself usually weaker, even when, as often happens, its irritability assumes the fallacious appearance of strength. It has become unusually sensitive to unusual stimuli and also, it is possible,—perhaps as a result of those conditions,—more liable to atavistic manifestations. An organism in this state becomes peculiarly apt to seize on the automatic sources of energy generated by emotion. The parched sexual instinct greedily drinks up and absorbs the force it obtains by applying abnormal stimuli to its emotional apparatus. It becomes largely, if not solely, dependent on the energy thus secured. The abnormal organism in this respect may become as dependent on anger or fear, and for the same reason, as in other respects it may become dependent on alcohol.

We see the process very well illustrated by the occasional action of the emotion of anger. In animals the connection between love and anger is so close that even normally, as Groos points out, in some birds the sight of an enemy may call out the gestures of courtship.[139] As Krafft-Ebing remarks, both love and anger "seek their object, try to possess themselves of it, and naturally exhaust themselves in a physical effect on it; both throw the psychomotor sphere into the most intense excitement, and by means of this excitement reach their normal expression."[140] Féré has well remarked that the impatience of desire may itself be regarded as a true state of anger, and Stanley Hall, in his admirable study of anger, notes that "erethism of the breasts or sexual parts" was among the physical manifestations of anger occurring in some of his cases, and in one case a seminal emission accompanied every violent outburst.[141]Thus it is that anger may be used to reinforce a weak sexual impulse, and cases have been recorded in which coitus could only be performed when the man had succeeded in working himself up into an artificial state of anger.[142] On the other hand, Féré has recorded a case in which the sexual excitement accompanying delayed orgasm was always transformed into anger, though without any true sadistic manifestations.[143]

As a not unexpected complementary phenomenon to this connection of anger and sexual emotion in the male, it is sometimes found that the spectacle of masculine anger excites pleasurable emotion in women. The case has been recorded of a woman who delighted in arousing anger for the pleasure it gave her, and who advised another woman to follow her example and excite her husband's anger, as nothing was so enjoyable as to see a man in a fury of rage[144]; Lombroso mentions a woman who was mostly frigid, but experienced sexual feelings when she heard anyone swearing; and a medical friend tells me of a lady considerably past middle age who experienced sexual erethism after listening to a heated argument between her husband and a friend on religious topics. The case has also been recorded of a masochistic man who found sexual satisfaction in masturbating while a woman, by his instructions, addressed him in the lowest possible terms of abuse.[145] Such a feeling doubtless underlies that delight in teasing men which is so common among young women. Stanley Hall, referring to the almost morbid dread of witnessing manifestations of anger felt by many women, remarks: "In animals, females are often described as watching with complacency the conflict of rival males for their possession, and it seems probable that the intense horror of this state, which many females report, is associated more or less unconsciously with the sexual rage which has followed it."[146] The dread may well be felt at least as much as regards the emotional state in themselves as in the males.

Even when the emotion aroused is disgust it may still act as a sexual stimulant. Stcherbak has narrated the instructive case of a very intelligent and elegant married lady of rather delicate constitution, an artist of some talent, who never experienced any pleasure in sexual intercourse, but ever since sexual feelings first began to be manifested at all (at the age of 18) has only experienced them in relation to disgusting things. Anything that is repulsive, like vomit, etc., causes vague but pleasurable feelings which she gradually came to recognize as sexual. The sight of a crushed frog will cause very definite sexual sensations. She has had many admirers and she has observed that a declaration of love by a disagreeable or even repulsive man sexually excites her, though she has no desire for sexual intercourse with him.[147]

After all that has gone before it is easy to see how the emotion of fear may act in an analogous manner to anger. Just as anger may reinforce the active forms of the sexual impulse to which it is allied, so fear may reinforce the passive forms of that impulse. The following observations, written by a lady, very well show how we may thus explain the sexual attractiveness of whipping: "The fascination of whipping, which has always greatly puzzled me, seems to be a sort of hankering after the stimulus of fear. In a wild state animals live in constant fear. In civilized life one but rarely feels it. A woman's pleasure in being afraid of a husband or lover may be an equivalent of a man's love of adventure; and the fear of children for their parents may be the dawning of the love of adventure. In a woman this desire of adventure receives a serious check when she begins to realize what she might be subjected to by a man if she gratified it. Excessive fear is demoralizing, but it seems to me that the idea of being whipped gives a sense of fear which is not excessive. It is almost the only kind of pain (physical) which is inflicted on children or women by persons whom they can love and trust, and with a moral object. Any other kind of bodily ill treatment suggests malignity and may rouse resentment, and, in extreme cases, an excess of fear which goes beyond the limits of pleasurable excitement. Given a hereditary feeling of this sort, I think it is helped by the want of actual experience, as the association with excitement is freed from the idea of pain as such." In his very valuable and suggestive study of fears, Stanley Hall, while recognizing the evil of excessive fear, has emphasized the emotional and even the intellectual benefits of fear, and the great part played by fear in the evolution of the race as "the rudimentary organ on the full development and subsequent reduction of which many of the best things in the soul are dependent." "Fears that paralyze some brains," he remarks, "are a good tonic for others. In some form and degree all need it always. Without the fear apparatus in us, what a wealth of motive would be lost!"[148]

It is on the basis of this tonic influence of fear that in some morbidly sensitive natures fear acts as a sexual stimulant. Cullerre has brought together a number of cases in both men and women, mostly neurasthenic, in which fits of extreme anxiety and dread, sometimes of a religious character and often in highly moral people, terminate in spontaneous orgasm or in masturbation.[149]

Professor Gurlitt mentions that his first full sexual emission took place in class at school, when he was absorbed in writing out the life of Aristides and very anxious lest he should not be able to complete it within the set time.[150]

Dread and anxiety not only excite sexual emotion, but in the more extreme morbid cases they may suppress and replace it. Terror, say Fliess, is transmuted coitus, and Freud believes that the neurosis of anxiety always has a sexual cause, while Ballet, Capgras, Löwenfeld, and others, though not regarding a sexual traumatism as the only cause, still regard it as frequent.

It is worthy of note that not only fear, but even so depressing an emotion as grief, may act as a sexual stimulant, more especially in women. This fact is not sufficiently recognized, though probably everyone can recall instances from his personal knowledge, such cases being generally regarded as inexplicable. It is, however, not more surprising that grief should be transformed into sexual emotion than that (as in a case recorded by Stanley Hall) it should manifest itself as anger. In any case we have to bear in mind the frequency of this psychological transformation in the presence of cases which might otherwise seem to call for a cynical interpretation.

The case has been recorded of an English lady of good social position who fell in love with an undertaker at her father's funeral and insisted on marrying him. It is known that some men have been so abnormally excited by the funeral trappings of death that only in such surroundings have they been able to effect coitus. A case has been recorded of a physician of unimpeachable morality who was unable to attend funerals, even of his own relatives, on account of the sexual excitement thus aroused. Funerals, tragedies at the theater, pictures of martyrdom, scenes of execution, and trials at the law-courts have been grouped together as arousing pleasure in many people, especially women. (C. F. von Schlichtegroll, *Sacher-Masoch und der Masochismus*, pp. 30-31.) Wakes and similar festivals may here find their psychological basis, and funerals are an unquestionable source of enjoyment among some people, especially of so-called "Celtic" race. The stimulating reaction after funerals is well known to many, and Leigh Hunt refers to this (in his *Autobiography*) as affecting the sincerely devoted friends who had just cremated Shelley.

It may well be, as Kiernan has argued (*Alienist and Neurologist*, 1891; *ibid.*, 1902, p. 263), that in the disturbance of emotional balance caused by grief the primitive instincts become peculiarly apt to respond to stimulus, and that in the aboulia of grief the mind is specially liable to become the prey to obsessions.

"When my child died at the age of 6 months," a correspondent writes, "I had a violent paroxysm of weeping and for some days I could not eat. When I kissed the dead boy for the last time (I had never seen a corpse before) I felt I had reached the depths of misery and could never smile or have any deep emotions again. Yet that night, though my thoughts had not strayed to sexual subjects since the child's death, I had a violent erection. I felt ashamed to desire carnal things when my dead child was still in the house, and explained to my wife. She was sympathetic, for her idea was that our common grief had intensified my love for her. I feel convinced, however, that my desire was the result of a stimulus propagated to the sexual centers from the centers affected by my grief, the transference of my emotion from one set of nerves to another. I do not perhaps express my meaning clearly."

How far the emotional influence of grief entered into the following episode it is impossible to say, for here it is probable that we are mainly concerned with one of those almost irresistible impulses by which adolescent girls are sometimes overcome. The narrative is from the lips of a reliable witness, a railway guard, who, some thirty years ago, when a youth of 18, in Cornwall, lodged with a man and woman who had a daughter of his own age. Some months later, when requiring a night's lodging, he called at the house, and was greeted warmly by the woman, who told him her husband had just died and that she and her daughter were very nervous and would be glad if he would stay the night, but that as the corpse occupied the other bedroom he would have to share their bed ("We don't think very much of that among us," my informant added). He agreed, and went to bed, and when, a little later, the two women also came to bed, the girl, at her own suggestion, lay next to the youth. Nothing happened during the night, but in the morning, when the mother went down to light the fire, the daughter immediately threw off the bedclothes, exposing her naked person, and before the youth had realized what was happening she had drawn him over on to her. He was so utterly surprised that nothing whatever happened, but the incident made a life-long impression on him.

In this connection reference may be made to the story of the Ephesian matron in Petronius; the story of the widow, overcome by grief, who watches by her husband's tomb, and very speedily falls into the arms of the soldier who is on guard. This story, in very various forms, is found in China and India, and has occurred repeatedly in European literature during the last two thousand years. The history of the wanderings of this story has been told by Grisebach (Eduard Grisebach, *Die Treulose Witwe*, third edition, 1877). It is not probable, however, that all the stories of this type are actually related; in any case it would seem that their vitality is due to the fact that they have been found to show a real correspondence to life; one may note, for instance, the curious tone of personal emotion with which George Chapman treated this theme in his play, *Widow's Tears*.

It may be added that, in explaining the resort to pain as an emotional stimulus, we have to take into account not only the biological and psychological considerations here brought forward, but also the abnormal physiological conditions under which stimuli usually felt as painful come specially to possess a sexually exciting influence. The neurasthenic and neuropathic states may be regarded as conditions of more or less permanent fatigue. It is true that under the conditions we are considering there may be an extreme sensitiveness to stimuli not usually felt as of sexual character, a kind of hyperesthesia; but hyperesthesia, it has well been said, is nothing but the beginning of anesthesia.[151] Sergeant Bertrand, the classical example of necrophily,[152] began to masturbate at the age of 9, stimulating a sexual impulse which may have been congenitally feeble by accompanying thoughts of ill-treating women. It was not till subsequently that he began to imagine that the women were corpses. The sadistic thoughts were only incidents in the emotional evolution, and the real object throughout was to procure strong emotion and not to inflict cruelty. Some observations of Féré's as to the conditions which influence the amount of muscular work accomplished with the ergograph are instructive from the present point of view: "Although sensibility diminishes in the course of fatigue," Féré found that "there are periods during which the excitability increases before it disappears. As fatigue increases, the perception of the intercurrent excitation is retarded; an odor is perceived as exciting before it is perceived as a differentiated sensation; the most fetid odors arouse feelings of well-being before being perceived as odors, and their painful quality only appears afterward, or is not noticed at all." And after recording a series of results with the ergograph obtained under the stimulus of unpleasant odors he remarks: "We are thus struck by two facts: the diminution of work during painful excitation, and its increase when the excitation has ceased. When the effects following the excitation have disappeared the diminution is more rapid than in the ordinary state. When the fatigue is manifested by a notable diminution, if the same excitation is brought into action again, no diminution is produced, but a more or less durable increase, exactly as though there had been an agreeable excitation. Moreover, the stimulus which appears painful in a state of repose loses that painful character either partially or completely when acting on the same subject in a more and more fatigued state." Féré defines a painful stimulus as a strong excitation which causes displays of energy which the will cannot utilize; when, as a result of diminished sensibility, the excitants are attenuated, the will can utilize them, and so there is no pain.[153] These experiments had no reference to the sexual instinct, but it will be seen at once that they have an extremely significant bearing on the subject before us, for they show us the mechanism of the process by which in an abnormal organism pain becomes a sexual stimulant.

[136]

Erasmus Darwin, *Zoönomia*, vol. i, p. 496.

[137]

K. Groos, *Spiele der Menschen*, pp. 200-210.

[138]

Hirn, *Origins of Art*, p. 54. Reference may here perhaps be made to the fact that unpleasant memories persist in women more than in men (*American Journal of Psychology*, 1899, p. 244). This had already been pointed out by Coleridge. "It is a remark that I have made many times," we find it said in one of his fragments (*Anima Poetæ*, p. 89), "and many times, I guess, shall repeat, that women are infinitely fonder of clinging to and beating about, hanging upon and keeping up, and reluctantly letting fall any doleful or painful or unpleasant subject, than men of the same class and rank."

[139]

Groos, *Spiele der Thiere*, p. 251. Maeder (*Jahrbuch für Psychoanalytische Forschungen*, 1909, vol. i, p. 149) mentions an epileptic girl of 22 who masturbates when she is in a rage with anyone.

[140]

Krafft-Ebing, *Psychopathia Sexualis*, English translation of tenth edition, p. 78.

[141]

Stanley Hall, "A Study of Anger," *American Journal of Psychology*, July, 1899, p. 549.

[142]

Krafft-Ebing refers to such a case as recorded by Schulz, *Psychopathia Sexualis*, p. 78.

[143]

Féré, *L'Instinct sexuel*, p. 213.

[144]

C. F. von Schlichtegroll, *Sacher-Masoch und der Masochismus*, p. 31.

[145]

Archivio di Psichiatria, vol. xv, p. 120. Mention may also be made of the cases (described as hysterical mixoscopia by Kiernan, *Alienist and Neurologist*, May, 1903) in which young women address to themselves anonymous letters of an abusive and disgusting character, and show them to others.

[146]

Stanley Hall, *loc. cit.*, p. 587.

[147]

Archives de Neurologie, Oct., 1907.

[148]

G. Stanley Hall, "A Study of Fears," *American Journal of Psychology*, vol. viii, No. 2.

[149]

A. Cullerre, "De l'Excitation Sexuelle dans les Psychopathies Anxieuses,"*Archives de Neurologie*, Feb., 1905.

[150]

L. Gurlitt (*Die Neue Generation*, July, 1909). Moll (*Sexualleben des Kindes*, p. 84) also give examples of the connection between anxiety and sexual excitement. Freud (*Der Wahn und die Traüme in Jensen's Gradiva*, p. 52) considers that in dream-interpretation we may replace "terror" by "sexual excitement." In noting the general sexual effects of fear, we need not strictly separate the group of cases in which the sexual effects are physical only, and fail to be circuited through the brain.

[151]

See the article on "Neurasthenia" by Rudolf Arndt in Tuke's *Dictionary of Psychological Medicine*.

[152]

Lunier, *Annales Médico-psychologiques*, 1849, p. 153.

[153]

Féré, *Comptes-rendus de la Société de Biologie*, December 15 and 22, 1900; *id.*, *Année Psychologique*, seventh year, 1901, pp. 82-129; more especially the same author's *Travail et Plaisir*, 1904.

VII.

Summary of Results Reached—The Joy of Emotional Expansion—The Satisfaction of the Craving for Power—The Influence of Neurasthenic and Neuropathic Conditions—The Problem of Pain in Love Largely Constitutes a Special Case of Erotic Symbolism.

It may seem to some that in our discussion of the relationships of love and pain we have covered a very wide field. This was inevitable. The subject is peculiarly difficult and complex, and if we are to gain a real insight into its nature we must not attempt to force the facts to fit into any narrow and artificial formulas of our own construction. Yet, as we have unraveled this seemingly confused mass of phenomena it will not have escaped the careful reader that the apparently diverse threads we have disentangled run in a parallel and uniform manner; they all have a like source and they all converge to a like result. We have seen that the starting-point of the whole group of manifestations must be found in the essential facts of courtship among animal and primitive human societies. Pain is seldom very far from some of the phases of primitive courtship; but it is not the pain which is the essential element in courtship, it is the state of intense emotion, of tumescence, with which at any moment, in some shape or another, pain may, in some way or another, be brought into connection. So that we have come to see that in the phrase "love and pain" we have to understand by "pain" a state of intense emotional excitement with which pain in the stricter sense may be associated, but is by no means necessarily associated. It is the strong emotion which exerts the irresistible fascination in the lover, in his partner, or in both. The pain is merely the means to that end. It is the lever which is employed to bring the emotional force to bear on the sexual impulse. The question of love and pain is mainly a question of emotional dynamics.

In attaining this view of our subject we have learned that any impulse of true cruelty is almost outside the field altogether. The mistake was indeed obvious and inevitable. Let us suppose that every musical instrument is sensitive and that every musical performance involves the infliction of pain on the instrument. It would then be very difficult indeed to realize that the pleasure of music lies by no means in the infliction of pain. We should certainly find would-be scientific and analytical people ready to declare that the pleasure of music is the pleasure of giving pain, and that the emotional effects of music are due to the pain thus inflicted. In algolagnia, as in music, it is not cruelty that is sought; it is the joy of being plunged among the waves of that great primitive ocean of emotions which underlies the variegated world of our everyday lives, and pain—a pain which, as we have seen, is often deprived so far as possible of cruelty, though sometimes by very thin and feeble devices—is merely the channel by which that ocean is reached.

If we try to carry our inquiry beyond the point we have been content to reach, and ask ourselves why this emotional intoxication exerts so irresistible a fascination, we might find a final reply in the explanation of Nietzsche—who regarded this kind of intoxication as of great significance both in life and in art—that it gives us the consciousness of energy and the satisfaction of our craving for power.[154] To carry the inquiry to this point would be, however, to take it into a somewhat speculative and metaphysical region, and we have perhaps done well not to attempt to analyze further the joy of emotional expansion. We must be content to regard the profound satisfaction of emotion as due to a widespread motor excitement, the elements of which we cannot yet completely analyze.[155]

It is because the joy of emotional intoxication is the end really sought that we have to regard the supposed opposition between "sadism" and "masochism" as unimportant and indeed misleading. The emotional value of pain is equally great whether the pain is inflicted, suffered, witnessed, or merely exists as a mental imagination, and there is no reason why it should not coexist in all these forms in the same person, as, in fact, we frequently find it.

The particular emotions which are invoked by pain to reinforce the sexual impulse are more especially anger and fear, and, as we have seen, these two very powerful and primitive emotions are—on the active and passive sides, respectively—the emotions most constantly brought into play in animal and early human courtship; so that they naturally constitute the emotional reservoirs from which the sexual impulse may still most easily draw. It is not difficult to show that the various forms in which "pain"—as we must here understand pain—is employed in the service of the sexual impulse are mainly manifestations or transformations of anger or fear, either in their simple or usually more complex forms, in some of which anger and fear may be mingled.

We thus accept the biological origin of the psychological association between love and pain; it is traceable to the phenomena of animal courtship. We do not on this account exclude the more direct physiological factor. It may seem surprising that manifestations that have their origin in primeval forms of courtship should in many cases coincide with actual sensations of definite anatomical base today, and still more surprising that these traditional manifestations and actual sensations should so often be complementary to each other in their active and passive aspects: that is to say, that the pleasure of whipping should be matched by the pleasure of being whipped, the pleasure of mock strangling by the pleasure of being so strangled, that pain inflicted is not more desirable than pain suffered. But such coincidence is of the very essence of the whole group of phenomena. The manifestations of courtship were from the first conditioned by physiological facts; it is not strange that they should always tend to run *pari passu* with physiological facts. The manifestations which failed to find anchorage in physiological relationships might well tend to die out. Even under the most normal circumstances, in healthy persons of healthy heredity, the manifestations we have been considering are liable to make themselves felt. Under such circumstances, however, they never become of the first importance in the sexual process; they are often little more than play. It is only under neurasthenic or neuropathic conditions—that is to say, in an organism which from acquired or congenital causes, and usually perhaps both, has become enfeebled, irritable, "fatigued"—that these manifestations are liable to flourish vigorously, to come to the forefront of sexual consciousness, and even to attain such seriously urgent importance that they may in themselves constitute the entire end and aim of sexual desire. Under these pathological conditions, pain, in the broad and special sense in which we have been obliged to define it, becomes a welcome tonic and a more or less indispensable stimulant to the sexual system.

It will not have escaped the careful reader that in following out our subject we have sometimes been brought into contact with manifestations which scarcely seem to come within any definition of pain. This is undoubtedly so, and the references to these manifestations were not accidental, for they serve to indicate the real bearings of our subject. The relationships of love and pain constitute a subject at once of so much gravity and so much psychological significance that it was well to devote to them a special study. But pain, as we have here to understand it, largely constitutes a special case of what we shall later learn to know as erotic symbolism: that is to say, the psychic condition in which a part of the sexual process, a single idea or group of ideas, tends to assume unusual importance, or even to occupy the whole field of sexual consciousness, the part becoming a symbol that stands for the whole. When we come to the discussion of this great group of abnormal sexual manifestations it will frequently be necessary to refer to the results we have reached in studying the sexual significance of pain.

[154]
See, for instance, the section "Zur Physiologie der Kunst" in Nietzsche's fragmentary work, *Der Wille zur Macht*, Werke, Bd. xv. Groos (*Spiele der Menschen*, p. 89) refers to the significance of the fact that nearly all races have special methods of procuring intoxication. *Cf.* Partridge's study of the psychology of alcohol (*American Journal of Psychology*, April, 1900). "It is hard to imagine," this writer remarks of intoxicants, "what the religious or social consciousness of primitive man would have been without them."

[155]
The muscular element is the most conspicuous in emotion, though it is not possible, as a careful student of the emotions (H. R. Marshall, *Pain, Pleasure, and Æsthetics*, p. 84) well points out, "to limit the physical activities involved with the emotions to such effects of voluntary innervation or alteration of size of blood-vessels or spasm of organic muscle, as Lange seems to think determines them; nor to increase or decrease of muscle-power, as Féré's results might suggest; nor to such changes, in relation of size of capillaries, in

voluntary innervation, in respiratory and heart functioning, as Lehmann has observed. Emotions seem to me to be coincidents of reactions of the whole organism tending to certain results."

THE SEXUAL IMPULSE IN WOMEN.

A special and detailed study of the normal characters of the sexual impulse in men seems unnecessary. I have elsewhere discussed various aspects of the male sexual impulse, and others remain for later discussion. But to deal with it broadly as a whole seems unnecessary, if only because it is predominantly open and aggressive. Moreover, since the constitution of society has largely been in the hands of men, the nature of the sexual impulse in men has largely been expressed in the written and unwritten codes of social law. The sexual instinct in women is much more elusive. This, indeed, is involved at the outset in the organic psychological play of male and female, manifesting itself in the phenomena of modesty and courting. The same elusiveness, the same mocking mystery, meet us throughout when we seek to investigate the manifestations of the sexual impulse in women. Nor is it easy to find any full and authentic record of a social state clearly founded in sexual matters on the demands of woman's nature.

An illustration of our ignorance and bias in these matters is furnished by the relationship of marriage, celibacy, and divorce to suicide in the two sexes. There can be no doubt that the sexual emotions of women have a profound influence in determining suicide. This is indicated, among other facts, by a comparison of the suicide-rate in the sexes according to age; while in men the frequency of suicide increases progressively throughout life, in women there is an arrest after the age of 30; that is to say, when the period of most intense sexual emotion has been passed. This phenomenon is witnessed among peoples so unlike as the French, the Prussians, and the Italians. Now, how do marriage and divorce affect the sexual liability to suicide? We are always accustomed to say that marriage protects women, and it is even asserted that men have self-sacrificingly maintained the institution of marriage mainly for the benefit of women. Professor Durkheim, however, who has studied suicide elaborately from the sociological standpoint, so far as possible eliminating fallacies, has in recent years thrown considerable doubt on the current assumption. He shows that if we take the tendency to suicide as a test, and eliminate the influence of children, who are an undoubted protection to women, it is not women, but men, who are protected by marriage, and that the protection of women from suicide increases regularly as divorces increase. After discussing these points exhaustively, "we reach a conclusion," he states, "considerably removed from the current view of marriage and the part it plays. It is regarded as having been instituted for the sake of the wife and to protect her weakness against masculine caprices. Monogamy, especially, is very often presented as a sacrifice of man's polygamous instincts, made in order to ameliorate the condition of woman in marriage. In reality, whatever may have been the historical causes which determined this restriction, it is man who has profited most. The liberty which he has thus renounced could only have been a source of torment to him. Woman had not the same reasons for abandoning freedom, and from this point of view we may say that in submitting to the same rule it is she who has made the sacrifice." (E. Durkheim, *Le Suicide*, 1897, pp. 186-214, 289-311.)

There is possibly some significance in the varying incidence of insanity in unmarried men and unmarried women as compared with the married. At Erlangen, for example, Hagen found that among insane women the preponderance of the single over the married is not nearly so great as among insane men, marriage appearing to exert a much more marked prophylactic influence in the case of men than of women. (F. W. Hagen, *Statistische Untersuchungen über Geisteskrankheiten*, 1876, p. 153.) The phenomena are here, however, highly complex, and, as Hagen himself points out, the prophylactic influence of marriage, while very probable, is not the only or even the chief factor at work.

It is worth noting that exactly the same sexual difference may be traced in England. It appears that, in ratio to similar groups in the general population (taking the years 1876-1900, inclusive), the number of admissions to asylums is the same for both sexes among married people (*i.e.*, 8.5), but for the single it is larger among the men (4.8 to 4.5), as also it is among the widowed (17.9 to 13.9) (*Fifty-sixth Annual Report of the Commissioners in Lunacy, England and Wales*, 1902, p. 141). This would seem to indicate that when living apart from men the tendency to insanity is less in women, but is raised to the male level when the sexes live together in marriage.

Much the same seems to hold true of criminality. It was long since noted by Horsley that in England marriage decidedly increases the tendency to crime in women, though it decidedly decreases it in men. Prinzing has shown (*Zeitschrift für Sozialwissenschaft*, Bd. ii, 1899) that this is also the case in Germany.

Similarly marriage decreases the tendency of men to become habitual drunkards and increases that of women. Notwithstanding the fact that the average age of the men is greater than that of the women, the majority of the men admitted to the inebriate reformatories under the English Inebriates Acts are single; the majority of the women are married; of 865 women so admitted 32 per cent, were single, 50 per cent, married, and 18 per cent, widows. (*British Medical Journal*, Sept. 2, 1911, p. 518.)

It thus happens that even the elementary characters of the sexual impulse in women still arouse, even among the most competent physiological and medical authorities,—not least so when they are themselves women,—the most divergent opinions. Its very existence even may be said to be questioned. It would generally be agreed that among men the strength of the sexual impulse varies within a considerable range, but that it is very rarely altogether absent, such total absence being abnormal and probably more or less pathological. But if applied to women, this statement is by no means always accepted. By many, sexual anesthesia is considered natural in women, some even declaring that any other opinion would be degrading to women; even by those who do not hold this opinion it is believed that there is an unnatural prevalence of sexual frigidity among civilized women. On these grounds it is desirable to deal generally with this and other elementary questions of allied character.

I.

The Primitive View of Women—As a Supernatural Element in Life—As Peculiarly Embodying the Sexual Instinct—The Modern Tendency to Underestimate the Sexual Impulse in Women—This Tendency Confined to Recent Times—Sexual Anæsthesia—Its Prevalence—Difficulties in Investigating the Subject—Some Attempts to Investigate it— Sexual Anesthesia must be Regarded as Abnormal—The Tendency to Spontaneous Manifestations of the Sexual Impulse in Young Girls at Puberty.

From very early times it seems possible to trace two streams of opinion regarding women: on the one hand, a tendency to regard women as a supernatural element in life, more or less superior to men, and, on the other hand, a tendency to regard women as especially embodying the sexual instinct and as peculiarly prone to exhibit its manifestations.

In the most primitive societies, indeed, the two views seem to be to some extent amalgamated; or, it should rather be said, they have not yet been differentiated; and, as in such societies it is usual to venerate the generative principle of nature and its embodiments in the human body and in human functions, such a co-ordination of ideas is entirely rational. But with the development of culture the tendency is for this homogeneous conception to be split up into two inharmonious tendencies. Even apart from Christianity and before its advent this may be noted. It was, however, to Christianity and the Christian ascetic spirit that we owe the complete differentiation and extreme development which these opposing views have reached. The condemnation of sexuality involved the glorification of the virgin; and indifference, even contempt, was felt for the woman who exercised sexual functions. It remained open to anyone, according to his own temperament, to identify the typical average woman with the one or with the other type; all the fund of latent sexual emotion which no ascetic rule can crush out of the human heart assured the picturesque idealization alike of the angelic and the diabolic types of woman. We may trace the same influence subtly lurking even in the most would-be scientific statements of anthropologists and physicians today.[156]

It may not be out of place to recall at this point, once more, the fact, fairly obvious indeed, that the judgments of men concerning women are very rarely matters of cold scientific observation, but are colored both by their own sexual emotions and by their own moral attitude toward the sexual impulse. The ascetic who is unsuccessfully warring with his own carnal impulses may (like the voluptuary) see nothing in women but incarnations of sexual impulse; the ascetic who has subdued his own carnal impulses may see no elements of sex in women at all. Thus the opinions regarding this matter are not only tinged by elements of primitive culture, but by elements of individual disposition. Statements about the sexual impulses of women often tell us less about women than about the persons who make them.

The curious manner in which for men women become incarnations of the sexual impulse is shown by the tendency of both general and personal names for women to become applicable to prostitutes only. This is the case with the words "garce" and "fille" in French, "Mädchen" and "Dirne" in German, as well as with the French "catin" (Catherine) and the German "Metze" (Mathilde). (See, *e.g.,* R. Kleinpaul, *Die Räthsel der Sprache,* 1890, pp. 197-198.)

At the same time, though we have to recognize the presence of elements which color and distort in various ways the judgments of men regarding women, it must not be hastily assumed that these elements render discussion of the question altogether unprofitable. In most cases such prejudices lead chiefly to a one-sided solution of facts, against which we can guard.

While, however, these two opposing currents of opinion are of very ancient origin, it is only within quite recent times, and only in two or three countries, that they have led to any marked difference of opinion regarding the sexual aptitude of women. In ancient times men blamed women for concupiscence or praised them for chastity, but it seems to have been reserved for the nineteenth century to state that women are apt to be congenitally incapable of experiencing complete sexual satisfaction, and peculiarly liable to sexual anesthesia. This idea appears to have been almost unknown to the eighteenth century. During the last century, however, and more especially in England, Germany, and Italy, this opinion has been frequently set down, sometimes even as a matter of course, with a tincture of contempt or pity for any woman afflicted with sexual emotions.

In the treatise *On Generation* (chapter v), which until recent times was commonly ascribed to Hippocrates, it is stated that men have greater pleasure in coitus than women, though the pleasure of women lasts longer, and this opinion, though not usually accepted, was treated with great respect by medical authors down to the end of the seventeenth century. Thus A. Laurentius (Du Laurens), after a long discussion, decides that men have stronger sexual desire and greater pleasure in coitus than women. (*Historia Anatomica Humani Corporis,* 1599, lib. viii, quest, ii and vii.)

About half a century ago a book entitled *Functions and Disorders of the Reproductive Organs,* by W. Acton, a surgeon, passed through many editions and was popularly regarded as a standard authority on the subjects with which it deals. This extraordinary book is almost solely concerned with men; the author evidently regards the function of reproduction as almost exclusively appertaining to men. Women, if "well brought up," are, and should be, he states, in England, absolutely ignorant of all matters concerning it. "I should say," this author again remarks, "that the majority of women (happily for society) are not very much troubled with sexual feeling of any kind." The supposition that women do possess sexual feelings he considers "a vile aspersion."

In the article "Generation," contained in another medical work belonging to the middle of the nineteenth century,—Rees's *Cyclopedia,*—we find the following statement: "That a mucous fluid is sometimes found in coition from the internal organs and vagina is undoubted; but this only happens in lascivious women, or such as live luxuriously."

Gall had stated decisively that the sexual desires of men are stronger and more imperious than those of women. (*Fonctions du Cerveau,* 1825, vol. iii, pp. 241-271.)

Raciborski declared that three-fourths of women merely endure the approaches of men. (*De la Puberté chez la Femme,* 1844, p. 486.)

"When the question is carefully inquired into and without prejudice," said Lawson Tait, "it is found that women have their sexual appetites far less developed than men."

(Lawson Tait, "Remote Effects of Removal of the Uterine Appendages,"*Provincial Medical Journal*, May, 1891.) "The sexual instinct is very powerful in man and comparatively weak in women," he stated elsewhere (*Diseases of Women*, 1889, p. 60).

Hammond stated that, leaving prostitutes out of consideration, it is doubtful if in one-tenth of the instances of intercourse they [women] experience the slightest pleasurable sensation from first to last (Hammond, *Sexual Impotence*, p. 300), and he considered (p. 281) that this condition was sometimes congenital.

Lombroso and Ferrero consider that sexual sensibility, as well as all other forms of sensibility, is less pronounced in women, and they bring forward various facts and opinions which seem to them to point in the same direction. "Woman is naturally and organically frigid." At the same time they consider that, while erethism is less, sexuality is greater than in men. (Lombroso and Ferrero, *La Donna Delinquente, la Prostituta, e la Donna Normale*, 1893, pp. 54-58.)

"It is an altogether false idea," Fehling declared, in his rectorial address at the University of Basel in 1891, "that a young woman has just as strong an impulse to the opposite sex as a young man.... The appearance of the sexual side in the love of a young girl is pathological." (H. Fehling, *Die Bestimmung der Frau*, 1892, p. 18.) In his *Lehrbuch der Frauenkrankheiten* the same gynecological authority states his belief that half of all women are not sexually excitable.

Krafft-Ebing was of opinion that women require less sexual satisfaction than men, being less sensual. (Krafft-Ebing, "Ueber Neurosen und Psychosen durch sexuelle Abstinenz," *Jahrbücher für Psychiatrie*, 1888, Bd. viii, ht. I and 2.)

"In the normal woman, especially of the higher social classes," states Windscheid, "the sexual instinct is acquired, not inborn; when it is inborn, or awakes by itself, there is abnormality. Since women do not know this instinct before marriage, they do not miss it when they have no occasion in life to learn it." (F. Windscheid, "Die Beziehungen zwischen Gynäkologie und Neurologie," *Zentralblatt für Gynäkologie*, 1896, No. 22; quoted by. Moll, *Libido Sexualis*, Bd. i, p. 271.)

"The sensuality of men," Moll states, "is in my opinion very much greater than that of women." (A. Moll, *Die Konträre Sexualempfindung*, third edition, 1899, p. 592.)

"Women are, in general, less sensual than men," remarks Näcke, "notwithstanding the alleged greater nervous supply of their sexual organs." (P. Näcke, "Kritisches zum Kapitel der Sexualität," *Archiv für Psychiatrie*, 1899, p. 341.)

Löwenfeld states that in normal young girls the specifically sexual feelings are absolutely unknown; so that desire cannot exist in them. Putting aside the not inconsiderable proportion of women in whom this absence of desire may persist and be permanent, even after sexual relationships have begun, thus constituting absolute frigidity, in a still larger number desire remains extremely moderate, constituting a state of relative frigidity. He adds that he cannot unconditionally support the view of Fürbringer, who is inclined to ascribe sexual coldness to the majority of German married women. (L. Löwenfeld, *Sexualleben und Nervenleiden*, 1899, second edition, p. 11.)

Adler, who discusses the question at some length, decides that the sexual needs of women are less than those of men, though in some cases the orgasm in quantity and quality greatly exceeds that of men. He believes, not only that the sexual impulse in women is absolutely less than in men, and requires stronger stimulation to arouse it, but that also it suffers from a latency due to inhibition, which acts like a foreign body in the brain (analogous to the psychic trauma of Breuer and Freud in hysteria), and demands great skill in the man who is to awaken the woman to love. (O. Adler, *Die Mangelhafte Geschlechtsempfindung des Weibes*, 1904, pp. 47, 126 *et seq.*; also enlarged second edition, 1911; *id.*, "Die Frigide Frau," *Sexual-Probleme*, Jan., 1912.)

It must not, however, be supposed that this view of the natural tendency of women to frigidity has everywhere found acceptance. It is not only an opinion of very recent growth, but is confined, on the whole, to a few countries.

"Turn to history," wrote Brierre de Boismont, "and on every page you will be able to recognize the predominance of erotic ideas in women." It is the same today, he adds, and he attributes it to the fact that men are more easily able to gratify their sexual impulses. (*Des Hallucinations*, 1862, p. 431.)

The laws of Manu attribute to women concupiscence and anger, the love of bed and of adornment.

The Jews attributed to women greater sexual desire than to men. This is illustrated, according to Knobel (as quoted by Dillmann), by *Genesis*, chapter iii, v. 16.

In Greek antiquity the romance and sentiment of love were mainly felt toward persons of the same sex, and were divorced from the more purely sexual feelings felt for persons of opposite sex. Theognis compared marriage to cattle-breeding. In love between men and women the latter were nearly always regarded as taking the more active part. In all Greek love-stories of early date the woman falls in love with the man, and never the reverse. Æschylus makes even a father assume that his daughters will misbehave if left to themselves. Euripides emphasized the importance of women; "The Euripidean woman who 'falls in love' thinks first of all: 'How can I seduce the man I love?'" (E. F. M.Benecke, *Antimachus of Colophon and the Position of Women in Greek Poetry*, 1896, pp. 34, 54.)

The most famous passage in Latin literature as to the question of whether men or women obtain greater pleasure from sexual intercourse is that in which Ovid narrates the legend of Tiresias (*Metamorphoses*, iii, 317-333). Tiresias, having been both a man and a woman, decided in favor of women. This passage was frequently quoted down to the eighteenth century.

In a passage quoted from a lost work of Galen by the Arabian biographer, Abu-l-Faraj, that great physician says of the Christians "that they practice celibacy, that even many of their women do so." So that in Galen's opinion it was more difficult for a woman than for a man to be continent.

The same view is widely prevalent among Arabic authors, and there is an Arabic saying that "The longing of the woman for the penis is greater than that of the man for the vulva."

In China, remarks Dr. Coltman, "when an old gentleman of my acquaintance was visiting me my little daughter, 5 years old, ran into the room, and, climbing upon my knee, kissed me. My visitor expressed his surprise, and remarked: 'We never kiss our daughters when they are so large; we may when they are very small, but not after they are 3 years old,' said he, 'because it is apt to excite in them bad emotions.'" (Coltman, *The Chinese*, 1900, p. 99.)

The early Christian Fathers clearly show that they regard women as more inclined to sexual enjoyment than men. That was, for instance, the opinion of Tertullian (*De Virginibus Velandis*, chapter x), and it is clearly implied in some of St. Jerome's epistles.

Notwithstanding the influence of Christianity, among the vigorous barbarian races of medieval Europe, the existence of sexual appetite in women was not considered to be, as it later became, a matter to be concealed or denied. Thus in 1068 the ecclesiastical historian, Ordericus Vitalis (himself half Norman and half English), narrates that the wives of the Norman knights who had accompanied William the Conqueror to England two years earlier sent over to their husbands to say that they were consumed by the fierce names of desire ("sæva libidinis face urebantur"), and that if their husbands failed to return very shortly they proposed to take other husbands. It is added that this threat brought a few husbands back to their wanton ladies ("lascivis dominabus suis").

During the medieval period in Europe, largely in consequence, no doubt, of the predominance of ascetic ideals set up by men who naturally regarded woman as the symbol of sex, the doctrine of the incontinence of woman became firmly fixed, and it is unnecessary and unprofitable to quote examples. It is sufficient to mention the very comprehensive statement of Jean de Meung (in the *Roman de la Rose*, 9903):—

"Toutes estes, serés, ou fûtesDe fait ou de volunté putes."

The satirical Jean de Meung was, however, a somewhat extreme and untypical representative of his age, and the fourteenth century Johannes de Sancto Amando (Jean de St. Amand) gives a somewhat more scientifically based opinion (quoted by Pagel,*Neue litterarische Beiträge zur Mittelalterlichen Medicin*, 1896, p. 30) that sexual desire is stronger in women than in men.

Humanism and the spread of the Renaissance movement brought in a spirit more sympathetic to women. Soon after, especially in Italy and France, we begin to find attempts at analyzing the sexual emotions, which are not always without a certain subtlety. In the seventeenth century a book of this kind was written by Venette. In matters of love, Venette declared, "men are but children compared to women. In these matters women have a more lively imagination, and they usually have more leisure to think of love. Women are much more lascivious and amorous than men." This is the conclusion reached in a chapter devoted to the question whether men or women are the more amorous. In a subsequent chapter, dealing with the question whether men or women receive more pleasure from the sexual embrace, Venette concludes, after admitting the great difficulty of the question, that man's pleasure is greater, but woman's lasts longer. (N. Venette, *De la Génération de l'Homme ou Tableau de l'Amour Conjugal*, Amsterdam, 1688.)

At a much earlier date, however, Montaigne had discussed this matter with his usual wisdom, and, while pointing out that men have imposed their own rule of life on women and their own ideals, and have demanded from them opposite and contradictory virtues,—a statement not yet antiquated,—he argues that women are incomparably more apt and more ardent in love than men are, and that in this matter they always know far more than men can teach them, for "it is a discipline that is born in their veins." (Montaigne, *Essais*, book iii, chapter v.)

The old physiologists generally mentioned the appearance of sexual desire in girls as one of the normal signs of puberty. This may be seen in the numerous quotations brought together by Schurig, in his *Parthenologia*, cap. ii.

A long succession of distinguished physicians throughout the seventeenth century discussed at more or less length the relative amount of sexual desire in men and women, and the relative degree of their pleasure in coitus. It is remarkable that, although they usually attach great weight to the supposed opinion of Hippocrates in the opposite sense, most of them decide that both desire and pleasure are greater in women.

Plazzonus decides that women have more sources of pleasure in coitus than men because of the larger extent of surface excited; and if it were not so, he adds, women would not be induced to incur the pains and risks of pregnancy and childbirth. (Plazzonus,*De Partibus Generationi Inservientibus*, 1621, lib. ii, cap. xiii.)

"Without doubt," says Ferrand, "woman is more passionate than man, and more often torn by the evils of love." (Ferrand, *De la Maladie d'Amour*, 1623, chapter ii.)

Zacchia, mainly on *a priori* grounds, concludes that women have more pleasure in coitus than men. (Zacchia, *Quæstiones Medico-legales*, 1630, lib. iii, quest, vii.)

Sinibaldus, discussing whether men or women have more salacity, decides in favor of women. (J. B. Sinibaldus, *Geneanthropeia*, 1642, lib. ii, tract. ii, cap. v.)

Hornius believed that women have greater sexual pleasure than men, though he mainly supported his opinion by the authority of classical poets. (Hornius, *Historic Naturalis*, 1670, lib. iii, cap. i.)

Nenter describes what we may now call women's affectability, and considers that it makes them more prone than men to the sexual emotions, as is shown by the fact that, notwithstanding their modesty, they sometimes make sexual advances. This greater proneness of women to the sexual impulse is, he remarks, entirely natural and right, for the work of generation is mainly carried on by women, and love is its basis: "generationis fundamentum est amor." (G. P. Nenter, *Theoria Hominis Sani*, 1714, cap. v, memb. ii.)

The above opinions of seventeenth-century physicians are quoted from the original sources. Schurig, in his *Gynæcologia*, (pp. 46-50 and 71-81), quotes a number of passages on this subject from medical authorities of the same period, on which I have not drawn.

Sénancour, in his fine and suggestive book on love, first published in 1806, asks: "Has sexual pleasure the same power on the sex which less loudly demands it? It has more, at all events in some respects. The very vigor and laboriousness of men may lead them to neglect love, but the constant cares of maternity make women feel how important it must ever be to them. We must remember also that in men the special emotions of love only have a single focus, while in women the organs of lactation are united to those of conception. Our feelings are all determined by these material causes." (Sénancour, *De l'Amour*, fourth edition,

1834, vol. i, p. 68.) A later psychologist of love, this time a woman, Ellen Key, states that woman's erotic demands, though more silent than man's, are stronger. (Ellen Key, *Ueber Liebe und Ehe*, p. 138.)

Michael Ryan considered that sexual enjoyment "is more delicious and protracted" in women, and ascribed this to a more sensitive nervous system, a finer and more delicate skin, more acute feelings, and the fact that in women the mammæ are the seat of a vivid sensibility in sympathy with the uterus. (M. Ryan,*Philosophy of Marriage*, 1837, p. 153.)

Busch was inclined to think women have greater sexual pleasure than men. (D. W. H. Busch, *Das Geschlechtsleben des Weibes*, 1839, vol. i, p. 69.) Kobelt held that the anatomical conformation of the sexual organs in women led to the conclusion that this must be the case.

Guttceit, speaking of his thirty years' medical experience in Russia, says: "In Russia at all events, a girl, as very many have acknowledged to me, cannot resist the ever stronger impulses of sex beyond the twenty-second or twenty-third year. And if she cannot do so in natural ways she adopts artificial ways. The belief that the feminine sex feels the stimulus of sex less than the male is quite false." (Guttceit, *Dreissig Jahre Praxis*, 1873, theil i, p. 313.)

In Scandinavia, according to Vedeler, the sexual emotions are at least as strong in women as in men (Vedeler, "De Impotentia Feminarum," *Norsk Magazin for Laegevidenskaben*, March, 1894). In Sweden, Dr. Eklund, of Stockholm, remarking that from 25 to 33 per cent. of the births are illegitimate, adds: "We hardly ever hear anyone talk of a woman having been seduced, simply because the lust is at the worst in the woman, who, as a rule, is the seducing party." (Eklund, *Transactions of the American Association of Obstetricians*, Philadelphia, 1892, p. 307.)

On the opposite side of the Baltic, in the Königsberg district, the same observation has been made. Intercourse before marriage is the rule in most villages of this agricultural district, among the working classes, with or without intention of subsequent marriage; "the girls are often the seducing parties, or at least very willing; they seek to bind their lovers to them and compel them to marriage." In the Köslin district of Pomerania, where intercourse between the girls and youths is common, the girls come to the youths' rooms even more frequently than the youths to the girls'. In some of the Dantzig districts the girls give themselves to the youths, and even seduce them, sometimes, but not always, with a view of marriage. (Wittenberg, *Die geschlechtsittlichen Verhalten der Landbewohner im Deutschen Reiche*, 1895, Bd. i, pp. 47, 61, 83.)

Mantegazza devoted great attention to this point in several of theworks he published during fifty years, and was decidedly of the opinion that the sexual emotions are much stronger in women than in men, and that women have much more enjoyment in sexual intercourse. In his *Fisiologia del Piacere* he supports this view, and refers to the greater complexity of the genital apparatus in women (as well as its larger surface and more protected position), to what he considers to be the keener sensibility of women generally, to the passivity of women, etc.; and he considers that sexual pleasure is rendered more seductive to women by the mystery in which it is veiled for them by modesty and our social habits. In a more recent work (*Fisiologia della Donna*, cap. viii) Mantegazza returns to this subject, and remarks that long experience, while confirming his early opinion, has modified it to the extent that he now believes that, as compared with men, the sexual emotions of women vary within far wider limits. Among men few are quite insensitive to the physical pleasures of love, while, on the other hand, few are thrown by the violence of its emotional manifestations into a state of syncope or convulsions. Among women, while some are absolutely insensitive, others (as in cases with which he was acquainted) are so violently excited by the paradise of physical love that, after the sexual embrace, they faint or fall into a cataleptic condition for several hours.

"Physical sex is a larger factor in the life of the woman.... If this be true of the physical element, it is equally true of the mental element." (Dr. Elizabeth Blackwell, *The Human Element in Sex*, fifth edition, 1894, p. 47.)

"In the female sex," remarks Clouston, "reproduction is a more dominant function of the organism than in the male, and has far larger, if not more intense, relationships to feeling, judgment, and volition." (Clouston, *Neuroses of Development*, 1891.)

"It may be said," Marro states, "that in woman the visceral system reacts, if not with greater intensity, certainly in a more general manner, to all the impressions, having a sexual basis, which dominate the life of woman, if not as sexual emotions properly so called, as related emotions closely dependent on the reproductive instinct." (A. Marro, *La Pubertà*, 1898, p. 233.)

Forel also believed (*Die Sexuelle Frage*, p. 274) that women are more erotic than men.

The gynecologist Kisch states his belief that "The sexual impulse is so powerful in women that at certain periods of life its primitive force dominates her whole nature, and there can be no room left for reason to argue concerning reproduction; on the contrary, union is desired even in the presence of the fear of reproduction or when there can be no question of it." He regards absence of sexual feeling in women as pathological. (Kisch, *Sterilität des Weibes*, second edition, pp. 205-206.) In his later work (*The Sexual Life of Woman*) Kisch again asserts that sexual impulse always exists in mature women (in the absence of organic sexual defect and cerebral disease), though it varies in strength and may be repressed. In adolescent girls, however, it is weaker than in youths of the same age. After she has had sexual experiences, Kisch maintains, a woman's sexual emotions are just as powerful as a man's, though she has more motives than a man for controlling them.

Eulenburg is of the same opinion as Kisch, and sharply criticises the loose assertion of some authorities who have expressed themselves in an opposite sense. (A. Eulenburg, *Sexuale Neuropathie*, pp. 88-90; the same author has dealt with the point in the *Zukunft*, December 2, 1893.)

Kossmann states that the opinion as to the widespread existence of frigidity among women is a fable. (Kossmann, *Allgemeine Gynæcologie*, 1903, p. 362.)

Bloch concludes that "in most cases the sexual coldness of women is in fact only apparent, either due to the concealment of glowing sexuality beneath the veil of outward reticence prescribed by conventional morality, or else to the husband who has not succeeded in arousing erotic sensations which are complicated and with difficulty awakened.... The sexual sensibility of women is certainly different from that of men, but in strength it is at least as great." (Iwan Bloch, *Das Sexualleben unserer Zeit* 1907, ch. v.)

Nyström, also, after devoting a chapter to the discussion of the causes of sexual coldness in women, concludes: "My conviction, founded on experience, is, that only a small number of women would be without sexual feeling if sound views and teaching prevailed in respect to the sexual life, if due weight were given to inner devotion and tender caresses as the preliminaries of love in marriage, and if couples who wish to avoid pregnancy would adopt sensible preventive methods instead of *coitus interruptus*." (A. Nyström, *Das Geschlichtsleben und seine Gesetze*, eighth edition, 1907, p. 177.)

We thus find two opinions widely current: one, of world-wide existence and almost universally accepted in those ages and centers in which life is lived most nakedly, according to which the sexual impulse is stronger in women than in men; another, now widely prevalent in many countries, according to which the sexual instinct is distinctly weaker in women, if, indeed, it may not be regarded as normally absent altogether. A third view is possible: it may be held that there is no difference at all. This view, formerly not very widely held, is that of the French physiologist, Beaunis, as it is of Winckel; while Rohleder, who formerly held that sexual feeling tends to be defective in women, now believes that men and women are equal in sexual impulse.

At an earlier period, however, Donatus (*De Medica Historia Mirabili*, 1613, lib. iv, cap. xvii) held the same view, and remarked that sometimes men and sometimes women are the more salacious, varying with the individual. Roubaud (*De l'Impuissance*, 1855, p. 38) stated that the question is so difficult as to be insoluble.

In dealing with the characteristics of the sexual impulse in women, it will be seen, we have to consider the prevalence in them of what is commonly termed (in its slightest forms) frigidity or hyphedonia, and (in more complete form) sexual anesthesia or anaphrodism, or erotic blindness, or anhedonia.[157]

Many modern writers have referred to the prevalence of frigidity among women. Shufeldt believes (*Pacific Medical Journal*, Nov., 1907) that 75 per cent, of married women in New York are afflicted with sexual frigidity, and that it is on the increase; it is rare, however, he adds, among Jewish women. Hegar gives 50 per cent, as the proportion of sexually anesthetic women; Fürbringer says the majority of women are so. Effertz (quoted by Löwenfeld, *Sexualleben und Nervenleiden*, p. 11, apparently with approval) regards 10 per cent, among women generally as sexually anesthetic, but only 1 per cent, men. Moll states (Eulenburg's *Encyclopädie*, fourth edition, art. "Geschlechtstrieb") that the prevalence of sexual anesthesia among German women varies, according to different authorities, from 10 to 66 per cent. Elsewhere Moll (*Konträre Sexualempfindung*, third edition, 1890, p. 510) emphasizes the statement that "sexual anesthesia in women is much more frequent than is generally supposed." He explains that he is referring to the physical element of pleasure and satisfaction in intercourse, and of desire for intercourse. He adds that the psychic side of love is often more conspicuous in women than in men. He cannot agree with Sollier that this kind of sexual frigidity is a symptom of hysteria. Féré (*L'Instinct Sexuel*, second edition, p. 112), in referring to the greater frequency of sexual anesthesia in women, remarks that it is often associated with neuropathic states, as well as with anomalies of the genital organs, or general troubles of nutrition, and is usually acquired. Some authors attribute great importance to amenorrhea in this connection; one investigator has found that in 4 out of 14 cases of absolute amenorrhea sexual feeling was absent. Löwenfeld, again (*Sexualleben und Nervenleiden*), referring to the common misconception that nervous disorder is associated with increased sexual desire, points out that nervously degenerate women far more often display frigidity than increased sexual desire. Elsewhere (*Ueber die Sexuelle Konstitution*) Löwenfeld says it is only among the upper classes that sexual anesthesia is common. Campbell Clark, also, showed some years ago that, in young women with a tendency to chlorosis and a predisposition to insanity, defects of pelvic and mammary development are very prevalent. (*Journal of Mental Science*, October, 1888.)

As regards the older medical authors, Schurig (*Spermatologia*, 1720, p. 243, and *Gynæcologia*, 1730, p. 81) brought together from the literature and from his own knowledge cases of women who felt no pleasure in coitus, as well as of some men who had erections without pleasure.

There is, however, much uncertainty as to what precisely is meant by sexual frigidity or anesthesia. All the old medical authors carefully distinguish between the heat of sexual desire and the actual presence of pleasure in coitus; many modern writers also properly separate *libido* from *voluptas*, since it is quite possible to experience sexual desires and not to be able to obtain their gratification during sexual intercourse, and it is possible to hold, with Mantegazza, that women naturally have stronger sexual impulses than men, but are more liable than men to experience sexual anesthesia. But it is very much more difficult than most people seem to suppose, to obtain quite precise and definite data concerning the absence of either *voluptas* or *libido* in a woman. Even if we accept the statement of the woman who asserts that she has either or both, the statement of their absence is by no means equally conclusive and final. As even Adler—who discusses this question fully and has very pronounced opinions about it—admits, there are women who stoutly deny the existence of any sexual feelings until such feelings are actually discovered.[158] Some of the most marked characteristics of the sexual impulse in women, moreover,—its association with modesty, its comparatively late development, its seeming passivity, its need of stimulation,—all combine to render difficult the final pronouncement that a woman is sexually frigid. Most significant of all in this connection is the complexity of the sexual apparatus in women and the corresponding psychic difficulty—based on the fundamental principle of sexual selection— of finding a fitting mate. The fact that a woman is cold with one man or even with a succession of men by no means shows that she is not apt to experience sexual emotions; it merely shows that these men have not been able to arouse them. "I recall two very striking cases," a distinguished gynecologist, the late Dr. Engelmann, of Boston, wrote to me, "of very attractive young married women—one having had a child, the other a miscarriage— who were both absolutely cold to their husbands, as told me by both husband and wife. They could not understand desire or passion, and would not even believe that it existed. Yet, both these women with other men developed ardent passion, all the stronger perhaps because it had been so long latent." In such cases it is scarcely necessary to invoke Adler's theory of a morbid inhibition, or "foreign body in consciousness," which has to be

113

overcome. We are simply in the presence of the natural fact that the female throughout nature not only requires much loving, but is usually fastidious in the choice of a lover. In the human species this natural fact is often disguised and perverted. Women are not always free to choose the man whom they would prefer as a lover, nor even free to find out whether the man they prefer sexually fits them; they are, moreover, very often extremely ignorant of the whole question of sex, and the victims of the prejudice and false conventions they have been taught. On the one hand, they are driven into an unnatural primness and austerity; on the other hand, they rebound to an equally unnatural facility or even promiscuity. Thus it happens that the men who find that a large number of women are not so facile as they themselves are, and as they have found a large number of women to be, rush to the conclusion that women tend to be "sexually anesthetic." If we wish to be accurate, it is very doubtful whether we can assert that a woman is ever absolutely without the aptitude for sexual satisfaction.[159] She may unquestionably be without any conscious desire for actual coitus. But if we realize to how large an extent woman is a sexual organism, and how diffused and even unconscious the sexual impulses may be, it becomes very difficult to assert that she has never shown any manifestation of the sexual impulse. All we can assert with some degree of positiveness in some cases is that she has not manifested sexual gratification, more particularly as shown by the occurrence of the orgasm, but that is very far indeed from warranting us to assert that she never will experience such gratification or still less that she is organically incapable of experiencing it.[160] It is therefore quite impossible to follow Adler when he asks us to accept the existence of a condition which he solemnly terms *anæsthesia sexualis completa idiopathica*, in which there is no mechanical difficulty in the way or psychic inhibition, but an "absolute" lack of sexual sensibility and a complete absence of sexual inclination.[161]

It is instructive to observe that Adler himself knows no "pure" case of this condition. To find such a case he has to go back nearly two centuries to Madame de Warens, to whom he devotes a whole chapter. He has, moreover, had the courage in writing this chapter to rely entirely on Rousseau's *Confessions*, which were written nearly half a century later than the episodes they narrated, and are therefore full of inaccuracies, besides being founded on an imperfect and false knowledge of Madame de Warens's earlier life, and written by a man who was, there can be no doubt, not able to arouse women's passions. Adler shows himself completely ignorant of the historical investigations of De Montet, Mugnier, Ritter, and others which, during recent years, have thrown a flood of light on the life and character of Madame de Warens, and not even acquainted with the highly significant fact that she was hysterical.[162] This is the basis of "fact" on which we are asked to accept *anæsthesia sexualis completa idiopathica*.[163]

"In dealing with the alleged absence of the sexual impulse," a well-informed medical correspondent writes from America, "much caution has to be used in accepting statements as to its absence, from the fact that most women fear by the admission to place themselves in an impure category. I am also satisfied that influx of women into universities, etc., is often due to the sexual impulse causing restlessness, and that this factor finds expression in the prurient prudishness so often presenting itself in such women, which interferes with coeducation. This is becoming especially noticeable at the University of Chicago, where prudishness interferes with classical, biological, sociological, and physiological discussion in the classroom. There have been complaints by such women that a given professor has not left out embryological facts not in themselves in any way implying indelicacy. I have even been informed that the opinion is often expressed in college dormitories that embryological facts and discussions should be left out of a course intended for both sexes." Such prudishness, it is scarcely necessary to remark, whether found in women or men, indicates a mind that has become morbidly sensitive to sexual impressions. For the healthy mind embryological and allied facts have no emotionally sexual significance, and there is, therefore, no need to shun them.

Kolischer, of Chicago ("Sexual Frigidity in Women," *American Journal of Obstetrics*, Sept., 1905), points out that it is often the failure of the husband to produce sexual excitement in the wife which leads to voluntary repression of sexual sensation on her part, or an acquired sexual anesthesia. "Sexual excitement," he remarks, "not brought to its natural climax, the reaction leaves the woman in a very disagreeable condition, and repeated occurrences of this kind may even lead to general nervous disturbances. Some of these unfortunate women learn to suppress their sexual sensation so as to avoid all these disagreeable sequelæ. Such a state of affairs is not only unfortunate, because it deprives the female partner of her natural rights, but it is also to be deplored because it practically brings down such a married woman to the level of the prostitute."

In illustration of the prevalence of inhibitions of various kinds, from without and from within, in suppressing or disguising sexual feeling in women, I may quote the following observations by an American lady concerning a series of women of her acquaintance:—

"Mrs. A. This woman is handsome and healthy. She has never had children, much to the grief of herself and her husband. The man is also handsome and attractive. Mrs. A. once asked me if love-making between me and my husband ever originated with me. I replied it was as often so as not, and she said that in that event she could not see how passion between husband and wife could be regulated. When I seemed not to be ashamed of the matter, but rather to be positive in my views that it should be so, she at once tried to impress me with the fact that she did not wish me to think she 'could not be aroused.' This woman several times hinted that she had learned a great amount that was not edifying at boarding school, and I always felt that, with proper encouragement, she would have retailed suggestive stories.

"Mrs. B. This woman lives to please her husband, who is a spoiled man. She gave birth to a child soon after marriage, but was left an invalid for some years. She told me coition always hurt her, and she said it made her sick to see her husband nude. I was therefore surprised, years afterward, to hear her say, in reply to a remark of another person, 'Yes; women are not only as passionate as men, I am sure they are more so.' I therefore questioned the lack of passion she had on former occasions avowed, or else felt convinced her improvement in health had made intercourse pleasant.

"Miss C. A teacher. She is emotional and easily becomes hysterical. Her life has been one of self-sacrifice and her rearing most Puritanical. She told me she thought women did not crave sexual satisfaction unless it had been aroused in them. I consider her one who physically is injured by not having it.

"Mrs. D. After being married a few years this person told me she thought intercourse 'horrid.' Some years after this, however, she fell in love with a man not her husband, which caused their separation. She always fancied men in love with her, and she told me that she and her husband tried to live without intercourse, fearing more children, but they could not do it; she also told of trying to refrain, for the same purpose, until safe parts of the menstrual month, but that 'was just the time she cared least for it.' These remarks made me doubt the sincerity of the first.

"Mrs. E. said she enjoyed intercourse as well as her husband, and she 'didn't see why she should not say so.' This same woman, whether using a current phrase or not, afterward said her husband 'did not bother her very often.'

"Mrs. F., the mother of several children, was married to a man she neither loved nor respected, but she said that when a strange man touched her it made her tremble all over.

"Mrs. G., the mother of many children, divorced on account of the dissipation, drinking and otherwise, of her husband. She is of the creole type, but large and almost repulsive. She is a brilliant talker and she supports herself by writing. She has fallen in love with a number of young men, 'wildly, madly, passionately,' as one of them told me, and I am sure she suffers greatly from the lack of satisfaction. She would no doubt procure it if it were possible.

"I believe," the writer concludes, "women are as passionate as men, but the enforced restraint of years possibly smothers it. The fear of having children and the methods to prevent conception are, I am sure, potent factors in the injury to the emotions of married women. Perhaps the lack of intercourse acts less disastrously upon a woman because of the renewed feeling which comes after each menstrual period."

As bearing on the causes which have led to the disguise and misinterpretation of the sexual impulse in women I may quote the following communication from another lady:—

"I do think the coldness of women has been greatly exaggerated. Men's theoretically ideal woman (though they don't care so much about it in practice) is passionless, and women are afraid to admit that they have any desire for sexual pleasure. Rousseau, who was not very straight-laced, excuses the conduct of Madame de Warens on the ground that it was not the result of passion: an aggravation rather than a palliation of the offense, if society viewed it from the point of view of any other fault. Even in the modern novels written by the 'new woman' the longing for maternity, always an honorable sentiment, is dragged in to veil the so-called 'lower' desire. That some women, at any rate, have very strong passions and that great suffering is entailed by their repression is not, I am sure, sufficiently recognized, even by women themselves.

"Besides the 'passionless ideal' which checks their sincerity, there are many causes which serve to disguise a woman's feelings to herself and make her seem to herself colder than she really is. Briefly these are:—

"1. Unrecognized disease of the reproductive organs, especially after the birth of children. A friend of mine lamented to me her inability to feel pleasure, though she had done so before the birth of her child, then 3 years old. With considerable difficulty I persuaded her to see a doctor, who told her all the reproductive organs were seriously congested; so that for three years she had lived in ignorance and regret for her husband's sake and her own.

"2. The dread of recommencing, once having suffered them, all the pains and discomforts of child-bearing.

"3. Even when precautions are taken, much bother and anxiety is involved, which has a very dampening effect on excitement.

"4. The fact that men will never take any trouble to find out what specially excites a woman. A woman, as a rule, is at some pains to find out the little things which particularly affect the man she loves,—it may be a trick of speech, a rose in her hair, or what not,—and she makes use of her knowledge. But do you know one man who will take the same trouble? (It is difficult to specify, as what pleases one person may not another. I find that the things that affect me personally are the following: [a] Admiration for a man's mental capacity will translate itself sometimes into direct physical excitement. [b] Scents of white flowers, like tuberose or syringa. [c] The sight of fireflies. [d] The idea or the reality of suspension. [e] Occasionally absolute passivity.)

"5. The fact that many women satisfy their husbands when themselves disinclined. This is like eating jam when one does not fancy it, and has a similar effect. It is a great mistake, in my opinion, to do so, except very rarely. A man, though perhaps cross at the time, prefers, I believe, to gratify himself a few times, when the woman also enjoys it, to many times when she does not.

"6. The masochistic tendency of women, or their desire for subjection to the man they love. I believe no point in the whole question is more misunderstood than this. Nearly every man imagines that to secure a woman's love and respect he must give her her own way in small things, and compel her obedience in great ones. Every man who desires success with a woman should exactly reverse that theory."

When we are faced by these various and often conflicting statements of opinion it seems necessary to obtain, if possible, a definite basis of objective fact. It would be fairly obvious in any case, and it becomes unquestionable in view of the statements I have brought together, that the best-informed and most sagacious clinical observers, when giving an opinion on a very difficult and elusive subject which they have not studied with any attention and method, are liable to make unguarded assertions; sometimes, also, they become the victims of ethical or pseudoethical prejudices, so as to be most easily influenced by that class of cases which happens to fit in best with their prepossessions.[164] In order to reach any conclusions on a reasonable basis it is necessary to take a series of unselected individuals and to ascertain carefully the condition of the sexual impulse in each.

At present, however, this is extremely difficult to do at all satisfactorily, and quite impossible, indeed, to do in a manner likely to yield absolutely unimpeachable results. Nevertheless, a few series of observations have been made. Thus, Dr. Harry Campbell[165] records the result of an investigation, carried on in his hospital practice, of 52 married women of the poorer class; they were not patients, but ordinary, healthy working-class women, and the inquiry was not made directly, but of the husbands, who were patients.

Sexual instinct was said to be present in 12 cases before marriage, and absent in 40; in 13 of the 40 it never appeared at all; so that it altogether appeared in 39, or in the ratio of something over 75 per cent. Among the 12 in whom it existed before marriage it was said to have appeared in most with puberty; in 3, however, a few years before puberty, and in 2 a few years later. In 2 of those in whom it appeared before puberty, menstruation began late; in the third it rose almost to nymphomania on the day preceding the first menstruation. In nearly all the cases desire was said to be stronger in the husband than in the wife; when it was stronger in the wife, the husband was exceptionally indifferent. Of the 13 in whom desire was absent after marriage, 5 had been married for a period under two years, and Campbell remarks that it would be wrong to conclude that it would never develop in these cases, for in this group of cases the appearance of sexual instinct was sometimes a matter of days, sometimes of years, after the date of marriage. In two-thirds of the cases there was a diminution of desire, usually gradual, at the climacteric; in the remaining third there was either no change or exaltation of desire. The most important general result, Campbell concludes, is that "the sexual instinct is very much less intense in woman than in man," and to this he elsewhere adds a corollary that "the sexual instinct in the civilized woman is, I believe, tending to atrophy."

An eminent gynecologist, the late Dr. Matthews Duncan, has (in his work on *Sterility in Women*) presented a table which, although foreign to this subject, has a certain bearing on the matter. Matthews Duncan, believing that the absence of sexual desire and of sexual pleasure in coitus are powerful influences working for sterility, noted their presence or absence in a number of cases, and found that, among 191 sterile women between the ages of 15 and 45, 152, or 79 per cent., acknowledged the presence of sexual desire; and among 196 sterile women (mostly the same cases), 134, or 68 per cent., acknowledged the presence of sexual pleasure in coitus. Omitting the cases over 35 years of age, which were comparatively few, the largest proportion of affirmative answers, both as regards sexual pleasure and sexual desire, was from between 30 and 34 years of age. Matthews Duncan assumes that the absence of sexual desire and sexual pleasure in women is thoroughly abnormal.[166]

An English non-medical author, in the course of a thoughtful discussion of sexual phenomena, revealing considerable knowledge and observation,[167] has devoted a chapter to this subject in another of its aspects. Without attempting to ascertain the normal strength of the sexual instinct in women, he briefly describes 11 cases of "sexual anesthesia" in Women (in 2 or 3 of which there appears, however, to be an element of latent homosexuality) from among the circle of his own friends. This author concludes that sexual coldness is very common among English women, and that it involves questions of great social and ethical importance.

I have not met with any series of observations made among seemingly healthy and normal women in other countries; there are, however, various series of somewhat abnormal cases in which the point was noted, and the results are not uninstructive. Thus, in Vienna at Krafft-Ebing's psychiatric clinic, Gattel (*Ueber die sexuellen Ursachen der Neurasthenie und Angstneurose*, 1898) carefully investigated the cases of 42 women, mostly at the height of sexual life,—*i.e.*, between 20 and 35,—who were suffering from slight nervous disorders, especially neurasthenia and mild hysteria, but none of them from grave nervous or other disease. Of these 42, at least 17 had masturbated, at one time or another, either before or after marriage, in order to obtain relief of sexual feelings. In the case of 4 it is stated that they do not obtain sexual satisfaction in marriage, but in these cases only *coitus interruptus* is practised, and the fact that the absence of sexual satisfaction was complained of seems to indicate an aptitude for experiencing it. These 4 cases can therefore scarcely be regarded as exceptions. In all the other cases sexual desire, sexual excitement, or sexual satisfaction is always clearly indicated, and in a considerable proportion of cases it is noted that the sexual impulse is very strongly developed. This series is valuable, since the facts of the sexual life are, as far as possible, recorded with much precision. The significance of the facts varies, however, according to the view taken as to the causation of neurasthenia and allied conditions of slight nervous disorder. Gattel argues that sexual irregularities are a peculiarly fruitful, if not invariable, source of such disorders; according to the more commonly accepted view this is not so. If we accept the more usual view, these women fairly correspond to average women of lower class; if, however, we accept Gattel's view, they may possess the sexual instinct in a more marked degree than average women.

In a series of 116 German women in whom the operation of removing the ovaries was performed, Pfister usually noted briefly in what way the sexual impulse was affected by the operation ("Die Wirkung der Castration auf den Weiblichen Organismus,"*Archiv für Gynäkologie*, 1898, p. 583). In 13 cases (all but 3 unmarried) the presence of sexual desire at any time was denied, and 2 of these expressed disgust of sexual matters. In 12 cases the point is left doubtful. In all the other cases sexual desire had once been present, and in 2 or 3 cases it was acknowledged to be so strong as to approach nymphomania. In about 30 of these (not including any in which it was previously very strong) it was extinguished by castration, in a few others it was diminished, and in the rest unaffected. Thus, when we exclude the 12 cases in which the point was not apparently investigated, and the 10 unmarried women, in whom it may have been latent or unavowed, we find that, of 94 married women, 91 women acknowledged the existence of sexual desire and only 3 denied it.

Schröter, again in Germany, has investigated the manifestations of the sexual impulse among 402 insane women in the asylum at Eichberg in Rheingau. ("Wird bei jungen Unverheiratheten zur Zeit der Menstruation stärkere sexuelle Erregheit beobaehtet?"*Allgemeine Zeitschrift für Psychiatrie*, vol. lvi, 1899, pp. 321-333.) There is no reason to suppose that the insane represent a class of the community specially liable to sexual emotion, although its manifestations may become unrestrained and conspicuous under the influence of insanity; and at the same time, while the appearance of such manifestations is evidence of the aptitude for sexual emotions, their absence may be only due to disease, seclusion, or to an intact power of self-control.

Of the 402 women, 166 were married and 236 unmarried. Schröter divided them into four groups: (1) those below 20; (2) those between 20 and 30; (3) those between 30 and 40; (4) those from 40 to the menopause. The patients included persons from the lowest class of the population, and only about a quarter of them could fairly be regarded as curable. Thus the manifestations of sexuality were diminished, for with advance of mental disease sexual manifestations cease to appear. Schröter only counted those cases in which the sexual manifestations were decided and fairly constant at the menstrual epoch; if not visibly manifested, sexual feeling was not taken into account. Sexual phenomena accompanied the entry of the menstrual epoch in 141 cases: *i.e.*, in 20 (or in the proportion of 72 per cent.) of the first group, consisting entirely of unmarried women; in 33 (or 28 per cent.) of the second group; in 55 (or 35 per cent.) of the third group; and in 33 (or 33 per cent.) of the fourth group. It was found that 181 patients showed no sexual phenomena at any time, while 80 showed sexual phenomena frequently between the menstrual epochs, but only in a slight degree, and not at all during the period. At all ages sexual manifestations were more prevalent among the unmarried than among the married, though this difference became regularly and progressively less with increase in age.

Schröter inclines to think that sexual excitement is commoner among insane women belonging to the lower social classes than in those belonging to the better classes. Among 184 women in a private asylum, only 13 (6.13 per cent.) showed very marked and constant excitement at menstrual periods. He points out, however, that this may be due to a greater ability to restrain the manifestations of feeling.

There is some interest in Schröter's results, though they cannot be put on a line with inquiries made among the sane; they only represent the prevalence of the grossest and strongest sexual manifestations when freed from the restraints of sanity.

As a slight contribution toward the question, I have selected a series of 12 cases of women of whose sexual development I possess precise information, with the following results: In 2 cases distinct sexual feeling was experienced spontaneously at the age of 7 and 8, but the complete orgasm only occurred some years after puberty; in 5 cases sexual feeling appeared spontaneously for a few months to a year after the appearance of menstruation, which began between 12 and 14 years of age, usually at 13; in another case sexual feeling first appeared shortly after menstruation began, but not spontaneously, being called out by a lover's advances; in the remaining 4 cases sexual emotion never became definite and conscious until adult life (the ages being 26, 27, 34, 35), in 2 cases through being made love

118

to, and in 2 cases through self-manipulation out of accident or curiosity. It is noteworthy that the sexual feelings first developed in adult life were usually as strong as those arising at puberty. It may be added that, of these 12 women, 9 had at some time or another masturbated (4 shortly after puberty, 5 in adult life), but, except in 1 case, rarely and at intervals. All belong to the middle class, 2 or 3 leading easy, though not idle, lives, while all the others are engaged in professional or other avocations often involving severe labor. They differ widely in character and mental ability; but, while 2 or 3 might be regarded as slightly abnormal, they are all fairly healthy.

I am inclined to believe that the experiences of the foregoing group are fairly typical of the social class to which they belong. I may, however, bring forward another series of 35 women, varying in age from 18 to 40 (with 2 exceptions all over 25), and in every respect comparable with the smaller group, but concerning whom my knowledge, though reliable, is usually less precise and detailed. In this group 5 state that they have never experienced sexual emotion, these being all unmarried and leading strictly chaste lives; in 18 cases the sexual impulse may be described as strong, or is so considered by the subject herself; in 9 cases it is only moderate; in 3 it is very slight when evoked, and with difficulty evoked, in 1 of these only appearing two years after marriage, in another the exhaustion and worry of household cares being assigned for its comparative absence. It is noteworthy that all the more highly intelligent, energetic women in the series appear in the group of those with strong sexual emotions, and also that severe mental and physical labor, even when cultivated for this purpose, has usually had little or no influence in relieving sexual emotion.

An American physician in the State of Connecticut sends me the following notes concerning a series of 13 married women, taken, as they occurred, in obstetric practice. They are in every way respectable and moral women:—

"Mrs. A. says that her husband does not give her sufficient sexual attention, as he fears they will have more children than he can properly care for. Mrs. B. always enjoys intercourse; so does Mrs. C. Mrs. D. is easily excited and very fond of sexual attention. Mrs. E. likes intercourse if her husband is careful not to hurt her. Mrs. F. never had any sexual desire until after second marriage, but it is now very urgent at times. Mrs. G. is not easily excited, but has never objected to her husband's attention. Mrs. H. would prefer to have her husband exhibit more attention. Mrs. I. never refused her husband, but he does not trouble her much. Mrs. J. thinks that three or four times a week is satisfactory, but would not object to nightly intercourse. Mrs. K. does not think that her husband could give her more than she would like. Mrs. L. would prefer to live with a woman if it were not for sexual intercourse. Mrs. M., aged 40, says that her husband, aged 65, insists upon intercourse three times every night, and that he keeps her tired and disgusted. She each time has at least one orgasm, and would not object to reasonable attention."

It may be remarked that, while these results in English women of the middle class are in fair agreement with the German and Austrian observations I have quoted, they differ from Campbell's results among women of the working class in London. This discrepancy is, perhaps, not difficult to explain. While the conditions of upper-class life may possibly be peculiarly favorable to the development of the sexual emotions, among the working classes in London, where the stress of the struggle for existence under bad hygienic conditions is so severe, they may be peculiarly unfavorable. It is thus possible that there really are a smaller number of women experiencing sexual emotion among the class dealt with by Campbell than among the class to which my series belong.[168]

A more serious consideration is the method of investigation. A working man, who is perhaps unintelligent outside his own work, and in many cases married to a woman who is superior in refinement, may possibly be able to arouse his wife's sexual emotions, and also able to ascertain what those emotions are, and be willing to answer questions truthfully on this point, to the best of his ability, but he is by no means a witness whose evidence is final. While, however, Campbell's facts may not be quite unquestionable, I am inclined to agree with his conclusion, and Mantegazza's, that there is a very great range of variation in this matter, and that there is no age at which the sexual impulse in women may not appear. A lady who has received the confidence of very many women tells me that she has never found a woman who was without sexual feeling. I should myself be inclined to say that it is extremely difficult to find a woman who is without the aptitude for sexual emotion, although a great variety of circumstances may hinder, temporarily or permanently, the development of this latent aptitude. In other words, while the latent sexual aptitude may always be present, the sexual impulse is liable to be defective and the aptitude to remain latent, with consequent deficiency of sexual emotion, and absence of sexual satisfaction.

This is not only indicated by the considerable proportion of my cases in which there is only moderate or slight sexual feeling. I have ample evidence that in many cases the element of pain, which may almost be said to be normal in the establishment of the sexual function, is never merged, as it normally is, in pleasurable sensations on the full establishment of sexual relationships. Sometimes, no doubt, this may be due to dyspareunia. Sometimes there may be an absolute sexual anesthesia, whether of congenital or hysterical origin. I have been told of the case of a married lady who has never been able to obtain sexual pleasure, although she has had relations with several men, partly to try if she could obtain the experience, and partly to please them; the very fact that the motives for sexual relationships arose from no stronger impulse itself indicates a congenital defect on the psychic as well as on the physical side. But, as a rule, the sexual anesthesia involved is not absolute, but lies in a disinclination to the sexual act due to various causes, in a defect of strong sexual impulse, and an inaptitude for the sexual orgasm.

I am indebted to a lady who has written largely on the woman question, and is herself the mother of a numerous family, for several letters in regard to the prevalence among women of sexual coldness, a condition which she regards as by no means to be regretted. She considers that in all her own children the sexual impulse is very slightly developed, the boys being indifferent to women, the girls cold toward men and with no desire to marry, though all are intelligent and affectionate, the girls showing a very delicate and refined kind of beauty. (A large selection of photographs accompanied this communication.) Something of the same tendency is said to mark the stocks from which this family springs, and they are said to be notable for their longevity, healthiness, and disinclination for excesses of all kinds. It is scarcely necessary to remark that a mother, however highly intelligent, is by no means an infallible judge as to the presence or absence in her children of so shy, subtle, and elusive an impulse as that of sex. At the same time I am by no means disposed to question the existence in individuals, and even in families or stocks, of a relatively weak sexual impulse, which, while still enabling procreation to take place, is accompanied by no strong attraction to the opposite sex and no marked inclination for marriage. (Adler, *op. cit.*, p. 168, found such a condition transmitted from mother to daughter.) Such persons often possess a delicate type of beauty. Even, however, when the health is good there seems usually to be a certain lack of vitality.

It seems to me that a state of sexual anesthesia, relative or absolute, cannot be considered as anything but abnormal. To take even the lowest ground, the satisfaction of the reproductive function ought to be at least as gratifying as the evacuation of the bowels or bladder; while, if we take, as we certainly must, higher ground than this, an act which is at once the supreme fact and symbol of love and the supreme creative act cannot under normal conditions be other than the most pleasurable of all acts, or it would stand in violent opposition to all that we find in nature.

How natural the sexual impulse is in women, whatever difficulties may arise in regard to its complete gratification, is clearly seen when we come to consider the frequency with which in young women we witness its more or less instinctive manifestations. Such manifestations are liable to occur in a specially marked manner in the years immediately following the establishment of puberty, and are the more impressive when we remember the comparatively passive part played by the female generally in the game of courtship, and the immense social force working on women to compel them to even an unnatural extension of that passive part. The manifestations to which I allude not only occur with most frequency in young girls, but, contrary to the common belief, they seem to occur chiefly in innocent and unperverted girls. The more vicious are skillful enough to avoid the necessity for any such open manifestations. We have to bear this in mind when confronted by flagrant sexual phenomena in young girls.

"A young girl," says Hammer ("Ueber die Sinnlichkeit gesunder Jungfrauen," *Die Neue Generation,* Aug., 1911), "who has not previously adopted any method of self-gratification experiences at the beginning of puberty, about the time of the first menstruation and the sprouting of the pubic hair, in the absence of all stimulation by a man, spontaneous sexual tendencies of both local and psychic nature. On the psychic side there is a feeling of emptiness and dissatisfaction, a need of subjection and of serving, and, if the opportunity has so far been absent, the craving to see masculine nudity and to learn the facts of procreation. Side by side with these wishes, there are at the same time inhibitory desires, such as the wish to keep herself pure, either for a man whom she represents to herself as the 'ideal,' or for her parents, who must not be worried, or as a member of a chosen people in whose spirit she must live and die, or out of love to Jesus or to some saint. On the physical side, there is the feeling of fresh power and energy, of enterprise; the agreeable tension of the genital regions, which easily become moist. Then there is the feeling of overirritability and excess of tension, and the need of relieving the tension through pinches, blows, tight lacing, and so forth. If the girl remains innocent of sex satisfaction, there takes place during sleep, at regular intervals of about three days, more or less the relief and emission of the tense glands, not corresponding to the menstrual period, but to intercourse, and serving better than sexual instruction to represent to her the phenomena of intercourse. If at this period actual intercourse takes place, it is, as a rule, free from pain, as also is the introduction of the speculum. Without any seduction from without, the chaste girl now frequently finds a way to relieve the excessive tension without the aid of a man. It is self-abuse that leads gradually to the production of pain in defloration. The menstrual phenomena correspond to birth; self-gratification or relief during sleep to intercourse." This statement of the matter is somewhat too absolute and unqualified. Under the artificial conditions of civilization the inhibitory influences of training speedily work powerfully, and more or less successfully, in banishing sexual phenomena into the subconscious, sometimes to work all the mischief there which Freud attributes to them. It must also be said (as I have pointed out in the discussion of Auto-erotism in another volume) that sexual dreams seem to be the exception rather than the rule in innocent girls. It remains true that sexual phenomena in girls at puberty must not be regarded as morbid or unnatural. There is also very good reason for believing (even apart from the testimony of so experienced a gynecologist as Hammer) that on the physical side sexual processes tend to be accomplished with a facility that is often lost in later years with prolonged chastity. This is true alike of intercourse and of childbirth. (See vol. vi of these *Studies,* ch. xii.)

Even, however, in the case of adults the active part played by women in real life in matters of love by no means corresponds to the conventional ideas on these subjects. No doubt nearly every woman receives her sexual initiation from an older and more experienced man. But, on the other hand, nearly every man receives his first initiation through the active and designed steps taken by an older and more experienced woman. It is too often forgotten by those who write on these subjects that the man who seduces a woman has usually himself in the first place been "seduced" by a woman.

A well-known physician in Chicago tells me that on making inquiry of 25 middle-class married men in succession be found that 16 had been first seduced by a woman. An officer in the Indian Medical Service writes to me as follows: "Once at a club in Burma we were some 25 at table and the subject of first intercourse came up. All had been led astray by servants save 2, whom their sisters' governesses had initiated. We were all men in the 'service,' so the facts may be taken to be typical of what occurs in our stratum of society. All had had sexual relations with respectable unmarried girls, and most with the wives of men known to their fathers, in some instances these being old enough to be their lovers' mothers. Apparently up to the age of 17 none had dared to make the first advances, yet from the age of 13 onward all had had ample opportunity for gratifying their sexual instincts with women. Though all had been to public schools where homosexuality was known to occur, yet (as I can assert from intimate knowledge) none had given signs of inversion or perversion in Burma."

In Russia, Tchlenoff, investigating the sexual life of over 2000 Moscow students of upper and middle class (*Archives d'Anthropologie Criminelle,* Oct.-Nov., 1908), found that in half of them the first coitus took place between 14 and 17 years of age; in 41 per cent, with prostitutes, in 39 per cent, with servants, and in 10 per cent, with married women. In 41 per cent, the young man declared that he had taken the initiative, in 25 per cent, the women took it, and in 23 per cent, the incitement came from a comrade.

The histories I have recorded in Appendix B (as well as in the two following volumes of these *Studies*) very well illustrate the tendency of young girls to manifest sexual impulses when freed from the constraint which they feel in the presence of adult men and from the fear of consequences. These histories show especially how very frequently nurse-maids and servant-girls effect the sexual initiation of the young boys intrusted to them. How common this impulse is among adolescent girls of low social class is indicated by the fact that certainly the majority of middle-class men can recall instances from their own childhood. (I here leave out of account the widespread practice among nurses of soothing very young children in their charge by manipulating the sexual organs.)

A medical correspondent, in emphasizing this point, writes that "many boys will tell you that, if a nurse-girl is allowed to sleep in the same room with them, she will attempt sexual manipulations. Either the girl gets into bed with the boy and pulling him on to her tickles the penis and inserts it into the vulva, making the boy imitate sexual movements, or she simply masturbates the child, to get him excited and interested, often showing him the female sexual opening in herself or in his sisters, teaching him to finger it. In fact, a nurse-girl may ruin a boy, chiefly, I think, because she has been brought up to regard the sexual organs as a mystery, and is in utter ignorance about them. She thus takes the opportunity of investigating the boy's penis to find out how it works, etc., in order to satisfy her curiosity. I know of a case in which a nurse in a fashionable London Square garden used to collect all the boys and girls (gentlemen's children) in a summer-house when it grew dark, and, turning up her petticoats, invite all the boys to look at and feel her vulva, and also incite the older boys of 12 or 14 to have coitus with her. Girls are afraid of pregnancy, so do not allow an adult penis to operate. I think people should take on a far higher class of nurses, than they do."

"Children ought never to be allowed, under any circumstances whatever," wrote Lawson Tait (*Diseases of Women*, 1889, p. 62), "to sleep with servants. In every instance where I have found a number of children affected [by masturbation] the contagion has been traced to a servant." Freud has found (*Neurologisches Centralblatt*, No. 10, 1896) that in cases of severe youthful hysteria the starting point may frequently be traced to sexual manipulations by servants, nurse-girls, and governesses.

"When I was about 8 or 9," a friend writes, "a servant-maid of our family, who used to carry the candle out of my bedroom, often drew down the bedclothes and inspected my organs. One night she put the penis in her mouth. When I asked her why she did it her answer was that 'sucking a boy's little dangle' cured her of pains in her stomach. She said that she had done it to other little boys, and declared that she liked doing it. This girl was about 16; she had lately been 'converted.' Another maid in our family used to kiss me warmly on the naked abdomen when I was a small boy. But she never did more than that. I have heard of various instances of servant-girls tampering with boys before puberty, exciting the penis to premature erection by manipulation, suction, and contact with their own parts." Such overstimulation must necessarily in some cases have an injurious influence on the boy's immature nervous system. Thus, Hutchinson (*Archives of Surgery*, vol. iv, p. 200) describes a case of amblyopia in a boy, developing after he had been placed to sleep in a servant-girl's room.

Moll (*Konträre Sexualempfindung*, third edition, 1899, p. 325) refers to the frequency with which servant-girls (between the ages of 18 and 30) carry on sexual practices with young boys (between 5 and 13) committed to their care. More than a century earlier Tissot, in his famous work on onanism, referred to the frequency with which servant-girls corrupt boys by teaching them to masturbate; and still earlier, in England, the author of *Onania* gave many such cases. We may, indeed, go back to the time of Rabelais, who (as Dr. Kiernan reminds me) represents the governesses of Gargantua, when he was a child, as taking pleasure in playing with his penis till it became wet, and joking with each other about it. (*Gargantua*, book i, chapter ix.)

The prevalence of such manifestations among servant-girls witnesses to their prevalence among lower-class girls generally. In judging such acts, even when they seem to be very deliberate, it is important to remember that at this age unreasoning instinct plays a very large part in the manifestations of the sexual impulse. This is clearly indicated by the phenomena observed in the insane. Thus, as we have seen (page 214), Schröter has found that, among girls of low social class under 20 years of age, spontaneous periodical sexual manifestations at menstrual epochs occurred in as large a proportion as 72 per cent. Among girls of better social position these impulses are inhibited, or at all events modified, by good taste or good feeling, the influences of tradition or education; it is only to the latter that children should be intrusted.

Hoche mentions a case in which a man was accused of repeatedly exhibiting his sexual organs to the servant-girl at a house; she enjoyed the spectacle (*Neurologisches Centralblatt*, 1896, No. 2). It may well be that in some cases of self-exhibition the offender has good reason, on the ground of previous experience, for thinking that he is giving pleasure. "When we used to go to bathe while I was at school," writes a correspondent, "girls from a poor quarter of the lower town (some quite 16) often followed us and stood to watch about a hundred yards from the river. They used to 'giggle' and 'pass remarks.' I have seen girls of this class peeping through chinks of a palisade around a bathing-place on the Thames." A correspondent who has given special attention to the point tells me of the great interest displayed by young girls of the people in Italy in the sexual organs of men.

Curiosity—whether in the form of the desire for knowledge or the desire for sensation—is, of course, not confined to young girls and women of lower social strata, though in them it is less often restrained by motives of self-respect and good feeling. "At the age of 8," writes a correspondent, "I was one day playing in a spare room with a girl of about 12 or 13. She gave me a penholder, and, crouching upon her hands and knees, with her posterior toward me, invited me to introduce the instrument into the vulva. This was the first time I had seen the female parts, and, as I appeared to be somewhat repelled, she coaxed me to comply with her desire. I did as she directed, and she said that it gave her pleasure. Several times after I repeated the same act at her request. A friend tells me that when he was 10 a girl of 16 asked him to lace up her boots. While he was kneeling at her feet his hand touched her ankle. She asked him to put his hand higher, and repeated 'Higher, higher,' till he touched the pudenda, and finally, at her request, put his finger into the vestibule. This girl was very handsome and amiable, and a favorite of the boy's mother. No one suspected this propensity." Again, a correspondent (a man of science) tells me of a friend who lately, when dining out, met a girl, the daughter of a country vicar; he was not specially attracted to her and paid her no special attention. "A few days afterward he was astonished to receive a call from her one afternoon (though his address is not discoverable from any recognized source). She sat down as near to him as she could, and rested her hand on his thigh, etc., while talking on different subjects and drinking tea. Then without any verbal prelude she asked him to have connection with her. Though not exactly a Puritan, he is not the man to jump at such an offer from a woman he is not in love with, so, after ascertaining that the girl was *virgo intacta*, he declined and she went away. A fortnight or so later he received a letter from her in the country, making no reference to what had passed, but giving an account of her work with her Sunday-school class. He did not reply, and then came a curt note asking him to return her letter. My friend feels sure she was devoted to auto-erotic performances, but, having become attracted to him, came to the conclusion she would like to try normal intercourse."

Wolbarst, studying the prevalence of gonorrhea among boys in New York (especially, it would appear, in quarters where the foreign-born elements—mainly Russian Jew and south Italian—are large), states: "In my study of this subject there have been observed 3 cases of gonorrheal urethritis, in boys aged, respectively, 4, 10, and 12 years, which were acquired in the usual manner, from girls ranging between 10 and 12 years of age. In each case, according to the story told by the victim, the girl made the first advances, and in 1 case, that of the 4-year-old boy, the act was consummated in the form of an assault, by a girl 12 years old, in which the child was threatened with injury unless he performed his part." (A. L. Wolbarst, *Journal of the American Medical Association*, Sept. 28, 1901.) In a further series of cases

(*Medical Record*, Oct. 29, 1910) Wolbarst obtained similar results, though he recognizes also the frequency of precocious sexuality in the young boys themselves.

Gibb states, concerning assaults on children by women: "It is undeniably true that they occur much more frequently than is generally supposed, although but few of the cases are brought to public notice, owing to the difficulty of proving the charge." (W. T. Gibb, article "Indecent Assaults upon Children," in A. McLane Hamilton's *System of Legal Medicine*, vol. i, p. 651.) Gibb's opinion carries weight, since he is medical adviser for the New York Society for the Protection of Children, and compelled to sift the evidence carefully in such cases.

It should be mentioned that, while a sexual curiosity exercised on younger children is, in girls about the age of puberty, an ill-regulated, but scarcely morbid, manifestation, in older women it may be of pathological origin. Thus, Kisch records the case of a refined and educated lady of 30 who had been married for nine years, but had never experienced sexual pleasure in coitus. For a long time past, however, she had felt a strong desire to play with the genital organs of children of either sex, a proceeding which gave her sexual pleasure. She sought to resist this impulse as much as possible, but during menstruation it was often irresistible. Examination showed an enlarged and retroflexed uterus and anesthesia of vagina. (Kisch, *Die Sterilität des Weibes*, 1886, p. 103.) The psychological mechanism by which an anesthetic vagina leads to a feeling of repulsion for normal coitus and normal sexual organs, and directs the sexual feelings toward more infantile forms of sexuality, is here not difficult to trace.

It is not often that the sexual attempts of girls and young women on boys—notwithstanding their undoubted frequency—become of medico-legal interest. In France in the course of ten years (1874 to 1884) only 181 women, who were mostly between 20 and 30 years of age, were actually convicted of sexual attempts on children below 15. (Paul Bernard, "Viols et attentats a la Pudeur," *Archives de l'Anthropologie Criminelle*, 1887.) Lop ("Attentats à la Pudeur commis par des Femmes sur des Petits Enfants," *id.*, Aug., 1896) brings together a number of cases chiefly committed by girls between the ages of 18 and 20. In England such accusations against a young woman or girl may easily be circumvented. If she is under 16 she is protected by the Criminal Law Amendment Act and cannot be punished. In any case, when found out, she can always easily bring the sympathy to her side by declaring that she is not the aggressor, but the victim. Cases of violent sexual assault upon girls, Lawson Tait remarks, while they undoubtedly do occur, are very much rarer than the frequency with which the charge is made would lead us to suspect. At one time, by arrangement with the authority, 70 such charges at Birmingham were consecutively brought before Lawson Tait. These charges were all made under the Criminal Law Amendment Act. In only 6 of these cases was he able to advise prosecution, in all of which cases conviction was obtained. In 7 other cases in which the police decided to prosecute there was either no conviction or a very light sentence. In at least 26 cases the charge was clearly trumped up. The average age of these girls was 12. "There is not a piece of sexual argot that ever had before reached my ears," remarks Mr. Tait, "but was used by these children in the descriptions given by them of what had been done to them; and they introduced, in addition, quite a new vocabulary on the subject. The minute and detailed descriptions of the sexual act given by chits of 10 and 11 would do credit to the pages of Mirabeau. At first sight it is a puzzle to see how children so young obtained their information." "About the use of the word 'seduced,'" the same writer remarks, "I wish to say that the class of women from amongst whom the great bulk of these cases are drawn seem to use it in a sense altogether different from that generally employed. It is not with them a process in which male villainy succeeds by various arts in overcoming female virtue and reluctance, but simply a date at which an incident in their lives occurs for the first time; and, according to their use of the phrase, the ancient legend of the Sacred Scriptures, had it ended in the more ordinary and usual way by the virtue of Joseph yielding to the temptation offered, would have to read as a record of the seduction of Mrs. Potiphar."

With reference to Lawson Tait's observation that violent assaults on women, while they do occur, are very much rarer than the frequency with which such charges are made would lead us to believe, it may be remarked that many medico-legal authorities are of the same opinion. (See, *e.g.*, G. Vivian Poore's *Treatise on Medical Jurisprudence*, 1901, p. 325. This writer also remarks: "I hold very strongly that a woman may rape a man as much as a man may rape a woman.") There can be little doubt that the plea of force is very frequently seized on by women as the easiest available weapon of defense when her connection with a man has been revealed. She has been so permeated by the current notion that no "respectable" woman can possibly have any sexual impulses of her own to gratify that, in order to screen what she feels to be regarded as an utterly shameful and wicked, as well as foolish, act, she declares it never took place by her own will at all. "Now, I ask you, gentlemen," I once heard an experienced counsel address the jury in a criminal case, "as men of the world, have you ever known or heard of a woman, a single woman, confess that she had had sexual connection and not declare that force had been used to compel her to such connection?" The statement is a little sweeping, but in this matter there is some element of truth in the "man of the world's" opinion. One may refer to the story (told by Etienne de Bourbon, by Francisco de Osuna in a religious work, and by Cervantes in *Don Quixote*, part ii, ch. xlv) concerning a magistrate who, when a girl came before him to complain of rape, ordered the accused young man either to marry her or pay her a sum of money. The fine was paid, and the magistrate then told the man to follow the girl and take the money from her by force; the man obeyed, but the girl defended herself so energetically that he could not secure the money. Then the judge, calling the parties before him again, ordered the fine to be returned: "Had you defended your chastity as well as you have defended your money it could not have been taken away from you." In most cases of "rape," in the case of adults, there has probably been some degree of consent, though that partial assent may have been basely secured by an appeal to the lower nervous centers alone, with no participation of the intelligence and will. Freud (*Zur Psychopathologie des Alltagslebens*, p. 87) considers that on this ground the judge's decision in *Don Quixote* is "psychologically unjust," because in such a case the woman's strength is paralyzed by the fact that an unconscious instinct in herself takes her assailant's part against her own conscious resistance. But it must be remembered that the factor of instinct plays a large part even when no violence is attempted.

Such facts and considerations as these tend to show that the sexual impulse is by no means so weak in women as many would lead us to think. It would appear that, whereas in earlier ages there was generally a tendency to credit women with an unduly large share of the sexual impulse, there is now a tendency to unduly minimize the sexual impulse in women.

[156]
I have had occasion to refer to the historic evolution of male opinion regarding women in previous volumes, as, *e.g.*, *Man and Woman*, chapter i, and the appendix on "The Influence of Menstruation on the Position of Women" in the first volume of these *Studies*.

[157]
The terminology proposed by Ziehen ("Zur Lehre von den psychopathischen Konstitutionen," *Charité Annalen*, vol. xxxiii, 1909) is as follows: For absence of sexual feeling, *anhedonia*; for diminution of the same, *hyphedonia*; for excess of sexual feeling, *hyperhedonia*; for qualitative sexual perversions, *parhedonia*. "Erotic blindness" was suggested by Nardelli.

[158]
O. Adler, *Die Mangelhafte Geschlechtsempfindung des Weibes*, 1904, p. 146.

[159]
A correspondent tells me that he knows a woman who has been a prostitute since the age of 15, but never experienced sexual pleasure and a real, non-simulated orgasm till she was 23; since then she has become very sensual. In other similar cases the hitherto indifferent prostitute, having found the man who suits her, abandons her profession, even though she is thereby compelled to live in extreme poverty. "An insensible woman," as La Bruyère long ago remarked in his chapter "Des Femmes," "is merely one who has not yet seen the man she must love."

[160]
Guttceit (*Dreissig Jahre Praxis*, vol. i, p. 416) pointed out that the presence or absence of the orgasm is the only factor in "sexual anesthesia" of which we can speak at all definitely;

and he believed that anaphrodism, in the sense of absence of the sexual impulse, never occurs at all, many women having confided to him that they had sexual desires, although those desires were not gratified by coitus.

[161]

Op. cit., p. 164.

[162]

Havelock Ellis, "Madame de Warens," *The Venture*, 1903.

[163]

It is interesting to observe that finally even Adler admits (*op. cit.*, p. 155) that there is no such thing as *congenital* lack of aptitude for sexual sensibility.

[164]

"I am not entirely satisfied with the testimony as to the alleged sexual anesthesia," a medical correspondent writes. "The same principle which makes the young harlot an old saint makes the repentant rake a believer in sexual anesthesia. Most of the medical men who believe, or claim to believe, that sexual anesthesia is so prevalent do so either to flatter their hysterical patients or because they have the mentality of the Hyacinthe of Zola's *Paris*."

[165]

Differences in the Nervous Organization of Man and Woman, 1891; chapter xiii, "Sexual Instinct in Men and Women Compared."

[166]

Matthews Duncan considered that "the healthy performance of the functions of child-bearing is surely connected with a well-regulated condition of desire and pleasure." "Desire and pleasure," he adds, "may be excessive, furious, overpowering, without bringing the female into the class of maniacs; they may be temporary, healthy, and moderate; they may be absent or dull." (Matthews Duncan, *Goulstonian Lectures on Sterility in Woman*, pp. 91, 121.)

[167]

Geoffrey Mortimer, *Chapters on Human Love*, 1898, ch. xvi.

[168]

I do not, however, attach much weight to this possibility. The sexual instinct among the lower social classes everywhere is subject to comparatively weak inhibition, and Löwenfeld is probably right in believing the women of the lower class do not suffer from sexual anesthesia to anything like the same extent as upper-class women. In England most women of the working class appear to have had sexual intercourse at some time in their lives, notwithstanding the risks of pregnancy, and if pregnancy occurs they refer to it calmly as an "accident," for which they cannot be held responsible; "Well, I couldn't help that," I have heard a young widow remark when mildly reproached for the existence of her illegitimate child. Again, among American negresses there seems to be no defect of sexual passion, and it is said that the majority of negresses in the Southern States support not only their children, but their lovers and husbands.

II.

Special Characters of the Sexual Impulse in Women—The More Passive Part Played by Women in Courtship—This Passivity only Apparent—The Physical Mechanism of the Sexual Process in Women More Complex—The Slower Development of Orgasm in Women—The Sexual Impulse in Women More Frequently Needs to be Actively Aroused—The Climax of Sexual Energy Falls Later in Women's Lives than in Men's—Sexual Ardor in Women Increased After the Establishment of Sexual Relationships—Women bear Sexual Excesses better than Men—The Sexual Sphere Larger and More Diffused in Women—The Sexual Impulse in Women Shows a Greater Tendency to Periodicity and a Wider Range of Variation.

So far I have been discussing the question of the sexual impulse in women on the ground upon which previous writers have usually placed it. The question, that is, has usually presented itself to them as one concerning the relative strength of the impulse in men and women. When so considered, not hastily and with prepossession, as is too often the case, but with a genuine desire to get at the real facts in all their aspects, there is no reason, as we have seen, to conclude that, on the whole, the sexual impulse in women is lacking in strength.

But we have to push our investigation of the matter further. In reality, the question as to whether the sexual impulse is or is not stronger in one sex than in the other is a somewhat crude one. To put the question in that form is to reveal ignorance of the real facts of the matter. And in that form, moreover, no really definite and satisfactory answer can be given.

It is necessary to put the matter on different ground. Instead of taking more or less insolvable questions as to the strength of the sexual impulse in the two sexes, it is more profitable to consider its differences. What are the special characters of the sexual impulse in women?

There is certainly one purely natural sexual difference of a fundamental character, which lies at the basis of whatever truth may be in the assertion that women are not susceptible of sexual emotion. As may be seen when considering the phenomena of modesty, the part played by the female in courtship throughout nature is usually different from that played by the male, and is, in some respects, a more difficult and complex part. Except when the male fails to play his part properly, she is usually comparatively passive; in the proper playing of her part she has to appear to shun the male, to flee from his approaches—even actually to repel them.[169]

Courtship resembles very closely, indeed, a drama or game; and the aggressiveness of the male, the coyness of the female, are alike unconsciously assumed in order to bring about in the most effectual manner the ultimate union of the sexes. The seeming reluctance of the female is not intended to inhibit sexual activity either in the male or in herself, but to increase it in both. The passivity of the female, therefore, is not a real, but only an apparent, passivity, and this holds true of our own species as much as of the lower animals. "Women are like delicately adjusted alembics," said a seventeenth-century author. "No fire can be seen outside, but if you look underneath the alembic, if you place your hand on the hearts of women, in both places you will find a great furnace."[170] Or, as Marro has finely put it, the passivity of women in love is the passivity of the magnet, which in its apparent immobility is drawing the iron toward it. An intense energy lies behind such passivity, an absorbed preoccupation in the end to be attained.

Tarde, when exercising magistrate's functions, once had to inquire into a case in which a young man was accused of murder. In questioning a girl of 18, a shepherdess, who appeared before him as a witness, she told him that on the morning following the crime she had seen the footmarks of the accused up to a certain point. He asked how she recognized them, and she replied, ingenuously but with assurance, that she could recognize the footprints of every young man in the neighborhood, even in a plowed field.[171] No better illustration could be given of the real significance of the sexual passivity of women, even at its most negative point.

"The women I have known," a correspondent writes, "do not express their sensations and feelings as much as I do. Nor have I found women usually anxious to practise 'luxuries.' They seldom care to practice *fellatio*; I have only known one woman who offered to do *fellatio* because she liked it. Nor do they generally care to masturbate a man; that is, they do not care greatly to enjoy the contemplation of the other person's excitement. (To me, to see the woman excited means almost more than my own pleasure.) They usually resist *cunnilinctus*, although they enjoy it. They do not seem to care to touch or look at a man's parts so much as he does at theirs. And they seem to dislike the tongue-kiss unless they feel very sexual or really love a man." My correspondent admits that his relationships have been numerous and facile, while his erotic demands tend also to deviate from the normal path. Under such circumstances, which not uncommonly occur, the woman's passions fail to be deeply stirred, and she retains her normal attitude of relative passivity.

It is owing to the fact that the sexual passivity of women is only an apparent, and not a real, passivity that women are apt to suffer, as men are, from prolonged sexual abstinence. This, indeed, has been denied, but can scarcely be said to admit of doubt. The only question is as to the relative amount of such suffering, necessarily a very difficult question. As far back as the fourteenth century Johannes de Sancto Amando stated that women are more injured than men by sexual abstinence. In modern times Maudsley considers that women "suffer more than men do from the entire deprivation of sexual intercourse" ("Relations between Body and Mind," *Lancet*, May 28, 1870). By some it has been held that this cause may produce actual disease. Thus, Tilt, an eminent gynecologist of the middle of the nineteenth century, in discussing this question, wrote: "When we consider how much of the lifetime of woman is occupied by the various phases of the generative process, and how terrible is often the conflict within her between the impulse of passion and the dictates of duty, it may be well understood how such a conflict reacts on the organs of the sexual economy in the unimpregnated female, and principally on the ovaria, causing an orgasm, which, if often repeated, may *possibly* be productive of subacute ovaritis." (Tilt, *On Uterine and Ovarian Inflammation*, 1862, pp. 309-310.) Long before Tilt, Haller, it seems, had said that women are especially liable to suffer from privation of sexual intercourse to which they have been accustomed, and referred to chlorosis, hysteria, nymphomania, and simple mania curable by intercourse. Hegar considers that in women an injurious result follows the nonsatisfaction of the sexual impulse and of the "ideal feelings," and that symptoms thus arise (pallor, loss of flesh, cardialgia, malaise, sleeplessness, disturbances of menstruation) which are diagnosed as "chlorosis." (Hegar, *Zusammenhang der Geschlechtskrankheiten mit nervösen Leiden*, 1885, p. 45.) Freud, as well as Gattel, has found that states of anxiety (*Angstzustände*) are caused by sexual abstinence. Löwenfeld, on careful examination of his own cases, is able to confirm this connection in both sexes. He has specially noticed it in young women who marry elderly husbands. Löwenfeld believes, however, that, on the whole, healthy unmarried women bear sexual abstinence better than men. If, however, they are of at all neuropathic disposition, ungratified sexual emotions may easily lead to various morbid conditions, especially of a hysteroneurasthenic character. (Löwenfeld, *Sexualleben und Nervenleiden*, second edition, 1899, pp. 44, 47, 54-60.) Balls-Headley considers that unsatisfied sexual desires in women may lead to the following conditions: general atrophy, anemia, neuralgia and hysteria, irregular menstruation, leucorrhea, atrophy of sexual organs. He also refers to the frequency of myoma of the uterus among those who have not become pregnant or who have long ceased to bear children. (Balls-Headley, art. "Etiology of Diseases of Female Genital Organs," Allbutt and Playfair, *System of Gynæcology*, 1896, p. 141.) It cannot, however, be said that he brings forward substantial evidence in favor of these beliefs. It may be added that in America, during recent years, leading gynecologists have recorded a number of cases in which widows on remarriage have shown marked improvement in uterine and pelvic conditions.

The question as to whether men or women suffer most from sexual abstinence, as well as the question whether definite morbid conditions are produced by such abstinence, remains, however, an obscure and debated problem. The available data do not enable us to answer it decisively. It is one of those subtle and complex questions which can only be investigated properly by a gynecologist who is also a psychologist. Incidentally, however, we have met and shall have occasion to meet with evidence bearing on this question. It is sufficient to say here, briefly, that it is impossible to believe, even if no evidence were forthcoming, that the exercise or non-exercise of so vastly important a function can make no difference to the organism generally. So far as the evidence goes, it may be said to indicate that the results of the abeyance of the sexual functions in healthy women in whom the sexual emotions have never been definitely aroused tend to be diffused and unconscious, as the sexual impulse itself often is, but that, in women in whom the sexual emotions have been definitely aroused and gratified, the results of sexual abstinence tend to be acute and conscious.

These acute results are at the present day very often due to premature ejaculation by nervous or neurasthenic husbands, the rapidity with which detumescence is reached in the husband allowing insufficient time for tumescence in the wife, who consequently fails to reach the orgasm. This has of late been frequently pointed out. Thus Kafemann (*Sexual-Probleme*, March, 1910, p. 194 *et seq.*) emphasizes the prevalence of sexual incompetence in men. Ferenczi, of Budapest (*Zentralblatt für Psychoanalyse*, 1910, ht. 1 and 2, p. 75), believes that the combination of neurasthenic husbands with resultantly nervous wives is extraordinarily common; even putting aside the neurasthenic, he considers it may be said that the whole male sex in relation to women suffer from precocious ejaculation. He adds that it is often difficult to say whether the lack of harmony may not be due to retarded orgasm in the woman. He regards the influence of masturbation in early life as tending to quicken orgasm in man, while when practised by the other sex it tends to slow orgasm, and thus increases the disharmony. He holds, however, that the chief cause lies in the education of women with its emphasis on sexual repression; this works too well and the result is that when the external impediments to the sexual impulse are removed the impulse has become incapable of normal action. Porosz (*British Medical Journal*, April 1, 1911) has brought forward cases of serious nervous trouble in women which have been dispersed when the sexual weakness and premature ejaculation of the husband have been cured.

The true nature of the passivity of the female is revealed by the ease with which it is thrown off, more especially when the male refuses to accept his cue. Or, if we prefer to accept the analogy of a game, we may say that in the play of courtship the first move belongs to the male, but that, if he fails to play, it is then the female's turn to play.

Among many birds the males at mating time fall into a state of sexual frenzy, but not the females. "I cannot call to mind a single case," states an authority on birds (H. E. Howard, *Zoölogist*, 1902, p. 146), "where I have seen anything approaching frenzy in the female of any species while mating."

Another great authority on birds, a very patient and skillful observer, Mr. Edmund Selous, remarks, however, in describing the courting habits of the ruffs and reeves (*Machetes pugnax*) that, notwithstanding the passivity of the females beforehand, their movements during and after coitus show that they derive at least as much pleasure as the males. (E. Selous, "Selection in Birds,"*Zoölogist*, Feb. and May, 1907.)

The same observer, after speaking of the great beauty of the male eider duck, continues: "These glorified males—there were a dozen of these, perhaps, to some six or seven females—swam closely about the latter, but more in attendance upon them than as actively pursuing them, for the females seemed themselves almost as active agents in the sport of being wooed as were their lovers in wooing them. The male bird first dipped down his head till his beak just touched the water, then raised it again in a constrained and tense manner,—the curious rigid action so frequent in the nuptial antics of birds,—at the same time uttering his strange haunting note. The air became filled with it; every moment one or other of the birds—sometimes several together—with upturned bill would softly laugh or exclaim, and while the males did this, the females, turning excitedly, and with little eager demonstrations from one to another of them, kept lowering and extending forward the head and neck in the direction of each in turn.... I noticed that a female would often approach a male bird with her head and neck laid flat along the water as though in a very 'coming on' disposition, and that the male bird declined her advances. This, taken in conjunction with the actions of the female when courted by the male, appears to me to raise a doubt as to the universal application of the law that throughout nature the male, in courtship, is eager, and the female coy. Here, to all appearances, courtship was proceeding, and the birds had not yet mated. The female eider ducks, however,—at any rate, some of them,—appeared to be anything but coy." (*Bird Watching*, pp. 144-146.)

Among moor-hens and great-crested grebes sometimes what Selous terms "functional hermaphroditism" occurs and the females play the part of the male toward their male companions, and then repeat the sexual act with a reversion to the normal order, the whole to the satisfaction of both parties. (E. Selous, *Zoölogist*, 1902, p. 196.)

It is not only among birds that the female sometimes takes the active part, but also among mammals. Among white rats, for instance, the males are exceptionally eager. Steinach, who has made many valuable experiments on these animals (*Archiv für die Gesammte Physiologie*, Bd. lvi, 1894, p. 319), tells us that, when a female white rat is introduced into the cage of a male, he at once leaves off eating, or whatever else he may be doing, becomes indifferent to noises or any other source of distraction, and devotes himself entirely to her. If, however, he is introduced into her cage the new environment renders him nervous and suspicious, and then it is she who takes the active part, trying to attract him in every way.

The impetuosity during heat of female animals of various species, when at length admitted to the male, is indeed well known to all who are familiar with animals.

I have referred to the frequency with which, in the human species,—and very markedly in early adolescence, when the sexual impulse is in a high degree unconscious and unrestrainedly instinctive,—similar manifestations may often be noted. We have to recognize that they are not necessarily abnormal and still less pathological. They merely represent the unseasonable apparition of a tendency which in due subordination is implied in the phases of courtship throughout the animal world. Among some peoples and in some stages of culture, tending to withdraw the men from women and the thought of women, this phase of courtship and this attitude assume a prominence which is absolutely normal. The literature of the Middle Ages presents a state of society in which men were devoted to war and to warlike sports, while the women took the more active part in love-making. The medieval poets represent women as actively encouraging backward lovers, and as delighting to offer to great heroes the chastity they had preserved, sometimes entering their bed-chambers at night. Schultz (*Das Höfische Leben*, Bd. i, pp. 594-598) considers that these representations are not exaggerated. *Cf.* Krabbes, *Die Frau im Altfranzösischen Karls-Epos*, 1884, p. 20 *et seq.*; and M. A. Potter, *Sohrab and Rustem*, 1902, pp. 152-163.

Among savages and barbarous races in various parts of the world it is the recognized custom, reversing the more usual method, for the girl to take the initiative in courtship. This is especially so in New Guinea. Here the girls almost invariably take the initiative, and in consequence hold a very independent position. Women are always regarded as the seducers: "Women steal men." A youth who proposed to a girl would be making himself ridiculous, would be called a woman, and be laughed at by the girls. The usual method by which a girl proposes is to send a present to the youth by a third party, following this up by repeated gifts of food; the young man sometimes waits a month or two, receiving presents all the time, in order to assure himself of the girl's constancy before decisively accepting her advances. (A. C. Haddon, *Cambridge Expedition to Torres Straits*, vol. v, ch. viii;*id.*, "Western Tribes of Torres Straits," *Journal of the Anthropological Institute*, vol. xix, February, 1890, pp. 314, 356, 394, 395, 411, 413; *id.*, *Head Hunters*, pp. 158-164; R. E. Guise, "Tribes of the Wanigela River," *Journal of the Anthropological Institute*, new series, vol. i, February-May, 1899, p. 209.) Westermarck gives instances of races among whom the women take the initiative in courtship. (*History of Marriage*, p. 158; so also Finck, *Primitive Love and Love-stories*, 1899, p. 109 *et seq.*; and as regards Celtic women, see Rhys and Brynmor Jones, *The Welsh People*.)

There is another characteristic of great significance by which the sexual impulse in women differs from that in men: the widely unlike character of the physical mechanism involved in the process of coitus. Considering how obvious this difference is, it is strange that its fundamental importance should so often be underrated. In man the process of tumescence and detumescence is simple. In women it is complex. In man we have the more or less spontaneously erectile penis, which needs but very simple conditions to secure the ejaculation which brings relief. In women we have in the clitoris a corresponding apparatus on a small scale, but behind this has developed a much more extensive mechanism, which also demands satisfaction, and requires for that satisfaction the presence of various conditions that are almost antagonistic. Naturally the more complex mechanism is the more easily disturbed. It is the difference, roughly speaking, between a lock and a key. This analogy is far from indicating all the difficulties involved. We have to imagine a lock that not only requires a key to fit it, but should only be entered at the right moment, and, under the best conditions, may only become adjusted to the key by considerable use. The fact that the man takes the more active part in coitus has increased these difficulties; the woman is too often taught to believe that the whole function is low and impure, only to be submitted to at her husband's will and for his sake, and the man has no proper knowledge of the mechanism involved and the best way of dealing with it. The grossest brutality thus may be, and not infrequently is, exercised in all innocence by an ignorant husband who simply believes that he is performing his "marital duties." For a woman to exercise this physical brutality on a man is with difficulty possible; a man's pleasurable excitement is usually the necessary condition of the woman's sexual gratification. But the reverse is not the case, and, if the man is sufficiently ignorant orsufficiently coarse-grained to be satisfied with the woman's submission, he may easily become to her, in all innocence, a cause of torture.

To the man coitus must be in some slight degree pleasurable or it cannot take place at all. To the woman the same act which, under some circumstances, in the desire it arouses and the satisfaction it imparts, will cause the whole universe to shrivel into nothingness, under other circumstances will be a source of anguish, physical and mental. This is so to some extent even in the presence of the right and fit man. There can be no doubt whatever that the mucus which is so profusely poured out over the external sexual organs in woman during the excitement of sexual desire has for its end the lubrication of the parts and the facilitation of the passage of the intromittent organ. The most casual inspection of the cold, contracted, dry vulva in its usual aspect and the same when distended, hot, and moist suffices to show which condition is and which is not that ready for intercourse, and until the proper condition is reached it is certain that coitus should not be attempted.

The varying sensitiveness of the female parts again offers difficulties. Sexual relations in women are, at the onset, almost inevitably painful; and to some extent the same experience may be repeated at every act of coitus. Ordinary tactile sensibility in the female genitourinary region is notably obtuse, but at the beginning of the sexual act there is normally a hyperesthesia which may be painful or pleasurable as excitement culminates, passing into a seeming anesthesia, which even craves for rough contact; so that in sexual excitement a woman normally displays in quick succession that same quality of sensibility to superficial pressure and insensibility to deep pressure which the hysterical woman exhibits simultaneously.

Thus we see that a highly important practical result follows from the greater complexity of the sexual apparatus in women and the greater difficulty with which it is aroused. In coitus the orgasm tends to occur more slowly in women than in men. It may easily happen that the whole process of detumescence is completed in the man before it has begun in his partner, who is left either cold or unsatisfied. This is one of the respects in which women remain nearer than men to the primitive stage of humanity.

In the Hippocratic treatise, *Of Generation,* it is stated that, while woman has less pleasure in coitus than man, her pleasure lasts longer. (*Œuvres d'Hippocrate,* edition Littré, vol. vii, p. 477.)

Beaunis considers that the slower development of the orgasm in women is the only essential difference in the sexual process in men and women. (Beaunis, *Les Sensations Internes,* 1889, p. 151.) This characteristic of the sexual impulse in women, though recognized for so long a period, is still far too often ignored or unknown. There is even a superstition that injurious results may follow if the male orgasm is not effected as rapidly as possible. That this is not so is shown by the experiences of the Oneida community in America, who in their system of sexual relationship carried prolonged intercourse without ejaculation to an extreme degree. There can be no doubt whatever that very prolonged intercourse gives the maximum amount of pleasure and relief to the woman. Not only is this the very decided opinion of women who have experienced it, but it is also indicated by the well-recognized fact that a woman who repeats the sexual act several times in succession often experiences more intense orgasm and pleasure with each repetition.

This point is much better understood in the East than in the West. The prolongation of the man's excitement, in order to give the woman time for orgasm, is, remarks Sir Richard Burton (*Arabian Nights,* vol. v, p. 76), much studied by Moslems, as also by Hindoos, who, on this account, during the orgasm seek to avoid overtension of muscles and to preoccupy the brain. During coitus they will drink sherbet, chew betel-nut, and even smoke. Europeans devote no care to this matter, and Hindoo women, who require about twenty minutes to complete the act, contemptuously call them "village cocks." I have received confirmation of Burton's statements on this point from medical correspondents in India.

While the European desires to perform as many acts of coitus in one night as possible, Breitenstein remarks, the Malay, as still more the Javanese, wishes, not to repeat the act many times, but to prolong it. His aim is to remain in the vagina for about a quarter of an hour. Unlike the European, also, he boasts of the pleasure he has given his partner far more than of his own pleasure. (Breitenstein, *21 Jahre in India,* theil i, "Borneo," p. 228.)

131

Jäger (*Entdeckung der Seele*, second edition, vol. i, 1884, p. 203), as quoted by Moll, explains the preference of some women for castrated men as due, not merely to the absence of risk of impregnation, but to the prolonged erections that take place in the castrated. Aly-Belfàdel remarks (*Archivio di Psichiatria*, 1903, p. 117) that he knows women who prefer old men in coitus simply because of their delay in ejaculation which allows more time to the women to become excited.

A Russian correspondent living in Italy informs me that a Neapolitan girl of 17, who had only recently ceased to be a virgin, explained to him that she preferred *coitus in ore vulvæ* to real intercourse because the latter was over before she had time to obtain the orgasm (or, as she put it, "the big bird has fled from the cage and I am left in the lurch"), while in the other way she was able to experience the orgasm twice before her partner reached the climax. "This reminds me," my correspondent continues, "that a Milanese cocotte once told me that she much liked intercourse with Jews because, on account of the circumcised penis being less sensitive to contact, they ejaculate more slowly then Christians. 'With Christians,' she said, 'it constantly happens that I am left unsatisfied because they ejaculate before me, while in coitus with Jews I sometimes ejaculate twice before the orgasm occurs in my partner, or, rather, I hold back the second orgasm until he is ready.' This is confirmed," my correspondent continues, "by what I was told by a Russian Jew, a student at the Zürich Polytechnic, who had a Russian comrade living with a mistress, also a Russian student, or pseudostudent. One day the Jew, going early to see his friend, was told to enter by a woman's voice and found his friend's mistress alone and in her chemise beside the bed. He was about to retire, but the young woman bade him stay and in a few minutes he was in bed with her. She told him that her lover had just gone away and that she never had sexual relief with him because he always ejaculated too soon. That morning he had left her so excited and so unrelieved that she was just about to masturbate—which she rarely did because it gave her headache—when she heard the Jew's voice, and, knowing that Jews are slower in coitus than Christians, she had suddenly resolved to give herself to him."

I am informed that the sexual power of negroes and slower ejaculation (see Appendix A) are the cause of the favor with which they are viewed by some white women of strong sexual passions in America, and by many prostitutes. At one time there was a special house in New York City to which white women resorted for these "buck lovers"; the women came heavily veiled and would inspect the penises of the men before making their selection.

It is thus a result of the complexity of the sexual mechanism in women that the whole attitude of a woman toward the sexual relationship is liable to be affected disastrously by the husband's lack of skill or consideration in initiating her into this intimate mystery. Normally the stage of apparent repulsion and passivity, often associated with great sensitiveness, physical and moral, passes into one of active participation and aid in the consummation of the sexual act. But if, from whatever cause, there is partial arrest on the woman's side of this evolution in the process of courtship, if her submission is merely a mental and deliberate act of will, and not an instinctive and impulsive participation, there is a necessary failure of sexual relief and gratification. When we find that a woman displays a certain degree of indifference in sexual relationships, and a failure of complete gratification, we have to recognize that the fault may possibly lie, not in her, but in the defective skill of a lover who has not known how to play successfully the complex and subtle game of courtship. Sexual coldness due to the shock and suffering of the wedding-night is a phenomenon that is far too frequent.[172] Hence it is that many women may never experience sexual gratification and relief, through no defect on their part, but through the failure of the husband to understand the lover's part. We make a false analogy when we compare the courtship of animals exclusively with our own courtships before marriage. Courtship, properly understood, is the process whereby both the male and the female are brought into that state of sexual tumescence which is a more or less necessary condition for sexual intercourse. The play of courtship cannot, therefore, be considered to be definitely brought to an end by the ceremony of marriage; it may more properly be regarded as the natural preliminary to every act of coitus.

Tumescence is not merely a more or less essential condition for proper sexual intercourse. It is probably of more fundamental significance as one of the favoring conditions of impregnation. This has, indeed, been long recognized. Van Swieten, when consulted by the childless Maria Theresa, gave the opinion "Ego vero censeo, vulvam Sacratissimæ Majestatis ante coitum diutius esse titillandam," and thereafter she had many children. "I think it very nearly certain," Matthews Duncan wrote (*Goulstonian Lectures on Sterility in Woman*, 1884, p. 96), "that desire and pleasure in due or moderate degree are very important aids to, or predisposing causes of, fecundity," as bringing into action the complicated processes of fecundation. Hirst (*Text-book of Obstetrics*, 1899, p. 67) mentions the case of a childless married woman who for six years had had no orgasm during intercourse; then it occurred at the same time as coitus, and pregnancy resulted.

Kisch is very decidedly of the same opinion, and considers that the popular belief on this point is fully justified. It is a fact, he states, that an unfaithful wife is more likely to conceive with her lover than with her husband, and he concludes that, whatever the precise mechanism may be, "sexual excitement on the woman's part is a necessary link in the chain of conditions producing impregnation." (E. H. Kisch, *Die Sterilität des Weibes*, 1886, p. 99.) Kisch believes (p. 103) that in the majority of women sexual pleasure only appears gradually, after the first cohabitation, and then develops progressively, and that the first conception usually coincides with its complete awakening. In 556 cases of his own the most frequent epoch of first impregnation was found to be between ten and fifteen months after marriage.

The removal of sexual frigidity thus becomes a matter of some importance. This removal may in some cases be effected by treatment through the husband, but that course is not always practicable. Dr. Douglas Bryan, of Leicester, informs me that in several cases he has succeeded in removing sexual coldness and physical aversion in the wife by hypnotic suggestion. The suggestions given to the patient are "that all her womanly natural feelings would be quickly and satisfactorily developed during coitus; that she would experience no feeling of disgust and nausea, would have no fear of the orgasm not developing; that there would be no involuntary resistance on her part." The fact that such suggestions can be permanently effective tends to show how superficial the sexual "anesthesia" of women usually is.

Not only, therefore, is the apparatus of sexual excitement in women more complex than in men, but—in part, possibly as a result of this greater complexity—it much more frequently requires to be actively aroused. In men tumescence tends to occur almost spontaneously, or under the simple influence of accumulated semen. In women, also, especially in those who live a natural and healthy life, sexual excitement also tends to occur spontaneously, but by no means so frequently as in men. The comparative rarity of sexual dreams in women who have not had sexual relationships alone serves to indicate this sexual difference. In a very large number of women the sexual impulse remains latent until aroused by a lover's caresses. The youth spontaneously becomes a man; but the maiden—as it has been said—"must be kissed into a woman."

One result of this characteristic is that, more especially when love is unduly delayed beyond the first youth, this complex apparatus has difficulty in responding to the unfamiliar demands of sexual excitement. Moreover, delayed normal sexual relations, when the sexual impulse is not absolutely latent, tend to induce all degrees of perverted or abnormal sexual gratification, and the physical mechanism when trained to respond in other ways often fails to respond normally when, at last, the normal conditions of response are presented. In all these ways passivity and even aversion may be produced in the conjugal relationship. The fact that it is almost normally the function of the male to arouse the female, and that the greater complexity of the sexual mechanism in women leads to more frequent disturbance of that mechanism, produces a simulation of organic sexual coldness which has deceived many.

An instructive study of cases in which the sexual impulse has been thus perverted has been presented by Smith Baker ("The Neuropsychical Element in Conjugal Aversion," *Journal of Nervous and Mental Disease*, vol. xvii, September, 1892). Raymond and Janet, who believes that sexual coldness is extremely frequent in marriage, and that it plays an important part in the causation of physical and moral troubles, find that it is most often due to masturbation. (*Les Obsessions*, vol. ii, p. 307.) Adler, after discussing the complexity of the feminine sexual mechanism, and the difficulty which women find in obtaining sexual gratification in normal coitus, concludes that "masturbation is a frequent, perhaps the most frequent, cause of defective sexual sensibility in women." (*Op. cit.*, p. 119.) He remarks that in women masturbation usually has less resemblance to normal coitus than in men and involves very frequently the special excitation of parts which are not the chief focus of excitement in coitus, so that coitus fails to supply the excitation which has become habitual (pp. 113-116). In the discussion of "Auto-erotism" in the first volume of these *Studies*, I had already referred to the divorce between the physical and the ideal sides of love which may, especially in women, be induced by masturbation.

Another cause of inhibited sexual feeling has been brought forward. A married lady with normal sexual impulse states (*Sexual-Probleme*, April, 1912, p. 290) that she cannot experience orgasm and sexual satisfaction when the intercourse is not for conception. This is a psychic inhibition independent of any disturbance due to the process of prevention. She knows other women who are similarly affected. Such an inhibition must be regarded as artificial and abnormal, since the final result of sexual intercourse, under natural and normal conditions, forms no essential constituent of the psychic process of intercourse.

As a result of the fact that in women the sexual emotions tend not to develop great intensity until submitted to powerful stimulation, we find that the maximum climax of sexual emotion tends to fall somewhat later in a woman's life than in a man's. Among animals generally there appears to be frequently traceable a tendency for the sexual activities of the male to develop at a somewhat earlier age than those of the female. In the human, species we may certainly trace the same tendency. As the great physiologist, Burdach, pointed out, throughout nature, with the accomplishment of the sexual act the part of the male in the work of generation comes to an end; but that act represents only the beginning of a woman's generative activity.

A youth of 20 may often display a passionate ardor in love which is very seldom indeed found in women who are under 25. It is rare for a woman, even though her sexual emotions may awaken at puberty or earlier, to experience the great passion of her life until after the age of 25 has been passed. In confirmation of this statement, which is supported by daily observation, it may be pointed out that nearly all the most passionate love-letters of women, as well as their most passionate devotions, have come from women who had passed, sometimes long passed, their first youth. When Heloise wrote to Abelard the first of the letters which have come down to us she was at least 32. Mademoiselle Aissé's relation with the Chevalier began when she was 32, and when she died, six years later, the passion of each was at its height. Mary Wollstonecraft was 34 when her love-letters to Imlay began, and her child was born in the following year. Mademoiselle de Lespinasse was 43 when she began to write her letters to M. de Guibert. In some cases the sexual impulse may not even appear until after the period of the menopause has been passed.[173]

In Roman times Ovid remarked (*Ars Amatoria*, lib. ii) that a woman fails to understand the art of love until she has reached the age of 35. "A girl of 18," said Stendhal (*De l'Amour*, ch. viii), "has not the power to crystallize her emotions; she forms desires that are too limited by her lack of experience in the things of life, to be able to love with such passion as a woman of 28." "Sexual needs," said Restif de la Bretonne (*Monsieur Nicolas*, vol. xi, p. 221), "often only appears in young women when they are between 26 and 27 years of age; at least, that is what I have observed."

Erb states that it is about the middle of the twenties that women begin to suffer physically, morally, and intellectually from their sexual needs. Nyström (*Das Geschlechtsleben*, p. 163) considers that it is about the age of 30 that a woman first begins to feel conscious of sex needs. In a case of Adler's (*op. cit.*, p. 141), sexual feelings first appeared after the birth of the third child, at the age of 30. Forel (*Die Sexuelle Frage*, 1906, p. 219) considers that sexual desire in woman is often strongest between the ages of 30 and 40. Leith Napier (*Menopause*, p. 94) remarks that from 28 to 30 is often an important age in woman who have retained their virginity, erotism then appearing with the full maturity of the nervous system. Yellowlees (art. "Masturbation," *Dictionary of Psychological Medicine*), again, states that at about the age of 33 some women experience great sexual irritability, often resulting in masturbation. Audiffrent (*Archives d'Anthropologie Criminelle*, Jan. 15, 1902, p. 3) considers that it is toward the age of 30 that a woman reaches her full moral and physical development, and that at this period her emotional and idealizing impulses reach a degree of intensity which is

134

sometimes irresistible. It has already been mentioned that Matthews Duncan's careful inquiries showed that it is between the ages of 30 and 34 that the largest proportion of women experience sexual desire and sexual pleasure. It may be remarked, also, that while the typical English novelists, who have generally sought to avoid touching the deeper and more complex aspects of passion, often choose very youthful heroines, French novelists, who have frequently had a predilection for the problems of passion, often choose heroines who are approaching the age of 30.

Hirschfeld (*Von Wesen der Liebe*, p. 26) was consulted by a lady who, being without any sexual desires or feelings, married an inverted man in order to live with him a life of simple comradeship. Within six months, however, she fell violently in love with her husband, with the full manifestation of sexual feelings and accompanying emotions of jealousy. Under all the circumstances, however, she would not enter into sexual relationship with her husband, and the torture she endured became so acute that she desired to be castrated. In this connection, also, I may mention a case, which has been communicated to me from Glasgow, of a girl—strong and healthy and menstruating regularly since the age of 17—who was seduced at the age of 20 without any sexual desire on her part, giving birth to a child nine months later. Subsequently she became a prostitute for three years, and during this period had not the slightest sexual desire or any pleasure in sexual connection. Thereafter she met a poor lad with whom she has full sexual desire and sexual pleasure, the result being that she refuses to go with any other man, and consequently is almost without food for several days every week.

The late appearance of the great climax of sexual emotion in women is indicated by a tendency to nervous and psychic disturbances between the ages of 25 and about 33, which has been independently noted by various alienists (though it may be noted that 25 to 30 is not an unusual age for first attacks of insanity in men also). Thus, Krafft-Ebing states that adult unmarried women between the ages of 25 and 30 often show nervous symptoms and peculiarities. (Krafft-Ebing, "Ueber Neurosen und Psychosen durch Sexuelle Abstinenz," *Jahrbücher für Psychiatrie*, Bd. viii, ht. 1-4, 1888.) Pitres and Régis find also (*Comptes-rendus XIIe Congrès International de Médecine*, Moscow, 1897, vol. iv, p. 45) that obsessions, which are commoner in women than in men and are commonly connected in their causation with strong moral emotion, occur in women chiefly between the ages of 26 and 30, though in men much earlier. The average age at which in England women inebriates begin drinking in excess is 26. (*British Medical Journal*, Sept. 2, 1911, p. 518.)

A case recorded by Sérieux is instructive as regards the development of the sexual impulse, although it comes within the sphere of mental disorder. A woman of 32 with bad heredity had in childhood had weak health and become shy, silent, and fond of solitude, teased by her companions and finding consolation in hard work. Though very emotional, she never, even in the vaguest form, experienced any of those feelings and aspirations which reveal the presence of the sexual impulse. She had no love of dancing and was indifferent to any embraces she might chance to receive from young men. She never masturbated or showed inverted feelings. At the age of 23 she married. She still, however, experienced no sexual feelings; twice only she felt a faint sensation of pleasure. A child was born, but her home was unhappy on account of her husband's drunken habits. He died and she worked hard for her own living and the support of her mother. Then at the age of 31 a new phase occurs in her life: she falls in love with the master of her workshop. It was at first a purely psychic affection, without any mixture of physical elements; it was enough to see him, and she trembled when she touched anything that belonged to him. She was constantly thinking about him; she loved him for his eyes, which seemed to her those of her own child, and especially for his intelligence. Gradually, however, the lower nervous centers began to take part in these emotions; one day in passing her the master chanced to touch her shoulder; this contact was sufficient to produce sexual turgescence. She began to masturbate daily, thinking of her master, and for the first time in her life she desired coitus. She evoked the image of her master so constantly and vividly that at last hallucinations of sight, touch, and hearing appeared, and it seemed to her that he was present. These hallucinations were only with difficulty dissipated. (P. Sérieux, *Les Anomalies de L'Instinct Sexuel*, 1888, p. 50.) This case presents in an insane form a phenomenon which is certainly by no means uncommon and is very significant. Up to the age of 31 we should certainly have been forced to conclude that this woman was sexually anesthetic to an almost absolute degree. In reality, we see this was by no means the case. Weak health, hard work, and a brutal husband had prolonged the latency of the sexual emotions; but they were there, ready to explode with even insane intensity (this being due to the unsound heredity) in the presence of a man who appealed to these emotions.

In connection with the late evolution of the sexual emotions in women reference may be made to what is usually termed "old maid's insanity," a condition not met with in men. In these cases, which are not, indeed, common, single women who have led severely strict and virtuous lives, devoting themselves to religious or intellectual work, and carefully repressing the animal side of their natures, at last, just before the climacteric, experience an awakening of the erotic impulse; they fall in love with some unfortunate man, often a clergyman, persecute him with their attentions, and frequently suffer from the delusion that he reciprocates their affections.

When once duly aroused, there cannot usually be any doubt concerning the strength of the sexual impulse in normal and healthy women. There would, however, appear to be a distinct difference between the sexes at this point also. Before sexual union the male tends to be more ardent; after sexual union it is the female who tends to be more ardent. The sexual energy of women, under these circumstances, would seem to be the greater on account of the long period during which it has been dormant.

Sinibaldus in the seventeenth century, in his *Geneanthropeia*, argued that, though women are cold at first, and aroused with more difficulty and greater slowness than men, the flame of passion spreads in them the more afterward, just as iron is by nature cold, but when heated gives a great degree of heat. Similarly Mandeville said of women that "their passions are not so easily raised nor so suddenly fixed upon any particular object; but when this passion is once rooted in women it is much stronger and more durable than in men, and rather increases than diminishes by enjoying the person of the beloved." (*A Modest Defence of Public Stews*, 1724, p. 34.) Burdach considered that women only acquire the full enjoyment of their general strength after marriage and pregnancy, while it is before marriage that men have most vigor. Schopenhauer also said that a man's love decreases with enjoyment, and a woman's increases. And Ellen Key has remarked (*Love and Marriage*) that "where there is no mixture of Southern blood it is a long time, sometimes indeed not till years after marriage, that the senses of the Northern women awake to consciousness."

Even among animals this tendency seems to be manifested. Edmund Selous (*Bird Watching*, p. 112) remarks, concerning sea-gulls: "Always, or almost always, one of the birds—and this I take to be the female—is more eager, has a more soliciting manner and tender begging look than the other. It is she who, as a rule, draws the male bird on. She looks fondly up at him, and, raising her bill to his, as though beseeching a kiss, just touches with it, in raising, the feathers of the throat—an action light, but full of endearment. And in every way she shows herself the most desirous, and, in fact, so worries and pesters the poor male gull that often, to avoid her importunities, he flies away. This may seem odd, but I have seen other instances of it. No doubt, in actual courting, before the sexes are paired, the male bird is usually the most eager, but after marriage the female often becomes the wooer. Of this I have seen some marked instances." Selous mentions especially the plover, kestrel hawk, and rook.

In association with the fact that women tend to show an increase of sexual ardor after sexual relationships have been set up may be noted the probably related fact that sexual intercourse is undoubtedly less injurious to women than to men. Other things being equal, that is to say, the threshold of excess is passed very much sooner by the man than by the woman. This was long ago pointed out by Montaigne. The ancient saying, "*Omne animal post coitum triste*," is of limited application at the best, but certainly has little reference to women.[174] Alacrity, rather than languor, as Robin has truly observed,[175] marks a woman after coitus, or, as a medical friend of my own has said, a woman then goes about the house singing.[176] It is, indeed, only after intercourse with a woman for whom, in reality, he feels contempt that a man experiences that revulsion of feeling described by Shakespeare (sonnet cxxix). Such a passage should not be quoted, as it sometimes has been quoted, as the representation of a normal phenomenon. But, with equal gratification on both sides, it remains true that, while after a single coitus the man may experience a not unpleasant lassitude and readiness for sleep, this is rarely the case with his partner, for whom a single coitus is often but a pleasant stimulus, the climax of satisfaction not being reached until a second or subsequent act of intercourse. "Excess in venery," which, rightly or wrongly, is set down as the cause of so many evils in men, seldom, indeed, appears in connection with women, although in every act of venery the woman has taken part.[177]

That women bear sexual excesses better than men was noted by Cabanis and other early writers. Alienists frequently refer to the fact that women are less liable to be affected by insanity following such excesses. (See, *e.g.*, Maudsley, "Relations between Body and Mind," *Lancet*, May 28, 1870; and G. Savage, art. "Marriage and Insanity" in *Dictionary of Psychological Medicine*.) Trousseau remarked on the fact that women are not exhausted by repeated acts of coitus within a short period, notwithstanding that the nervous excitement in their case is as great, if not greater, and he considered that this showed that the loss of semen is a cause of exhaustion in men. Löwenfeld (*Sexualleben und Nervenleiden*, pp. 74, 153) states that there cannot be question that the nervous system in women is less influenced by the after-effects of coitus than in men. Not only, he remarks, are prostitutes very little liable to suffer from nervous overstimulation, and neurasthenia and hysteria when occurring in them be easily traceable to other causes, but "healthy women who are not given to prostitution, when they indulge in very frequent sexual intercourse, provided it is practised normally, do not experience the slightest injurious effect. I have seen many young married couples where the husband had been reduced to a pitiable condition of nervous prostration and general discomfort by the zeal with which he had exercised his marital duties, while the wife had been benefited and was in the uninterrupted enjoyment of the best health." This experience is by no means uncommon.

A correspondent writes: "It is quite true that the threshold of excess is less easily reached by women than by men. I have found that women can reach the orgasm much more frequently than men. Take an ordinary case. I spend two hours with ——. I have the orgasm 3 times, with difficulty; she has it 6 or 8, or even 10 or 12, times. Women can also experience it a second or third time in succession, with no interval between. Sometimes the mere fact of realizing that the man is having the orgasm causes the woman to have it also, though it is true that a woman usually requires as many minutes to develop the orgasm as a man does seconds." I may also refer to the case recorded in another part of this volume in which a wife had the orgasm 26 times to her husband's twice.

Hutchinson, under the name of post-marital amblyopia (*Archives of Surgery*, vol. iv, p. 200), has described a condition occurring in men in good health who soon after marriage become nearly blind, but recover as soon as the cause is removed. He mentions no cases in women due to coitus, but finds that in women some failure of sight may occur after parturition.

Näcke states that, in his experience, while masturbation is, apparently, commoner in insane men than in insane women, masturbation repeated several times a day is much commoner in the women. (P. Näcke, "Die Sexuellen Perversitäten in der Irrenanstalt," *Psychiatrische Bladen*, 1899, No. 2.)

Great excesses in masturbation seem also to be commoner among women who may be said to be sane than among men. Thus, Bloch (*New Orleans Medical Journal*, 1896) records the case of a young married woman of 25, of bad heredity, who had suffered from almost life-long sexual hyperesthesia, and would masturbate fourteen times daily during the menstrual periods.

With regard to excesses in coitus the case may be mentioned of a country girl of 17, living in a rural district in North Carolina where prostitution was unknown, who would cohabit with men almost openly. On one Sunday she went to a secluded school-house and let three or four men wear themselves out cohabiting with her. On another occasion, at night, in a field, she allowed anyone who would to perform the sexual act, and 25 men and boys then had intercourse with her. When seen she was much prostrated and with a tendency to spasm, but quite rational. Subsequently she married and attacks of this nature became rare.

Mr. Lawson made an "attested statement" of what he had observed among the Marquesan women. "He mentions one case in which he heard a parcel of boys next morning count over and *name* 103 men who during the night had intercourse with *one* woman." (*Medico-Chirurgical Review*, 1871, vol. ii, p. 360, apparently quoting Chevers.) This statement seems open to question, but, if reliable, would furnish a case which must be unique.

There is a further important difference, though intimately related to some of the differences already mentioned, between the sexual impulse in women and in men. In women it is at once larger and more diffused. As Sinibaldus long ago said, the sexual pleasure of men is intensive, of women extensive. In men the sexual impulse is, as it were, focused to a single point. This is necessarily so, for the whole of the essentially necessary part of the male in the process of human procreation is confined to the ejaculation of semen into the vagina. But in women, mainly owing to the fact that women are the child-bearers, in place of one primary sexual center and one primary erogenous region, there are at least three such sexual centers and erogenous regions: the clitoris (corresponding to the penis), the vaginal passage up to the womb, and the nipple. In both sexes there are other secondary and reflex centers, but there is good reason for believing that these are more numerous and more widespread in women than in men.[178] How numerous the secondary sexual centers in women may be is indicated by the case of a woman mentioned by Moraglia, who boasted that she knew fourteen different ways of masturbating herself.

This great diffusion of the sexual impulse and emotions in women is as visible on the psychic as on the physical side. A woman can find sexual satisfaction in a great number of ways that do not include the sexual act proper, and in a great number of ways that apparently are not physical at all, simply because their physical basis is diffused or is to be found in one of the outlying sexual zones.

It is, moreover, owing to the diffused character of the sexual emotions in women that it so often happens that emotion really having a sexual origin is not recognized as such even by the woman herself. It is possible that the great prevalence in women of the religious emotional state of "storm and stress," noted by Professor Starbuck,[179] is largely due to unemployed sexual impulse. In this and similar ways it happens that the magnitude of the sexual sphere in woman is unrealized by the careless observer.

A number of converging facts tend to indicate that the sexual sphere is larger, and more potent in its influence on the organism, in women than in men. It would appear that among the males and females of lower animals the same difference may be found. It is stated that in birds there is a greater flow of blood to the ovaries than to the testes.

In women the system generally is more affected by disturbances in the sexual sphere than in men. This appears to be the case as regards the eye. "The influence of the sexual system upon the eye in man," Power states, "is far less potent, and the connection, in consequence, far less easy to trace than in woman." (H. Power, "Relation of Ophthalmic Disease to the Sexual Organs," *Lancet*, November 26, 1887.)

The greater predominance of the sexual system in women on the psychic side is clearly brought out in insane conditions. It is well known that, while satyriasis is rare, nymphomania is comparatively common. These conditions are probably often forms of mania, and in mania, while sexual symptoms are common in men, they are often stated to be the rule in women (see, *e.g.*, Krafft-Ebing, *Psychopathia Sexualis*, tenth edition, English translation, p. 465). Bouchereau, in noting this difference in the prevalence of sexual manifestations during insanity, remarks that it is partly due to the naturally greater dependence of women on the organs of generation, and partly to the more active, independent, and laborious lives of men; in his opinion, satyriasis is specially apt to develop in men who lead lives resembling those of women. (Bouchereau, art. "Satyriasis," *Dictionnaire Encyclopédique des Sciences Médicales.*) Again, postconnubial insanity is very much commoner in women than in men, a fact which may indicate the more predominant part played by the sexual sphere in women. (Savage, art. "Marriage and Insanity," *Dictionary of Psychological Medicine.*)

Insanity tends to remove the artificial inhibitory influences that rule in ordinary life, and there is therefore significance in such a fact as that the sexual appetite is often increased in general paralysis and to a notable extent in women. (Pactet and Colin, *Les Aliénés devant la Justice*, 1902, p. 122.)

Näcke, from his experiences among the insane, makes an interesting and possibly sound distinction regarding the character of the sexual manifestations in the two sexes. Among men he finds these manifestations to be more of a reflex and purely spinal nature and chiefly manifested in masturbation; in women he finds them to be of a more cerebral character, and chiefly manifested in erotic gestures, lascivious conversation, etc. The sexual impulse would thus tend to involve to a greater extent the higher psychic region in women than in men.

Forel likewise (*Die Sexuelle Frage*, 1906, p. 276), remarking on the much greater prevalence of erotic manifestations among insane women than insane men (and pointing out that it is by no means due merely to the presence of a male doctor, for it remains the same when the doctor is a woman), considers that it proves that in women the sexual impulse resides more prominently in the higher nervous centers and in men in the lower centers. (As regards the great prevalence of erotic manifestations among the female insane, I may also refer to Claye Shaw's interesting observations, "The Sexes in Lunacy," *St. Bartholomew's Hospital Reports*, vol. xxiv, 1888; also quoted in Havelock Ellis, *Man and Woman*, p. 370 *et seq.*) Whether or not we may accept Näcke's and Forel's interpretation of the facts, which is at least doubtful, there can be little doubt that the sexual impulse is more fundamental in women. This is indicated by Näcke's observation that among idiots sexual manifestations are commoner in females than in males. Of 16 idiot girls, of the age of 16 and under, 15 certainly masturbated, sometimes as often as fourteen times a day, while the remaining girl probably masturbated; but of 25 youthful male idiots only 1 played with his penis. (P. Näcke, "Die Sexuellen Perversitäten in der Irrenanstalt," *Psychiatrische Bladen*, 1899, No. 2, pp. 9, 12.) On the physical side Bourneville and Sollier found (*Progrès médical*, 1888) that puberty is much retarded in idiot and imbecile boys, while J. Voisin (*Annales d'Hygiène Publique*, June, 1894) found that in idiot and imbecile girls, on the contrary, there is no lack of full sexual development or retardation of puberty, while masturbation is common. In women, it may be added, as Ball pointed out (*Folie érotique*, p. 40), sexual hallucinations are especially common, while under the influence of anesthetics erotic manifestations and feelings are frequent in women, but rare in men. (Havelock Ellis, *Man and Woman*, p. 256.)

The fact that the first coitus has a much more profound moral and psychic influence on a woman than on a man would also seem to indicate how much more fundamental the sexual region is in women. The fact may be considered as undoubted. (It is referred to by Marro, *La Pubertà*, p. 460.) The mere physical fact that, while in men coitus remains a merely exterior contact, in women it involves penetration into the sensitive and virginal interior of the body would alone indicate this difference.

We are told that in the East there was once a woman named Moârbeda who was a philosopher and considered to be the wisest woman of her time. When Moârbeda was once asked: "In what part of a woman's body does her mind reside?" she replied: "Between her thighs." To many women,—perhaps, indeed, we might even say to most women,—to a certain extent may be applied—and in no offensive sense—the dictum of the wise woman of the East; in a certain sense their brains are in their wombs. Their mental activity may sometimes seem to be limited; they may appear to be passing through life always in a rather inert or dreamy state; but, when their sexual emotions are touched, then at once they spring into life; they become alert, resourceful, courageous, indefatigable. "But when I am not in love I am nothing!" exclaimed a woman when reproached by a French magistrate for living with a thief. There are many women who could truly make the same statement, not many men. That emotion, which, one is tempted to say, often unmans the man, makes the woman for the first time truly herself.

"Women are more occupied with love than men," wrote De Sénancour (*De l'Amour*, vol. ii, p. 59); "it shows itself in all their movements, animates their looks, gives to their gestures a grace that is always new, to their smiles and voices an inexpressible charm; they live for love, while many men in obeying love feel that they are forgetting themselves."

Restif de la Bretonne (*Monsieur Nicolas*, vol. vi, p. 223) quotes a young girl who well describes the difference which love makes to a woman: "Before I vegetated; now all my actions have a motive, an end; they have become important. When I wake my first thought is 'Someone is occupied with me and desires me.' I am no longer alone, as I was before; another feels my existence and cherishes it," etc.

"One is surprised to see in the south," remarks Bonstetten, in his suggestive book, *L'Homme du Midi et l'Homme du Nord* (1824),—and the remark by no means applies only to the south,—"how love imparts intelligence even to those who are most deficient in ideas. An Italian woman in love is inexhaustible in the variety of her feelings, all subordinated to the supreme emotion which dominates her. Her ideas follow one another with prodigious rapidity, and produce a lambent play which is fed by her heart alone. If she ceases to love, her mind becomes merely the scoria of the lava which yesterday had been so bright."

Cabanis had already made some observations to much the same effect. Referring to the years of nubility following puberty, he remarks: "I have very often seen the greatest fecundity of ideas, the most brilliant imagination, a singular aptitude for the arts, suddenly develop in girls of this age, only to give place soon afterward to the most absolute mental mediocrity." (Cabanis, "De l'Influence des Sexes," etc., *Rapports du Physique et du Morale de l'Homme.*)

This phenomenon seems to be one of the indications of the immense organic significance of the sexual relations. Woman's part in the world is less obtrusively active than man's, but there is a moment when nature cannot dispense with energy and mental vigor in women, and that is during the reproductive period. The languidest woman must needs be alive when her sexual emotions are profoundly stirred. People often marvel at the infatuation which men display for women who, in the eyes of all the world, seem commonplace and dull. This is not, as we usually suppose, always entirely due to the proverbial blindness of love. For the man whom she loves, such a woman is often alive and transformed. He sees a woman who is hidden from all the world. He experiences something of that surprise and awe which Dostoieffsky felt when the seemingly dull and brutish criminals of Siberia suddenly exhibited gleams of exquisite sensibility.

In women, it must further be said, the sexual impulse shows a much more marked tendency to periodicity than in men; not only is it less apt to appear spontaneously, but its spontaneous manifestations are in a very pronounced manner correlated with menstruation. A woman who may experience almost overmastering sexual desire just before, during, or after the monthly period may remain perfectly calm and self-possessed during the rest of the month. In men such irregularities of the sexual impulse are far less marked. Thus it is that a woman may often appear capricious, unaccountable, or cold, merely because her moments of strong emotion have been physiologically confined within a limited period. She may be one day capable of audacities of which on another the very memory might seem to have left her.

Not only is the intensity of the sexual impulse in women, as compared to men, more liable to vary from day to day, or from week to week, but the same greater variability is marked when we compare the whole cycle of life in women to that of men. The stress of early womanhood, when the reproductive functions are in fullest activity, and of late womanhood, when they are ceasing, produces a profound organic fermentation, psychic as much as physical, which is not paralleled in the lives of men. This greater variability in the cycle of a woman's life as compared with a man's is indicated very delicately and precisely by the varying incidence of insanity, and is made clearly visible in a diagram prepared by Marro showing the relative liability to mental diseases in the two sexes according to age.[180] At the age of 20 the incidence of insanity in both sexes is equal; from that age onward the curve in men proceeds in a gradual and equable manner, with only the slightest oscillation, on to old age. But in women the curve is extremely irregular; it remains high during all the years from 20 to 30, instead of falling like the masculine curve; then it falls rapidly to considerably below the masculine curve, rising again considerably above the masculine level during the climacteric years from 40 to 50, after which age the two sexes remain fairly close together to the end of life. Thus, as measured by the test of insanity, the curve of woman's life, in the sudden rise and sudden fall of its sexual crisis, differs from the curve of man's life and closely resembles the minor curve of her menstrual cycle.

The general tendency of this difference in sexual life and impulse is to show a greater range of variation in women than in men. Fairly uniform, on the whole, in men generally and in the same man throughout mature life, sexual impulse varies widely between woman and woman, and even in the same woman at different periods.

[169]
Ovid remarks (*Ars Amatoria*, bk. i) that, if men were silent, women would take the active and suppliant part.

[170]
Ferrand, *De la Maladie d'Amour*, 1623, ch. ii.

[171]
Tarde, *Archives d'Anthropologie Criminelle*, May 15, 1897. Marro, who quotes this observation (*Pubertà*, p. 467; in French edition, p. 61), remarks that his own evidence lends some support to Lombroso's conclusion that under ordinary circumstances woman's sensory acuteness is less than that of man. He is, however, inclined to impute this to defective attention; within the sexual sphere women's attention becomes concentrated, and their sensory perceptions then go far beyond those of men. There is probably considerable truth in this subtle observation.

[172]
A well-known gynecologist writes from America: "Abhorrence due to suffering on first nights I have repeatedly seen. One very marked case is that of a fine womanly young woman with splendid figure; she is a very good woman, and admires her husband, but, though she tries to develop desire and passion, she cannot succeed. I fear the man will some day appear who will be able to develop the latent feelings."

[173]
It is curious that, while the sexual impulse in women tends to develop at a late age more frequently than in men, it would also appear to develop more frequently at a very early age than in the other sex. The majority of cases of precocious sexual development seems to be in female children. W. Roger Williams ("Precocious Sexual Development," *British Gynæcological Journal*, May, 1902) finds that 80 such cases have been recorded in females and only 20 in males, and, while 13 is the earliest age at which boys have proved virile, girls have been known to conceive at 8.

[174]
I find the same remark made by Plazzonus in the seventeenth century.

[175]
Art. "Fécondation," *Dictionnaire Encyclopédique des Sciences Médicales*.

[176]
This also is an ancient remark, for in the early treatise *De Secretis Mulierum*, once attributed to Michael Scot, it is stated, concerning the woman who finds pleasure in coitus, "cantat libenter."

[177]
It is scarcely necessary to add that prostitutes can furnish little evidence one way or the other. Not only may prostitutes refuse to participate in the sexual orgasm, but the evils of a prostitute's life are obviously connected with causes quite other than mere excess of sexual gratification.

[178]
This is, for instance, indicated by the experiments of Gualino concerning the sexual sensitiveness of the lips (*Archivio di Psichiatria*, 1904, fasc. 3). He found that mechanical irritation applied to the lips produced more or less sexual feeling in 12 out of 20 women, but in only 10 out of 25 men, *i.e.*, in three-fifths of the women and two-fifths of the men.

[179]
"Adolescence is for women primarily a period of storm and stress, while for men it is in the highest sense a period of doubt," (Starbuck, *Psychology of Religion*, p. 241.) It is interesting to note that in the religious sphere, also, the emotions of women are more diffused than those of men; Starbuck confirms the conclusion of Professor Coe that, while

women have at least as much religious emotion as men, in them it is more all pervasive, and they experience fewer struggles and acute crises. (*Ibid.*, p. 80.)

[180]

Marro, *La Pubertà*, p. 233. This table covers all those cases, nearly 3000, of patients entering the Turin asylum, from 1886 to 1895, in which the age of the first appearance of insanity was known.

III.

Summary of Conclusions.

In conclusion it may be worth while to sum up the main points brought out in this brief discussion of a very large question. We have seen that there are two streams of opinion regarding the relative strength of the sexual impulse in men and women: one tending to regard it as greater in men, the other as greater in women. We have concluded that, since a large body of facts may be brought forward to support either view, we may fairly hold that, roughly speaking, the distribution of the sexual impulse between the two sexes is fairly balanced.

We have, however, further seen that the phenomena are in reality too complex to be settled by the usual crude method of attempting to discover quantitative differences in the sexual impulse. We more nearly get to the bottom of the question by a more analytic method, breaking up our mass of facts into groups. In this way we find that there are certain well-marked characteristics by which the sexual impulse in women differs from the same impulse in men: 1. It shows greater apparent passivity. 2. It is more complex, less apt to appear spontaneously, and more often needing to be aroused, while the sexual orgasm develops more slowly than in men. 3. It tends to become stronger after sexual relationships are established. 4. The threshold of excess is less easily reached than in men. 5. The sexual sphere is larger and more diffused. 6. There is a more marked tendency to periodicity in the spontaneous manifestations of sexual desire. 7. Largely as a result of these characteristics, the sexual impulse shows a greater range of variation in women than in men, both as between woman and woman and in the same woman at different periods.

It may be added that a proper understanding of these sexual differences in men and women is of great importance, both in the practical management of sexual hygiene and in the comprehension of those wider psychological characteristics by which women differ from men.

APPENDICES.

APPENDIX A.
THE SEXUAL INSTINCT IN SAVAGES.
I.

In the eighteenth century, when savage tribes in various parts of the world first began to be visited, extravagantly romantic views widely prevailed as to the simple and idyllic lives led by primitive peoples. During the greater part of the nineteenth century the tendency of opinion was to the opposite extreme, and it became usual to insist on the degraded and licentious morals of savages.[181]

In reality, however, savage life is just as little a prolonged debauch as a prolonged idyll. The inquiries of such writers as Westermarck, Frazer, and Crawley are tending to introduce a sounder conception of the actual, often highly complex, conditions of primitive life in its relations to the sexual instinct.

At the same time it is not difficult to account for the belief, widely spread during the nineteenth century, in the unbridled licentiousness of savages. In the first place, the doctrine of evolution inevitably created a prejudice in favor of such a view. It was assumed that modesty, chastity, and restraint were the finest and ultimate flowers of moral development;

therefore at the beginnings of civilization we must needs expect to find the opposite of these things. Apart, however, from any mere prejudice of this kind, a superficial observation of the actual facts necessarily led to much misunderstanding. Just as the nakedness of many savage peoples led to the belief that they were lacking in modesty, although, as a matter of fact, modesty is more highly developed in savage life than in civilization,[182] so the absence of our European rules of sexual behavior among savages led to the conclusion that they were abandoned to debauchery. The widespread custom of lending the wife under certain circumstances was especially regarded as indicating gross licentiousness. Moreover, even when intercourse was found to be free before marriage, scarcely any investigator sought to ascertain what amount of sexual intercourse this freedom involved. It was not clearly understood that such freedom must by no means be necessarily assumed to involve very frequent intercourse. Again, it often happened that no clear distinction was made between peoples contaminated by association with civilization, and peoples not so contaminated. For instance, when prostitution is attributed to a savage people we must usually suppose either that a mistake has been made or that the people in question have been degraded by intercourse with white peoples, for among unspoilt savages customs that can properly be called prostitution rarely prevail. Nor, indeed, would they be in harmony with the conditions of primitive life.

It has been seriously maintained that the chastity of savages, so far as it exists at all, is due to European civilization. It is doubtless true that this is the case with individual persons and tribes, but there is ample evidence from various parts of the world to show that this is by no means the rule. And, indeed, it may be said—with no disregard of the energy and sincerity of missionary efforts—that it could not be so. A new system of beliefs and practices, however excellent it may be in itself, can never possess the same stringent and unquestionable force as the system in which an individual and his ancestors have always lived, and which they have never doubted the validity of. That this is so we may have occasion to observe among ourselves. Christian teachers question the wisdom of bringing young people under free-thinking influence, because, although they do not deny the morals of free-thinkers, they believe that to unsettle the young may have a disastrous effect, not only on belief, but also on conduct. Yet this dangerously unsettling process has been applied by missionaries on a wholesale scale to races which in some respect are often little more than children. When, therefore, we are considering the chastity of savages we must not take into account those peoples which have been brought into close contact with Europeans.

In order to understand the sexual habits of savages generally there are two points which always have to be borne in mind as of the first importance: (1) the checks restraining sexual intercourse among savages, especially as regards time and season, are so numerous, and the sanctions upholding those checks so stringent, that sexual excess cannot prevail to the same extent as in civilization; (2) even in the absence of such checks, that difficulty of obtaining sexual erethism which has been noted as so common among savages, when not overcome by the stimulating influences prevailing at special times and seasons, and which is probably in large measure dependent on hard condition of life as well as an insensitive quality of nervous texture, still remains an important factor, tending to produce a natural chastity. There is a third consideration which, though from the present point of view subsidiary, is not without bearing on our conception of chastity among savages: the importance, even sacredness, of procreation is much more generally recognized by savage than by civilized peoples, and also a certain symbolic significance is frequently attached to human procreation as related to natural fruitfulness generally; so that a primitive sexual orgy, instead of being a mere manifestation of licentiousness, may have a ritual significance, as a magical means of evoking the fruitfulness of fields and herds.[183]

When a savage practises extraconjugal sexual intercourse, the act is frequently not, as it has come to be conventionally regarded in civilization, an immorality or at least an illegitimate indulgence; it is a useful and entirely justifiable act, producing definite benefits, conducing alike to cosmic order and social order, although these benefits are not always such as we in civilization believe to be caused by the act. Thus, speaking of the northern tribes of central Australia, Spencer and Gillen remark: "It is very usual amongst all of the tribes to allow considerable license during the performance of certain of their ceremonies when a large number of natives, some of them coming often from distant parts, are gathered together—in fact, on such occasions all of the ordinary marital rules seem to be more or less set aside for the time being. Each day, in some tribes, one or more women are told off whose duty it is to attend at the corrobboree grounds,—sometimes only during the day, sometimes at night,—and all of the men, except those who are fathers, elder and younger brothers, and sons, have access to them.... The idea is that the sexual intercourse assists in some way in the proper performance of the ceremony, causing everything to work smoothly and preventing the decorations from falling off."[184]

It is largely this sacred character of sexual intercourse—the fact that it is among the things that are at once "divine" and "impure," these two conceptions not being differentiated in primitive thought—which leads to the frequency with which in savage life a taboo is put upon its exercise. Robertson Smith added an appendix to his *Religion of the Semites* on "Taboo on the Intercourse of the Sexes."[185] Westermarck brought together evidence showing the frequency with which this and allied causes tended to the chastity of savages.[186] Frazer has very luminously expounded the whole primitive conception of sexual intercourse, and showed how it affected chastity.[187] Warriors must often be chaste; the men who go on any hunting or other expedition require to be chaste to be successful; the women left behind must be strictly chaste; sometimes even the whole of the people left behind, and for long periods, must be chaste in order to insure the success of the expedition. Hubert and Maus touched on the same point in their elaborate essay on sacrifice, pointing out how frequently sexual relationships are prohibited on the occasion of any ceremony whatever.[188] Crawley, in elaborating the primitive conception of taboo, has dealt fully with ritual and traditional influences making for chastity among savages. He brings forward, for instance, a number of cases, from various parts of the world, in which intercourse has to be delayed for days, weeks, even months, after marriage. He considers that the sexual continence prevalent among savages is largely due to a belief in the enervating effects of coitus; so dangerous are the sexes to each other that, as he points out, even now sexual separation of the sexes commonly occurs.[189]

There are thus a great number of constantly recurring occasions in savage life when continence must be preserved, and when, it is firmly believed, terrible risks would be incurred by its violation—during war, after victory, after festivals, during mourning, on journeys, in hunting and fishing, in a vast number of agricultural and industrial occupations.

It might fairly be argued that the facility with which the savage places these checks on sexual intercourse itself bears witness to the weakness of the sexual impulse. Evidence of another order which seems to point to the undeveloped state of the sexual impulse among savages may be found in the comparatively undeveloped condition of their sexual organs, a condition not, indeed, by any means constant, but very frequently noted. As regards women, it has in many parts of the world been observed to be the rule, and the data which Ploss and Bartels have accumulated seem to me, on the whole, to point clearly in this direction.[190]

At another point, also, it may be remarked, the repulsion between the sexes and the restraints on intercourse may be associated with weak sexual impulse. It is not improbable that a certain horror of the sexual organs may be a natural feeling which is extinguished in the intoxication of desire, yet still has a physiological basis which renders the sexual organs—disguised and minimized by convention and by artistic representation—more or less disgusting in the absence of erotic emotion.[191] And this is probably more marked in cases in which the sexual instinct is constitutionally feeble. A lady who had no marked sexual desires, and who considered it well bred to be indifferent to such matters, on inspecting her sexual parts in a mirror for the first time in her life was shocked and disgusted at the sight. Certainly many women could record a similar experience on being first approached by a man, although artistic conventions present the male form with greater truth than the female. Moreover,—and here is the significant point,—this feeling is by no means restricted to the refined and cultured. "When working at Michelangelo," wrote a correspondent from Italy, "my upper gondolier used to see photographs and statuettes of all that man's works. Stopping one day before the Night and Dawn of S. Lorenzo, sprawling naked women, he exclaimed: 'How hideous they are!' I pressed him to explain himself. He went on: 'The ugliest man naked is handsomer than the finest woman naked. Women have crooked legs,

144

and their sexual organs stink. I only once saw a naked woman. It was in a brothel, when I was 18. The sight of her "natura" made me go out and vomit into the canal. You know I have been twice married, but I never saw either of my wives without clothing.' Of very rank cheese he said one day: 'Puzza come la natura d'una donna.'" This man, my correspondent added, was entirely normal and robust, but seemed to regard sexual congress as a mere evacuation, the sexual instinct apparently not being strong.

It seems possible that, if the sexual impulse had no existence, all men would regard women with this *horror feminæ*. As things are, however, at all events in civilization, sexual emotions begin to develop even earlier, usually, than acquaintance with the organs of the other sex begins; so that this disgust is inhibited. If, however, among savages the sexual impulse is habitually weak, and only aroused to strength under the impetus of powerful stimuli, often acting periodically, then we should expect the*horror*to be a factor of considerable importance.

The weakness of the physical sexual impulse among savages is reflected in the psychic sphere. Many writers have pointed out that love plays but a small part in their lives. They practise few endearments; they often only kiss children (Westermarck notes that sexual love is far less strong than parental love); love-poems are among some primitive peoples few (mostly originating with the women), and their literature often gives little or no attention to passion.[192] Affection and devotion are, however, often strong, especially in savage women.

It is not surprising that jealousy should often, though not by any means invariably, be absent, both among men and among women. Among savages this is doubtless a proof of the weakness of the sexual impulse. Spencer and Gillen note the comparativeabsence of jealousy in men among the Central Australian tribes they studied.[193]Negresses, it is said by a French army surgeon in his *Untrodden Fields of Anthropology*, do not know what jealousy is, and the first wife will even borrow money to buy the second wife. Among a much higher race, the women in a Korean household, it is said, live together happily, as an almost invariable rule, though it appears that this was not always the case among a polygamous people of European race, the Mormons.

The tendency of the sexual instinct in savages to periodicity, to seasonal manifestations, I do not discuss here, as I have dealt with it in the first volume of these*Studies*.[194] It has, however, a very important bearing on this subject. Periodicity of sexual manifestations is, indeed, less absolute in primitive man than in most animals, but it is still very often quite clearly marked. It is largely the occurrence of these violent occasional outbursts of the sexual instinct—during which the organic impulse to tumescence becomes so powerful that external stimuli are no longer necessary—that has led to the belief in the peculiar strength of the impulse in savages.[195]

[181]

Thus, Lubbock (Lord Avebury), in the *Origin of Civilization*, fifth edition, 1889, brings forward a number of references in evidence of this belief. More recently Finck, in his *Primitive Love and Love-stories*, 1899, seeks to accumulate data in favor of the unbounded licentiousness of savages. He admits, however, that a view of the matter opposed to his own is now tending to prevail.

[182]

See "The Evolution of Modesty" in the first volume of these *Studies*.

[183]

The sacredness of sexual relations often applies also to individual marriage. Thus, Skeat, in his *Malay Magic*, shows that the bride and bridegroom are definitely recognized as sacred, in the same sense that the king is, and in Malay States the king is a very sacred person. See also, concerning the sacred character of coitus, whether individual or collective, A. Van Gennep,*Rites de Passage, passim*.

[184]

Spencer and Gillen, *Northern Tribes of Central Australia*, p. 136.

[185]

Religion of the Semites, second edition, 1894, p. 454 *et seq*.

[186]

History of Marriage, pp. 66-70, 150-156, etc.

[187]

Golden Bough, third edition, part ii, *Taboo and the Perils of the Soul.* Frazer has discussed taboo generally. For a shorter account of taboo, see art. "Taboo" by Northcote Thomas in *Encyclopædia Britannica*, eleventh edition, 1911. Freud has lately (*Imago*, 1912) made an attempt to explain the origin of taboo psychologically by comparing it to neurotic obsessions. Taboo, Freud believes, has its origin in a forbidden act to perform which there is a strong unconscious tendency; an ambivalent attitude, that is, combining the opposite tendencies, is thus established. In this way Freud would account for the fact that tabooed persons and things are both sacred and unclean.

[188]

"Essai sur le Sacrifice," *L'Année Sociologique*, 1899, pp. 50-51.

[189]

The Mystic Rose, 1902, p. 187 *et seq.*, 215 *et seq.*, 342 *et seq.*

[190]

Das Weib, vol. i, section 6.

[191]

This statement has been questioned. It should, however, be fairly evident that the sexual organs in either sex, when closely examined, can scarcely be regarded as beautiful except in the eyes of a person of the opposite sex who is in a condition of sexual excitement, and they are not always attractive even then. Moreover, it must be remembered that the snake-like aptitude of the penis to enter into a state of erection apart from the control of the will puts it in a different category from any other organ of the body, and could not fail to attract the attention of primitive peoples so easily alarmed by unusual manifestations. We find even in the early ages of Christianity that St. Augustine attached immense importance to this alarming aptitude of the penis as a sign of man's sinful and degenerate state.

[192]

Lubbock, *Origin of Civilization*, fifth edition, pp. 69, 73; Westermarck,*History of Marriage*, p. 357; Grosse, *Anfänge der Kunst*, p. 236; Herbert Spencer, "Origin of Music," *Mind*, Oct., 1890.

[193]

Spencer and Gillen, *Native Tribes of Central Australia*, p. 99; *cf.* Finck,*Primitive Love and Love-stories*, p. 89 *et seq.*

[194]

"The Phenomena of Sexual Periodicity." The subject has also been more recently discussed by Walter Heape, "The 'Sexual Season' of Mammals,"*Quarterly Journal of Microscopical Science*, vol. xliv, 1900. See also F. H. A. Marshall, *The Physiology of Reproduction*, 1910.

[195]

This view finds a belated supporter in Max Marcuse ("Geschlechtstrieb des Urmenschens," *Sexual-Problem*, Oct., 1909), who, on grounds which I cannot regard as sound, seeks to maintain the belief that the sexual instinct is more highly developed among savage than among civilized peoples.

II.

The facts thus seem to indicate that among primitive peoples, while the magical, ceremonial, and traditional restraints on sexual intercourse are very numerous, very widespread, and nearly always very stringent, there is, underlying this prevalence of restraints on intercourse, a fundamental weakness of the sexual instinct, which craves less, and craves less frequently, than is the case among civilized peoples, but is liable to be powerfully manifested at special seasons. It is perfectly true that among savages, as Sutherland states, "there is no ideal which makes chastity a thing beautiful in itself"; but when the same writer goes on to state that "it is untrue that in sexual license the savage has everything to learn," we must demand greater precision of statement.[196]Travelers, and too often would-be scientific writers, have been so much impressed by the absence among savages of the

146

civilized ideal of chastity, and by the frequent freedom of sexual intercourse, that they have not paused to inquire more carefully into the phenomena, or to put themselves at the primitive point of view, but have assumed that freedom here means all that it would mean in a European population.

In order to illustrate the actual circumstances of savage life in this respect from the scanty evidence furnished by the most careful observers, I have brought together from scattered sources a few statements concerning primitive peoples in very various parts of the world.[197]

Among the Andamanese, Portman, who knows them well, says that sexual desire is very moderate; in males it appears at the age of 18, but, as "their love for sport is greater than their passions, these are not gratified to any great extent till after marriage, which rarely takes place till a man is about 26."[198]

Although chastity is not esteemed by the Fuegians, and virginity is lost at a very early age, yet both men and women are extremely moderate in sexual indulgence.[199]

Among the Eskimo at the other end of the American continent, according to Dr. F. Cook, the sexual passions are suppressed during the long darkness of winter, as also is the menstrual function usually, and the majority of the children are born nine months after the appearance of the sun.[200]

Among the Indians of North America it is the custom of many tribes to refrain from sexual intercourse during the whole period of lactation, as also D'Orbigny found to be the case among South American Indians, although suckling went on for over three years.[201] Many of the Indian tribes have now been rendered licentious by contact with civilization. In the primitive condition their customs were entirely different. Dr. Holder, who knows many tribes of North American Indians well, has dealt in some detail with this point. "Several of the virtues," he states, "and among them chastity, were more faithfully practised by the Indian race before the invasion from the East than these same virtues are practised by the white race of the present day.... The race is less salacious than either the negro or white race.... That the women of some tribes are now more careful of their virtue than the women of any other community whose history I know, I am fully convinced."[202] It is not only on the women that sexual abstinence is imposed. Among some branches of the Salish Indians of British Columbia a young widower must refrain from sexual intercourse for a year, and sometimes lives entirely apart during that period.[203]

In many parts of Polynesia, although the sexual impulse seems often to have been highly developed before the arrival of Europeans, it is very doubtful whether license, in the European sense, at all generally prevailed. The Marquesans, who have sometimes been regarded as peculiarly licentious, are especially mentioned by Foley as illustrating his statement that sexual erethism is with difficulty attained by primitive peoples except during sexual seasons.[204] Herman Melville's detailed account in *Typee* of the Marquesans (somewhat idealized, no doubt) reveals nothing that can fairly be called licentiousness. At Rotuma, J. Stanley Gardiner remarks, before the missionaries came sexual intercourse before marriage was free, but gross immorality and prostitution and adultery were unknown. Matters are much worse now.[205] The Maoris of New Zealand, in the old days, according to one who had lived among them, were more chaste than the English, and, though a chief might lend his wife to a friend as an honor, it would be very difficult to take her (*private communication*).[206]Captain Cook also represented these people as modest and virtuous.

Among the Papuans of New Guinea and Torres Straits, although intercourse before marriage is free, it is by no means unbridled, nor is it carried to excess. There are many circumstances restraining intercourse. Thus, unmarried men must not indulge in it during October and November at Torres Straits. It is the general rule also that there should be no sexual intercourse during pregnancy, while a child is being suckled (which goes on for three or four years), or even until it can speak or walk.[207] In Astrolabe Bay, New Guinea, according to Vahness, a young couple must abstain from intercourse for several weeks after marriage, and to break this rule would be disgraceful.[208]

As regards Australia, Brough Smyth wrote: "Promiscuous intercourse between the sexes is not practised by the aborigines, and their laws on the subject, particularly those of New South Wales, are very strict. When at camp all the young unmarried men are stationed by themselves at the extreme end, while the married men, each with his family, occupy the center. No conversation is allowed between the single men and the girls or the married women. Infractions of these laws were visited by punishment; ... five or six warriors threw from a comparatively short distance several spears at him [the offender]. The man was often severely wounded and sometimes killed."[209] This author mentions that a black woman has been known to kill a white man who attempted to have intercourse with her by force. Yet both sexes have occasional sexual intercourse from an early age. After marriage, in various parts of Australia, there are numerous restraints on intercourse, which is forbidden not merely during menstruation, but during the latter part of pregnancy and for one moon after childbirth.[210]

Concerning the people of the Malay Peninsula, Hrolf Vaughan Stevens states: "The sexual impulse among the Belendas is only developed to a slight extent; they are not sensual, and the husband has intercourse with his wife not oftener than three times a month. The women also are not ardent.... The Orang Lâut are more sensual than the Dyaks, who are, however, more given to obscene jokes than their neighbors.... With the Belendas there is little or no love-play in sexual relations".[211] Skeat tells us also that among Malays in war-time strict chastity must be observed in a stockade, or the bullets of the garrison will lose their power.[212]

It is a common notion that the negro and negroid races of Africa are peculiarly prone to sexual indulgence. This notion is not supported by those who have had the most intimate knowledge of these peoples. It probably gained currency in part owing to the open and expansive temperament of the negro, and in part owing to the extremely sexual character of many African orgies and festivals, though those might quite as legitimately be taken as evidence of difficulty in attaining sexual erethism.

A French army surgeon, speaking from knowledge of the black races in various French colonies, states in his *Untrodden Fields of Anthropology* that it is a mistake to imagine that the negress is very amorous. She is rather cold, and indifferent to the refinements of love, in which respects she is very unlike the mulatto. The white man is usually powerless to excite her, partly from his small penis, partly from his rapidity of emission; the black man, on account of his blunter nervous system, takes three times as long to reach emission as the white man. Among the Mohammedan peoples of West Africa, Daniell remarks, as well as in central and northern Africa, it is usual to suckle a child for two or more years. From the time when pregnancy becomes apparent to the end of weaning no intercourse takes place. It is believed that this would greatly endanger the infant, if not destroy it. This means that for every child the woman, at all events, must remain continent for about three years.[213] Sir H. H. Johnston, writing concerning the peoples of central Africa, remarks that the man also must remain chaste during these periods. Thus, among the Atonga the wife leaves her husband at the sixth month of pregnancy, and does not resume relations with him until five or six months after the birth of the child. If, in the interval, he has relations with any other woman, it is believed his wife will certainly die. "The negro is very rarely vicious," Johnston says, "after he has attained to the age of puberty. He is only more or less uxorious. The children are vicious, as they are among most races of mankind, the boys outrageously so. As regards the little girls over nearly the whole of British Central Africa, chastity before puberty is an unknown condition, except perhaps among the A-nyanja. Before a girl is become a woman it is a matter of absolute indifference what she does, and scarcely any girl remains a virgin after about 5 years of age."[214] Among the Bangala of the upper Congo a woman suckles her child for six to eighteen months and during all this period the husband has no intercourse with his wife, for that, it is believed, would kill the child.[215]

Among the Yoruba-speaking people of West Africa A. B. Ellis mentions that suckling lasts for three years, during the whole of which period the wife must not cohabit with her husband.[216]

Although chastity before marriage appears to be, as a rule, little regarded in Africa, this is not always so. In some parts of West Africa, a girl, at all events if of high birth, when found guilty of unchastity may be punished by the insertion into her vagina of bird pepper, a kind of capsicum, beaten into a mass; this produces intense pain and such acute inflammation that the canal may even be obliterated.[217]

Among the Dahomey women there is no coitus during pregnancy nor during suckling, which lasts for nearly three years. The same is true among the Jekris and other tribes on the Niger, where it is believed that the milk would suffer if intercourse took place during lactation.[218]

In another part of Africa, among the Suaheli, even after marriage only incomplete coitus is at first allowed and there is no intercourse for a year after the child's birth.[219]

Farther south, among the Ba Wenda of north Transvaal, says the Rev. R. Wessmann, although the young men are permitted to "play" with the young girls before marriage, no sexual intercourse is allowed. If it is seen that a girl's labia are apart when she sits down on a stone, she is scolded, or even punished, as guilty of having had intercourse.[220]

Among the higher races in India the sexual instinct is very developed, and sexual intercourse has been cultivated as an art, perhaps more elaborately than anywhere else. Here, however, we are far removed from primitive conditions and among a people closely allied to the Europeans. Farther to the east, as among the Cambodians, strict chastity seems to prevail, and if we cross the Himalayas to the north we find ourselves among wild people to whom sexual license is unknown. Thus, among the Turcomans, even a few days after the marriage has been celebrated, the young couple are separated for an entire year.[221]

All the great organized religions have seized on this value of sexual abstinence, already consecrated by primitive magic and religion, and embodied it in their system. It was so in ancient Egypt. Thus, according to Diodorus, on the death of a king, the entire population of Egypt abstained from sexual intercourse for seventy-two days. The Persians, again, attached great value to sexual as to all other kinds of purity. Even involuntary seminal emissions were severely punishable. To lie with a menstruatingwoman, according to the *Vendidad*, was as serious a matter as to pollute holy fire, and to lie with a pregnant woman was to incur a penalty of 2000 strokes. Among the modern Parsees a man must not lie with his wife after she is four months and ten days pregnant. Mohammedanism cannot be described as an ascetic religion, yet long and frequent periods of sexual abstinence are enjoined. There must be no sexual intercourse during the whole of pregnancy, during suckling, during menstruation (and for eight days before and after), nor during the thirty days of the Ramedan fast. Other times of sexual abstinence are also prescribed; thus among the Mohammedan Yezidis of Mardin in northern Mesopotamia there must be no sexual intercourse on Wednesdays or Fridays.[222]

In the early Christian Church many rules of sexual abstinence still prevailed, similar to those usual among savages, though not for such prolonged periods. In Egbert's Penitential, belonging to the ninth century, it is stated that a woman must abstain from intercourse with her husband three months after conception and for forty days after birth. There were a number of other occasions, including Lent, when a husband must not know his wife.[223] "Some canonists say," remarks Jeremy Taylor, "that the Church forbids a mutual congression of married pairs upon festival days.... The Council of Eliberis commanded abstinence from conjugal rights for three or four or seven days before the communion. Pope Liberius commanded the same during the whole time of Lent, supposing the fast is polluted by such congressions."[224]

[196]
A. Sutherland, *Origin and Growth of the Moral Instinct*, vol. i, pp. 8, 187. As has been shown by, for instance, Dr. Iwan Bloch (*Beiträge zur Ætiologie der Psychopathia Sexualis*, Erster Theil, 1902), every perverse sexual practice may be found, somewhere or other, among savages or barbarians; but, as the same writer acutely points out (p. 58), these devices bear witness to the need of overcoming frigidity rather than to the strength of the sexual impulse.
[197]
Ploss and Bartels have brought together in *Das Weib* a large number of facts in the same sense, more especially under the headings of *Abstinenz-Vorschriften* and *Die Fernhaltung der Schwangeren*. I have not drawn upon their collection.
[198]
Journal of the Anthropological Institute, May, 1896, p. 369.
[199]

Hyades and Deniker, *Mission Scientifique du Cap Horn*, vol. vii, p. 188.

[200]

F. Cook, *New York Journal of Gynecology and Obstetrics*, 1894.

[201]

A. d'Orbigny, *L'Homme Américain*, 1839, vol. i, p. 47.

[202]

A. B. Holder, "Gynecic Notes Among the American Indians," *American Journal of Obstetrics*, 1892, vol. xxvi, No. 1.

[203]

Journal of the Anthropological Institute, 1905, p. 139.

[204]

Foley, *Bulletin de la Société d' Anthropologie*, Paris, November 6, 1879.

[205]

J. S. Gardiner, *Journal of the Anthropological Institute*, February, 1898, p. 409.

[206]

As regards the modern Maoris, a medical correspondent in New Zealand writes: "It is nothing for members of both sexes to live in the same room, and for promiscuous intercourse to take place between father and daughter or brother and sister. Maori women, who will display a great deal of modesty when in the presence of male Maoris, will openly ask strange Europeans to have sexual intercourse with them, and without any desire for reward. The men, however, seem to prefer their own women, and even when staying in towns, where they can obtain prostitutes, they will remain continent until they return home again, a period of perhaps a month."

[207]

Schellong, *Zeitschrift für Ethnologie*, 1889, i, pp. 17, 19; Haddon, *Journal of the Anthropological Institute*, February, 1890, pp. 316, 397; Guise, *ib.*, February and May, 1899, p. 207; Seligmann, *ib.*, 1902, pp. 298, 301-302;*Reports Cambridge Expedition*, vol. v, pp. 199-200, 275.

[208]

Zeitschrift für Ethnologie, 1900, ht. v, p. 414.

[209]

R. Brough Smyth, *The Aborigines of Victoria*, vol. ii, p. 318.

[210]

Journal of the Anthropological Institute, 1894, pp. 170, 177, 187.

[211]

Zeitschrift für Ethnologie, 1896, iv, pp. 180-181.

[212]

W. W. Skeat, *Malay Magic*, p. 524.

[213]

W. F. Daniell, *Medical Topography of Gulf of Guinea*, 1849, p. 55.

[214]

Sir H. H. Johnston, *British Central Africa*, 1899, pp. 409, 414.

[215]

Rev. J. H. Weeks, *Journal of the Anthropological Institute*, 1910, p. 418.

[216]

Sir A. B. Ellis, *Yoruba-Speaking Peoples*, p. 185.

[217]

W. F. Daniell, *op. cit.*, p. 36.

[218]

Journal of the Anthropological Institute, August and November, 1898, p. 106.

[219]

Zeitschrift für Ethnologie, 1899, ii and iii, p. 84; Velten, *Sitten und Gebraüche der Suaheli*, p. 12.

[220]

Zeitschrift für Ethnologie, 1896, p. 364.

[221]

Vambery, *Travels in Central Asia*, 1864, p. 323.

[222]

Heard, *Journal of the Anthropological Institute*, Jan.-June, 1911, p. 210. The same rule is also observed by the Christians of this district.

[223]

Haddon and Stubbs, *Councils and Ecclesiastical Documents*, vol. iii, p. 423.

[224]

Jeremy Taylor, *The Rule of Conscience*, bk. iii, ch. iv, rule xx.

III.

Thus it would seem probable that, contrary to a belief once widely prevalent, the sexual instinct has increased rather than diminished with the growth of civilization. This fact was clear to the insight of Lucretius, though it has often been lost sight of since.[225] Yet even observation of animals might have suggested the real bearing of the facts. The higher breeds of cattle, it is said, require the male more often than the inferior breeds.[226] Thorough-bred horses soon reach sexual maturity, and I understand that since pains have been taken to improve cart-horses the sexual instincts of the mares have become less trustworthy. There is certainly no doubt that in our domestic animals generally, which live under what may be called civilized conditions, the sexual system and the sexual needs are more developed than in the wild species most closely related to them.[227] All observers seem to agree on this point, and it is sufficient to refer to the excellent summary of the question furnished by Heape in the study of "The 'Sexual Season' of Mammals," to which reference has already been made. He remarks, moreover, that, "while the sexual activity of domestic animals and of wild animals in captivity may be more frequently exhibited, it is not so violent as is shown by animals in the wild state."[228] So that, it would seem, the greater periodicity of the instinct in the wild state, alike in animals and in man, is associated with greater violence of the manifestations when they do appear. Certain rodents, such as the rat and the mouse, are well known to possess both great reproductive power and marked sexual proclivities. Heape suggests that this also is "due to the advantages derived from their intimate relations with the luxuries of civilization." Heape recognizes that, as regards reproductive power, the same development may be traced in man: "It would seem highly probable that the reproductive power of man has increased with civilization, precisely as it may be increased in the lower animals by domestication; that the effect of a regular supply of good food, together with all the other stimulating factors available and exercised in modern civilized communities, has resulted in such great activity of the generative organs, and so great an increase in the supply of the reproductive elements, that conception in the healthy human female may be said to be possible almost at any time during the reproductive period."

"People of sense and reflection are most apt to have violent and constant passions," wrote Mary Wollstonecraft, "and to be preyed on by them."[229] It is that fact which leads to the greater importance of sexual phenomena among the civilized as compared to savages. The conditions of civilization increase the sexual instinct, which consequently tends to be more intimately connected with moral feelings. Morality is bound up with the development of the sexual instinct. The more casual and periodic character of the impulse in animals, since it involves greater sexual indifference, tends to favor a loose tie between the sexes, and hence is not favorable to the development of morals as we understand morals. In man the ever-present impulse of sex, idealizing each sex to the other sex, draws men and women together and holds them together. Foolish and ignorant persons may deplore the full development which the sexual instinct has reached in civilized man; to a finer insight that development is seen to be indissolubly linked with all that is most poignant and most difficult, indeed, but also all that is best, in human life as we know it.

[225]

De Rerum Naturâ, v, 1016.

[226]

151

Raciborski (*Traité de la Menstruation,* p. 43) quotes the observation of an experienced breeder of choice cattle to this effect.

[227]

"The organs which in the feral state," as Adlerz remarks (*Biologisches Centralblatt,* No. 4, 1902; quoted in *Science,* May 16, 1902), "are continually exercised in a severe struggle for existence, do not under domestication compete so closely with one another for the less needed nutriment. Hence, organs like the reproductive glands, which are not so directly implicated in self-preservation, are able to avail themselves of more food."

[228]

Quarterly Journal of Microscopical Science, vol. xliv, 1900, p. 12, 31, 39.

[229]

"Love," in *Thoughts on the Education of Daughters.*

APPENDIX B.
THE DEVELOPMENT OF THE SEXUAL INSTINCT.

It is a very remarkable fact that, although for many years past serious attempts have been made to elucidate the psychology of sexual perversions, little or no endeavor has been made to study the development of the normal sexual emotions. Nearly every writer seems either to take for granted that he and his readers are so familiar with all the facts of normal sex psychology that any detailed statement is altogether uncalled for, or else he is content to write a few fragmentary remarks, mostly made up of miscellaneous extracts from anatomical, philosophical, and historical works.

Yet it is as unreasonable to take normal phenomena for granted here as in any other region of science. A knowledge of such phenomena is as necessary here as physiology is to pathology or anatomy to surgery. So far from the facts of normal sex development, sex emotions, and sex needs being uniform and constant, as is assumed by those who consider their discussion unnecessary, the range of variation within fairly normal limits is immense, and it is impossible to meet with two individuals whose records are nearly identical.

There are two fundamental reasons why the endeavor should be made to obtain a broad basis of clear information on the subject. In the first place, the normal phenomena give the key to the abnormal phenomena, and the majority of sexual perversions, including even those that are most repulsive, are but exaggerations of instincts and emotions that are germinal in normal human beings. In the second place, we cannot even know what is normal until we are acquainted with the sexual life of a large number of healthy individuals. And until we know the limits of normal sexuality we are not in position to lay down any reasonable rules of sexual hygiene.

On these grounds I have for some time sought to obtain the sexual histories, and more especially the early histories, of men and women who, on *prima facie* grounds, may fairly be considered, or are at all events by themselves and others considered, ordinarily healthy and normal.

There are many difficulties about such a task, difficulties which are sufficiently obvious. There is, first of all, the natural reticence to reveal facts of so intimately personal a character. There is the prevailing ignorance and unintelligence which leads to the phenomena being obscure to the subject himself. When the first difficulty has been overcome, and the second is non-existent, there is still a lack of sufficiently strong motive to undertake the record, as well as a failure to realize the value of such records. I have, however, received a large number of such histories, for the most part offered spontaneously with permission to make such further inquiries as I thought desirable. Some of these histories are extremely interesting and instructive. In the present Appendix, and in a corresponding Appendix to the two following volumes of these *Studies,* I bring forward a varied selection of these narratives. In a few cases, it will be seen, the subjects are, to say the least, on the borderland of the abnormal, but they do not come before us as patients desiring treatment. They are playing their, usually active, sometimes even distinguished, part in the world, which knows nothing of their intimate histories.

HISTORY I.—E. T. (I reproduce this history, written in the third person, as it reached my hands.) T.'s earliest recollections of ideas of a sexual character are vaguely associated with thoughts upon whipping inflicted on companions by their parents, and sometimes upon his own person. About the age of 7 T. occasionally depicted to himself the appearance of the bare nates and genitalia of boys during flagellation. Reflection upon whipping gave rise to slight curious sensations at the base of the abdomen and in the nerves of the sexual system. The sight of a boy being whipped upon the bare nates caused erection before the age of 9. He cannot account for these excitations, as at the time he had not learned the most rudimentary facts of sex. The spectacle of the boy's nudity had no attraction for him, while the beating aroused his indignation against the person who administered it. T. knew a boy and girl of about his own age whose imaginations dwelt somewhat morbidly upon whipping. The three used to talk together about such chastisement, and the little girl liked to read "stories that had whippings in them." None of these children delighted in cruelty; the fascination in the theme of castigation seemed to be in imagining the spectacle of the exposed nates, though actual witnessing of the whipping made them angry at the time.

Accustomed to watch a young sister being bathed, T. had no distinct curiosity concerning the differences in sex until the age of 9. About this time he asked his father where babies came from, and was told to be quiet. When he persisted in the inquiry his father threatened to box his ears. His mother told him subsequently that doctors brought babies to mothers. He credited the story so far as to carefully watch the doctor who came when his mother "was going to have a new baby," in the hope of seeing a bundle in his arm. T. was 9 when he interrogated a servant-girl of 16 about babies and their origin. She laughed and said that one day she would tell him how children came. One Sunday this servant took T. for a country walk and initiated him in sexual intercourse, telling him he was too young to be a father, but that was the way babies were made. The girl took him into a field, saying she would show him how to do something which would make him "feel as though he was in heaven," informing him that she had often done this with young men. She then succeeded in causing erection and instructed him how to act. His feeling at the time was one of disgust; the appearance and odor of the female genitalia repelled him. Afterward, however, he wished to repeat the experience with girls of his own age. Finding the boy unresponsive, the girl took the masculine position and embraced him with great passion. T. can recall the expression of the girl's face, the perspiration on her forehead, and the whispered query whether it pleased him. The embrace lasted for about ten minutes, when the girl said it had "done her good." Later the same day they met a girl cousin of this servant about 10 or 12 years old. The three went to a lonely part of the seashore. The servant there suggested that T. should repeat the act with the little girl. T. was too shy, though the girl seemed quite willing and experienced. The older girl told the younger to keep watch a few yards away, while she again brought about intercourse in the same way. The servant told T. not to tell anyone. Intercourse with the servant was never repeated after that day; from shame he kept the promise for many years.

After this episode T. began to speculate about sexual matters and to observe the coupling of dogs with newly acquired interest. At 10 years he often lay awake, listening to a woman of 25 singing to a piano accompaniment. The woman's voice seemed very beautiful, and so strongly impressed him that he fell in love with her and longed to embrace her sexually. This secret attachment was much more romantic than sensual, though the idea of embracing the woman seemed to T. a natural part of the romance. He was beginning to invest the sex with angelic qualities. The thought of his adventure with the servant no longer caused repulsion, but rather pleasure. He reflected that if he could meet the girl now he could be very fond of her and understand things better. At this time he had not masturbated, nor even heard of the practice. One day, while playing with a girl of his own age, he succeeded in overcoming her shyness and induced her to expose herself, at the same time uncovering his own sexual parts. On this occasion and once afterward he succeeded in penetrating the vulva. Both he and the girl experienced imperfect enjoyment.

At boarding-school, where he was sent at 10, T. learned the vulgar phrases for sexual organs and sexual acts, and acquired the habit of moderate masturbation. Coarse talk and indecent jests about the opposite sex were common amusements of the playroom and dormitories. At first the obscene conversation was very distasteful; later he became more used to it, but thought it strange that sex intimacy should be a subject for ridicule and jest.

He began to read love-stories and think much about girls. At the same time he learned the nature of "the sin of fornication," and wondered why it should be considered so heinous. Parts of the Bible condemning intercourse between the unmarried alarmed him. Being of a serious as well as emotional and amorous nature, he became converted to evangelic belief. His mother warned him to beware of unclean companions at school. He tried to act as a Christian and think only pure thoughts about women. The talk, however, was always of girls and of being in love. His mind was often engrossed with amatory ideas of a poetic, sensuous nature, his sexual experiences having a firm hold on his imagination, while they gave him gratifying assurance of actual knowledge concerning things merely imagined by most of his companions.

His health was vigorous and he keenly enjoyed all outdoor games and excelled in daring and schoolboy mischief.

At 12 he fell deeply in love with a girl of corresponding age. He never felt any powerful sexual desire for his sweetheart, and never attempted anything but kissing and decorous caresses. He liked to walk and sit with the girl, to hold her hand, and stroke her soft hair. He felt real grief when separated from her. His thoughts of her were seldom sensual. A year or so afterward he had a temporary passion for a woman of 30, who used to flirt with him and allow kissing. T. thought her queen-like and very lovely, and wished to be her knight.

One day he saw, for a moment, in a friend's house, a dark, earnest-looking girl of 13, who made a very deep impression upon him, and, though he did not exchange a word with her, he often thought about her afterward. Five years later he met the dark girl again, and the pair were mutually drawn to one another. He proposed marriage and avowed a most desperate passion. A refusal on the plea of youth caused him the deepest misery. About eight years thereafter T. married the girl, and the marriage proved a very happy one for both.

When he was 15 T. made the acquaintance of a pretty blonde of the same age. She was a high-spirited hoiden. They were soon close friends and later lovers. They wrote a number of letters to each other and exchanged locks of hair and presents. Their talk about love was unreserved. One day she told T. that she had been sexually embraced by a former lover, a boy of 16, hinting very plainly that she would like T. to embrace her. This amour lasted for about six months. The lovers had many opportunities for clandestine intercourse. They used to consummate their passion in a part of a wood they called "the bower." Now and then one or the other would experience a pricking of conscience, but they were too passionately attached to each other to sever the intimacy. At length the girl began to dread the risk of conception and the intercourse ceased. Looking back upon this episode T. avers that the attachment and its physical expression seemed quite natural, poetic, and beautiful, though at times his religious principles condemned his conduct. He now thinks that the experience is by no means to be regretted either by the girl or himself. It was a wholesome youthful passion, as innocent as the mating of birds, and the insight which it gave to both of the hidden emotions of human nature was morally advantageous in after-life.

T. believes that his amative precocity was due to the early awakening of sex feeling by the servant-girl. But he also believes that the love passion would have asserted itself early in any case, since he inherits a warm temperament, had erectile power long before puberty, and has considerable seminal capacity. Having closely watched the effects of suppressed normal emotions and desires in youth at the time of pubescence, he maintains that such suppression is disastrous, causing unhealthy thoughts and leading to the formation of a habit of masturbation which may persist throughout life. He believes that temporary sexual intimacies between boys and girls under 20 from the period of puberty would be far less harmful than separation of the sexes until marriage, with its resultants: masturbation, hysteria, repressed and disordered functions in young women, seduction, prostitution, venereal affections, and many other evils.

154

HISTORY II.—The following narrative was written by a married lady: "My mother (herself a very passionate and attractive woman) recognized the difficulty for English girls of getting satisfactorily married, and determined, if possible, to shield us from disappointment by turning our thoughts in a different direction. Theoretically the idea was perhaps good, but in practice it proved useless. The natural desires were there. Disappointment and disillusion followed their repression none the less surely for having altered their natural shape. I think the love I had for my mother was almost sexual, as to be with her was a keen pleasure, and to be long away from her an almost unendurable pain. She used to talk to us a good deal on all sorts of subjects, but she never troubled about education in the ordinary sense. When 9 years old I had been taught nothing except to read and write. She never forbade us to read anything, but if by accident we got hold of a book of which she did not approve she used to say: 'I think that is rather a silly story, don't you?' We were so eager to come up to her standard of taste that we at once imagined we thought it silly, too. In the same way she discouraged ideas about love or marriage, not by suggesting there was anything wrong or improper about them, but by implying great contempt for girls who thought about lovers, etc. Up to the age of about 20 I had a vague general impression that love was very well for ordinary women, but far beneath the dignity of a somewhat superior person like myself. To show how little it entered my thoughts I may add that, up to 17, I fancied a woman got a child by being kissed on the lips by a man. Hence all the fuss in novels about the kiss on the mouth.

"When I was 9 years old I began to feel a great craving for scientific knowledge. *A Child's Guide to Science*, which I discovered at a second-hand book-stall (and which, by the way, informed me that heat is due to a substance called caloric), became a constant companion. In order to learn about light and gravitation, I saved up my money and ordered (of all books) Newton's*Principia*, shedding bitter tears when I found I could not understand a word of it. At the same time I was horribly ashamed of this desire for knowledge. I got such books as I could surreptitiously and hid them in odd corners. Why, I cannot imagine, as no one would have objected, but, on the contrary, I should have been helped to suitable books.

"My sisters and I were all violently argumentative, but our quarrels were all on abstract subjects. We saw little of other children and made no friendships, preferring each other's society to that of outsiders. When I was about 10 a girl of the same age came to stay with us for a few days. When we went to bed the first night she asked me if I ever played with myself, whereupon I took a great dislike to her. No sexual ideas or feelings were excited. When still quite a child, however, I had feelings of excitement which I now recognize as sexual. Such feelings always came to me in bed (at least I cannot remember them at any other time) and were generally accompanied by a gradually increasing desire to make water. For a long time I would not dare to get out of bed for fear of being scolded for staying awake, and only did so at last when actually compelled. In the mean time the sexual excitement increased also, and I believe I thought the latter was the result of the former, or, perhaps, rather, that both were the same thing. (This was when I was about 7 or 8 years old.) So far as I can recollect, the excitement did not recur when the desire to make water had been gratified. I seemed to remember wondering why thinking of certain things (I can't remember what these were) should make one want to urinate. (In later life I have found that, if the bladder is not emptied before coitus, pleasure is often more intense.) There were also feelings, which I now recognize as sexual, in connection with ideas of whipping.

"As a child and girl I had very strong religious feelings (I should have now if I could believe in the reality of religion), which were absent in my sisters. These feelings were much the same as I experienced later sexually; I felt toward God what I imagined I should like to feel to my husband if I married. This, I fancy, is what usually occurs. At 14 I went to a boarding-school where there were seventy girls between 7 and 19. I think it goes to show that there is but very little sexual precocity among English girls that during the three years I stayed there I never heard a word the strictest mother would have objected to. One or two of the older girls were occasionally a little sentimental, but on no occasion did I hear the physical side of things touched upon. I think this is partly due to the amount of exercise we took. When picturing my childhood I always see myself racing about, jumping walls, climbing trees. In France and Italy I have been struck by the greater sedateness of

Continental children. Our idea of naughtiness consisted chiefly in having suppers in our bedrooms and sliding down the banisters after being sent to bed. The first gratified our natural appetite, while the second supplied the necessary thrill in the fear of being caught.

"I made no violent friendships with the other girls, but I became much attached to the French governess. She was 30, and a born teacher, very strict with all of us, and doubly so with me for fear of showing favoritism. But she was never unjust, and I was rather proud of her severity and took a certain pleasure in being punished by her, the punishment always taking the form of learning by heart, which I rather liked doing. So I had my thrill, excitement, I don't quite know what to call it, without any very great inconvenience to myself. Just before we left school the sexual instinct began to show itself in enthusiasm for art with a capital A, Ouida's novels being mainly responsible. My sister and I agreed that we would spend our lives traveling about France, Italy, and the Continent, generally *à la Tricotrin*, with a violin in one pocket and an Atravante Dante in the other. To do this satisfactorily to ourselves we must be artists, and I resolved to go in for music and become a second Liszt. When my father offered to take us to Italy, the artist's Mecca, for a couple of years, we were wild with delight. We went, and disillusionment began. It may perhaps seem absurd, but we suffered acutely that first summer. Our villa was quite on the beach, the lowest of its flight of steps being washed by the Mediterranean. At the back were grounds which seemed a paradise. Long alleys covered over with vines and carpeted with long grass and poppies, grassy slopes dotted with olives and ilex, roses everywhere, and almost every flower in profusion, with, at night, the fireflies and the heavy scents of syringa and orange blossoms. In the midst of every possible excitement to the senses there was one thing wanting, and we did not know what that was.

"We attributed our restlessness and dissatisfaction to the slow progress in our artistic education, and consoled ourselves by thinking when once we had mastered the technical difficulties we should feel all right. And of course we did derive a very real pleasure from all the beauties of art and nature with which Italy abounds.

"It seems to me, however, that the art craze is one of the modern phases of woman's sexual life. When we were in Italy the great centers of the country were simply overrun with girls studying art, most of whom had very little talent, but who had mistaken the restlessness due to the first awakening of the sexual instinct for the divine flame of genius. In our case it did not matter, as we were not dependent upon our own exertions. But it must have been terribly hard for girls who had burned their boats and chosen art as a career, to have added to the repression of their natural desires the bitterness of knowing that in their chosen walk of life they were failures. The results as far as work goes might not be so bad if the passions, as in men, were occasionally gratified. It is the constant drudgery combined with the disappointment and finding that art alone does not satisfy which is so paralyzing. Besides, sexual gratification is always followed by exaltation of the mental faculties, with, in my experience, no depressing reaction such as follows pleasure excited by mental causes alone.

"At one time when living at the villa I met a man about 45, who took rather a fancy to me. I mention this because it woke me up; no emotion was excited, but I realized for the first time (I must have been nearly 20) that I was no longer a child, and that a man could think of me in connection with love. It was only after this, and not immediately after, either, that men's society began to have an interest for me, and that I began to think a man's love would be a pleasant thing to possess, after all.

"The sexual instinct, at any rate as regards consciousness, thus developed slowly and in what I believe to be a very usual sequence: religion, admiration for an older woman, and art. I am not sure that I have made quite enough of the first, yet I do not know that there is any more to say. There were very strong physical feelings connected with all these which were identical with those now connected with passion, but they were completely satisfied by the mental idea which excited them.

"The first time I can remember feeling keen physical pleasure was when I was between 7 and 8 years old. I can't recollect the cause, but I remember lying quite still in my little cot clasping the iron rails at the top. It may be said that this is hardly slow development, but I mean slow as regards (1) any connection of the idea with a man or (2) any physical means of excitation.

156

"I have laid stress on my desire for knowledge, as I think my sexual feelings were affected by it. A great part of my feeling for my mother was due to the stores of information she appeared to possess. The omniscience of God was to me his most striking attribute. My French teacher's capacity was her chief attraction. When, as a girl, I thought of marriage, I desired a man who 'could explain things to me.' One learns later to live one's mental and sexual life separately to a great extent. But at 20 I could not have done so; given the opportunity, I should have made the mistake of Dorothea in *Middlemarch*.

"I have spoken of the depressing after-effects of pleasure brought about by a purely mental cause, but I do not think this is the case in childhood and early youth. (Perhaps some women feel no such depression afterward, and this may account for their coldness in regard to men.) This may perhaps be accounted for by the fact that it occurs much more rarely, and also it is perhaps a natural process before the sexual organs fully develop, and so not harmful.

"I always find it difficult in expressing the different degrees of physical excitement even to myself, though I know exactly what I felt. As a child, from the time of the early experience already mentioned (about the age of 7 or 8), and as a young girl, the second stage (secretion of mucus) was always reached. The amount of secretion has always been excessive, but at first secretion only lasted a short time; later it began to last for several hours, or even sometimes the whole night, if the natural gratification has been withheld for a long time (say, three months). I do not remember ever feeling the third stage (complete orgasm) until I saw the first man I fancied I cared for. I do not think that mental causes alone have ever produced more than the first two stages (general diffuse excitement and secretion). I have sometimes wondered whether I could produce the third mechanically, but I have a curious unreasonable repugnance to trying the experiment; it would seem to materialize it too much. As a child and a girl I was contented to arrive at the second stage, possibly because I did not realize that there was any other, and perhaps this is why I have experienced no evil results.

"In dreams the third stage seems to come suddenly without any leading up to it, either mental or physical, of which I am conscious. I do not, however, remember having any such dreams before I was engaged. They came at a later period; even then, when great pleasure was experienced, it came, as a rule, suddenly and sharply, with no dreams leading up to it. The dreams generally take a sad form (an Evangeline and Gabriel business), where one vainly seeks the person who eludes one. I have, however, sometimes had pleasurable dreams of men who were quite indifferent to me and of whom I never thought when awake. The impression on waking is so strong one could almost fancy one's self really in love with them. I can quite understand falling in love with a person by dreaming of him in this way.

"The first time I remember experiencing the third stage in waking moments was at a picnic, when the man, to whom I have before referred as the first that I fancied I cared for, leaned against me accidentally in passing a plate or dish; but I was already in a violent state of excitement at being with him. There was no possibility of anything between us, as he was married. If he guessed my feelings, they were never admitted, as I did my best to hide them. I never experienced this, except at the touch of some one I loved. (I think the saying about the woman 'desiring the desire of the man' is just about as true as most epigrams. It is the man's personality alone which affects me. His feelings toward me are of—I was going to say—indifference, but at any rate quite secondary importance, and the gratification of my own vanity counts as nothing in such relations.)

"As a rule, to reach even the second stage the exciting ideas must be associated with some particular person, except in the case of a story, where one identifies one's self with one of the characters. In childhood and early youth it was, in the case of religion, the idea of God and the presence and the personality of God which aroused my feelings and always seemed very vivid to me. In the case of my governess, my feelings were aroused in exactly the same way as later they would be by one's lover. In the art craze I am rather vague as to how it came about, but I think, as a rule, there was rather a craving for pleasure than pleasure itself. I do not remember ever thinking much about the physical feeling. It seemed as natural that a pleasant emotion should produce pleasant physical effects as that a painful one should cause tears. As a child, one takes so much for granted, and later on my mind was so much occupied with worrying about the truth of religion that I hardly thought enough about anything else to analyze it carefully.

"I may summarize my own feelings thus: First, exciting ideas alone produce, as a rule, merely the first stage of sexual excitement. Second, the same ideas connected with a particular person will produce the second stage. Third, the same may be said of the presence of the beloved person. Fourth, actual contact appears necessary for the third stage. If the first stage only be reached, the sensation is not pleasurable in reality, or would not be but for its association. If produced, as I have sometimes found it to be, by a sense of mental incapacity, it is distinctly disagreeable, especially if one feels that the energy which might have been used in coping with the difficulty is being thus dissipated. If it be produced, as it may be, as the result of physical or mental restraint, it is also unpleasant unless the restraint were put upon one by a person one loves. Then, however, the second stage would probably be reached, but this would depend a good deal on one's mood. If the first stage only were reached, I think it would be disagreeable; it would mean a conflict between one's will and sexual feeling. Perhaps women who feel actual repugnance to the sexual act with a man they love have never gone beyond the first stage, when their dislike to it would be quite intelligible to me.

"Some time after the life in Italy had come to an end I became engaged. There was considerable difficulty in the way of marriage, but we saw a good deal of each other. My *fiancé* often dined with us, and we met every day. The result of seeing him so frequently was that I was kept in a constant state of strong, but suppressed, sexual excitement. This was particularly the case when we met in the evening and wandered about the moonlit garden together. When this had gone on about three months I began to experience a sense of discomfort after each of his visits. The abdomen seemed to swell with a feeling of fullness and congestion; but, though these sensations were closely connected with the physical excitement, they were not sufficiently painful to cause me any alarm or make me endeavor to avoid their pleasurable cause. The symptoms got worse, however, and no longer passed off quickly as at first. The swelling increased; considerable pain and a dragged-down sensation resulted the moment I tried to walk even a short distance. I was troubled with constant indigestion, weight in the chest, pain in the head and eyes, and continual slight diarrhea. This went on for about nine months, and then my *fiancé* was called away from the neighborhood. After his departure I got a trifle better, but the symptoms remained, though in less acute form. A few months later the engagement was broken off, and for some weeks I was severely ill with influenza and was on my back for several weeks. When I could get about a little, though very weak, all the swelling was gone, but pain returned whenever I tried to walk or stand for long. The indigestion and diarrhea were also very troublesome. I was treated for both by a physician, but without success. Next year I became engaged to my husband and was shortly after married. The indigestion and diarrhea disappeared soon after. The pain and dragging feeling in the abdomen bothered me much in walking or any kind of exercise. One day I came across a medical work, *The Elements of Social Science*, in which I found descriptions of symptoms like those I suffered from ascribed to uterine disease. I again applied to a doctor, telling him I thought there was displacement and possibly congestion. He confirmed my opinion and told me to wear a pessary. He ascribed the displacement to the relaxing climate, and said he did not think I should ever get quite right again. After the pessary had been placed in position every trace of pain, etc., left me. A year later I thought I would try and do without the pessary, and to my great satisfaction none of the old trials came back after its removal, in spite of much trouble, anxiety, sick nursing, and fatigue. I attribute the disorder entirely to violent sexual excitement which was not permitted its natural gratification and relief.

"I have reason to believe that suppression acts very injuriously on a woman's mental capacity. When excitement is naturally relieved the mind turns of its own accord to another subject, but when suppressed it is unable to do this. Personally, in the latter event, I find the greatest difficulty in concentrating my thoughts, and mental effort becomes painful. Other women have complained to me of the same difficulty. I have tried mechanical mental work, such as solving arithmetical or algebraic problems, but it does no good; in fact, it seems only to increase the excitement. (I may remark here that my feelings are always very strong not only before and after the monthly period, but also during the time itself; very unfortunately, as, of course, they cannot then be gratified. This only applies to desire from within, as I am strongly susceptible to influences from without at any time.) There seems nothing to be done but to bow to the storm till it passes over. Anything I do during the time it lasts, even household work, is badly done. The brain seems to become addled for the time being, while after gratification of desire it seems to attain an additional quickness and cleverness. Perhaps this cause contributes to the small amount of intellectual and artistic work done by women, admitting their natural inferiority to men in artistic impulse. A woman whose passions are satisfied generally has her strength sapped by maternity, while her attention is drawn from abstract ideas to her children."

HISTORY III.—B. states that his first sexual thoughts and acts were curiously connected with whipping. At 12 he and another boy used to beat each other with a cricket bat upon the bare nates, and afterward indulge in mutual masturbation. He cannot remember the beginning of his sexual speculation as a child, nor how he learned masturbation. When he was 13 he used to discuss erotic matters with a schoolfellow who was in the habit of engaging in vulvar intercourse with a girl of his own age. The intercourse was practised on the way home from school, and in a standing posture. B. embraced the girl in the same way. He is not interested in the psychological aspects of the sexual emotion. Although his sex passion was early kindled, he never had commerce with prostitutes. He thinks that his youthful experiences had no ill effect upon him morally, mentally, or physically. He practised masturbation in moderation till he married, at the age of 31.

HISTORY IV.—"I can remember" (writes the subject) "trotting away as a youngster about 5 with another boy to 'see a girl's legs'; the idea emanated from the other boy, but I was vaguely interested. How or where we were going to see the object in question I do not remember nor anything further than the intention. When 6 or 7 I remember being put to bed with the nurse girl and feeling her bare arm with undoubted sexual excitement; I remember, too, gradually feeling along the arm very cautiously, fearing the girl would wake and being bitterly disappointed to find it was merely the arm. I am almost certain I had then no idea of sex, but the disappointment was actual.

"These are the only early experiences of the sort I can remember. When about 9 I had others. On the coast of the north of England, which had then very few visitors and seemed to me very remote, I lived in a farm-house and used to assist the girls of the farm in looking after young cattle. These girls certainly instilled sexual ideas, though I did not realize them with precision. They used to talk about things a good many of which, I can now see, I did not then understand as they did. I liked to see these girls wading with their dresses tucked up. About this time I fell passionately in love with a girl cousin, but do not remember having any sensual ideas in regard to her. I cannot say that these early experiences had any influence on my later sexual development so far as I am consciously aware. I have always remembered them vaguely, never with sexual excitement.

"Sexual dreams took place first at about the age of 13; there was then emission and sensation in sleep. These were, however, not much associated with distinctly sexual dreams. All that I recall after them was the sensation, which, however, I did not even then absolutely localize. Masturbation was undoubtedly the direct result of these dreams. It was tried at first tentatively, out of curiosity to determine if the sensation of the dream could be so reproduced. Sexual dreams, such as I have described, occurred frequently, although I cannot say at what interval. I have never experienced the slightest attraction for the same sex."

HISTORY V.—"My maternal grandfather" (writes the subject of this history) "was a small farmer who kept a few beagles and greyhounds for hare-hunting. He had three daughters, one of whom became my mother. One of his sporting companions, a doctor of profligate habits and a drunkard, seduced my mother at the age of 20. When her condition was discovered she had to flee from the violence of her father, and I was born some distance from her home. After my grandfather's death I was reared by my grandmother, and saw nothing of my mother until I was nearly 16; she had left the country in shame and disgrace.

159

"I believe that in my heredity the transmission comes chiefly from my mother, who is now 58 years old. Although her life has been blameless in every particular since her youthful indiscretion, she has never got over it. I feel in my character a reflection of her overstrung condition during pregnancy.

"I can distinctly remember from the age of 9 years, and am sure that I had no sexual feelings before the age of 13, though always in the company of girls. I had many boyish passions for girls, always older than myself, but these were never accompanied by sexual desires. I deified all my sweethearts, and was satisfied if I got a flower, a handkerchief, or even a shred of clothing of my inamorata for the time being. These things gave me a strange idealistic emotion, but caused no sexual desire or erection.

"At 13 a 26-year-old sister of a boy companion once sat down on a sheaf of corn so as to expose the mons veneris and enticed me to copulate. There was slight erection, and after the act had been continued some time a pleasurable sensation of ejaculation, but without true emission. I had frequent relations with this woman after that.

"About this time the farm servant of a neighbor taught me masturbation. The mistress of the farm, a thin, willowy, dark woman, the mother of several children, treated me with such familiarity as once to urinate in my presence, so that I saw her very hirsute mons veneris. From that moment I conceived a great passion for her, and used to tremble as soon as I saw her. I had become well developed and virile, but, though I think she was a lustful woman, I never ventured to touch her. I found an extreme ecstasy in masturbating while gazing upon some article of her clothing. This gave me much greater sexual pleasure than actual connection with the ever-willing sister of my schoolfellow. I think I loved the married woman best because the mons veneris was more covered with hair.

"This has always had a peculiar attraction for me. Later, when accosted by prostitutes, I never would go with them unless I was assured the mons veneris was very hirsute. Never much addicted to masturbation, I derived no great enjoyment therefrom unless I had hair or part of the clothing of the woman with whom I was indulging in psychic coitus.

"At 16 I left school and went to a large city to learn a business. At this time the sexual appetite was very strong. I frequently had intercourse with three women in one evening.

"I have had but few lascivious dreams. In these the phantom partner was almost invariably a dead woman. (When about 8 I had seen the dead body of an aunt who died at 24.)

"When 20 I went to London and took all the pleasure which came my way. I cared only for normal coitus. Offers of another type created disgust. I once allowed a woman to exhaust me sexually orally, but felt degraded thereby. Women with whom I had become very intimate often urged me to *cunnilingus*, but I could not do it. I have practised intermammary coitus a very few times.

"At 26 I married a pure, gentle woman, after having for ten months before marriage led a life of celibacy. My wife died when I was 30, and for about eight months I lived a celibate life. Lascivious dreams sometimes occurred, but I invariably awoke before ejaculation. Eventually I gave way to the cravings of my strong sexual nature, but never wished for anything out of the usual except intercourse from behind. A woman with marked development of the nates has great attraction for me. Solitary masturbation has for some time ceased, but a nude woman in the act of masturbation with her back to me gives me great pleasure. I am as strong sexually at 38 as I was at 20, only I never want women unless I am brought into actual contact with them and they are hairy and have large pelvic development. I am in excellent health. Genitals are well developed, and I am clothed with hair from the chin to the genitals. My skull is dolichocephalic. I am violent and tenacious in temper, high-strung, and rapid in thought and action. My digestion is good, but I have a tendency to constipation. Occasionally I have a twinge of pain below the occipital region.

"My early views of women have changed; I no longer deify them, though I study them. I have known very sensual women living at home in respectable middle-class society. One, in particular, a girl of 18, after coitus used to excite me lingually. I have had a sweetheart who remained *virgo intacta*. Had I seduced her, as I could have done, I should have lost all interest in her. I could never bear the presence of naked men, and would never go to a public swimming bath for that reason. I regard myself as a man of abnormally strong, but,

160

on the whole, healthy and wholesome, sexual feelings. As a rule, I have coitus twice or oftener in one week and I practise withdrawal. I am a total abstainer, and never could embrace a woman who smelled of drink."

HISTORY VI.—The writer of the following is a man of letters, married. "Quite early I remember a strange and romantic interest in the feminine. Certainly before I was 9 I had a strong affection for a little girl playmate; our family lost sight of hers, and I saw and heard nothing of her for sixteen years; then, hearing she was coming to town, I experienced quite a flutter of heart, so strong had been the impression caused at even the early age of our acquaintance. Not that I mean to say I never wavered in between! Through the whole of my boyhood I remember persistent romantic interests in girls and women, whose smooth, fair faces and sweet voices exercised ever a subtle attraction over me. Before I was 12 I had picked out my 'future wife' a dozen times at least! (A different one each time of course!) Curiosity as to the physical detail of sex and birth was singularly absent. Possibly this was partly due to the fact that the only younger member of our family was born when I was but 4 years old. Grave, shy, and reserved, I was never taken into the counsels of prurient schoolmates. I was unaware that there was such discussion between them—though it is, I suppose, not probable that our school was exempt. I was a great reader, and when about 12 or 13 I came across a reference to an illegitimate child which puzzled me. Ere long, however, in my random and extensive reading I hit on a book that touched on phallicism, and I learned that there were male and female organs of generation. I had neither shame nor curiosity; I jumped to the conclusion that during close caresses somehow a subtle aroma arose from the man to fertilize the woman; I left the subject at this, satisfied, and had no inkling of the real intimacy of the embrace.

"About 14, much interested in Bradlaugh, I bought both the Knowlton pamphlet and Mrs. Besant's population book. I found the physical details in scientific language so dull that I could not peruse them. By reading the argumentative passages I learned that *somehow* (I knew not how) children could be produced or not produced as desired; and in this stage of the matter it seemed to me so admirable that it should be so that I wondered why there should be cavil.

"About this age my elder brother believed it to be his duty to tell me the secrets of sex; I remember his talking to me, while I, bored and uninterested, thought of something else. When he finished I had heard nothing. Remember, I felt no shame on the matter— none at all. I was simply bored. This I attribute to two things: first, my preponderating interest in the romantic side of things; secondly (and this bears with it a strong moral), *the feeling that the knowledge lay always within my grasp kept me from that curiosity which so oft consumes those who think it is hidden away from them.*

"The changes of puberty came naturally and without startling me. Even the fact of emissions—which took place during sleep at intervals, unaccompanied by dreams or by any physical prostration afterward—has left on my memory no recollection of surprise; I knew it to be somehow connected with generation, but I had no physical trouble, and I am quite sure I did not bother further about it. The best possible proof of this lies in the fact that my memory is a blank on the matter. At the age of 21 (I take this from a diary, so I know it is correct) I was still ignorant as to intrinsic fact. Then I pulled myself together and felt it was really time I learned the actual details of the matter. I went to a clever friend of mine and asked him to tell me all about it. He expressed himself astounded at my not knowing; and he had very great shyness about telling me. In fact, I had to drag facts out of him by a real cross-examination, during which he persistently marveled at my ignorance. Though he had a great deal of false shame about the matter, I had none at all. His revelations considerably surprised me, because I had no idea that there was actual intromission. When I came to reflect on what I had learned the fact of this close physical intimacy appealed to me as being quite poetic and beautiful between two lovers; and I have had no reason since to change my opinion.

"*Summary.*—1. Romantic interest in girls and women commencing early and remaining persistently.

"2. Knowledge before puberty of the fact that this interest was based on the all-important process of reproduction.

"3. Absence of further physical curiosity even at puberty itself.

"4. Knowledge ultimately acquired without shock.

"The physical in sex has never been any bother to me, neither have I bothered about it. I have recognized it, frankly, and don't see why I shouldn't, but my unashamed recognition has probably been because the merely physical is less absorbing to me than to most. Mental and emotional interest in passion has absorbed me greatly, but the merely physical has sunk into what I call its natural place of subordination. Nature is kind. It is our 'conspiracy of silence' which tends to emphasize physical detail."

HISTORY VII.—G. D., who is a doctor and a man of science, writes: "There is a strong history of gout on the paternal side. No history of alcohol, tubercle, brain trouble, or of the arthropathies. There is some reason to believe that two of my maternal aunts were sexually frigid, and perhaps this was true to a less extent of my mother, who had a contracted pelvis, necessitating the induction of labor at the eighth month of pregnancy.

"About the age of 7 a German nursery governess, B., took charge of me, and I soon became devoted to her. I was then a delicate child, and used to suffer frequently from nightmare, waking up screaming and covered with sweat. When this happened, B. would sometimes take me into her bed and soothe me with kisses, etc. These I returned, and can remember that I was particularly fond of kissing her breasts.

"About this time a girl cousin, A., about a year older than myself, was one of my most frequent playmates. I endeavored to monopolize her company and attention, and on this account often came to blows with C., a cousin rather younger than myself, who has since told me that he was then 'in love' with A. and 'jealous' of me. I believe I was really jealous and in love at the time, but cannot remember that anything in the nature of caresses took place between A. and myself.

"Some time later, probably when I was about 9, something led up to B. saying that she was not built like I was, that she had no penis, etc. (I cannot remember my nursery term for penis.) I was incredulous, and demanded to be allowed to see if it was true; this was refused, and I made many plans to gratify my curiosity, such as slipping into her room when she was dressing, tipping up the chair she was sitting in, and trying to suddenly thrust my hand up under her skirts. I did not succeed in finding out, but have since thought that, although she did not allow me to attain the object of my efforts, the later game caused her pleasurable sensations. I regard these efforts as being prompted purely by curiosity; I had no feelings of warmth or irritations of the genitals, and I certainly never manipulated them, nor was I, as far as I can judge, an unusually prurient small boy. B. left when I was about 10, when I went to a preparatory school.

"At 12½ I was sent to a public school, and was then told by my father the chief facts of sex and warned to avoid masturbation. My first wet dream took place when I was 14. Rather before this I had begun to suffer with severe intermittent testicular neuralgia which practically defied all treatment and continued on and off for four or five years, the attacks gradually becoming fewer and less severe.

"When 15, circumstances compelled me to leave school and to live for two years at the seaside with no companions of my own age. I had, however, the run of a well-stocked library, and fished and collected insects energetically.

"At 16 I made love to the trained nurse attending my mother, but, owing more, I think, to my timidity than to the austerity of her virtue, got no further than kissing. About this time wet dreams became inconveniently frequent; they would occur three or four times weekly, and resisted the stock remedies. At 17 I was advised to try connection. This I did, and found but little pleasure in the act, there being a strong esthetic objection to the 'love that keeps awake for lure.'

"About this time I found in the United States Pharmacopœia a remedy for my emissions, which have, however, always remained rather more frequent than those of the average individual, judging from the experience of my friends. Emissions are generally

162

accompanied by lascivious dreams, but at times take place when I dream that I am hurrying to catch a train, or to micturate against time.

"I have of late years (not noticed till after 20) observed that the dream accompanying emission is shorter; so that, whereas up to, say, 21 I generally performed the whole physiological act with my dream-charmer, I now almost invariably emit and awake before intromission has taken place. There has been no alternation comparable to this in the performance of the act while I am awake.

"As regards my physique I should mention that all my reflexes are very brisk, though I am only slightly ticklish in the ordinary sense of the term. I sweat easily and am very shy, not only with women, but with any strangers. I have, however, trained myself not to show this. About averagely passionate, I should say, and extremely critical where women are concerned, the latter quality often keeping me chaste for months at a time."

HISTORY VIII.—"When I was about 8 years old" (states the lady who is the subject of the present observation) "I remember that, with several other children, we used to play in an old garden at being father and mother, unfastening our drawers and bringing the sexual parts together, as we imagined married people to do, but no sexual feelings were aroused, nor did the boys have erections." When about 10 years old she became conscious of a pleasurable sensation associated with the smell of leather, which has ever since persisted. At that age she was sometimes left to wait in the office of a wholesale business house full of leather-bound ledgers. She did not then notice the sensation particularly, and was certainly not conscious of any connection with sexual emotion. Menstruation was established at 13½ years. Distinct sexual feelings were first observed a few months later. "The first feelings of love which I ever felt were at the age of 14 for a nice, manly boy of my own age, who often came to our house. He liked me, but was not in love with me. It was very seldom that he would sit by me and hold my hand, as I wished him. This went on till I was about 17, when he went to the university. After his first term he came back and was then attracted to me; but, though I loved him very much, I was too proud to show it. When he tried to kiss me, I resisted, though I longed for it. Thinking I was greatly offended, he apologized, which only made me angry. All these years I was worshiping at his shrine and mixed him up with all my ideas of life." Whenever she was near him she experienced physical sensations, with moistening of the vulva. This continued till she was about 20, but the object of these emotions never again attempted any advances.

At 19 she became engaged to someone else. At the beginning she was physically indifferent to her lover, but when he first kissed her she became greatly excited. The engagement, however, was soon broken off from absence of strong affection on either side and chiefly, it would seem, from the cooling of the lover's ardor. She thinks he would have been more strongly attached to her if she had been colder to him, or pretended to be, instead of responding with simplicity and frankness.

During the next few years little occurred. She was working hard, and her amusements would mostly, she says, be regarded as rather childish. She was extremely fond of dancing, and she was always pleased when anyone paid her attention. She was frequently conscious of sexual feelings, sometimes tormented by them, and she regarded this as something to be ashamed of. The constant longing for love was affected little or not at all by hard work. "At about this time I was very fond of abandoning myself to day-dreams. I was very glad if I could get everyone out of the house and lie on an easy chair or the bed. I liked especially to read poetry, all the more if I did not quite understand it. This would lead me on to all sorts of dreams of love, which, however, never went beyond the preliminaries of actual love—as that was all I then knew of love." The only climax to her dream of love was founded on a piece of information volunteered by a married woman many years earlier, when she was about 12. This lady—evidently agreeing with Rousseau (who in *Emile* commended the mother's reply to the child's query whence babies come, "Les femmes les pissent, mon enfant, avec des grands douleurs") that the unknown should first be explained to the young in terms of the known—told her that the husband micturated into the wife. She therefore used to imagine a lover who would bear her away into a forest and do this on her as she lay at the foot of a tree. (At a later date she accidentally discovered that a full bladder tended to

163

enhance sexual feelings, and occasionally resorted to this physical measure of heightening excitement.) All the physical sensations of sexual desire were called out by these day-dreams, with abundant secretion, but never the orgasm. Her reveries never led to masturbation or to allied manifestations, which have never taken place. Such a method of relief has, indeed, never offered any temptation to her and she doubts even its possibility in her case. (At a later period of life, however, at the age of 31, masturbation began and was practised at intervals.) At the same time she remarks that, while no orgasm (of which, indeed, she was then ignorant) ever occurred, the sexual excitement produced by the day-dreams was sufficiently great to cause a feeling of relief afterward. These day-dreams were the only way in which the sexual erethism was discharged. She cannot recall having erotic dreams or any sexual manifestations during sleep.

Spontaneous sexual excitement was present a few days before menstruation, and fairly marked during and immediately after the period. It also tended to recur in the middle of the intermenstrual period.

The pleasurable sensation connected with the smell of leather became more marked as she approached adult age. It was especially pronounced about the age of 24, and the sexual emotion it produced (with moisture of the vulva) was then clearly conscious. No other odor produced this effect in such a marked degree. It was often associated with leather bags, but not with boots, though on rubbing the leather of shoes she found that this odor was given out. She cannot account for its origin, and does not connect any association with it. It never affected her conduct or led to fetichistic habits.

Some other odors affect her in the same way, though not to the same degree as leather. This is more especially the case with some flowers, especially white flowers with heavy odors, like gardenias. Many flowers, on the other hand, like primroses, seem rather opposed to sex effect, too fresh, though stimulating to the mind. Some artificial scents tend to produce sexual effects also. Personal odors have no influence of this kind. (At a later period the sexual influence of personal odors was occasionally experienced, but the present history deals only with the period before marriage.)

She believes that most beautiful things, however unconnected with sex, have a tendency to produce distinctively sexual feelings in a faint degree, although sometimes more marked, with secretion. She has, however, never experienced homosexual feeling, and, on first consideration, was inclined to believe that the sight of a beautiful woman had no sexual effect on her, though she could quite understand such an effect. Subsequently, on recalling as well as observing her experiences more carefully, she found that a lovely woman's face and figure (especially on one occasion the very graceful figure of a beautiful fairy in a ballet) produced distinct sexual sensations (with mucous emission). Music, however, has strongly emotional effects upon her, and she cannot recall that she ever felt any equally powerful influence of this kind in the absence of music.

Looking back on the development of her feelings she finds that, though in some respects they may have been slow, they were simple, natural, spontaneous, and correspond to "the dawning and progress which go on in the development of every girl. While it is going on in actual fact, the girl does not know or bother herself about trying to understand it. Afterward it seems quite clear and simple. Full occupation of the brain, and hands too, while it does not do away with desire, is a great help and safeguard to a growing girl, when combined with proper information about herself and her relation to man the animal, so that she may realize where she is and how to choose the right man—though under the best conditions failure may occur."

HISTORY IX.—The subject belongs to a large family having some neurotic members; she spent her early life on a large farm. She is vigorous and energetic, has intellectual tastes, and is accustomed to think for herself, from unconventional standpoints, on many subjects. Her parents were very religious, and not, she thinks, of sensual temperament. Her own early life was free from associations of a sexual character, and she can recall little that now seems to be significant in this respect. She remembers that in childhood and for some time later she believed that children were born through the navel. Her activities went chiefly into humanitarian and utopian directions, and she cherished ideas

164

of a large, healthy, free life, untrammeled by civilization. She regards herself as very passionate, but her sexual emotions appear to have developed very slowly and have been somewhat intellectualized. After reaching adult life she has formed several successive relationships with men to whom she has been attracted by affinity in temperament, in intellectual views, and in tastes. These relationships have usually been followed by some degree of disillusion, and so have been dissolved. She does not believe in legal marriage, though under fitting circumstances she would much like to have a child.

She never masturbated until the age of 27. At that time a married friend told her that such a thing could be done. She found it gave her decided pleasure, indeed, more than coitus had ever given her except with one man. She has never practised it to excess, only at rare intervals, and is of the opinion that it is decidedly beneficial when thus moderately indulged in. She has sometimes found, for instance, that, after the mental excitement produced by delivering a lecture, sleep would be impossible if masturbation were not resorted to as a sedative to relieve the tension.

Spontaneous sexual excitement is strongest just before the monthly period.

Definite sexual dreams and sexual excitement during sleep have not occurred except possibly on one or two occasions.

She has from girlhood experienced erotic day-dreams, imagining love-stories of which she herself was the heroine; the climax of these stories has developed with her own developing knowledge of sexual matters.

She is not inverted, and has never been in love with a woman. She finds, however, that a beautiful woman is distinctly a sexual excitation, calling out definite physical manifestations of sexual emotion. She explains this by saying that she thinks she instinctively puts herself in the place of a man and feels as it seems to her a man would feel.

She finds that music excites the sexual emotions, as well as many scents, whether of flowers, the personal odor of the beloved person, or artificial perfumes.

HISTORY X.—The subject is of German extraction on both sides. The father is of marked intellectual tastes, as also is she herself. There is no unhealthy strain in the family so far as she is aware, though they all have very strong passions. She is well developed, healthy, vigorous, and athletic, any trouble to which she is subject being mainly due to overwork.

Looking back on her childhood, she can now see various sexual manifestations occurring at a period when she was quite ignorant of sex matters. "The very first," she writes, "was at the age of 6. I remember once sitting astride a banister while my parents were waiting for me outside. I distinctly remember a pleasurable sensation—probably in part due to a physical feeling—in the thought of staying there when I knew I ought to have run out to them. From that year till the age of 10 I simply reveled in the idea of being tortured. I went gladly to bed every night to imagine myself a slave, chained, beaten, made to carry loads and do ignominious work. One of my imaginings, I remember, was that I was chained to a moldering skeleton." As she grew older these fancies were discontinued. At the same time there was a trace of sadistic tendency: "I used to frighten and tease a young child, driven to it by an irresistible impulse, and experiencing a certain pleasurable feeling in so doing. But this, I am glad to say, was rare, as I hate all cruelty."

One of her favorite imaginings as a child was that she was a boy, and especially that she was a knight rescuing damsels in distress. She was not fond of girls' occupations, and has always had a sort of chivalrous feeling toward women.

"When I first heard of the sexual act," she writes, "it appeared to me so absurd that I took little notice. About the age of 10 I discussed it a good deal with other girls, and we used to play childishly indecent games—out of pure mischief and not from any definite physical feeling."

About a year after menstruation was established she accidentally discovered the act of masturbation by leaning over a table. "I discovered it naturally; no one taught me; and the very naturalness of the impulse that led me to it often made me in later years question the harmfulness." Both her sisters masturbated from a very early age, but not, to her knowledge, her brother. The practice of masturbation was continued. "For many years, imbued with the old ideas of morality, I struggled against it in vain. The sight of animals copulating, the perusal of various books (Shakespeare, Rabelais, Gautier's *Mademoiselle de Maupin*, etc.), the sight of the nude in some Bacchanalian pictures (such as Rubens's), all aroused passion. Coexistent with this—perhaps (though I doubt it) due to it—arose a disgust for normal intercourse. I fell in love and enjoyed kisses, etc., but the mere thought of anything beyond disgusted me. Had my lover suggested such a thing I would have lost all love for him. But all this time I went on masturbating, though as seldom as possible and without thought of my lover. Love was to me a thing ideal and quite apart from lust, and I still think that it is false to try to connect the two. I fear that even now, if I fell in love, sexual intercourse would break the charm. At the age of 18 I came across Tolstoy's *Kreutzer Sonata* and was overjoyed to find all I had thought written down there. Gradually, through seeing a friend happily married, I have grown to a more normal view of things. I am very critical of men and have never met one liberal-minded and just enough to please me. Perhaps if I did I might take a perfectly healthy view of things."

In course of time various devices had been adopted to heighten sexual excitement when indulging in masturbation. Thus, for instance, she found that the effects of sexual excitement are increased by keeping the bladder full. But the chief method which she had devised for heightening and prolonging the preliminary excitement consisted in wearing tight stays (as a rule, she wears loose stays) and in painting her face. She cannot herself explain this. Self-excitement is completed by friction, or sometimes by the introduction of a piece of wood into the vagina. She finds that, the more frequently she masturbates, the more easily she is excited. Spontaneous sexual feeling is strongest before and after the menstrual period; not so much so during the periods.

There are various faint traces of homosexuality, it may be gathered, in the history of this subject's sexual development. Recently these have come to a climax in the formation of a homosexual relationship with a girl friend. This relationship has given her great pleasure and satisfaction. She does not, however, regard herself as being a really inverted person.

There have been vivid sexual dreams from about 17 (apparently about the period of the relationship with the lover). These dreams have not, however, had special reference to persons of either sex.

Apart from the influence of books and pictures already mentioned, she remarks that she is sexually affected by the personal odor of a beloved person, but is not consciously affected by any other odors.

HISTORY XI.—Widower, aged 40 years. Surgeon. "My experience of sexual matters began early. When I was about 10 years of age a boy friend who was staying with us told me that his sister made him uncover his person, with which she played and encouraged him to do the same for her. He said it was great fun, and suggested that we should take two of my sisters into an old barn and repeat his experience on them. This we did, and tried all we could to have connection with them; they were nothing loath and did all they could to help us, but nothing was effected and I experienced no pleasure in it.

"When I went back to school I attracted the attention of one of the big boys who slept in the same room with me; he came into my bed and began to play with my member, saying that it was the usual thing to do and would give me pleasure. I did not feel any pleasure, but I liked the attention, and rather enjoyed playing with his member, which was of large size, and surrounded by thick pubic hair. After I had played with him for some time I was surprised at his having an emission of sticky matter. Afterward he rubbed me again, saying that if I let him do it long enough he would produce the same substance from me. This he failed to do, however, though he rubbed me long and frequently, on that and many other occasions. I was very disappointed at not being able to have an emission, and on every occasion that offered I endeavored to excite myself to the extent of compassing this. I used to ask to go out of school two or three times a day, and retired to the closet, where I practised on myself most diligently, but to no purpose, at that time, though I began to have pleasurable emotions in the act.

"When I went home for the holidays I took a great interest in one of my father's maids, whose legs I felt as she ran upstairs one day. I was in great fear that she would complain of what I had done, but I was delighted to find that she did nothing of the sort; on the contrary, she took to kissing and fondling me, calling me her sweetheart and saying that I was a forward boy. This encouraged me greatly, and I was not long in getting to more intimate relations with her. She called me into her room one day when we were alone in the house, she being in a half-dressed condition, and put me on the bed and laid herself on me, kissing me passionately on the mouth. She next unbuttoned my trousers and fondled and kissed my member, and directed my hand to her privates. I became very much excited and trembled violently, but was able to do for her what she wanted in the way of masturbation until she became wet. After this we had many meetings in which we embraced and she let me introduce my member until she had satisfied herself, though I was too young to have an emission.

"On return to school I practised mutual masturbation with several of my schoolfellows, and finally, at the age of 14 years, had my first real emission. I was greatly pleased thereat, and, with this and the growth of hair which began to show on my pubis, began to feel myself quite a man. I loved lying in the arms of another boy, pressing against his body, and fondling his person and being fondled by him in return. We always finished up with mutual masturbation. We never indulged in any unnatural connections.

"After leaving school I had no opportunity of indulging in relations with my own sex, and, indeed, did not wish for such, as I became a slave to the charms of the other sex, and passed most of my time in either enjoying, or planning to enjoy, love passages with them.

"The sight of a woman's limbs or bust, especially if partly hidden by pretty underclothing, and the more so if seen by stealth, was sufficient to give a lustful feeling and a violent erection, accompanied by palpitation of the heart and throbbing in the head.

"I had frequent coitus at the age of 17, as well as masturbating regularly. I liked to perform masturbation on a girl, even more than I liked having connection with her; and this was especially so in the case of girls who had never had masturbation practised on them before; I loved to see the look of surprised pleasure appear on their faces as they felt the delightful and novel sensation.

"To gratify this desire I persuaded dozens of girls to allow me to take liberties with them, and it would surprise you to learn what a number of girls, many of them in good social position, permitted me the liberty I desired, though the supply was never equal to my demand.

"With a view to enlarging my opportunities I took up the study of medicine as a profession, and reveled in the chances it gave of being on intimate sexual terms with many who would have been, otherwise, out of my reach.

"At the age of 25 I married the daughter of an officer, a beautiful girl with a fully developed figure and an amorous disposition. While engaged, we used to pass hours wrapped in each other's arms, practising mutual masturbation, or I would kiss her passionately on the mouth, introducing my tongue into her mouth at intervals, with the invariable result that I had an emission and she went off into sighs and shivers. After marriage we practised all sorts of fancy coitus, *coitus reservatus*, etc., and rarely passed twenty-four hours without two conjunctions, until she got far on in the family way, and our play had to cease for a while.

"During this interval I went to stay at the house of an old schoolfellow, who had been one of my lovers of days gone by. It happened that on account of the number of guests staying in the house the bed accommodation was somewhat scanty, and I agreed to share my friend's bedroom. The sight of his naked body as he undressed gave rise to lustful feelings in me; and when he had turned out the light I stole across to his bed and got in beside him. He made no objection, and we passed the night in mutual masturbation and embraces, *coitus inter femora*, etc. I was surprised to find how much I preferred this state of affairs to coitus with my wife, and determined to enjoy the occasion to the full. We passed a fortnight together in the above fashion, and, though I afterward went back and did my duty by my wife, I never took the same pleasure in her again, and when she died, five years later, I felt no inclination to contract another marriage, but devoted myself heart and soul to my old school-friend, with whom I continued tender relations until his death by accident last year. Since then I have lost all interest in life."

"The patient," writes the well-known alienist to whom I am indebted for the above history, "consulted me lately. I found him a fairly healthy man to look at, suffering from some neurasthenia and a tendency to melancholia. Generative organs large, one testicle shows some wasting, pubic hair abundant, form of body distinctly masculine; temperament neurotic. He improved under treatment, and, after seeing me three times and writing out the above history, came no more."

HISTORY XII.—Mrs. B., aged 32. Father's family normal; mother's family clever, eccentric, somewhat neuropathic. She is herself normal, good-looking, usually healthy, highly intelligent, and with much practical ability, though at some periods of life, and especially in childhood, she has shared to some extent in the high-strung and supersensitive temperament of her mother's family. As a child she was sometimes spoiled and sometimes cuffed, and suffered tortures from nervousness. She has, however, acquired a large measure of self-control.

The first sensations which she now recognizes as sexual were experienced at the age of 3, when her mother gave her an injection; afterward she declared herself unable to relieve her bowels naturally in order to obtain a repetition of this experience, which was several times repeated. At the age of 7 a man pursued her with attentions and attempted to take liberties, but she rejected his advances in terror; four years later another man attempted to assault her, but she resisted vigorously, struck him, and escaped by running. Neither of these sexual attempts appears to have left any serious permanent impression on the child's mind.

At the age of 11, when her mother was giving her a bath, the sensation of her mother's fingers touching her private parts gave her what she now knows to be sexual feelings, and a year later when taking her bath she would pour hot water on to the sexual region in order to cause these sensations; this did not lead to masturbation, but she had a vague idea that it was "wrong."

At the age of 12 menstruation began; she suffered very severely from dysmenorrhea, the period sometimes lasting for ten days, and the pain being often extreme. She was not treated for this condition, her mother being of opinion that she would outgrow it. From the age of 14 or 15 until 23, or about the period of her marriage, she suffered from anemia.

She had little curiosity about sexual matters; her mother wished that she should always come to her for information about things she became acquainted with as to the general facts of sex; she did not, however, know definitely the facts of copulation until her marriage. She knew nothing of erection or semen, and thought that when a man and woman placed their organs together a child resulted. She hated talking about these subjects indecently, and would not listen to the sexual conversation of her schoolfellows. She never felt any homosexual attraction. Once another girl was much in love with her, but she despised and disliked her attentions; again, when a girl much older than herself, a friend of her mother's, slept with her and made advances, she repelled her and refused to sleep with her again.

She always got on well with men, and men were attracted to her. She was direct and sincere, without undue modesty. But she never allowed men to touch her or kiss her. She was a good dancer, and fond of dancing, but denies that it ever led to sexual feelings. She never felt any sexual attraction for a man until, at the age of 20, she fell in love with her future husband five years or more before marriage.

At this period she began to feel vague discomfort, which she knew to be localized near her sexual organs. She was aware, in a dim way, that it was connected with her love, and was of a sexual nature. But there was no definite idea of sexual intercourse. She felt nervous and depressed. If she had been asked to state what would relieve her, she could only have said B.'s presence and tenderness. A few days before he declared his love she experienced the nearest approach to sexual feeling she had ever had. It was summer and, with B. and some of her family, she had gone on a little expedition. One evening, in the train after a day's excursion, B. took her hand (unperceived by the others) and held it for some time. This aroused the strongest emotions in her; she closed her eyes, and, though she was not at the time aware that her sensations were localized in her sexual organs, she thinks, in the light of subsequent knowledge, that she then experienced the orgasm.

During the engagement, which lasted between two and three years, circumstances prevented frequent meetings. B. would kiss her, suck her nipples, which became erect, and lie on her. She allowed him to take these liberties, feeling that if she refused him all satisfaction he might have relations with other women. She still felt no definite desire for contact of the sexual organs. She longed rather to be embraced and kissed, and to lie in her lover's arms all night. A few months before marriage, however, she masturbated occasionally, just before or just after menstruation, imagining, while doing it, that she was in her lover's arms. The act was usually followed by a sick feeling. Just before marriage she underwent an operation for the relief of the dysmenorrhea. She was somewhat shocked and sickened by the experiences of the wedding night. It seemed to her that her husband approached her with the violence of an animal, and there was some difficulty in effecting entrance. Coitus, though incomplete, took place some seven times on this first night. The bleeding from rupture of the hymen continued, so that for two days she had to wear a towel. For two months subsequently there was great pain during intercourse, although she suppressed the indications of this.

There were several children born of the marriage and for some years she lived happily, on the whole, with her husband, notwithstanding various hardships and difficulties and some incompatibility of temper.

As regards her sexual feelings she considers, from what other women have told her, that her feelings are, if anything, stronger than the average. The orgasm, however, was not fully developed until about five years after marriage. Sexual feeling is most pronounced before, during, and after the menstrual period, more especially before and about the third day (the period usually lasts from five to seven days). There is more sexual desire during pregnancy, especially toward the end, than at any other time. She never refused normal intercourse to her husband, but any abnormal or perverted method of sexual gratification is repellent. She was awakened one night about the third month of pregnancy by her husband inserting his penis *in ore*; the child was born with palate defect and she is herself inclined to believe that this incident was the cause of the defect. Though she desires normal intercourse, she has seldom obtained complete gratification. For a long time she disliked seeing or touching the penis, and the feel, and especially the smell, of the semen produced nausea and even vomiting. (She has a very delicate sense of smell as well as of taste; though fond of the scent of flowers, no sexual feelings are thus aroused.) Withdrawal and the use of condoms are unsatisfactory to her, and mutual masturbation gives no relief and produces headache. Feelings of friendship for her husband have been most potent in arousing the sexual emotions, and she has had most pleasure in intercourse after a day spent in bicycling together. She has been for many months at a time without sexual intercourse, and during such periods has suffered much from pain in the head; this, however, she has now completely surmounted. She eventually discovered that her husband's abstinence from marital intercourse was due to infidelity. This led to a definite separation. She still occasionally experiences sexual desire, but has no inclination to masturbate. Her life is full and busy, affording ample scope for her energies and intelligence; moreover, she has her children to train and educate. She herself believes that her sexual life is at an end.

HISTORY XIII.—G. R., army officer. "I am 35 years of age. My parents married at the ages of 38 and 25, and my father is now 84 and my mother 71; both are particularly strong and healthy in body and mind. I am of old lineage on both sides, and know of no disease, defect, or abnormality among any of my ancestors or relations, except that my mother's family has a slight tendency to drink and excess, the present members of it all being considered eccentric. I have one brother and one sister living (brother unmarried, sister with several children) and am the youngest of a family of five. My brother is abnormal, but I don't know exactly in what way or from what cause. I have a strong suspicion that he masturbates to excess. My father is artistic and my mother musical. I have no aptitude for either, but appreciate both enormously, though not until about ten years ago. My principal reading is religion, science, and philosophy, with an occasional standard novel, or a modern novel of the 'improper' type by way of relaxation. I became a convinced and militant rationalist about five years ago, but have been an unbeliever since I left school. I was anemic and threatened with bowel complaint at the age of 7, and was in consequence taken abroad for my health. I am now strong and vigorous, with great powers of endurance, and enjoy all forms of sport and exercise, particularly hunting, pig-sticking, and polo. I drink a lot, and am never fitter than when eating, drinking, and taking exercise in what most people would call excess. It takes more alcohol than I can hold to make me drunk when in England; but not so in the East. I have been told that I am very good-looking.

"When I was about 4 or 5 I was constantly chaffed by my older companions about putting my hand down my trousers and playing with my privates. I don't remember getting an erection, nor at what age this first occurred with me. At one time my brother and I used to play about with my sister's underclothing, and took great pleasure in it, but we never saw her genitals. She told us that on carefully examining herself one day she was glad to find that she had a small penis like boys had—doubtless the clitoris. When in France, at the age of 8 to 10, I began to notice the sexual parts of animals, and was very keen to know what mares kept between their hind legs. Later on I took great pleasure with another boy in feeling the teats of a she-ass, and, by myself, the penis of a donkey, as I had seen the French grooms do; but I took no interest in my own penis. I used to put my finger as far up the anus as it would go, and got a vague satisfaction from it. I went to a small private school at the age of 11, having been previously told by my mother of the manner of birth of men and animals, of which I was quite ignorant till then. She made no mention of the part taken by the father, and I never thought about it. Even then I was left with the impression that one was born through the navel. I was initiated at school, and used to handle the penis of the boy who told me. On several occasions I did *fellatio* for him, and liked it, but he never offered to do the same for me, and I don't think he got much satisfaction out of it. Soon after this I became conscious of pleasurable sensations when lying on my stomach with an erection, and used occasionally to gratify myself that way, caring little for the school tradition that it was 'wicked' and bad for one. On one occasion, when talking at night with another boy, we compared our organs, both in erection, and I then for the first time thought of trying what I had heard vaguely mentioned, viz., two boys playing at man and woman. I lay on him with my penis on his stomach and almost at once had an orgasm with emission, and experienced acute pleasure, though both he and I supposed that I had involuntarily micturated. I was 13 when this happened. I did it once more with him before I left, this time the other way up, so as to spare him the unpleasantness. I used to like kissing and hugging the smaller boys, and had a great eye for good looks. On going home for the holidays I masturbated with my hand out of curiosity to see what happened when the orgasm occurred, and then only did I fully understand the nature of the act. After this the rush and strangeness of a large public school distracted my attention, but I heard about wet dreams, masturbation, and homosexuality from the other boys, and soon became thoroughly initiated. I believe the tone of my house, if not of the whole school, was exceptionally bad; though it may only be that I saw more of it because I was attracted by it, and that other schools are the same really. Things involving certain expulsion if found out were done more or less in public, and I have myself openly got into bed with or masturbated other boys, and on more than one occasion have helped forcibly to masturbate small boys or to hold them while others had connection with them, the idea of the last two acts being that the boy would thereby be seduced and become available for, and willing to perform, homosexuality. Before I became big enough to have boys myself I masturbated frequently (on one occasion three times in the day), and invariably by lying on my stomach without the use of the hands. In having connection with other boys I used to do it between the thighs or on the stomach, and I never heard of any other way at that school. *Pædicatio* would disgust me, and, moreover, would deprive me of the principal pleasure of intercourse, viz., the feeling of lying face to face and stomach to stomach. Of course, the satisfaction was to be mutual, but, though good-looking, I was never the passive party only, like some small boys who might be called professionals and whom I used to pay for their services. I went back after I had left and had a boy in the dark whom I had never seen before, having been told that he was all right. I used to have a very genuine affection for any party to my pleasure, though I took delight in torturing one in particular, but for what reason I cannot say. For one boy I developed a deep love, which lasted long after we

170

had left school and had ceased all sexual connection. This love was as strong as anything I have ever felt since.

"I don't remember whether it was while I was at school or later that I first began again to take a sexual interest in animals. I used to masturbate a good deal and was always trying to find new ways of doing it and new substances to lie on. It was while feeling the vulva of a young mare that the brilliant thought struck me of trying to copulate with her, and thus getting the advantage of the soft vagina. It afforded me great satisfaction and I had an emission, though I did not then, nor at any other time with any other animal, succeed in penetrating properly. I afterward did the same with other mares and with a certain cow whenever I got a safe opportunity, which was not as often as I could have wished. I have not had connection with an animal for about ten years, but would have no objection to doing so, and feel sure I could perform the act properly now. After I left school at 17, I occasionally had longings for boys, but it was the exception and not the rule. I continued to masturbate, but not to excess, and used to make ineffectual efforts to stop it, but never succeeded for very long. When I was confirmed, at the age of 15, I became intensely religious, and was so remorseful at my first lapse from virtue that I burnt my leg with a red-hot poker, and I bear the scar still. On leaving school I went to Germany and there had my first coitus with a woman, a fat old German who gave me very little satisfaction. My next, a Jewess, gave me more than I asked for, in the shape of a soft chancre. In my ignorance I never had it treated, but it must have been very mild, for it disappeared of its own accord. When cramming in England I occasionally went home with a prostitute, but did not care much about them and could not afford good ones. On one occasion I was impotent. It may have been through drink, but it disgusted me with myself. I liked seeing the women naked, and always insisted that they should strip, especially the breasts, which I liked large and full. I had not learned to kiss on the lips, and had no desire to kiss the body, except the breasts, which I was generally too shy to do. But as I nearly always wore a condom and found penetration difficult I did not much enjoy the actual coitus. I am fully convinced that if women had been more accessible, if I had not thought myself bound to use preventives in self-defense, and if the act had not been looked upon with such disfavor by those in authority over me, I should have masturbated less or not at all, and would not have been tempted to bestiality. When I was 22 I had coitus with a girl who was not a prostitute for the first time. I was violently excited and enjoyed it more than anything I had yet experienced, in spite of the facts that she would not undress and insisted on withdrawal before emission. On one other occasion only have I had coitus with a non-professional unmarried woman. Shortly after this I caught syphilis from a girl of the streets. I was circumcised and stayed in a private hospital for six weeks. It never went beyond the primary stage, and I have felt no ill effects from it, except that I have got a hydrocele in the right testicle. Of course, this incident necessitated the use of a condom on every occasion, and it greatly spoiled my pleasure. About this time a brother-officer older than myself made advances to me. He compared me to a Greek statue, and wanted to kiss me. I would have nothing to do with him, but was glad to have his confessions of homosexuality and somewhat surprised to learn that he was not alone in the regiment. I afterward fell in love with his sister, and he married and had children. He was bisexual in his inclinations, but was really in love with me for a short time.

"I had little to do with professionals until I went to South Africa, and though I was fond of ladies' society, and liked by ladies, I looked upon them as something apart, especially married women, and never attempted to take liberties with them; though I used to with shopgirls, etc., in my cramming days, and had often been in love. In South Africa I first began really to enjoy coitus, and on going to India continued to do so; in fact, I thought sexually of nothing else and rarely masturbated,—perhaps once in three weeks. I would go to brothels wherever they were available, Durban, Cape Town, Colombo, Calcutta, Bombay, and at one time preferred black women to white. I used to have horrible orgies with my brother-officers, and on one occasion I ordered six women to my bungalow in order to celebrate my birthday, and made a present of them to five of my friends after dinner. During this period, and until I went home, I rarely spoke to a lady, the chief exception being No. 1, a brother-officer's wife, with whom I began to be in love.

"Shortly after the South African War I fell violently in love with a young brother-officer, 'Z.' It amounted to a passion and I was forced to make overtures to him. He did not understand, being ignorant of homosexuality and quite virile, and would have nothing to do with me, though he was very nice about it. This lasted for about a year, and then, thinking no doubt that he had better stop it, as I was really making myself very ridiculous and was mad with love, he threw me up altogether. I was intensely miserable for some time, and then I recovered and we made it up, and are now firm friends. I still want to kiss and stroke him when I see him naked, but would do nothing more. I went home by way of Japan after several years' absence from home, taking the women of the Eastern ports as I went, until I contracted gonorrhea in the Tokio Yoshiwara. I could not get rid of it, and arrived home in that state, having been deprived of the pleasure of trying several new races on the way in consequence. In England I rushed into a society which I had quit on such different terms, and it received me with open arms. I very soon began a flirtation with a married woman, and she completed my education in kissing which had been begun by the Japanese harlots. I was just coming to the point with this woman when I met No. 1 again, and my love for her was at once renewed. I told her so, but I knew that she did not return it. I then became attracted to No. 2, a girl older than myself, whom I had known all my life. I kissed her and fondled her breasts; but she would not allow anything else, until one night, when in the train with her, I got my hand down farther than she intended. It ended in my performing *cunnilingus* on her first, and then obtaining satisfaction between her thighs—a large step to take after the former limitations. Previous to this I had on several occasions obtained an emission, without meaning to, by lying on her fully dressed. She was aware of my disease, which by that time had become a gleet and did not inconvenience me in any way. From that time until I went back to India we went through the same performance whenever possible, I masturbating her sometimes with the finger, sometimes with the tongue, and having connection with various parts of her body, including the breasts, but always with a condom on account of my disease. She used to strip for my edification, and we frequently spent the night in the same bed. I was attracted to her mentally, but not very much physically; that is to say, that if circumstances had not thrown us together I should never have picked her out from other girls as being sexually attractive to me. I returned to India, and to No. 1, though I kept faithful to No. 2 in word and deed for five months, but gradually the overmastering influence of No. 1 reasserted itself over me. And then I met No. 3. We were attracted to each other at first acquaintance, and the attraction was mental and sexual. She was married and in love with another man, but that did not prevent her from kissing me. I felt her breasts, masturbated her, and had emissions by lying on her, but she drew the line at one thing, viz., kissing on the lips; and I drew it at coitus. We arranged a trip together during which I went to bed with her, but never had coitus, though we both had frequent orgasms in other ways. Before starting on this trip I had thought that I should not see No. 1 again, and she let me kiss her, to my unspeakable joy. Circumstances, however, intervened, and I went straight to No. 1 after parting with No. 3, told her all I had done, and then kissed her again, leaving her just before her real lover, with whom she was then living, arrived. Later I returned again to No. 1, now in child to her lover. We lived together for three nights in spite of this. She then went home, and I had no connection with any woman for two years, except one black woman, being consumed with love and worship for No. 1. I was much in society, but never had any luck. At the end of this time I was traveling one night with a young officer ('X'), slight and effeminate and preferring men to women, with whom I had been until then on friendly but not intimate terms. I watched him undress and go to bed, and then, having myself undressed, went over to his bunk and put my hand under his clothes. He at once responded, and I got into his bed, both of us being in a frenzy of passion and surprise. But I was fairly sure of my ground or I would not have dared to take the risk. I used often to go to his bed after this, and on one occasion had coitus with a girl on a chair at a ball and the next night with my young officer. I scarcely knew the girl, and don't know her name now, but I took her measure, made her excited by manipulation and kissing, and then got her consent. I did not harm her, even if I had been the first, for orgasm occurred before I had penetrated beyond the lips. X surprised me by telling me that he had had connection with three other officers in my regiment, as well as with several others in the same station. He would not tell me their names, but I guessed easily enough. He used to drink heavily, and once I got into his bed when he was in a drunken stupor and he was quite unaware that I was there for some time. I myself was drinking too much at this time, and was frequently drunk before dinner. In the hot weather that followed I had one orgy in Bombay which lasted three nights. I started on a Greek and a Pole and finished up with a Japanese, two brother-officers accompanying me. Afterward I was much alone during the day in my bungalow, and used to become possessed by intense desire. I masturbated occasionally, but by this time took but little pleasure in it, always craving for the moist human vagina. I had often heard, and myself quoted, the Pathan proverb 'Women for breeding; boys for pleasure; melons for delight,' and one day when seeking for some novelty with which to masturbate, and my eye being caught by a melon put ready for me to eat, it flashed across me to try whether the proverb was in any way true. I found it most satisfactory, and practised it several times after that, the pepita (papaye or pawpaw) being the nearest approach to the human vagina. The opportune arrival of a fairly good-looking punkah woman, however, put an end to this form of enjoyment by providing me with what I wanted. Soon afterward I went home again, taking the Japanese at Bombay on my way.

"I had kept up a correspondence with No. 1 all this time, but we had made a compact that whatever each did until we met again was not to count, and I knew that she had had at least one liaison since our parting, and was in entire ignorance of the state of her feelings toward me. Therefore, while trying to arrange a meeting with her, I took the first thing that chance threw in my way, thinking a bird in the hand better than the off chance of a better one in the bush. This was No. 4, with whom I spent three days at the seaside after having first had coitus with her in my own home while she was in the monthly state. Immediately on parting from her I came home to receive No. 1. The first time we were alone she kissed me, and this was followed by mutual confessions and coitus, though at first she said my affair was too recent. I agreed not to have connection again with No. 4, and kept to this until when staying in the same house again with her I was tempted beyond my powers; and I may add that she gave me no assistance in keeping this promise, of which she was fully cognizant. I at once wrote and confessed to No. 1, and she very naturally would have nothing more to do with me. But I managed to reconcile her, and we afterward lived together for three days in the country, as well as in London and in her own house. Meanwhile No. 5 had been making advances to me which I could not well refuse, being a very old friend. Nos. 4 and 5 were on one occasion staying together at my house, just after I had been faithless to No. 1 with No. 4. I could not very well sleep with them both, so at the earnest entreaty of No. 4 I went to her room first, told her my reasons for not having connection with her, left her in tears, and then went and slept with No. 5. This is the only transaction I have ever concealed from No. 1; but No. 5 knows my whole story and accepts the situation of being only second so long as I give her satisfaction whenever possible. About this time I again met No. 3 and kissed and masturbated her in a cab, but she would not allow me to go home with her. At the bidding of No. 1 I now broke entirely with No. 4, to the great grief and astonishment of my sister, whose friend she was. Shortly after this I again returned to India, where I quarreled hopelessly with No. 1, and I don't know to this day what my fault was, except that she had got tired of me. Her influence over me is, however, too great to be so easily broken, and I would return to her tomorrow if she moved a finger in reconciliation. During the following hot weather I slowly but surely, albeit quite unconsciously, obtained an influence over No. 6, and it ended by her falling desperately in love with me and allowing me to do what I liked. I did not love her, and told her about No. 1, whose image always remained in the back of my vision, whatever I was doing. She also accepted the situation, and I don't think has any grievance against me. For my part I have nothing but thanks and gratitude and as much love as I am capable of to give her, and all the other women with whom I have had any sexual relations. The following is a short account of the above women:—

"No. 1. Had coitus before marriage, for love and with full knowledge of the nature of the act. Agreement with her husband not to have coitus rigidly adhered to by both. Has had connection with five other men since marriage. Very passionate, but faddy and particular. Slow at producing orgasm. Likes being in bed naked, and liked me once for having kissed her mons veneris. Thin, with undeveloped breasts. Brilliant, good-looking. Artistic and

173

highly intellectual. Never masturbated, and did not know of homosexuality among women; very sensitive to touch on the pudenda.

"No. 2. Has had sexual relations, but never coitus, with many men. Mutually masturbated with one man. Masturbated herself frequently, and took a long time to produce orgasm, even with *cunnilingus*, which delighted her immensely. After having it performed, she would stoop down and passionately kiss my lips. Fond of prolonged kisses, during which the tongue played a prominent part. Tall and fully developed, but no looks. Clever, masculine brain, and strong physically. Skillfully concealed her passionate nature, which, however, was long in developing and was long kept in check by maidenly modesty.

"No. 3. Innocent before marriage, and hated her *fiancé* even to touch her, which feeling still persists. Has had liaisons with many men, and several miscarriages, one legitimate, others illegitimate, and one illegitimate child. Does not masturbate herself, but readily yields to its seduction when performed by others. The most passionate woman I have ever met. Good, typical, womanly figure, but thin and weak. Not much looks, but very fascinating to men. Clever and intellectual.

"No. 4. Coitus only with her husband before myself. Not very passionate. I know nothing about masturbation or homosexuality in her case. Very broad hips, large breasts, and well-developed nates. Deserted by her husband. No children. Rather foolish and weak-minded. Penetration difficult owing to long labia majora.

"No. 5. Knows all about homosexuality of both sexes and wants to know more about everything. Probably masturbates. Several children. In love with her husband at first, but now tired of him and took to other men for variety and because her husband had ceased to give her sexual pleasure. Very passionate; has slow orgasm; likes nakedness and contact of body. Very large vagina. Broad hips and full breasts. Intellectual, but not so by nature. Artistic and very musical.

"No. 6. Absolutely innocent before marriage. Was practically raped by her husband on her marriage night. This disgusted her with the whole performance, and she could not bear her husband's caresses. During pregnancy she was frightened because she did not know what was going to happen, *i.e.*, how the child was going to be born; and no one enlightened her,—doctor, nurse, or mother. Did not know the meaning of the words sexual feeling, and never thought about sexual matters at all until marriage. I roused her passion, put things in their true light, made her have an orgasm, and told her what it meant. The orgasms at first made her cry and nearly faint, and she thereafter became intensely passionate. Very excited at cunnilingus, which I practised on her more than once. She confessed that the orgasm was stronger and more complete during coitus than during masturbation, which relieved my mind. She volunteered to strip naked and has but little shyness with me. Cannot bear her husband yet. She admits that she was only half a woman before she knew me, but now regrets her marriage. Short, thin, and slight, with narrow hips and no breasts. Quick woman's wit, but not intellectual.

"Of the prostitutes I have known, perhaps 60 in number, the Japanese easily take the palm. They are scrupulously clean, have charming manners and beautiful bodies, and take an intelligent interest in the proceedings. Also they are not always thinking about the money. Perhaps the Kashmiris come next, though the Chinese run them very close. Some of the more expensive London women are bearable, but they are such harlots! The white women in the East are insupportable, and small wonder, for they consist of the dregs of the European and American markets. My list comprises English, French, German, Italian, Spanish-American, American, Bengali, Punjabi, Kashmiri, Kaffir, Singhalese, Tamil, Burmese, Malay, Japanese, Chinese, Greek, and Pole.

"I naturally prefer to satisfy myself with a woman, a friend and a lady of my own class; but in the absence of the best I gladly take the next best available, down the scale from a lady for whom I do not care to prostitutes of all classes and colors, men, boys, animals, melons, and masturbation. I would as cheerfully have connection with my sister, or any other female relative. I have frequent erotic dreams about the most extraordinary subjects— male and female relations, casual acquaintances of both sexes, and animals. When I have got an intrigue in hand with a woman, I have no wish to masturbate, and often restrain myself when I know that I am going to have access before long to prostitutes. After coitus it takes a long time before I am ready for the next, sometimes two hours; and the first is always very quick, nearly always too quick for the woman. With a strange woman I have difficulty in maintaining erection at the instant of penetration, and this has often given me trouble.

"I know that most women like, and few dislike, being touched by me. My favorite colors are green and red, and I can whistle quite well.

"I would be very glad to know whether I may be considered sexually normal or not, but I do not desire any opinion on the morality of my acts, for the simple reason that without knowing all the circumstances it would be impossible to judge. But I cannot help saying that I do not consider anything I have done is wrong in itself, and I am quite certain that I have never harmed in any way any of the ladies with whom I have had relations. I am certain, if I had made promises which I knew I could not keep, I might have married one of them. But the result would have been great unhappiness to both, quarrels, and ultimate separation or divorce—and she realized that as well as I did. I may seem egotistical in my attitude and assurance toward ladies, but I only speak the honest truth; and I know that No. 6, for instance, has only gratitude and worship to give me for having opened her eyes. I have made her promise to have intercourse with her husband as soon as she can bear it, and I have satisfied myself that I have not started her on the road to sexual perversion. So much in self-explanation. I may add that I do not deliberately seek 'affaires de cœur,' and that, when they come my way, I do my utmost to use all consideration for the lady, thinking, as I do, that I owe them a far bigger debt than I shall ever be able to pay."

HISTORY XIV.—J. E., professional man, aged 32. Public school and university education, in which he did well. From age of 6 or 7 had strong sexual emotions, and from 9 sexually pleasurable dreams, though no emission till 12 or 13. He remembers the association of sexual excitement with whipping, either at sight or imagination of it, and this feeling was certainly shared by boys aged 9 to 12 at his private boarding-school and others at the public school later on. His nurse-maid used to invent excuses for beating his nates with a long lead-pencil when he wasaged about 7, and he saw occasional whippings with clothes removed in the family nursery.

When nearly 16 he was initiated into masturbation, which at once coincided with rapid mental development and success at school. He has practised it ever since under same conditions and restrictions as marital intercourse. Religion has never acted as any restraint, and the best restraint to all young people, in his opinion, is to warn them on hygienic grounds. (He became a freethinker at 17, partly on observing the inconsistency of religious persons in this connection. He was twice set upon by Catholics when 16, who attempted mutual masturbation.) He can vaguely remember some such warning when very young from his mother.

No intercourse with women till age of 19, though strong homosexual feelings from 10 upward, associated with feminine youths. These feelings were quite distinct from feelings of affection and friendship for more virile youths. An attack of gonorrhea at 21 was followed by an operation for circumcision, which had beneficial effects, but did not prevent an attack of syphilis at age of 23, caught at a guaranteed state establishment in France. Intercourse almost always with prostitutes, on prudential and worldly grounds, though what he approves would be greater laxity between boys and girls, with proper safeguards against undesired offspring. He is now happily married. He only indulges in masturbation at times when intercourse is impossible (e.g., childbirth). It is then practised once or twice a week in the early morning; overnight it causes troubled sleep, brain activity, and constipation. This seems ethically more desirable unless the wife were to condone physical infidelity, which she would not, and even then there might be risks of venereal disease. His general health and working power are in all respects excellent, as the venereal diseases were speedily and thoroughly cured. Homosexual feeling has entirely disappeared since marriage.

HISTORY XV.—G. D., English; aged 60. "My earliest essays in juvenile vice were due not so much to unguarded as to unguided ignorance. I slipped where my natural protectors suspected no danger, and I fell because I had never been warned of the treacherous nature of the ground. Before or soon after I was 7 years old, the example of an elder brother, who had lately begun to go to school as a day-boy, initiated me into the mysteries of masturbation, which seemed to me then as harmless as it was fascinating; and the novel pleasure was almost daily indulged in, after I had acquired sufficient dexterity to accomplish the act within a reasonable time, without a twinge of conscience, either in that brother's company or when alone. Decency demanded secrecy in the gratification of what soon became an imperiousdesire, and the preliminary operations included, almost from the first, mutual *fellatio* and approximation of the excited organs; but similar privacy was very properly sought during the performance of other bodily acts associated with those 'less honorable members,' and it appeared to me quite as natural and right for us to amuse ourselves together in that way as for a married couple to hide their most intimate embraces from the observation of others. Indeed, I went farther than that, and even came to regard the absence of all shame between us as akin to the primeval innocence which Adam and Eve exhibited before the Fall. I believed for long that we two were specially privileged and possessed a peculiar sense denied to other boys, for I had never heard of masturbation till I learnt, not the word indeed, but the thing itself.

"My curiosity about the real nature of sexual union in the case of human beings set my intelligence to work at the interesting problem, and by carefully studying certain parts of the Bible, Lemprière's classical and other dictionaries, as well as by persistently watching when I could the amorous proceedings of domestic animals, I learnt enough to make its most prominent features pretty clear before I was 11 years of age. I was then all eagerness to have the opportunity of inspecting at close quarters the genitals of women or young girls, and a stay at the seaside when I was 12 made the latter at least feasible. When the shore was nearly deserted, between 1 and 2 P.M., the daughters of the fisherfolk used to besiege the bathing machines and disport themselves in the water, bathing and paddling in various stages of nudity. I would pretend that my whole attention was being given to the making of miniature tunnels in the sand, while all the time I slyly peeped at what I most desired to see, whether in front or from behind, as the dancing damsels stood upright or stooped till their haunches were higher than their heads. I had already read something somewhere about the *clitoris*, and wanted especially to see it, but indistinct glimpses were all that I could obtain; nor was it until I visited an anatomical museum, which then existed at the top of the Haymarket in London, that I learned, a good many years later, from several life-sized models there displayed, the characteristic features of that part, as well as the abnormal modifications to which it is subject, either congenitally or in consequence of profligate habits. I was 15, I think, when I first came to know that girls can masturbate as well as boys.

"Long after I had realized why the terms male and female are so distinguished, my imagination was occupied with the possible postures in which the act of copulation may be accomplished by a man and woman; from Horace, Lucretius, Martial, Aristophanes, and, above all, from Ovid's *Ars Amatoria* I obtained much, but not always very clear, information while still a schoolboy. This was supplemented later by photographic pictures from Pompeiian brothels and photographs from life, purchased at Florence and gloated over one night, with twice-repeated masturbation, and afterward destroyed in a revulsion of shame.

"But while continuing to practise self-abuse (with a certain degree of restraint indeed, but seldom less often than once or even twice a week), after I had been made fully aware of its perils by Dr. Adam Clarke's alarming comments on Genesis xxxviii, 9, when I was about 12 or 13, I never had connection with a woman until I married somewhat late in life. This abstinence was not due to any frigidity of disposition, but from prudential and religious motives, and, to some extent perhaps, from the imperfect but genuine satisfaction afforded by solitary indulgence. My imagination, like that of young J. J. Rousseau, as set forth in his *Confessions*, was allowed free scope for its exercise, but in practice I confined myself to what seemed to me comparatively innocent as compared with fornication. I was never an unreserved 'exhibitionist' like Rousseau, but I have on more than one occasion turned toward a hedge and pretended to make water, when a girl had just passed me on the road, showing a *turgens cauda* if she should chance out of curiosity to look back, as once, at any rate, happened.

"I watched with interest the first indications of puberty in my own person. I had, of course, seen the pubic hair on many of my own sex, but I was 17 when I first saw a naked woman. She was standing at the door of her machine, wringing out her bathing-dress, as I swam past, and her face was hidden by the awning then used, so that she could not see me. A slight effusion of limpid mucus began to characterize the orgasm, at the age of 12 or 13 (before any ejaculation of semen was experienced), such as exuded later from the *urethra* when salacious excitement reached a certain pitch, even though the final climax might be postponed or prevented altogether. I found it a refinement of luxury to prolong the period of tumescence as far as possible, by frequently checking a too rapid progress toward the goal. By this practice of repeated arrest when the orgasm was imminent, and the mental debauchery which was its habitual accompaniment, I believe I did my nervous system more damage than by anything else—even the early age at which the dangerous indulgence became established. Nocturnal emissions (the sequel of lascivious dreams) commenced when I was about 15, at which age I had my first experience of an involuntary discharge when awake, under the influence of purely mental emotion; but this latter mode of escape did not often happen, and later on ceased altogether. My muscular strength was not impaired by too frequent indulgence, and I acquired some athletic prowess on the football field and on the running path, both as a boy and as a young man. Walking tours were for long my favorite recreation, even after the bicycle became an increasing attraction. My health, however, suffered in other ways from too constant absorption in lustful thoughts, which found vent in erotic verses and tales, generally destroyed soon after they were written. I have been subject since I was a boy to more or less prolonged fits of mental depression. How far I have inherited this tendency (my father and his father both married first cousins, and a neurotic diathesis has been characteristic of our family), or how far it has been aggravated by pernicious habits, I cannot say; cause and effect have no doubt acted and reacted on each other.

"As I grew toward adolescence I endeavored to make self-abuse as close an imitation as possible of sexual intercourse by such methods as may be easily imagined. My biological studies (I won a scholarship and took honors at my university) were directed with most intent predilection toward the reproductive system, particularly the modifications of the copulatory organs in different animals and the diverse manner of their employment. The sexual instinct, whether in its normal or abnormal manifestations, is a subject which has always had a strong attraction for me, nor has it lost its fascination with the growth of years (I am now 60) nor the competition of other interests.

"My very limited experience of the sexual system in women would lead me to believe that the *clitoris* is the only peculiarly sensitive part of the female *genitalia*, coition giving no pleasure unless 'the trigger of love' is simultaneously manipulated, as can be done when intromission is effected *a tergo*; that the mind of a normally healthy maiden is altogether free from sexual excitement of a physical kind, and that little curiosity is felt about the precise *modus operandi* of conjugal intercourse; but, nevertheless, I have good reason to believe that this, if not an unusual type, is by no means the only one that exists.

"As to sexual inversion my personal experience has been confined to two or three *grandes passions* for boys, the first of which possessed me when between the ages of 16 and 18, and involved, when I was 17, the most intense mental emotion, of a romantic kind, tinged with poignant jealousy and vexation at comparative coldness toward myself. These love passages never led me into indelicate behavior (I was once threatened with such treatment myself by a stranger whose acquaintance I made one day at the British Museum, when a lad of 15. He took me to his bedroom at an inn, locked the door, and showed me a collection of coins, giving me some, and, while doing so, attempted to take indecent liberties; but I pretended that I must catch a certain train, unlocked the door, and made a hasty escape), nor was any gratification sought beyond occasional kisses and other innocent endearments, though such caresses would sometimes excite an erection, which I carefully concealed. These amours were, however, no outcome of perverted instinct, nor were they any bar to fancies for the opposite sex which affected my imagination rather than my heart."

HISTORY XVI.—This history is given in the subject's own words: A. N., 34 years of age, a university graduate, devoted to learning and interested in philosophy and theology.

He is happily married and the father of an only daughter. Since puberty he has enjoyed excellent health.

"Looking back he finds the beginnings of sexual feeling obscure. This feeling is by no means identical in its progress with the knowledge of the phenomena of sex generally. The latter he acquired thus: His mother told him at a very early age the outlines of the phenomena of birth and explained to him (perhaps at that time unnecessarily) that the genital organs of little girls were different from his own. This piece of knowledge led to his asking, when 9 years old, a little girl cousin who came to live with the family (he was an only child) and who shared his bed to let him see her genitalia. This she readily did and also invited him to coitus, which she described as a 'nice game.' He complied, but without, of course, any feeling of pleasure or any understanding of the nature of what he was doing. Shortly after this he went to a day school, where, amid the extraordinarily coarse conversation of the boys, he was initiated into all the more obvious phenomena of sex. But still it was only a matter of intellectual curiosity. As such it had a strange fascination for him, and to this day he remembers many of the obscene words and phrases, as, for example, a set of indecent verses beginning 'William, the milkman, sat under a tree,' describing coitus, though some of the details were yet misunderstood by him. That up to his tenth or eleventh year no real sexual desire was awakened is plain from the fact that there was no desire for any repetition of attempts at coitus with his cousin, though he did indeed, again out of curiosity, finger her genitals sometimes, a thing which she, grown evidently more fastidious, reported to his mother, who gravely reprimanded him, telling him that it was the 'beginning of all evil.'

"Desire was awakened gradually and, as I have said, obscurely. Not only at school, but among his own cousins, especially two girls (other than the one above mentioned) and a boy, the conversation was lascivious in the extreme, though words never proceeded to deeds as between the boys and the girls. He was soon, however, about his fifteenth year, so far as he can remember, initiated into the practice of masturbation, first, sleeping with his boy cousin, the two used to play at 'husband and wife,' and then, more directly, a neighbor, a heavy, sensual type of boy, took him aside one day and drawing out his own penis asked him 'if he knew how to make some buttermilk.' Out of curiosity at first, and to obtain the new and voluptuous sensation afterward, he began assiduously to practise this vice, which, as he afterward found out, was very common, if not universal about him. That it was morally reprehensible he had not at that time the ghost of a notion; he considered that it belonged to the category of the 'dirty' only. His father quite neglected this development, believing, I suppose, in the superstition of the 'innocence of childhood.'

"This practice of masturbation went on assiduously to his sixteenth year, when its true nature and danger were revealed to him by a good clergyman who prepared him for confirmation. He had at this time gone far, in both solitary vice and vice 'à deux,' with his male cousin, with whom he practised even 'fellatio' and 'intromissio in anum.' But now he began to struggle against it and made some headway, but never entirely shook it off before his marriage at 26, so deeply rooted was the hold it had on him. Especially at the time between sleeping and waking, or while lying sleepless at night—when the monks prayed 'ne polluantur corpora'—did its attacks come insidiously upon him. He would struggle for weeks and then would come a relapse. On one occasion he slept with a young uncle who amused himself, thinking he was asleep, by playing with his penis until he had an emission. A. N. hailed the occasion with keen joy—he caustically argued that he experienced the pleasure without being culpable in its production! Then on 'coming to himself' he would agonize over his vice, remembering, for example, that, while *he* had rejoiced in what had been done, the very cousin who some time before used to share his sin was genuinely annoyed at the same uncle's attentions when it was he who suffered them.

"Looking back over the whole period of his youth and adolescence, he can trace the psychological effect of what was going on secretly, in his relations to girls and women. In a word, these relations were sentimental only. He often imagined himself in love; but it was imagination only. He was in love with a wraith, not a girl of flesh and blood. He hesitated to regard in any sexual way any girl of whom he had a high opinion; sexual desire and 'love' seemed for him to inhabit different worlds and that it would be a pollution to bring them together. In hours of relaxation from the very hard intellectual work which he was at this time engaged on at school and at the university, he was quite content with the society of quite young girls or even children when most of his friends would have sought out females of their own age. Nothing could have been farther from his desires or intention than any lascivious or, indeed, unseemly act toward any female in whose company he might be: no mother need have hesitated to trust her daughter in his company. I firmly believe that the discipline of the same bed which Gibbon (*Decline and Fall*, ed. Bury, vol. ii, p. 37) makes so merry over could have been endured by him without difficulty. His outward conduct was in all these respects most seemly and decorous, yet night after night he could masturbate, his imagination glowing with visions of female nakedness.

"Curiously the one and only actual female for whom he felt any desire at the earlier period (aged 14 to 16) began to be the cousin who lived in the house. On one occasion he touched her breasts, on another her naked thighs—and that was all! As she grew to puberty, she would have allowed far more liberties, but he contented himself with a sly glance now and again, when he could procure it, at her swelling bosom. The fear of putting her with child was ample to keep him away from her bed. Later on even so much as the foregoing occurred no more, and, as I have said, his outward life became absolutely decorous.

"Consequently he was in no danger of having dealings with prostitutes. The preliminaries, the conversation of such women, especially their drinking habits, would have been disgusting and repugnant to him in the extreme. He would have shunned the possibility of acquiring venereal disease like the plague. But he was never free from solitary vice; he secretly envied those who had occasions for coitus in what I may call a seemly and cleanly manner, friends in the country with farm girls, etc., of whom he had heard. He indulged also in lascivious reading, the obscene when he could procure it, rather than the merely suggestive, which has never been to his taste. He was familiar with quite a large number of Latin and Greek indecent passages, knew the broader farces of the *Canterbury Tales* and of the *Decameron*, and, later, the 'contes' of La Fontaine and the *Facetiæ* of Poggio. As Ste.-Beuve says of Gibbon, I think, he acquired an 'erudite and cold' sort of obscenity in this way.

"All this, of course, is only one half, and by no means always the dominant half, of his nature. He was often repentant for these delinquencies, and he was sincerely religious. He was also fond of serious learning and contrived to take a first-class university degree. Yet, ever and anon, the deeply sensual side of his nature made itself felt. Scotched for a time it could be, but killed never.

"Yet, I do not think it could be said that he had the sexual instinct in any really high degree. It was more like a small fly that makes a large buzz than any considerable factor in his constitution. He had a companion about this time of whom such a remark is even more true. This man's mind was replete with all manner of risky stories, all sorts of sexual details. He would take long walks with girls of loose character, talk with prostitutes at home and abroad, and yet, I believe, he never proceeded to coitus.

"Such then, was the subject of this notice up to the time of his marriage. Two men, one might say, in one skin. One learned, one merely obscene; one a pattern of decorousness, the other a self-polluter.

"On the sexual side he was as one knowing everything there is to know—yet knowing nothing. Like the boy-hero in Wedekind's*Frühling's Erwachen*, he had been long in Egypt, yet he had never seen the pyramids. He began to distress himself with questions as to whether he was yet capable; whether his recurring vice had not permanently injured him; whether he had made himself unfit for marriage. So shy and reserved was he about his secret that he could never have brought himself to mention it to a medical man. 'What! he! the good, the religious! the wholly moral and decorous!' (such was, indeed, the reputation he had among his friends); 'he, the victim of a vice so black!' No, no! '*Secretum meum mihi*,' he cried.

"Fortune, however, was kind to him. He was at an early age free from financial worries, which had almost crushed him earlier in his career, and he met in course of time the family from which he selected his excellent wife.

"The society in which he lived was of all English classes, I should suppose, the most reticent in matters of sex—the respectable, lower middle class; shopkeepers and the like, with a tradition of homely religion and virtue. The classes a little higher in the scale (to which, by the way, his mother had belonged) could far better sympathize with one in his position. Well, the family of his future wife was of a higher class and, what is far more, of foreign origin, for whom a large number of our English 'convenances' do not exist. To them sex was frankly recognized as a factor in life, and the mother of this household, as he grew more intimate, broached subjects which he had never, in such a manner, discussed before. It is unnecessary to give here any general history of his relationships with this household, as they have nothing to do with the matter in hand. After some time he became engaged to the youngest daughter, two years his senior, a woman of remarkable beauty and splendid development, one who attracted him as none other had done, both on account of her intellectual and social qualities and her physical beauty (he had hitherto despaired of finding the two combined in one person), for she is certainly the most beautiful woman with whom he has ever been acquainted.

"He now began to make the practical acquaintance of a woman—and one who, in impulses, temper, manner, and habit of thought, differed *toto cælo* from the girls he had known in his old home. Her sexual nature was ripe and developed, and it is lucky that the engagement was of short duration, or the strain and anticipation of that time might have been injurious to the health of both. As usual, in his outward relations toward women, so toward his *fiancée*, he was prepared for chaste caresses only. This, however, did not suffice for her hot and passionate nature. They went as far as possible short of actual coitus.

"After a few months, however, the marriage took place, and, at first, this brought him bitter disappointment and seemed to confirm his worst fears. He found himself quite unable to have pleasure or satisfactory coitus; quite incapable, with any erection that he could command, of introducing his well-developed penis into his wife's extremely narrow and contracted vagina. About a fortnight after the marriage, however, on his return from their short wedding tour, he felt much stronger and copulated with her, especially in the early mornings, so satisfactorily that she soon found herself with child. Coitus now began to be much more pleasurable for him, but to his wife still attended with pain.

"After nine months of married life, the child, the only offspring of the marriage, a healthy girl, was born. The stress of this time, the upsetting of his wife's health, her nervous breakdown and consequently uncertain temper, seemed for a period of nearly two years effectually to repress any sexual desire in the husband, and this period is perhaps the chastest of his life. Desire seemed to be the one thing absent. The revulsion of feeling in his wife was remarkable. The erstwhile amorous *fiancée*, who could hardly wait until marriage to test her lover, became now the wife and mother who hardly wished to be touched by her husband.

"Her health, however, gradually improved and a more normal state of affairs was brought about, which has continued to the present day, broken only by periods of abstention, chiefly caused by the attacks of anemia and menstrual irregularities from which his wife suffers from time to time. Ordinarily, he enjoys coitus once or twice in the month, hardly oftener, taking one month with another. At one time he exemplified in his own person the saying *omne animal post coitum triste*, but now happily this depression of spirits is rarely felt. Sometimes he has felt a depression of spirits, a general discontentedness, before experiencing a strong erection; in these cases coitus has cleared his spirits. He would naturally look upon coitus as an evacuation, although he recognizes the imperfectness of that view. For one thing he is constantly sorry, viz., that the act gives no pleasure to his wife, and that he has never been able to induce a crisis with her by normal means. In this state of affairs, knowing that 'après coup' she was still unsatisfied, he slipped into the practice of rubbing the clitoris with his fingers until the emission takes place. To do this, they assume the position 'ille sub, illa super.' From his own limited marital experience, he has never been able to understand the stories of women who masturbate several times a day, as his wife would be physically incapable (so he believes) of anything of the kind, and only easily reaches the crisis in any circumstances during the first few days after the menstrual flow has ceased. In fine, while agreeing theoretically with Sir Richard Burton and others that the eastern style of coitus (directed with a view to the pleasure of your partner) is the right one, it is one of his standing regrets that he is unable to practise it. In the place of the twenty minutes required by the women of India (according to Burton) he is happy if he can give two or three at the most, much as he would wish to prolong a pleasure as keen to himself as he could desire it to be to his dear and excellent spouse."

HISTORY XVII.—R. L., American; aged 43; height, 5 ft. 7 in.; weight, about 145 lbs.; occupation, teacher; somewhat neurotic; a slight myopia associated with acute astigmatism and muscular weakness of the eyes, producing a tendency to migraine. Uric acid diathesis, producing occasionally severe neuralgia, particularly in the intestines. These symptoms have been more or less constant since very early childhood. General health very good. Not inclined to indulge in athletic sports, but prefers sedentary occupations and recreations.

"My early ideas of sexual things are not very clear in recollection. I think that when 7 or 8 years of age I had a knowledge of the common or vulgar terms for intercourse and for the genital organs. Boys of my own age and slightly older would discuss sex relations, and I had a general knowledge that, in some way connected with the sexual act, 'babies were made.' We would tell, occasionally, lewd stories, and a few times attempted sexual practices with one another. Not till after puberty did I ever attempt masturbation. I must have been 9 or 10 years old before I learned that there was a difference in the sex organs of boys and girls. Up to this time I had supposed that intercourse was *per anum*. I attended a public school with both sexes. Talk among my boy associates was often nasty and concerned the sexual act with girls. At about 12 years I began to have erotic day dreams. I always had a sentimental attachment for some girl acquaintance whom I would idealize and with whom I would imagine myself having sex relations. As a matter of fact, there was no real sexual feeling about this. As I was very shy and timid naturally, I never made any kind of advances toward any of them, and they were entirely ignorant of any sentiments of affection in me.

"Pubertal changes commenced, I presume, about the age of 13½ years. I place it at this period from the following circumstances, which are fixed very strongly in my memory: I had, as a child, a soprano voice that was praised considerably by older friends, and about which I was inordinately conceited, I enjoyed greatly taking part in operettas, cantatas, etc. The dramatic instinct, if so it may be called, has always been marked with me, and amateur dramatics are still my chief diversion. When I was about the age mentioned above my voice changed quite rapidly, greatly to my distress of mind, as I was obliged to give up taking a part for which I had been cast in a school entertainment. The memory of that disappointment is still poignant. Other changes, such as the appearance of the pubertal hair, must have made no impression on my mind, as I cannot recollect anything in connection therewith. No involuntary emissions occurred. Indeed, during periods of continence in later life, when the sexual tension has been very strong, I have had very few such emissions.

"As a lad of 11 or 12, I had heard frequent allusions to masturbation by other boys who were older, but always in a way that indicated contempt. Yet there is no doubt now in my mind that the practice was very general. I think that I was probably about 15 when I decided to try the act. I think that there was little sex impulse in this decision. The animating purpose was rather curiosity. I succeeded in producing the complete orgasm and found it pleasurable, though there was a considerable shock of surprise at the ejaculation of semen. As nearly as I can estimate in my memory of an event as far back as this was, this was the beginning of definite sexual sensibility in me. I cannot but believe, however, that it would have been aroused sooner or later in some other way. Thereafter I would imagine myself embracing some of the girl friends to whom I have referred above, and, when excited, would masturbate. The act was in every instance a psychic intercourse. For some time I did not know that the practice was considered harmful. I indulged whenever I felt the inclination. This at times was rather frequent; again only at considerable intervals. I did know that it was looked upon as being unmanly, and never admitted, except to perhaps two or three boy friends, that I ever indulged. With these boys I practised mutual masturbation a few times. There was no homosexual feeling connected with these acts in any of us. It was only that the normal method of gratifying our desires was not available. I know the subsequent history of each of these boys, and there has been nothing to indicate any perverted instinct in any of them. About the age of 16 I heard a talk on sexual matters by a traveling evangelist, who portrayed the effects of masturbation in fearful colors. I now realize that he was an ignorant though well-intentioned man; but the general effect of his talk upon me was a bad one. One of the results of the habit, according to his statements, was insanity. Therefore I expected at any moment to lose my mind. I felt that I must stop the practice at once, but the matter became so great an obsession that again and again I broke my resolutions for reform. I undertook exercise, dieting, the reading of serious literature: all of which I had seen referred to in books as methods of lessening sexual desire. The object of these disciplinary practices was always the thing most prominently in mind, and so they were of no avail. Fortunately I entered college a little later, and the affairs of school life gradually took a commanding place in my thoughts, and the practice was not so much in mind. I did not, however, completely break away from it until almost the time of my marriage. If the present attitude of the scientific medical world toward the subject had been known to me, I do not believe that any evil would have come to me from the practice. At a later period of my life, say between 21 and 24, I would not indulge the habit for a considerable interval. At times I did not notice the presence or lack of desire. But then there would come periods when I would be under a severe sexual tension. This would be marked by intense nervousness, an inability to fix my attention upon any one thing, and a great desire to have intercourse. An act of masturbation at such a time would generally give relief. However, when I yielded to this form of relief, there would always follow feelings of profound self-reproach and of self-repugnance. Had I had nocturnal emissions they might have relieved me; but, as I have said before, they very rarely occurred. When, rarely, one did occur I would be greatly frightened, for I had the old, erroneous idea that they meant serious weakness and always ascribed them to my bad habit. That my habit of masturbation had any relation to the rarity of the involuntary emissions would, of course, be a matter of pure conjecture. In passing from the discussion of personal masturbation, I wish to say that my associations with boys as a pupil and as a teacher lead me to believe that the practice is practically universal. When discussing the hygienic evils of prostitution with boy pupils I have noted that, whereas not infrequently a boy will voluntarily protest that he has never had intercourse, there has always been a significant silence when masturbation is mentioned. I have never heard a boy make a denial, direct or indirect, that he had indulged in the practice. But it has seldom been a perversion. It has rather been, as in my own case, an available means of relieving a sexual impulse.

"During my college life I associated with many boys who had more or less regular sexual relations with prostitutes or with girls who were not virtuous. Their attitude toward the practice was an immoral one. The ethical aspect of irregular sexual relations never concerned them. It certainly did not concern me. What I have learned through my conversations on the subject with my pupils makes it evident to me that this is the common feeling of most boys of the adolescent period. I think of two things which operated strongly to prevent my entering into sexual relations with girls during this period of my life. One was an esthetic repugnance to the average prostitute. These are the women most easily available to the youth whose sexual desires are developed. I do not remember ever having seen an avowed prostitute who did not seem repulsive to me. I confess to an inclination to priggishness. I preferred to associate with people whom I called 'nice people.' It was fortunate for me that I was thrown into the society of a rather rough crowd of youths, who knocked a great deal of this snobbishness out of me. But it did act to prevent my having recourse to prostitution. A second preventive was my natural timidity in making advances to people. This has been a trait that I have never completely overcome. In my professional life this has been some detriment to my advancement. In the matter of sex relationship it tended to prevent my taking advantage of association with and even of advances from girls who, not prostitutes, were nevertheless not virtuous. There were a number of such in the town and neighborhood in which I lived, and I undoubtedly could have had sexual relations with them if I had only been able to overcome my shyness. The desire was not wanting. I really craved intercourse with them. It was simply a matter of cowardice. There was one girl whom I knew very well, with whom I was on friendly terms, who I knew had had sexual relations with other boys. She showed, at times, a marked preference for me, and I am sure would have welcomed any advances that I should have made. A number of times I sought her company with the intention of suggesting intercourse, but my resolution always failed.

"All through my college course I was much in the society of girls. We were in class together, associated very freely in society, frequently studied together. This is the most usual state of things in the western part of our country. But they were simply comrades: sex thoughts never arose in connection with such association. And I am quite certain that this was the general attitude of the other boys. Although the talk among the boy students was at times, very frankly and crudely, about sexual relations, no breath of scandal ever touched one of the college girls. Again my experience as teacher and student brings a conclusion that coeducation of the sexes does not affect, in one way or the other, the strictly sexual life of the male student. A very intimate friend who has had a varied experience in school work has told me recently that his conclusions are the same.

"When I was about 20 years old I became acquainted with a very beautiful girl, four years my junior. Our acquaintance very rapidly developed into deeper affection, and about five years later we were married. During all this time very little of the physical aspects of love entered into our attachment. My sweetheart had much of the same shyness as was so pronounced in my own character. For several years I think that the thought of marriage was never distinctly present in our minds. A formal betrothal between us did not take place until within a year and a half of our marriage. Yet each of us had a very distinct understanding of the feelings of the other. But until our betrothal there were none of even those very innocent expressions of endearment common, I imagine, to all lovers. I am sure that during this period of our attachment no thought of any physical relations between us was ever in my mind; or, at any rate, was promptly banished if it occurred. Yet all this time my sex desires were very strong and at times became an obsession. Never, though, were they directed toward my sweetheart. The first time that we engaged in the endearments and caresses allowed to lovers I became conscious, after a time, of a state of sexual excitement. I experienced an erection. It was absolutely reflex; no thought had entered into it. I was at once overwhelmed with a feeling of shame. I felt that I had been guilty of unthinkable indecency toward my betrothed. Then there arose a fear that it might be noticed. (Men at that time wore abominably tight clothing.) As a matter of fact, I now know that there was no real danger of this, for she was absolutely ignorant of the nature of the male sexual organs. But I made a pretext for withdrawing from the room and tried to adjust my clothing so that no exposure could occur. I was fearful of coming into close proximity to her again, lest there should be a recurrence of the feeling. As a matter of fact it did occur a number of times, but my good sense finally suggested the explanation and after a time it ceased to trouble me. The thought was latent in my mind that sexual excitement was necessarily more or less indecent at all times, and I could not reconcile its manifestation with a pure love.

"I have said that my sexual desire was strong. Up to the time of marriage it was never gratified in the normal manner. My esthetic abhorrence of prostitutes continued to prevent its gratification in that manner. No other opportunity offered. I am positive that moral considerations did not enter into the matter at all. I think now that it was strange that the thought that it would be disloyal to my promised wife to have connection with other women did not affect me. But I am sure that it did not. I am inclined to think that conscientious scruples very rarely enter into the average young man's considerations of contemplated sexual relations.

"As the time of my marriage drew near, thoughts of the physical relationship of husband and wife became, of course, more insistent. The idea of establishing sexual relations was not at all a pleasant one. I dreaded it as an ordeal. I wondered if it would be possible for us to retain the same love and affection for one another after such intimate relations were established. This was a recurrence of the fallacious notion that there was something inherently indecent in sexual things. I am in hopes that other ideas are replacing this wrong one, in the minds of the younger generation, as the result of the saner and franker discussion of sex. By a great effort, I had practically stopped masturbating. At times I felt almost maddened by desire. But never did the prospect of marriage seem desirable from this point of view. Up to the very day of our wedding my affection for my betrothed seemed free from sexual desire. But my physical being was craving sexual companionship.

"Theoretically I knew a great deal of the nature of intercourse. Practically I was absolutely ignorant. In some ways I was better informed, on matters that a new husband should know, than the average man entering the married life. A physician's library had been at my disposal, and I had read somewhat extensively on physiology and hygiene. My chosen lines of study had given me a theoretical knowledge of the anatomy of the female genital organs that was fairly thorough. I knew a little about the physiology of reproduction and rather less of intercourse. Fortunately, I learned in the course of my reading that the first sexual approaches were likely to be quite painful to a woman, and that great care should be exercised at this time. I tried to put into practice what little I had learned in theory and I imagine that we got through the introductory attempts with less than the average difficulties. Our first efforts were not satisfactory to either of us. My wife was absolutely unprepared so far as any definite knowledge of the act was concerned. I sincerely hope that the prudish notions of the past generations will give way to more sensible views in the future, and that the girl becoming a wife will be just as chaste, but wiser in matters of such importance to her happiness. I presume that my timidity was a valuable asset at this time; for I was afraid to force matters in any way, and time and repeated attempts finally overcame our difficulties. And when our sexual relations were once established, the whole tenor of my life was changed. All the former sexual unrest disappeared. My former feeling toward sexual relations was altered. They no longer seemed that which, though very desirable, was yet necessarily indecent. Fortunately, after the first few weeks, they have been quite pleasurable to my wife. I am sure that our sexual life since marriage has been a large factor in deepening the love that has made our married life an ideal one. As I look back at the first year of marriage, I wonder that we got through it so well. My knowledge of sexual hygiene was a strange mixture of fact and nonsense. If the frequency of acts of intercourse advocated by some of the authorities I have lately read is correct, then we must have passed the bounds of moderation. But it is certain that our general health has been very good: better in both cases than before marriage.

"In reviewing these phases of the development of my sexual life, one or two conclusions seem to me to be strongly emphasized. It was unfortunate that the real sexual desire was aroused as early and in the manner that it was. Whether this would have been prevented by more definite education in the hygiene and the purpose of the function, I can only conjecture. I believe that mine was and is the common experience of boys. I am decidedly of the opinion that there should be instruction given of the anatomy of the genital organs and of the hygiene of intercourse, and this shortly after the youth has reached puberty. How this is to be done is a grave question. It will require tact and knowledge not possessed by the average teacher and parent. However it is done, it should be honest, frank, and free from piosity.

"I am certain that, in my own case, rather frequent intercourse is decidedly beneficial. Any prolonged abstinence always brings about the same nervous disturbances that I have referred to above. It is fortunate for me that this repetition of the act is satisfactory to both concerned."

HISTORY XVIII.—E. W., dentist, aged 32, of New England Puritan stock. Height, 5 ft. 10½ in.; weight, 144 lbs. Spare and active, of nervobilious temperament.

"My earliest recollection is being punished for 'playing with myself' when I could not have been more than 3 or 4 years of age. I distinctly remember my exultation on discovering that I could excite myself (while my hands were tied behind my back for punishment) by rubbing my small but erect penis against the carpet while lying on my stomach. At this time, of course, I knew nothing of sex or of what I was doing. I did what my desires and instincts at that time prompted me to do. However, punishments and lectures failed utterly to break up this habit, and, though I always wished and tried faithfully to obey my parents, I soon grew to indulge quietly in bed when I was thought to be asleep. The matter apparently passed out of the minds of my parents as soon as they ceased to detect me further in the act, and they regarded it as abandoned. I now feel reasonably certain that this precocity was due to an adherent foreskin which covered the glans tightly almost to the meatus, and so kept up a continual irritation.

"I have no recollection that anyone ever taught me the habit, and I know beyond a doubt that no one ever learned of the habit or even a word as to the possibility of autoexcitement through word or deed of mine. My recollection of the sensations is that there was a short period of excitation, usually by rubbing, which was not particularly, often not at all, pleasurable, and this was followed by a single thrill of pleasure that extended all over my little body. The curious thing was, however, that there seemed to be no limit to the number of times I could consecutively produce this sensation. My recollection is perfectly clear of how I would lie in bed of a morning and thus excite myself time after time. As I grew older this condition, of course, changed. Masturbation was not a consuming passion with me at this or any other time. I enjoyed it and felt that in it I had a means of entertainment when other sources of enjoyment were not at hand.

"By the time I was 6 or 7 I had figured out the difference in sex in animals and suspected that 'all was not as it should be' in some portions of a girl's anatomy. This suspicion was suddenly confirmed one never-to-be-forgotten morning, when I induced my dearest playmate, a little girl, to urinate in my presence. I was more thunderstruck than excited over this discovery, and it led to no results in any other way, nor did we ever again unveil ourselves to each other. At this time I began to learn from the older boys the pitiful, childish vulgarities and common terms of sex, and to invent and exchange rhymes and stories that were pathetic in their attempts at vulgarity.

"At the age of 11 a buxom servant-girl threw out some vague hints to me,—I was very tall for my age,—and tried to induce me to take liberties with her, at least to the extent of telling her vulgar stories, but I would not rise to the lure. I believe that the thing which held me in check was fear of discovery by my parents and the consequent humiliation. A short time previous to this my father had enlightened me as to the means and manner of reproduction and had encouraged me to talk to him and to my mother on such subjects rather than with anyone else. I think this had a great influence for good, as it made me feel that I had some authoritative knowledge and that I was trusted by my parents. My determination not to prove entirely unworthy of their trust has been the anchor that has held through all the storms and temptations of youth and young manhood.

"About the age of puberty I began to long for more realistic experiences and tried through a period of a year or so the disgusting experiments of intercourse with animals, using hens and a cow for this purpose. Details are of no importance, and I spare myself their repetition. My better nature or general mental development soon overcame my desires in this direction, and the practice was abandoned.

"With the dawning of the power of emission I noticed that the adherent foreskin before alluded to, which had never been examined during all these years (as I had discovered that I was different from other boys and so was shy about exposing myself), began to trouble me by being painful during erections. Accordingly I took a buttonhook and tore all the adhesions loose. A very painful though ultimately entirely satisfactory operation!

"(I may mention in this connection that my two sons were afflicted with adherent foreskins to such an extent as to render circumcision necessary a few days after birth, in order that the function of urination might become fully established.)

"As my powers developed I had my first wet dream at about the age of 15, and was much surprised thereat. My father, however, told me not to be alarmed and soothed my anxious fears, which were easily aroused by my guilty feelings on account of my habit of masturbation, in which I still indulged from one to three times a week.

"Between the ages of 12 and 17 my father had the good judgment to require a large amount of active outdoor labor from me, as well as sending me to excellent schools. Certain kinds of study had a distinct effect upon the sexual organs, namely, difficult Latin and German translations and problems in fractions. I considered at the time that it was because my mind wandered from the subject I was studying. Now I am perfectly sure it was because my mind focused on the subject I was studying. At any rate the fact existed, and when alone in my room, wrestling with a knotty problem, I used almost as a rule to keep myself in the most violent state of erection for long periods—an hour or so—sometimes ending with an emission, but more often I forced myself to forego this climax through fear of overindulgence. During these years my curiosity as to the exact nature of the female organs was something terrible, and I wasted many hours and much ingenuity in the attempt to surreptitiously gratify it. My perseverance in the face of failure along this line was surely worthy of a nobler cause.

"I was much in the society of girls of my own age or older during these years and until I was 19. I found with them a keen and entirely pure and wholesome enjoyment utterly separate and apart from the desires and indulgences which I have been describing. I never cared for any girl who was 'forward' or in any way unladylike, and the idea of taking any undue liberties with any of my youthful sweethearts was as remote from my thoughts as a trip to the moon. Perhaps I can say this better and more distinctly by stating that I would be perfectly willing to have my wife know of, or my boys repeat, any action that I ever took with any woman.

"I spent my spare time in their society and lavished upon my girl companions every cent I could spare, but had no thought of immediate sex desire or gratification. At the age of 17 I went as an apprentice in my present profession of dentistry. Whenever it became necessary for me, in assisting at the operating chair, to touch a lady's hair or face, I would be seized with the utmost confusion and could with difficulty control my hands so that they did not tremble. This soon wore off as I came to a realization of the true professional spirit and attitude toward all patients, and, needless to say, has now become a matter of the utmost indifference to me.

"From 19 to 22 I attended a professional school in a large city, remote from my home, where I was an utter stranger. During these years I devoted myself to my professional studies and to music with much diligence. I took an active part in all student life and problems save only that of the 'eternal feminine.'

"Frequently I have been out with a crowd of 'the boys' when they headed for a brothel, and have been the only one to turn back or to remain on the sidewalk as the door closed behind my last companion. I say this not in self-praise, but in the same spirit of accuracy which has prompted me to put down everything concerning this greatest mystery of our natures as I have experienced it and worked it out.

"It was during these three years at school that I placed upon myself the most stringent and effective curbs to my sex nature. I somehow never could 'get my own consent' to go to a brothel or stay with a 'soiled dove,' for I had by this time firmly resolved that I would bring to my wife, whoever she might turn out to be, a clean body at least. I limited myself in my autoexcitement to one emission a week and on one or two occasions went two weeks without inducing an emission. Spontaneous nocturnal emissions were quite common during these years. I cannot state just how frequent they were, but perhaps one a week would be a fair average.

"Shortly after graduation at the age of 22 I became engaged to the woman who is now my wife. (She was 17 at the time of our engagement, brunette, well developed, and with a wisdom and charm that have held me a willing captive for ten years and no prospect of escape!)

"With our engagement began for each of us that divine and mysterious unfolding of the nature of one to the nature of the other. Our engagement lasted two years and a half and, ignorant as we both were, I am sure that it was none too long. Never shall I forget the surprise I felt—to say nothing of the delight—when I discovered that my sweetheart was as anxious to find out the uttermost facts about me as I was to explore the divine mystery of her sweet body.

"We lived in different towns and I used to spend Sundays at her home. I slept in a room adjoining that occupied by my betrothed and a friend. There was a transom with clear glass over the door which connected these two rooms, and to have stood upon the foot of the bed and looked through this transom would have been the easiest thing in the world, and was such an opportunity as I would have given years of my life to have obtained in my adolescence; but now that the chance was afforded me to freely spy upon the chamber of my future bride my soul revolted, for the feeling was upon me that not until it was revealed to me because she could no longer bear to keep it concealed from me would I look upon the blessed vision of her maiden loveliness. Nor was I disappointed, for gradually we became acquainted with each other's bodies, and this gradual unveiling of each to the other led, during the last months of our engagement, to mutual manual manipulations, excitement and

186

gratification. Intercourse did not take place until the second night after our marriage, and our first baby was born nine months and three days after our marriage, though my wife was ten days past the cessation of her period at the time of my first entering.

"Since marriage I have made it my first duty to study my wife's inclinations and desires with regard to our sexual relations, and can say that now, after seven years of married life, and after she has borne me two sons, we are enjoying a fullness of happiness that neither of us would have believed possible during the first year of our married life.

"I have found that the woman must have the entire charge of the time and number of approaches in a week or month, and that when she is for any reason disinclined to the sexual act the husband must keep away, no matter how he feels about the matter. Also the man must be sure that his wife reaches the orgasm or is at the point of it before he allows himself to 'let go.'

"Our meetings have averaged eight or nine a month. During the latter months of pregnancy they were *nil*, and in the month following an enforced separation of several weeks they were fourteen. We have never tried nor had the slightest curiosity to know how far we could indulge ourselves.

"For myself I seem to demand a gratification of the sexual desire rather oftener than my wife, and when I feel I cannot get a good night's rest without first being relieved of my seminal burden, while at the same time my wife is disinclined to the sexual act, I have her perform manual manipulation until relief is effected. Mind, I say *relief*, for the emission gives me very little pleasure under these circumstances, but it does give *relief*. In my present health I find I cannot sleep well if I go over more than two nights without an emission. My wife understands my condition, and is entirely willing to assist me in this way when she feels she cannot give me the gratification which I crave. We have come to see sex matters as they are, and respect and reverence have taken the place of ignorance and fear.

"To sum up, owing to lack of circumcision the sex instinct developed too soon and out of all proportion during my early youth. I cannot see that masturbation has ever had the slightest bad effect upon my health or mental state (except as I was constantly loathing myself more or less for being unable to stop it).

"The husband must subordinate himself to the wife in order to obtain the highest good and pleasure of both.

"I have always been successful in my undertakings. Stood at the head of my class at school, and in my professional work graduated with highest honors. I have a memory for prose or verse that is the cause of envy to many of my friends. The facts here set down are recorded in the interest of advancing study along this most important but neglected and ignored line. That they have been truthfully recorded without favor to the black or light on the white is my sincere belief."

HISTORY XIX.—E. B. Parents sound; strong constitution in mother, moderately so in father; vigorous and healthy, but of refined nature. Breast-milk for six months.

"*Age 4-5*. Took great delight in the little waterworks. Severely punished for this. Interest in the parts morbidly increased thereby.

"*Age 5*. Earliest recollection of 'counter-erection'—the penis shrinking tensely into itself, producing local and general discomfort. This resulted from certain kinds of *mauvaise-honte*,—having to kiss aged persons, having officious help at micturition, bathing, dressing, etc., which caused a sort of physical disgust. Toward puberty the experience grew rare. One such occasion was at about eighteen, when solicited on the street by a prostitute. The very *idea* of homosexual relations produces it. It would appear to be a powerful safeguard against promiscuous sex relations. I have met two men subject to the same thing, and have heard of one woman subject to something analogous. It might be called a nausea of the 'nether heart' in Georg Hirth's phrase.

"*Age 6-7*. Earliest recollection of erection. Unprovoked at first. A disposition to *punish* the organ and satisfaction in doing so. From this time erection took place whenever it was thought about.

"*Age 10*. Present at a discussion in the playground about the best way of intercourse, which I heard of for the first time. This was followed by enlightenment on the source of children. Concluded it must be very painful to both parties. 'Just the other way,' I was told. But the idea of pain to the genitals was 'interesting' to me. Pain felt by the other sex was 'interesting.' Pained looks captivated me—I liked to imagine some mysterious trouble; and, as I learned more, 'female complaints' interested me greatly in their subjects. I got a 'grateful pang' at the pit of the stomach at the thought, but neither erection nor the opposite. This hypogastric feeling has continued to associate itself with certain sexual impressions. The thought of a *woman mortifying herself* later on excited me sexually. Once, pulling a stay-string for fun (my wife never laced) gave me a powerful and quite unexpected erection.

"*Age 12.* A girl visitor of the same age got me talking about the genitals, and at bedtime came and proposed coitus. We failed to manage it. The vulva stripped back the foreskin, which was a voluptuous feeling; then we were alarmed by something and separated. I never saw her again. She too liked to 'punish' her vulva. She put whole pepper in it, and advised me to use the same. I continued greatly excited when she had gone; the hand flew to the phallus and worried it, and orgasm came on at once—the childish orgasm consisting of well-spaced spasms of the ejaculators, without the poignant preliminary nisus of the adult orgasm. There was no reaction or depression, except that the phallus—which did not subside at once—was painful to touch. A week or so later I tried again, but failed. A month later, being more excited, I succeeded. I found that I could only compass it about once in three weeks. There were no emissions. I used to have a spontaneous mental image of a small Grecian temple in a sunny park, which charmed me, and I had no scruples.

"*Age 12-13.* Masturbated once or twice a month.

"*Age 13-14.* Was sent to a small public school, where it happened that a very good tone prevailed. I learned that masturbation was bad form and unmanly. The proper thing was to save one's self up for women—at about 18. I dropped the practice easily, in spite of indulging my imagination about coitus. I thought of the initiation with prostitutes at 18, with the mixed feelings that even the most combative soldier must regard the fray. The hypogastric feeling above referred to would come on—which I liked and disliked at the same time. The first occasion on which I remember this feeling was when I got my first braces. Anything that harped on my sex produced it. Every time I received the sacrament, which I was forced to do very young, I repented of my intention of whoring at 18—as a man 'must' do—and afterward I relapsed to the expectation. Religion was a great reality to me, but it did not produce the radical effect that the development of the romantic sentiment did later on. (Both my wife and I became free-thinkers at about 30.)

"*Age 15-17.* Read poetry and romance. Conceived a high ideal of faithfulness and constancy. What a mockery all this loyalty is, I said to myself, if a man has stultified it beforehand. That was no mere castle-building. I had not understood what I was about in expecting to whore. The critical feelings were now awakening, and what they produced was revulsion against the abuse of sex, which got stronger every year. It became plain that there would be no whoring or the like for me; I was far too proud and fastidious. I neglected my tasks, which were uncongenial, and read a great deal of anatomy and physiology, which stood me in good stead later. As I rose in the school I was surprised to find the tone worse, but quite at the top it was better again, and with my latest companions sex was never even mentioned. At 14 I had a friend who importuned me to come into his bed, but I never would get under his bedclothes, for the male sex repels me powerfully in personal contact; he began to talk of masturbation, and now I can understand what he was aiming at. But my day-dreams of nymphs and dryads kept me in a state of perpetual tension, and erection was very frequent. The early morbid admiration of delicate women became replaced by admiration of health and strength combined with grace.

"*Age 17-18.* I was given a cubicle in which my neighbor on the right masturbated noisily two or three times a week, and the one on the left every night, using intermittent friction to drag it out longer. One night, kneeling at my bedside, saying prayers, my attention was divided between these and the occupation of my neighbor, when, after not having masturbated for four years,—the critical years of development,—the hand flew to the phallus and

"'pulses pounding through palms and trembling encircling fingers'

"procured, in Walt Whitman's language,

"'the wholesome relief,—repose, content.'

"I slept well and had a sense of elation at the proof of manhood, for we boys were anxious about whether we secreted semen or not. The sexual obsession was tempered, and about three weeks later I had my first 'pollution'—the 'angel of the night,' as Mantegazza with better sense calls it. From that time on I had pollutions every two or three weeks, with dreams sometimes of masturbation or of nymphs, or quite irrelevant matters. For a time these gave me perfect relief; then my 'dilectatio morosa' began to grow again, and the phallus would become so sensitive that working about on the belly would liberate the orgasm.

"*Age 18-19.* I had kept on persuading myself I was not masturbating—avoiding the use of the hand—but now I dropped this pretense, and frankly conceded the need to myself. I got done with it in a peremptory way and thought no more of it. I had no evil effects, moral or physical, and my mother would often compliment me on my bright appearance the morning after. At that time the appetite matured every seven to ten days, and, though I dreaded the idea of slavery to it, it would have been very hard to forego it. Headaches, which had begun to plague me from puberty on, grew rarer. Pollutions occurred in between, but were less effectual. I had up to this point accepted the incidental pleasure under a sort of protest; but now I got over that too and I allowed what I would prefer to call an idio-erotism (rather than an auto-erotism) its way, always picturing beautiful nymphs to myself. Surroundings of natural beauty moved me to this kind of reverie, partly perhaps because I had once secretly observed a lad basking naked on the sandy beach and toying with himself. The recollection is wholly unsullied to me. Happening on one occasion to check the stimulation about two-thirds way to orgasm, I experienced a miniature orgasm like the childish one, but with no declension of the tumescence, and I was able to repeat this maneuver several times before the full orgasm. This I later practised in *Coitus prolongatus*— giving the partner time to come up. I had already got into the way of poising the feeling on its climax. The ejaculator reflex, being habituated to this, seems to set in with its throbs when the maneuver is simulated, though no semen has yet been poured into the bulbous portion for the ejaculators to act upon. If this play be broken off before the critical spasm— as in the American 'Karezza,' etc.—there is no perceptible reaction, though an unsatisfied feeling remains. But when the act proceeds to emission and the poignant *undercurrent* of feeling sets in that ushers the ejaculation and may only last two to five seconds, it makes all the difference, and constitutional signs appear—perspiration, etc. This leads to the question whether the critical sensation specially involves the sympathetic nervous system? Up to that point the process is under control, but then automatic.

"An observation of practical importance to me at that time was this: I awoke in the morning after a pollution at night, with an acute headache of a specific kind, and erection. This had happened before, after pollution, and the erection suggested to me whether 'a hair of the dog that bit me' might not prove beneficial. As the excitation proceeded, the pain in the head was directly drained away, as if I were drawing it out. Other pain is also relieved for the moment, such as neuralgia, but to return soon with interest. This, however, was specific and pure benefit. The next time I got a bad headache of this character, without preceding pollution, I tried the remedy, at about 10 A. M. The semen was copious and watery, and the relief was marked, but in an hour's time the headache returned. I had never repeated the act at short interval, *i.e.*, while the organs were under the influence of a previous act, and now I tried the effect of that. The second emission was also profuse, but much thicker, and the relief much greater. In about three hours the headache was, however, again intolerable, and, the connection being now clear, I ventured on a third act, which proved to be the most voluptuous I had so far experienced, the nisus being far more intense. The semen was copious, but thick and ropy, with lumps as large as small peas that could scarcely be crushed with the finger, and yellow in color and rank in odor. After that I was perfectly well and kept so. (The urethra was blocked so that I could with difficulty stroke the masses out.) Later I have examined such semen microscopically and found the spermatozoa dead and disintegrating. My period in my best years—21 to 48—was twice a week, the odd number being an inconvenience, and I have since endeavored to avoid accumulations, emptying the receptacles on the fourth day, when I remembered the interval, even if the organs did not remind me. On the fifth day headache would otherwise appear and perhaps two acts be needful, or, if I forgot about it for a week, three acts running. That I did not abuse the function the fact proves that every year I would forget about it two to three times and have to resort to this drastic mode.[230] But there is quite a different headache that follows on indulgence during convalescence or when the system is otherwise much lowered. Railway traveling greatly accentuates the need with me; also riding. Girls aroused no physical desire, though I chiefly sought their society, and even after the genital tension was so pronounced, up to 20, I was troubled by the fact that women did not affect me sexually. About this time a buxom girl I liked and who liked me vehemently laid her hand on my arm, in trying to persuade me to give up shooting. The phallus leaped simultaneously. That was my first *sexual*experience—the proof that the *nexus* was established between the genital mechanism and the complex of feeling we call sexual.

"*Age 24*. At this age I went to stay at a house where there were two very pretty girls. I at once lost my heart to the elder, L. B., as she did to me (strong constitution, but refined nature; parents sound; brought up in the country; eleven months' breast-milk). 'What a mother she will make,' I said to myself. Now began a time of the spiritual and physical communion that I had pictured to myself....

"I am 60 now; she is 57. We are still like lovers. No; not *like*lovers; we *are* lovers. Of course, I do not mean to imply that sexual impressions have preponderated in our life, as they do in this account. Quite the contrary. We are both strong and, according to all accounts, unusually well preserved. We are very temperate. Since 48 I notice a gradual decline of the erotic propensity. It is now once in five or seven days. Since the menopause her propensity has declined markedly, but it is not extinct, and she delights as much as ever in my delight. She began to menstruate at 12, was regular till 17; then got chlorotic for a few months, soon recovered, though menstruation was often irregular, but never painful. Sexual experience began at 25. I have often wondered if a moderate self-gymnastic of the faculty, in Venturi's sense, would not have educated her genital sphere, and made her a still better comrade—excluded the periods of irregularity and frigidity. The stage of latency was too protracted. We often noticed that, when menstruation was due or nearly so, prolonged love-sports at bedtime would be followed by menstruation in the morning. We never were separated for longer than three months, and on that occasion, menstruation being delayed, she tried what masturbation would do to determine it, and with a positive result. My need, though less, is as imperative as ever. Seminal headaches—as I would call them—have ceased since 50; the accumulation only produces muddleheadedness. But I have not suffered accumulation over ten to at most twelve days. The quantity of semen is also less. The sensibility of the corpora has declined much; that of the glans is unimpaired. Erection is good. Orgasm takes two to four minutes to provoke, against forty to fifty seconds when young; it is in some respects even more enjoyable—perhaps less intense, but much more prolonged. I have no reaction from indulgence. But I never press it; it always presses me. For overaccumulation, with headache or muddleheadedness, the wifely hand is more efficacious than the vulva. Even the most vivid dream of coitus fails to compass the orgasm now. The peripheral stimulus is essential.

"In our case physical and psychical intensity of emotion have gone hand in hand. I have become specialized to one woman, despite an erotic endowment certainly not meager. The pervasive fragrance makes one adore the whole sex, but my wife does not interpret this homage in a sexually promiscuous sense. We both agree in the principle that if one cannot hold the affection of the other there is no title to it. Tarde says that constancy in love is rarely anything but a voyage of discovery round the beloved object. I am perpetually making fresh discoveries. But her constancy, I mean the high level of her passion, is independent of discoveries."

[230]
"A practical question arising out of the foregoing is whether such semen should be committed to the vagina? Its presence is known to me by constitutional symptoms (toxic). It is the last to be expelled, and its degenerate germ-cells have no chance against those of the normal fluid deposited in preceding acts, supposing that to be retained. But it may well happen that the prior emissions only reach the pouch, whereas the last is injected into the

womb itself. I have frequently had the sense of the orifices of meatus and cervix matching directly, especially when she had powerful orgasm (including two conceptions), and of the semen being sucked from me rather than occluded in its exit, as also happens, requiring me to relax the urge a little. At 18 to 19 the semen of a 'pollution' has left tender red patches where it dried on the neighboring skin, and deep straw-colored stains in the linen."